QUINTILIAN AND THE LAW

QUINTILIAN AND THE LAW

The Art of Persuasion in Law and Politics

Edited by

Olga Tellegen-Couperus

LEUVEN UNIVERSITY PRESS

© 2003 Universitaire Pers Leuven / Presses Universitaires de Louvain /
Leuven University Press
Blijde-Inkomststraat 5, B-3000 Leuven (Belgium)

ISBN 90 5867 301 4
D / 2003 / 1869 / 27
NUR : 635-683

CONTENTS

PREFACE

In September 2001, a unique meeting took place at the University of Tilburg (NL), convened by Willem Witteveen and me. Scholars from various disciplines and various countries came together to try and assess Quintilian's significance for students and practitioners of the art of persuasion in antiquity and in modern times. This book contains the result of their discussions. It is owing to several institutions and persons that this could happen.

The Royal Netherlands Academy of Arts and Sciences (KNAW) was willing to give a substantial grant for the meeting because of its innovative theme. The Department of Jurisprudence and Legal History of the Tilburg University, Faculty of Law, contributed not only personaliter in participating in the project but also materialiter in preparing this publication.

Two persons have been particularly helpful in preparing the text of this book. First of all, the editor for English texts at the Law Faculty of Tilburg University, Mrs. Ineke Sijtsma-van der Kruk M.A. must be mentioned. She deserves the utmost credit for her efforts to linguistically unify the texts and yet preserve the style and spirit of the originals. Eelkje van de Kuilen-Stap helped greatly by checking the layout of the essays and by making the source index.

Olga Tellegen-Couperus
Tilburg, Spring 2003

OLGA TELLEGEN-COUPERUS

INTRODUCTION

1. THE PURPOSE OF THIS BOOK

To win or not to win, that is the question in every political debate and in every law-suit, and the key to success is the art of persuasion. Therefore it is essential for politicians and lawyers to have a perfect command of that art. One may have a natural talent to move an audience, but in order to speak well when the occasion or the subject demands, one has to know the rules of rhetoric. When a politician wants his audience to make a certain decision, he can reach his goal, for instance, by offering two possible decisions - a 'good' one and a 'bad' one, by repeating his arguments and, above all, by using humour. A lawyer who wants to convince the judge must be able to present the facts of the case in such a manner that the judge not only believes him but also wants to believe him, and he must show that his arguments are not only legally but also morally better than those of his opponent.

Many books have been written on the subject, not only in recent times but also already when Western civilisation began to emerge. The names of Aristotle and Cicero spring to mind. Aristotle laid the basis for the theory of rhetoric and Cicero, the top-orator in Roman history, left an impressive number of rhetorical works. However, Aristotle's ideas have come down to us only in the form of lecture notes and Cicero's main work, *De oratore,* is on the orator rather than on rhetoric. Yet there is another author, whose name is less familiar, but whose work is in some respects even more interesting than that of Aristotle and Cicero. His name is Marcus Fabius Quintilianus, he lived in the first century AD, and his *magnum opus* is the *Institutionis oratoriae libri XII*, Twelve books on the education of the orator. This work is special because it contains a full and systematic survey of the rhetorical insights that had been developed in the previous centuries.

Quintilian did not write an ordinary textbook on rhetoric, but set out to design a complete educational programme for young Romans who were to become the leaders of the state. His orator had to be a good man, able to speak well. This implied not only artistic excellence but also moral goodness.

The main body of the *Institutio oratoria,* as the work is generally called, consists of the traditional parts of rhetoric. However, Quintilian does not only give his own version of the rhetorical system, but he evaluates the views of earlier authors as well. He formulates important insights in juridical argumentation, in the art of speech writing, and in the performative aspects of advocacy, and he also discusses the ethical problems involved. Moreover, he constantly enlivens his theory with examples from practice. In this way, he has succeeded in writing a book which offers a wealth of information and inspiration, even to the modern practitioners of law and politics.

The purpose of the present volume is to reintroduce Quintilian's *Institutio oratoria* to modern readers, and to show that the topics discussed in it are still very much alive today. To that end, modern experts of law and rhetoric present their views on the *Institutio oratoria*, each dealing with one of the twelve books of which it consists. The authors were free to choose their own way of working, so that some books are described in their entirety, others are discussed from one particular point of view, and others still are treated only with regard to a particular section. The result is meant to be instructive and entertaining, but of course it can never equal the work of the master himself.

In the next part of this introduction I will place the art of persuasion in law and politics in a historical context. Then I will give a short survey of Quintilian's life and of the *Institutio oratoria*. Finally, I will introduce the essays, not in the order of the books but according to the themes discussed in them. I will also use that section to briefly discuss the Roman law of procedure in criminal and civil trials.

2. THE RELATIONSHIP BETWEEN RHETORIC, LAW, AND POLITICS IN HISTORY

The art of persuasion or, as Quintilian preferred to call it, the art of speaking well, came into being in Greece in the 5th century BC, within the framework of law and politics.[1] In the Greek city-states, and particularly in the democratic polis of Athens, all adult male citizens were members of the popular assembly and, as such, took part in all major decisions concerning the city. The courts of law were also organised in a democratic way: in most criminal and civil trials, justice was administered by large juries consisting of 200-500 citizens. Since communication was mainly oral, it was very important for citizens to be able to speak well in public. It was the sophists who offered education in rhetoric, particularly in argumentation and style. Of these sophists, Gorgias from the Sicilian town of Leontini was the most important one. He lived from ca. 480 to ca. 380 BC.

In a philosophical sense, the sophists were 'relativists': they assumed that there is no absolute truth but only probabilities. They also denied the existence of ethically abstract qualities like good and just. For them, laws were conventional, variable rules, and therefore they insisted that every interpretation of the law is defendable. Their attitude triggered a violent reaction: philosophers like Socrates (469-399 BC) and Plato (427-347 BC) accused the sophists of being immoral and wicked. In their view, the sophists promoted a world full of appearances and deceit. By using beautiful words and stylistic tricks, they deliberately misled people. Moreover, it would be dangerous to teach the art of rhetoric to a large number of people because it could enable a bad person to damage society. Gorgias, on the other hand, held that it would

---

[1]   For a full survey, see G.A. Kennedy, *A New History of Classical Rhetoric*, Princeton: Princeton University Press 1994, with bibliography. G.A. Kennedy, *Classical Rhetoric and its Christian and Secular Tradition from Ancient to Modern Times*, 2nd edition, revised and enlarged, Chapel Hill and London: University of North Carolina Press 1999, is less profound but contains 'new' elements like the contribution of women to the history of rhetoric.

be dangerous to restrict the art of rhetoric to a small number of people because then only a few would be able to recognise bad arguments and deceitful purposes.

Aristotle (384-322 BC) took a middle course: he distinguished between the art of rhetoric, which was morally neutral, and the orator, whose duty it was to act in a morally just manner. In this way, he could include the theory of rhetoric in the philosophical system, which he taught at his school. Of course, the orator should try and persuade his audience with objective, straightforward arguments. However, people usually do not decide in a purely rational manner. Therefore, Aristotle developed the notions of *ethos* (referring to the character of the speaker), *pathos* (the arousal of emotions in the audience) and *logos* (the use of argument that shows or seems to show something). Aristotle's views, expounded in his *Rhetorica*, had a large impact throughout antiquity.

When the Macedonian king Alexander the Great (ca. 330 BC) had put end to Greek freedom and democracy and Hellenistic kings began to rule the Eastern part of the Mediterranean, the need to speak well in public lost its importance. Yet, rhetoric kept its place in education because it was considered as a useful, intellectual, and artistic training for the leading classes. The high value put on learning in this period stimulated the further development of theories of rhetoric. Many professional teachers wrote books about stylistic devices and about the theory of the stasis, i.e. the method to identify the question at issue in a speech. The most famous one was Hermagoras of Temnos who lived in the middle of the 2nd century BC and whose status theory held the lead for several centuries. The rhetoric of this period is usually called Hellenistic.

In the 2nd century BC, the Romans conquered Greece, but – to paraphrase Horace - at the same time, the Greeks conquered Rome by introducing the art of oratory.[2] Of course, there had been public debate in Rome before that time, for instance, in the senate and the popular assemblies, but soon Hellenistic oratory was recognised as being superior to the old-fashioned Roman way of speaking. Members of the ruling class hired Greek teachers for their sons to train them in rhetoric with a view to their having a career in politics.

Since the important political decisions were made in the senate, it was imperative to try and become a member of that austere body. The only way to achieve this goal, at least during the Republic, was to fulfil some public office, magistracy. The assembly of the male Roman citizens chose the magistrates. Therefore, a candidate had to obtain fame among the citizens and he had to build a reputation of being able to speak well in public. One of the ways to do so was by serving as an advocate. In later life, he could profit from this experience because, as a politician, he often had to appear in court for friends or clients.

The first Roman to make a complete study of Hellenistic rhetoric was M. Tullius Cicero (106-43 BC). In his *De oratore* he tried to devise a synthesis of rhetoric and philosophy. In his opinion, the perfect orator or politician is a wise man *and* an excellent speaker, who also commands a vast knowledge of law and history. Therefore, in his view, rhetoric and law were closely connected.

---

[2]   Horace, *Epistulae*, II.156-157.

In practice, in the late Republic, not all politicians may have been able to meet the high standards formulated by Cicero, but they must have had a basic knowledge of rhetoric and law. If they did not, they could, for instance, not participate in the senate, nor work as a magistrate, nor function as a provincial governor. Only a small number of politicians specialised in law. They gave advise on legal problems, helped people formulate legal documents, and acted as advocate or judge. They also collected their opinions or verdicts and published them. These politicians are now called jurists.[3] Of course one cannot say that all politicians were jurists, but there is no reason either to assume, as is often done nowadays, following Mommsen, that, generally speaking, politicians did not have a basic knowledge of the law at all.[4]

The connection between rhetoric, politics, and law continued into the early Empire. However, times had changed. Magistrates were no longer chosen by the Roman people but were often appointed by the emperor. Besides, freedom of speech began to be curtailed, particularly under despotic emperors like Nero and Domitian, so that oratory was no longer useful as a means of persuasion in political assemblies. However, in the courts of law it still was: criminal as well as civil trials were dominated by oratory. Vivid descriptions of such trials are to be found in the letters of Pliny the Younger.[5] Consequently, rhetoric remained an important part of education but it was now provided in rhetorical schools. Another difference was that style was gaining importance over argumentation. *Declamationes* were held, not only in schools for exercise but also in public for entertainment. Quintilian (ca. 40 – ca.100) criticizes the use of bizarre subjects, swollen style, and unrealistic conventions in the declamations and pleads for using proper names, more complicated cases, a simpler style, and more humour.[6] In his eyes, Cicero was the example of the perfect orator and he often quotes him in his *Institutio oratoria*.

The close connection between rhetoric, on the one hand, and law and politics, on the other, did not survive antiquity. After the fall of the Western Roman Empire, what was left of civilisation was kept alive by the church.[7] Rhetoric together with grammar and dialectic were the three subjects (*trivium*) which were taught. Law and politics subsisted on an elementary level only. Of the few Romans keeping up classical learning, mention must be made of Boethius who, in the 6th century, was a leading politician-orator at the Ostrogothic court. In his book *De differentiis topicis*, he compared rhetoric with dialectic in such a way that he narrowed rhetoric down to its function of *inventio* and then concluded that rhetoric was subordinate to dialectic.

---

[3]   For a modern view on the Roman jurists, see J.A. Crook, *Legal Advocacy in the Roman World*, London: Duckworth 1995.

[4]   See, for instance, J.J. May and J. Wisse in the introduction to their translation of Cicero's *De oratore*: *On the Ideal Orator*, New York-Oxford: Oxford University Press 2001, p. 5.

[5]   See, for instance, Pliny's Letter VI 33 on the trial of Attia Viriola who contested her father's will before the court of the *centumviri*, and his two letters on the extortion trials against Marius Priscus (Letter II 11) and Junius Bassus (Letter IV 9).

[6]   See, e.g., *Inst. or.* II.10.2-5 and 9; IV.3.2; V.13.36-47; VII.2. 54-56.

[7]   Kennedy (see note 1), pp. 196-225. See also A. Michel, 'La rhétorique, sa vocation et ses problèmes: sources antiques et médiévales', in: M. Fumaroli (ed.), *Histoire de la rhétorique dans l'Europe moderne 1450-1950*, Paris: Presses Universitaires de France 1999, pp. 32-44.

In the 13th century this book was used for teaching rhetoric at the university of Paris and it consequently had a rather negative effect on rhetorical studies.[8]

In the 12th century, the world of Western Europe changed fundamentally. A rapid population growth, trade, guilds, the Church becoming a powerful institution, the rise of strong, centralized monarchies, and the emergence of a strong urban civilisation, first in Flanders and Northern Italy but soon also in other regions, were new phenomena.[9] Civil and ecclesiastical administration called for well-trained personnel, which led to the emergence of universities all over Europe.

The school of law at Bologna, where Roman law and canon law were taught, was particularly successful.[10] The recent rediscovery of Justinian's Digest – a 6th century compilation of legal texts dating mainly from the early Roman empire - and of the works of Aristotle gave a formidable impetus to this success. Students who had completed the trivium, here learned to explain and analyse the texts of Roman law with the help of a system of logical distinctions derived from the works of Aristotle. The Roman jurists in antiquity had also used logic, but with much more freedom: if they thought that a logical, rational solution to a legal problem would go against justice, tradition, or the interest of the Roman people, they would not hesitate to drop logic and solve the problem in a socially acceptable way. The medieval jurists, however, saw legal science as a rational method to analyse texts and to argue on the basis of texts. For them, the law books of Justinian were a goldmine of arguments. The fact that they had been issued by a Roman emperor gave them extra authority. It is obvious that there was no room for rhetoric in the law schools of the middle ages.

For many centuries, this situation did not basically change. Of course, the humanists revived interest for rhetoric, but they were not able to shake the jurists out of their medieval habits. No doubt the most interesting person in this connection is Lorenzo Valla, professor of grammar and rhetoric in Rome, Florence, and Pavia (1407-1457).[11] He praised the correct and elegant style used by the classical Roman jurists and criticized the modern jurists for writing bad Latin.[12] He also blamed them for detaching Roman law from common sense as well as from its historical context. In Pavia, he even attacked the most famous jurist of his time, Bartolus di Saxoferrata, which caused so much commotion that he had to leave town.[13] One of his favourite themes was to condemn the separation of dialectics and rhetoric, which had taken place in the previous centuries, and to restore dialectics to its original

---

[8]   So J.J. Murphy, *Rhetoric in the Middle Ages, A History of Rhetorical Theory from St. Augustine to the Renaissance,* Berkeley-Los Angeles-London: University of California Press 1974, pp. 67-71.

[9]   J.M. Kelly, *A Short History of Western Legal Theory,* Oxford: Clarendon Press 1992, pp. 114-158.

[10]   P. Stein, *Roman Law in European History,* Cambridge: Cambridge University Press 1999, pp. 45- 70.

[11]   C. Vasoli, 'L'humanisme rhétorique en Italie au XVe siècle, in: *Histoire de la rhétorique* (see note 7), pp. 61-74.

[12]   L. Valla, 'Elegantiae Latini Sermonis', III, foreword, in: E. Garin (ed.), *Opera omnia* I, Turin: Bottega d'Erasmo 1962, pp. 79-81. See also D.R. Kelley, *Foundations of Modern Historical Scholarship: Language, Law and History in the French Renaissance,* New York-London: Columbia University Press 1970, pp. 39-43.

[13]   L. Valla, 'In Bartoli de insignis et armis libellum ad Candidum Decembrem epistula', in: *Opera omnia* I (see note 12), pp. 633-643.

place as a part of rhetoric. In fact, rhetoric in general should not only control grammar but also historiography, theology and the exegesis of sacred texts. It seemed this would include law as well.[14] In short, like Cicero, Valla thought that the art of oratory was superior to all other arts. For him, the best guide for rhetoric was Quintilian's *Institutio oratoria*, the complete text of which had been rediscovered in 1416. Valla's works have exercised a profound influence on philology and rhetoric, but hardly on legal science or politics.[15]

As from the 17th century, rhetoric went through an impressive period of new developments, in close connection with philosophy and philology.[16] One of them was caused by the 'new logic' introduced by Descartes in his 'Discours de la Méthode' (1637). This famous philosopher rejected the originally sophist idea that there are only probabilities, and he insisted that persuasion should be based on hard evidence, to be obtained by means of a mathematical model of knowledge. For rhetoric, this theory had far-reaching consequences, for it made some of its major subjects like the finding of arguments (*inventio*) and the use of emotions totally irrelevant. Rhetoric was reduced to style and, with the emergence of national states, it was used to help develop the national literature of those states. Consequently, rhetoric played only a minor part in politics and law; in the 19th century, under the influence of the German Historical School, it was even strictly separated from law.

Apart from its merits, this Historical School had one rather detrimental effect, namely, on the research of the Roman law of antiquity. According to Savigny, the founder of this school, the fundamental principle governing the practice and application of law was logic. Since German law was not artificially constructed (like French rational law) but had grown gradually from Roman and Germanic law in the course of history, it was necessary, for a proper understanding of this law, to try and reconstruct classical Roman law. It was only to be expected that the legal historians who undertook this job took over the ideas of the Historical School with regard to law and legal science: they assumed that logic ruled the law and that rhetoric had nothing to do with it. Consequently, they distinguished between juridical sources and non-juridical sources: they regarded the first category, including Justinian's *Corpus Iuris* and the Institutions of Gaius, as useful, but the second category, containing, for instance the rhetorical works by Cicero and Quintilian, as irrelevant because orators/rhetors knew little or nothing about Roman law and their works did not provide reliable information on this subject. The effect of this approach was that the 'non-juridical' sources were ignored or, if used, misinterpreted.[17]

---

[14] Valla states in one of his scholia on Quintilian (no. 17), that the task of orators to make laws is by far superior to that of jurists to interpret laws. See J. Fernandez Lopez, *Rétorica, Humanismo y Filología: Quintiliano y Lorenzo Valla*, Logroño: Instituto de Estudios Riojanos 1999, pp. 145-148.

[15] Valla did have a large impact on later legal science in that he laid the foundations of the 16th century historical school of law in France. However, this legal humanism did not have any real influence on legal practice. Stein (see note 10), pp. 75-86.

[16] Kennedy (see note 1), pp. 269-270. More information on this part of the history of rhetoric is to be found in F. Hallyn, 'Dialectique et rhétorique devant la "nouvelle science" du XVIIe siecle', in: *Histoire de la rhétorique* (see note 7), pp. 601-628.

[17] On this subject, see J.W. Tellegen and O.E. Tellegen-Couperus, 'Law and Rhetoric in the *Causa Curiana*', *Orbis iuris romani* 6 (2000) pp. 171-202.

It was not until the middle of the 20th century that attempts were made to restore the connection between rhetoric, politics, and law. The impetus came from the alpha and gamma disciplines. The American linguist Kenneth Burke showed that rhetorical analysis not only throws light on literary texts but also on politics as an expression of human relations.[18] He developed a highly original dramatic interpretation of the American constitution; his 'Grammar of Motives' opened the way for later hermeneutic and rhetorical study of constitutional interpretation. At the same time, in Belgium, the philosophers Perelman and Olbrechts-Tyteca argued that decisions in politics or courts of law are often not taken in a rational manner, but on the basis of accidental, probable, or plausible arguments.[19] They therefore tried to find a non-formal way of argumentation in law and in the habit of referring to precedent as a rational basis for decisions. Of course, this 'nouvelle rhétorique' is not the same as the traditional rhetoric which was developed in antiquity. Yet it is important to recognise that it is not realistic to apply the rationalism of Descartes and the logic of Savigny to decisions taken in politics and law. Rhetoric can be useful in politics as 'cement' in the unification of Europe and as a tool to improve the communication in (inter)national fora. In law, it can improve the quality of pleading and enhance the acceptance of judgments. It will be interesting to see that those tools, which were made in antiquity and which were described in detail by Quintilian, can still be used today.

3. M. FABIUS QUINTILIANUS

Quintilian was a Roman citizen who was born in Calagurris (now Calahorra), a town in Northern Spain, about AD 35.[20] He was sent to Rome for his education, where, like all boys from the upper class, he was trained in rhetoric. He chose as his mentor Cn. Domitius Afer, an orator who originally had made his fortune as a professional informer (*delator*) but who by this time had boosted his reputation and had become one of the leading orators. The fact that Quintilian published a speech 'led by a youthful desire for fame' (*Inst. or.* VII.2.24) suggests that, at this time, he had already started practice in the law courts and that he was doing quite well. Sometime around the year AD 60 he went back to Spain. There he had a successful career, maybe as a teacher of rhetoric or as an advocate or in both qualities. He made a very good impression on the governor of Northern Spain, Ser. Sulpicius Galba. This is the same Galba who, after the death of Nero in 68, became emperor of the Roman Empire, be it only for a short time. It was Galba who brought Quintilian to Rome.

---

[18]   K. Burke, *A Grammar of Motives*, New York: Prentice Hall 1945; rpt. Berkeley: University of California Press 1969, and *A Rhetoric of Motives*, New York: Prentice-Hall 1950; rpt. Berkeley: University of California Press 1969.
[19]   Ch. Perelman and L. Olbrechts-Tyteca, *La nouvelle rhétorique; traité de l'argumentation*, 2 Vols., Paris: Presses Universitaires de France 1958, 2nd edition, Brussels: Editions de l'Institut de sociologie 1970; rpt. 1988.
[20]   G.A. Kennedy, *Quintilian*, New York: Twayne Publishers 1969 and Id., *A New History* (see note 1), pp. 177-186. See also O. Seel, *Quintilian, oder die Kunst des Redens und Schweigens*, 2nd edition, Munich: Deutscher Taschenbuch Verlag 1987.

In Rome, the political situation was very chaotic and dangerous. It was one year and three emperors later that general Vespasian succeeded in keeping power and restoring law and order. By this time, Quintilian may have turned to teaching rhetoric and, when possible in this turbulent time, he may have practised as an advocate in civil and criminal cases. He must have acquired an excellent reputation for, a few years later, Emperor Vespasian appointed him as the first professor of Latin rhetoric who was to receive a salary from the imperial treasury. He held this office for twenty years. Among his pupils was Pliny the Younger and probably also Tacitus. It is more than likely that he also taught some of the persons whom we know as jurists; they all had important political careers, so they must have learned how to speak well in public.

In addition to his work at the school, Quintilian also appeared regularly in the law courts to plead cases for his clients. In the *Institutio oratoria,* he refers only to four particular cases in which he delivered a speech, but from the way he describes, for instance, how to prepare and deliver a speech, how to deal with clients, and how to examine witnesses, it can be inferred that he must have appeared as an advocate in many lawsuits.[21]

In the early 80s, Quintilian married a young woman who bore him two sons. Unfortunately, she died at the age of 18, soon to be followed by the younger son. Ten years later, in 92, Quintilian retired from teaching and, urged by friends, he decided to use his experience as a teacher and an orator to write a book on rhetoric. While he was working at it, Emperor Domitian gave him the honourable task of helping to educate the two grandsons of his sister, whom he had adopted. However, his good fortune ran out for, a short time later, his only surviving son fell seriously ill and died. In the introduction to Book 6, which actually is partly about the use of pathos, he gives a touching description of his dying son.

In utter misery and loneliness, Quintilian kept working at his book, his life's work. The *Institutio oratoria* was published at the turn of the year 95/96. At this time he was also given the *ornamenta consularia,* i.e., the status of a former consul without the obligations attached to it. Quintilian died a few years later. We do not know when this happened, but it was probably around AD 100.

Shortly before the *Institutio oratoria,* Quintilian had published a treatise on the causes of corrupted eloquence (*De causis corruptae eloquentiae*), in which he may have criticized teachers of rhetoric for tolerating artificiality and not making declamation an exercise in argumentation. Much earlier, he had published the speech mentioned above, which he had held as a young advocate in defence of a certain Naevius from Arpinum. Naevius was accused of murdering his wife by throwing her from some height, possibly from a window, but Quintilian successfully proved that he was innocent and that the wife had jumped. Other speeches circulated in Rome under his name, as well as two series of lecture notes, but Quintilian had nothing to do with their publication. Unfortunately, all these works are lost. The two collections of declamations, which have come down to us and which are attributed to Quintilian, are certainly not from his hand.

---

[21]   The four cases are mentioned in *Inst. or.* IV.1.19, VI.1.39, VII.2.24, and IX.2.73.

As a person, Quintilian seems to have been a humane and kind teacher, with a lot of common sense. In modern literature, some authors reproach Quintilian for flattering Emperor Domitian who, particularly in the last years of his life - the same years when Quintilian finished *his Institutio oratoria* - had turned into a despotic ruler.[22] However, nowadays, those remarks are usually explained in connection with Quintilian's personal situation – he owed his rise to the Flavian house – and to the circumstances of the time. Besides, Quintilian never took an active part in politics nor did he use his abilities as a *delator*. He did what he was good at: to teach and practise rhetoric.

4. THE *INSTITUTIO ORATORIA*

In the *Institutio oratoria*, Quintilian gives a full survey of the rhetorical system as it had been developed in the previous centuries. The book is special for various reasons, of which I shall mention a few. First, it is unique in that neither before nor after Quintilian a complete survey of rhetoric has been written. Moreover, of every subject he deals with, Quintilian mentions the views of other authors and evaluates them. Another special feature is the fact that Quintilian often lards his theoretical discussion of a subject with examples from practice. Since he could draw from his own experience, these examples are not only very useful, they also enliven the book and make it understandable even for people who know nothing about rhetoric or law. What makes the book extra interesting is that Quintilian sometimes describes subjects for which there is no parallel. A famous example is Book X, which is devoted to how an orator can develop an 'abundance' of ideas and words by reading and writing. In this connection, Quintilian provides his students with a complete history of Greek and Latin literature to help them decide what to read and what not to read.

Quintilian divided his *Institutio oratoria* into twelve books, beginning with the education of the young child and ending with suggestions on how the orator who has retired from public life should spend his time. In Book I, Quintilian describes the early childhood of the future orator, in particular, his lessons in Latin and literature. Next, in Book II, the young student - he is approximately fourteen years old now - is engaged in learning rhetoric. Quintilian discusses the duties of teacher and student, as well as the use and method of declamations, and he finishes by trying to find out what exactly rhetoric is. The first part of Book III contains a history of rhetoric. Then follow two major divisions, which were traditionally made in rhetoric: the three types of speeches (ceremonial, political, and judicial), and the five duties of the orator. It is to these five duties of the orator that the main part of the *Institutio oratoria* is devoted, beginning at Book III.6 and ending at Book XI.1. These duties are: to find the question - together with the proper arguments - to be discussed (*inventio*,

---

[22] On this discussion, see J. Adamietz, 'Quintilians "Institutio oratoria" ', in: H. Temporini and W. Haase (eds.), *Aufstieg und Niedergang der römischen Welt* II, 32, Berlin-New York: Walter de Gruyter 1986, pp. 2230-2231 with references. See also T. Morgan, 'A 'Good Man Skilled in Politics: Quintilian's Political Theory', in: Y.L. Too and N. Livingstone (eds.), *Pedagogy and Power, Rhetorics of Classical Learning*, Cambridge: Cambridge University Press 1998, pp. 245-262, particularly pp. 253-256, on Quintilian's attitude towards the emperor.

Book III.6 to Book VI), to order the arguments in the most effective way (*disposi-tio*, Book VII), to choose the most effective words and style (*elocutio*, Books VIII, IX, and X), to memorize the speech (*memoria*, Book XI Chapters 1 and 2) and to present it (*action*, Book XI.3). In Book XII, Quintilian turns to the most difficult part of his work, i.e., the person of the orator. He begins by asserting that it is not enough to say that the orator must be a good man, but that no man can be a good orator unless he is a good man (XII.1.1-3). He then expounds on the orator's character, his philosophical training, his knowledge of law and history, and questions like whether an orator should take on all cases or not. Quintilian reassures those who think that becoming a good orator is too difficult and ends the book expressing the hope that, if the knowledge of the principles of rhetoric proves to be of small practical utility to the young student, it will at least produce what he values more - the will to do what is good.

In the course of time, the *Institutio oratoria* has been appreciated in very differ-ent ways. In antiquity, it seems not to have been very popular; it was probably regarded as too large and too scientific.[23] Quintilian's ideas about the perfect orator have had no influence at all. Only from the late 3rd to 5th centuries, Quintilian was famous, but then particularly for his writings on education and rhetoric. In the 6th century, after the fall of the Western empire, Boethius and Cassiodorus used the *Institutio oratoria* for their work, and so did Isidore of Seville in the 7th century. However, later on, most of the manuscripts mouldered away: even whole books were lost.[24]

It was in the 14th century that Quintilian's work really became popular, thanks to the enthusiasm of Petrarch, although he had only a fragmentary text at his dis-posal. In 1416, a complete manuscript was discovered by Poggio Bracciolini, a sec-retary to the pope, who during the Council of Konstanz (1414-1417) had the oppor-tunity to visit the monastery of Sankt Gallen to search for classical texts. From then on, many handwritten copies were made of the *Institutio oratoria*, and, in 1470, the first printed edition was published.

The book was highly appreciated by the Italian humanists, not only as before, for Quintilian's ideas on education, but now also for his providing standards for writing proper Latin. According to Lorenzo Valla, it was at least as important as the works of Virgil and Cicero, or maybe even more so. In the 15th and 16th centuries, the *Institutio oratoria* became famous in Northern Europe as well. Authors like Agricola and Erasmus refer to it many times, and even Luther appreciated it as the perfect combination of education and eloquence. However, in the following century, the star of the *Institutio oratoria* began to decline. The book was still appreciated for Quin-tilian's literary criticism, for instance, by Montaigne and Lessing, but otherwise it was hardly read. By the end of the 19th century, the *Institutio oratoria* had become obsolete. Yet, this was not the end: in the middle of the 20th century, it was redis-covered by students of education, by students of speech and rhetoric, especially in

---

[23]   Adamietz (see note 22), pp. 2226ff., in particular p. 2266.
[24]   See L.D. Reynolds and N.G. Wilson, *Scribes and Scholars. A Guide to the Transmission of Greek and Latin Literature*, 3rd edition, Oxford: Clarendon Press 1991, pp. 82-83 and pp. 100-101.

the USA, and by students of classical antiquity. Now it is time for students of law to rediscover Quintilian.

Since 1470, several editions of the *Institutio oratoria* have been published.[25] Still the edition, which is now generally in use is the one published by Winterbottom in 1970.[26] Translations of Quintilian's work into English, French, Italian, and German, and recently into Dutch, have helped make it accessible to a larger group of readers.[27]

5. ORATORY, POLITICS, AND LAW IN THE INSTITUTIO ORATORIA

Over the past ten years, many studies about the *Institutio oratoria* have been published, dealing mainly with its educational and linguistic aspects.[28] This book is the first to be dedicated to law and politics in Quintilian's work. It consists of more than twenty essays, each dealing with the legal or rhetorical aspects of one particular book of the *Institutio oratoria*. The essays are arranged in the order of the *Institutio oratoria*. However, it is also interesting to relate the essays to each other in so far as they deal with a similar theme. This introduction is the most appropriate place to do so. The essays deal with (one of) six themes: (1) the ideal orator in a historical perspective, (2) his education, (3) rhetoric and communication, (4) argumentation, (5) Roman law in the *Institutio oratoria*, and (6) emotions in the courtroom.

5.1 The ideal orator in a historical perspective

In the two books at the beginning and the two books at the end of the work, and scattered throughout the others, Quintilian describes the nature and the expectations of the ideal orator; he makes it clear that the ideal orator is educated to rule. Four essays are dedicated to this theme. Jorge Fernandez deals with the notion of authority, which the ideal orator will need in order to be able to rule. In Book I of the *Insti-*

---

[25] More information on the text tradition, on the various editions and comments, in Adamietz (see note 22), pp. 2249-2252.

[26] M. Winterbottom (ed.), *M. Fabii Quintiliani Institutionis oratoriae libri XII*, 2 Vols., Oxford: Clarendon Press 1970, rpt 1990-91.

[27] *The Institutio Oratoria of Quintilian*, edited and translated by H.E. Butler, 4 Vols., Cambridge (Mass)-London: Cambridge University Press and W. Heinemann 1920; rpt 1979-1986. Last year, a new English translation has been published: *Quintilian. The Orator's Education*, Edited and translated by D.A. Russell, 5 Vols., Cambridge (Mass)-London: Harvard University Press and W. Heinemann 2002. Other translations are: *Quintilien, Institution oratoire*, texte établi et traduit par J. Cousin, 7 Vols., Paris: Les Belles Lettres 1975-1980; *L'istituzione oratoria di M.F. Quintiliano*, a cura di R. Faranda, Turin: UTET 1968; *M.F. Quintilianus, Ausbildung des Redners, Zwölf Bücher*, herausgegeben und übersetzt von H. Rahn, I, Darmstadt: Wissenschaftliche Buchgesellschaft 1972; II, Darmstadt: Wissenschaftliche Buchgesellschaft 1975; *Quintilianus, De opleiding tot redenaar*, vertaald, ingeleid en van aantekeningen voorzien door P. Gerbrandy, Groningen: Historische Uitgeverij 2001.

[28] In 1995, *Rhetorica. A Journal of the History of Rhetoric*, Vol. 19, dedicated two issues (2 and 3) to Quintilian; in 1998, a large international conference was held in Spain in commemoration of the 19th centenary of the *Institutio oratoria*. The proceedings of this conference were published in: T. Albaladejo, E. del Rio and J.A. Caballero (eds.), *Quintiliano: historia y actualidad de la retórica*, 3 Vols., Logroño: Ediciones Instituto de Estudios Riojanos 1998.

tutio oratoria, Quintilian uses two notions of authority, one deriving from the author's *ethos* and the other from his linguistic correctness. However, Quintilian acknowledges that it depends on the audience whether the orator's authority is accepted. Therefore, the orator may have to appeal to emotion in order to persuade his audience. According to Fernandez, this paradox has consequences for the kind of world in which Quintilian's ideal orator would fit.

In Book XII, Quintilian returns explicitly to the ideal orator. Vincenzo Scarano Ussani shows that Quintilian's educational programme for the ideal orator was completely in accordance with imperial policy: the role of philosophy was minimized, whereas law was made an important feature. Moreover, when Quintilian deals with the ethical values to be taught to the young orator, he makes it clear that, in his view, the most important one is the *communis utilitas,* which, in his time, was identical with the interest and will of the emperor

The ideal orator also became a model for the court orator in later times. From the 15th century, the educational system included rhetoric as a necessary subject for access to advanced university studies. This did not change forensic oratory, but it led to the publication of several treatises about how to write and speak in court. In his paper, Giovanni Rossi discusses several of those treatises and shows that precepts given by Quintilian, for instance, in Book IV, were used by Italian lawyers in the 17th and 18th centuries.

Willem Witteveen advocates the return of the legal professions to the ideal of a general jurisprudence, for which he finds inspiration in Quintilian. He focuses on two themes that are important for 'reflective practitioners' of law: the relation between communicative and strategic interaction, manifesting itself in the ethics of advocacy and the education of the good jurist. For the first theme, he discusses a number of texts from Book IV on ethical dilemmas that arise for the orator when formulating the *exordium* and the *narratio.* For the second theme, he describes the programme of exercises in Book II and the value, for the aspiring orator, of reading good books, comparing Quintilian's views on this subject in book X with those advocated by the *Law & Literature* movement of modern times.

5.2 The education of the orator

Although actually all papers refer to this theme - it is the title of Quintilian's work - some authors discuss 'their' book from a particular educational perspective. Serena Querzoli first deals with the subjects which, according to Quintilian (Book II), should be taught to the young orator. She concludes that the *Institutio oratoria* is much more comprehensive than other educational books of antiquity like, for instance, that of Vitruvius on architecture. She then discusses Quintilian's attitude towards the law and the jurists. She does so by comparing one of the exercises for young orators, i.e., the praise and denunciation of laws, with Theon's handbook on preparatory exercises, and by comparing Quintilian's definition of rhetoric with that given by Plato in his Gorgias.

Emotions can also be the subject of education. In the *proemium* or preface to Book VI, Quintilian describes the death of his only surviving son. Maria-Silvana

Celentano points out that Quintilian's description of his grief and of his hope to be able to overcome it with the help of rhetorical studies is a highly effective pedagogic instrument. The distressing personal experience and the consolation expressed in the *proemium* are reflected in the peroration, the emotions, humour, and the other technical subjects of rhetoric described in Book VI itself.

In Book X, after having treated invention, disposition, and style, Quintilian returns to the education of the orator and deals with the question of how improvisation can become second nature to the adult speaker who has mastered all these subjects. According to Quintilian, the adult orator has to practise constantly in writing, reading, speaking, and listening. James Murphy explains why listening was part of this programme and, after giving a short summary of Quintilian's instructions, he strongly recommends reading Book X for its practical advice and its memorable aphorisms, which express the everyday problems of the adult orator. He concludes his paper by giving some sample statements.

Sanne Taekema focuses on one particular aspect of the education of the orator, viz., on reading as a means of enhancing his capacity for improvisation. In Book X, Quintilian gives advice about the literary works a young orator should read. Taekema relates this advice to the discussions within the modern *Law & Literature* movement about which books lawyers should read and why. She finds that Quintilian's ideas are still relevant not only because reading multi-layered and well-written texts may help modern lawyers to improve their standards of writing and speaking, but also because it may help them to develop their judgment in ethical matters.

5.3 Rhetoric and communication

This theme is approached both from a linguistic and a general rhetorical point of view. Tomás Albaladejo discusses the communicative aspects of the three kinds of oratory as presented in the *Institutio oratoria* (Book III) He therefore analyses the relationships between the political and legal components of rhetorical discourses and their textual-linguistic organisation and communicative structure. The role of orators, hearers, and discourses themselves is examined in order to explain the deliberative, forensic, and epideictic speeches. According to Albaladejo, rhetoric offers the means for political and legal components of discourse to be cast in persuasive communication. He compares the role of the orator, the audei.

Rhetoric is the domain of linguistic communication and, more in general, of symbolic representation. Van Heusden argues that, whereas rhetoric is prominent in the theories of post-structuralism, it is virtually absent from contemporary European culture. The quest for a new form of rhetoric may have directed our attention toward Quintilian. His way of argumentation reflects a deeply rhetorical way of thinking to which we are no longer used. His rhetoric, however, is one of caution and discretion. As it strongly focuses on both style and argument, on the role of figures of speech and thought in particular, it can even be characterised, in a sense, as an anti-rhetorical rhetoric. Stressing the openness and earnestness of the orator, Quintilian always tries to avoid the cheap, the too overtly rhetorical. No tricks, no lying, at least in principle. With him, Van Heusden argues, we must plead for a revival of social communication, a revival of the serious debate on opinions, values, and tradition, as well as for a careful (in both senses of the word) use of linguistic signs.

Francisco Chico-Rico studies the concept of *elocutio* as described and explained in Book VIII of the *Institutio oratoria* from a semiotic point of view. He analyses its syntactic, semantic, and pragmatic aspects in order to get a better knowledge of the process of the micro-structure of rhetorical discourse in close connection with the general processes of textual construction and rhetorical communication between orators and hearers. *Latinitas, perspicuitas ornatus*, and *decorum*, in these general processes, serve *utilitas* and constitute qualities of rhetorical discourse manifestation which Chico-Rico discusses from the perspective of the relationships between *elocutio* and the other rhetorical operations, including *intellectio*, and between the same rhetorical operation and the components of the general process of rhetorical communication.

Generally speaking, *actio* or the delivery of a speech also belongs to the theme of rhetoric and communication. Quintilian is the only classical author who wrote a systematic treatise on this subject. One of its aspects is *gestus* or gestures. In his essay, Peter Wülfing focuses on Quintilian's description of hand, arm, and finger movements in *Inst. or.* XI.3.84-124: how should they be performed and in which part of the speech are they most effective? He also discusses modern literature on what is now called 'body language', and concludes that Quintilian's treatise may not suffice for application in modern times, but that it certainly has some advantages, which do not have their equal today.

5.4 Argumentation

Three essays are dedicated to this theme. In Book V, Quintilian deals with proofs as essential part of every speech, with arguments as a form of reasoning, and with places as reservoirs of ideas where the arguments are stored. Belén Saiz points out that particularly Quintilian's theory of places (*loci* or *topoi*) is at once oratorical and educational: he provides the young orator with a classification which stands out in consistency, but at the same time he makes it clear that his classification can only be used fruitfully by a naturally gifted orator.

When the orator has found his arguments, it is essential that he orders them in an appropriate way (*dispositio*). According to Quintilian, the best way to do this is by raising the right questions because then the orator can identify the key point on which the case hinges. Therefore, in Book VII, he develops a complex and comprehensive classification of questions, *status*. David Pujante discusses the different types of questions, and even provides schemes of the four *status*: *coniectura, definitio, qualitas*, and *translatio*.

Maarten Henket investigates to what extent Quintilian's system of *status* and *loci* can be useful for a modern theory of adjudication and for the training and practice of the modern judge. Most modern legal theorists assume that the average case does not demand any creativity or choice from the judge and that therefore argumentation is not necessary. Henket contests this view and argues that knowledge of *status* and *loci* will help the judge in making and formulating a reasoned decision and in convincing the appellate court, the legal community, and, if possible, the parties that his decision is right. The *Institutio oratoria*, and particularly Book VII, is a valuable source of inspiration in this respect.

5.5 Roman law

It is evident that Roman law plays an important part in the *Institutio oratoria*. The young orator will have to build his career in the courts of law and, when a senator, he will be involved in making laws. Consequently, Quintilian lards his instructions with many examples from legal practice. For a proper understanding of these examples, it is necessary to have a basic knowledge of the procedures as they took place in the first century AD. Therefore, I shall first give a rough sketch of these procedures and then I shall return to the essays about Roman law in the *Institutio oratoria*.

5.5.1.

In Quintilian's day, there were a large variety of procedures, in cases concerning criminal law as well as in cases on civil law. This variety was caused by the fact that emperor Augustus had introduced a new procedure for all cases, the *cognitio extraordinaria*, without abolishing the old Republican procedures, which differed according to the type of case.[29]

Since about 150 BC, there had been a limited number of courts for criminal cases, which could decide on specific offences like murder and poisoning, high treason, bribery during elections, etc.[30] Every respectable citizen, not only the injured party, could lodge a complaint against someone. If the praetor accepted the complaint, a jury was set up by drawing lots. The course of the lawsuit was not determined by the judge, as in Anglo-American law, but by the parties and their lawyers. The plaintiff had to prove that the defendant had committed the crime. If he was unsuccessful, he ran the risk of being accused himself because he had knowingly lodged a false complaint. If he was successful, he received a considerable reward. It was the jury who decided whether the accused was guilty or not and what the penalty would be, if that was not evident from the law. It was in the criminal courts that orators could show off their talents and try to gain popularity, as, for instance, Cicero did in his speech in defence of Roscius from Amerino and in his speech against Verres.

Civil cases were dealt with in a different way.[31] Usually a judge, i.e. a citizen who belonged to the nobility, was chosen by the parties to solve their dispute. The judge sat alone, and the contending parties had no right of appeal against his decision. A civil procedure took place on the basis of a *formula*, a written document in which the parties had summarised their claims. The drawing up of the *formula* and

---

[29]   See O. Tellegen-Couperus, *A Short History of Roman Law*, London: Routledge 1993, pp. 88-93.
[30]   For a modern overview, see O.F. Robinson, *The Criminal Law of Ancient Rome*, London: Duckworth 1995 and B. Santalucia, *Diritto e processo penale nell'antica Roma*, 2nd edition, Milan: Giuffrè 1998.
[31]   For detailed information, see M. Kaser and K. Hackl, *Das römische Zivilprozessrecht*, 2nd edition, Munich: Beck 1996.

the choosing of a judge took place under the supervision of the praetor. Although the advocates usually could not colour their speeches by using a grand style or emotional appeals, Cicero's speech *Pro Caecina* shows that legal arguments do not have to make a speech dull. A different procedure was used for lawsuits about large inheritances and possibly also about ownership of land and guardianship: they took place before a court of approximately 100 judges, the *centumviri*. Splendid speeches were delivered at these trials; here orators could make or break their reputations.

The *cognitio extrordinaria* had originated during the Republic and was first used in the provinces. The administration of justice was one of the tasks of the provincial governor. In 27 BC, when a number of provinces came directly under his control, Augustus delegated this task to officials in his service. This example was followed in the other provinces and – although not on a regular basis yet – also in Italy and Rome. The *cognitio extraordinaria* brought about a number of changes, for instance, the introduction of the right of appeal. The judge was now an official who worked in a hierarchical structure headed by the emperor, so parties could appeal to a senior judge or to the emperor himself. It must be mentioned that there was not always a strict distinction between the cognition procedure and the formulary system. From the beginning of the Empire, it sometimes happened that parties that had fought each other in the framework of a formulary procedure, appealed to the emperor or his subordinate against the sentence that had been pronounced. The introduction of the cognition procedure was not unfavourable for the orators, since the judges were no longer bound by all kinds of rules like the formula in civil cases and fixed penalties in criminal cases. The fact that they had such a wide competence made it extra interesting for the orators to try and influence the judges' feelings.

5.5.2.
The examples from legal practice with which Quintilian lards his instructions do not always refer to his own time but are often drawn from Cicero and from Greek mythology. Therefore, the first thing students of Roman law have to know is whether these examples provide trustworthy information. Two authors offer their views on this question.

Olivia Robinson takes Book III to demonstrate how useful Quintilian can be as a source of law, and also how dangerous. She discusses texts that confirm or increase our knowledge of Roman law, but also texts that are misleading. Her conclusion is that the *Institutio oratoria* is a valuable source, not to be ignored, but that it must be used with caution for discovering the substantive law or procedure of the first century AD.

Jan Willem Tellegen focuses on one example mentioned in Book VII, which Quintilian drew from the rhetorical works by Cicero, viz., the *causa Curiana*. Modern interpretations of this famous case contradict what Cicero and Quintilian wrote about it and this discrepancy is explained by the assumption that Cicero and Quintilian were orators and that their work therefore is unreliable. Tellegen, however, shows that Cicero's description of the case becomes absolutely clear with the help of

Quintilian, whereas what Quintilian writes on the subject only becomes meaningful in the light of Cicero's description. He concludes therefore that the *Institutio oratoria* is reliable and a valuable source of our knowledge about Roman law.

In other examples, Quintilian refers to lawsuits that took place in his own time. Because these references are often very brief, they are difficult to understand for modern readers. According to Olga Tellegen-Couperus, one can explain these references properly, but only when one takes account of their rhetorical context. She demonstrates this view with examples from the two books on style, VIII and IX. In VIII.5.19, Quintilian quotes a *sententia*, a striking sentence, which refers to the *lex Iulia et Papia* and which so far has not been satisfactorily explained. By using another reference to the same case (in VIII.5.17), she shows that the advocate in question had argued that it was unfair that the mistress of a young man could inherit a quarter of his inheritance since the *lex Iulia et Papia* allowed only a tenth of a husband's estate to his wife.

In IX 2.73-74, Quintilian describes how he won a case about an inheritance by using a particular figure of thought, *emphasis*. A wife was charged with forging her husband's will. In fact, the heirs had drawn up a document in which they promised to pay over the inheritance to the wife, and they had shown this document to the husband on his deathbed. Olga Tellegen-Couperus argues that the case had nothing to do with the *lex Iulia et Papia* as is generally assumed; Quintilian could clear the woman from the accusation by stressing the fact that the heirs had offered the document to the husband, and at the same time avoiding to refer to any reaction of him.

In his paper, Andrew Lewis draws attention to a phrase in the context of Quintilian's discussion on argumentation in Book V. In Chapter13, Quintilian deals with the refutation by the defendant. There are several strategies, one being the plea for mercy. In V.13.7, Quintilian concludes that it is ridiculous to ask for mercy from a judge who has to decide '*secundum legem*' in the case of those who admit liability. Lewis argues that *lex* in this phrase must be interpreted as the *formula* which determines exactly what the judge may do.

The law of procedure is also referred to in Book XI of the *Institutio oratoria*, which is dedicated to *elocutio*, style, and in particular to *apte dicere*. In the first chapter, Quintilian discusses the best wording of a speech in delicate cases where tact is required. One of his examples is that of an orator who has to address the same judges from whom he has appealed (XI.1.76). Esperanza Osaba explains that, since sentences were appealed mainly because of judges' lack of skill or unfairness, judges tended to consider appeals against their sentences as injurious and therefore took it out on the appealing party or his advocate. According to Quintilian, the orator should apologise to the judge and employ every means to induce him to feel compunction for his anger. From later legal texts, it appears that the problem of the angry judges had grown worse and that appeals could even be dangerous. Osaba thinks that Quintilian's text may be the first to refer to this problem.

5.6 Emotions in the courtroom

The last but perhaps most fascinating theme are the psychological strategies to be used in order to convince the judge. Quintilian gives instructions on such strategies throughout the *Institutio oratoria,* but particularly so at the beginning of Book IV and in Chapter 2 of Book VI. One even gets the impression that these instructions constitute a framework for his treatise of the *inventio,* which takes up Books IV to VI.

Ida Mastrorosa concentrates on the rhetorical rules and psychological strategies described in Book IV. According to Quintilian, influencing the emotions of the judge can be useful already in the introduction of a speech, namely, to rouse the judge's interest and make him prepared to accept the facts as the orator will describe them in the *narratio.* The orator is even allowed to twist the truth when describing the facts of the case, provided there is a good reason for doing so. Such a reason may be the wish to prevent an unskilled judge from falling into error.

The use of emotions in order to convince the judge is essential in the *peroratio* or epilogue of the speech. Quintilian writes about it in Book VI.2. Since this chapter forms the basis of several papers in this book, it is useful to have the full text in English at one's disposal. Jeroen Bons and Robert Taylor Lane have undertaken to prepare a new English translation of Chapter VI.2. Jeroen Bons also wrote a commentary.

Richard Katula interprets Chapter 2 of Book VI from a lawyer's point of view. He discusses Quintilian's advice on the purpose of emotional proof, the presentation of an emotional appeal and the strategic use of emotion in a trial. He then compares the Roman courtroom with the modern courtroom, arguing that emotional proof is still a vital force in today's judicial environment, but in a less conscious and more insidious manner.

Did the use of emotions distinguish the jurists from the orators? José-Domingo Rodríguez Martín uses Book VI of the *Institutio oratoria* to discuss the controversial topic of the relationship between jurists and orators in Quintilian's day. He explains that, whereas jurists were mainly working on private law where there was little room for emotions, orators preferred criminal cases where they could better display their skills. Still, jurists could play a part in convincing the judge, namely, by providing the ammunition for the battle that the orators had to undertake. In Quintilian's time, however, legal techniques were considered far less effective in convincing the judge than playing on his feelings.

It will now be clear that the essays in this book reflect the wide range of subjects discussed by Quintilian in his *Institutio oratoria.* They also show that many of the basic issues and dilemmas of the orators in first century Rome are still topical matters today. Therefore, politicians as well as legal professionals such as advocates and judges may find inspiration and support in the *Institutio oratoria,* which, as they will find, is even richer than this book.

J. FERNÁNDEZ LÓPEZ

THE CONCEPT OF AUTHORITY IN THE *INSTITUTIO ORATORIA*, BOOK I

1. INTRODUCTION

The first book of Quintilian's *Institutio oratoria* is, together with the twelfth and last, the one which deals with more general issues. In fact, it is the only book that does not deal with rhetoric properly speaking, as the development of the system of rhetoric is left for the remainder of the work. Nonetheless, allusions are of course made and fundamental questions directly related to rhetoric are dealt with. As a result of this, it is also the book in which the presence of the world of law is the least evident. Accordingly and significantly enough, Quintilian's Book I is quoted only once by F. Lanfranchi in his classical study on the relationship between law and rhetoric in the Roman world.[1]

Nevertheless, among the twelve books of the *Institutio*, Book I is arguably the one that is the most appealing to the modern reader, at least in some of its parts, and that is the reason why F. H. Colson started his worthy edition of this book stating that 'seldom have sixty pages of equal importance and interest lain so long neglected'.[2] The aim of the *Institutio*, as we recall, is to give as many and as detailed instructions as possible to describe the steps needed to form an ideal orator, who, in a famous formula traceable down to Cato the censor (third to second centuries BC), should be a *uir bonus dicendi peritus* (XII.1.25), that is to say, a good person, in the moral sense, who is an expert with words.

Book I of Quintilian's *Institutio oratoria* is devoted to presenting the first stages of the education that such a perfect orator-to-be should receive, and Quintilian's open and, one might say, advanced views on pedagogy have often found applause and recognition by later generations.[3] These pages contain allusions to the pedagogical value of contact with other students (I.2.18-22), to the merits of multilingual education (I.1.12-14), to the benefits of material and toy aids (I.1.24-26), to the stu-

[1] F. Lanfranchi, *Il diritto nei retori romani. Contributo alla storia dello sviluppo del diritto romano*, Milan: Giuffrè 1938, p. 32 n. 1.
[2] F.H. Colson (ed.), M. Fabii *Quintiliani Institutionis oratoriae liber I*, Cambridge: Cambridge University Press, 1924, p. i.
[3] See, among others, R. Johnson, 'Quintilian's Place in European Education', in: M.N. Kelly (ed.), *For Service to Classical Studies: Essays in Honour of Francis Letters*, Melbourne: Cheshire 1966, pp. 79-101 and V.E. Alfieri, 'La pedagogia di Quintiliano', *Athenaeum 42* (Omaggio a E. Malcovati) 1964, pp. 400-415; for a view which may somehow overemphasize Quintilian's weaknesses but that is a useful corrective to the exaggerated praise often lavished upon the *Institutio*, see G. Kennedy, 'An Estimate of Quintilian', *American Journal of Philology* 83 (1962) pp. 130-146.

dents' need for relaxation (I.3.8 and I.1.20), to the uselessness of corporal punishment (I.3.13-18), and so on. It is there where the appeal to modern readers is more
evident, and it is there where much of the interest that Colson alluded to can be
found: in Quintilian's broad idea of an orator's formation. This is also the reason
why the absence of almost any reference to legal aspects in these pages is still more
striking. Quintilian even recommends a series of disciplines to be studied in the preliminary stages of a rhetor's formation, and he includes music (I.10.9-33), geometry
(I.10.34-49), and even some acting techniques (I.11.1-19), notwithstanding the terrible social reputation that actors had at the time. However, as Lana rightly points out
in an article on the study of law at the rhetor's school, 'there was no place for the
study of law.'[4] The first lines of Lana's article are quite illustrative for our concerns:

> 'È noto che la scuola romana non riservava nessun posto specifico allo studio sistem-
> atico del diritto. Una società e una cultura come quella romana, che pure si affermarono
> specialmente per la sapienza giuridica, non ritenevano che fosse necessario impartire ai
> giovani una formazione giuridica sistematica e rigorosa. Non s'intende dire, con ciò,
> che gli studenti fossero totalmente digiuni di conoscenze giuridiche; ma che, in linea
> generale, quello che apprendevano intorno al diritto, lo apprendevano esclusivamente
> alla scuola del retore e giungeva loro filtrato attraverso le dottrine retoriche.'[5]

Despite all this, and as Lana points out,[6] Quintilian (XII.3) underlines that the orator
should master the study of law, at least so as to avoid having to have constant
recourse to the *iuris periti*, and he even acknowledges, though not explicitly
(III.6.59), that the usual practice was precisely the one he wanted to avoid. Anyhow,
for Quintilian, jurists are just failed orators, who even admit such a situation, as he
states in the last book of the *Institutio* (XII.3.9-10):

> *Quod si plerique desperata facultate agendi ad discendum ius declinaverunt, quam id
> scire facile est oratori quod discunt qui sua quoque confessione oratores esse non pos-
> sunt!*
> Moreover, if the class of legal experts is as a rule drawn from those who, in despair of
> making successful pleaders, have taken refuge with the law, how easy it must be for an
> orator to know what those succeed in learning, who by their own confession are inca-
> pable of becoming orators![7]

2. AUTHORITY

However, there is a concept that, at different levels and from diverse points of view,
is pervasive throughout this first book of the *Institutio*, and that can be linked very
directly with the world of law. I am referring to the idea of authority or, in Latin,
auctoritas.[8]

---

[4]   'Per lo studio del diritto non c'era posto.' I. Lana, 'Il primo approccio degli studenti romani con la
legge alla scuola del retore', *Klio* 61 (1979) pp. 89-95, at p. 89.
[5]   Lana (see note 4), p. 89.
[6]   See note 4, p. 94.
[7]   I use the text edition by Winterbottom (see Introduction, note 26) and the English translation by Butler (see Introduction, note 27).
[3]   On the importance of this concept in the Roman world, see R. Heinze, '*Auctoritas*', *Hermes* 60 (1925)
pp. 348-366.

Apart from its more technical juridical sense, which is the first one considered in the entry of the *Thesaurus linguae latinae*,[9] *auctoritas* as a quality possessed by people has two main general meanings. The first one would be the idea of an intrinsic quality, something very close to dignity, or gravity.[10] The other one takes more into account the importance of the audience who grants such authority, and would be something closer to influence or exemplarity.[11] Throughout the *Institutio*, we find both senses of the word, together with its frequent appearance in more technical contexts, where the authority just defined is considered as a means of persuasion. Authority thus becomes a quality of style or tone,[12] but above all it is one of the orator's persuasive strengths, which should be obtained or preserved almost at any cost.[13]

Thus, I would like to focus on how the idea of *auctoritas* plays a fundamental role in two fields that are widely treated in the first book of the *Institutio*.[14] The first one concerns linguistic authority. The verbal skills of the orator should address many issues of choice, lexical above all, but not exclusively, and in such instances authority is a crucial discriminating criterion, as we will see. The second one is more general, and concerns the very conception of the perfect orator which permeates over the whole work: the ideal orator conceived by Quintilian will only be able to fulfil his ideal role in society if he appears endowed with a considerable degree of authority based on his moral character or, to use the Greek word, on his *êthos*. Let us now consider both aspects of *auctoritas*.

3. LANGUAGE AND AUTHORITY

As we have already noted, Quintilian's first book does not deal with rhetoric in its technical sense, but with the preliminary educational stages a student should go through before entering the rhetor's school. One of them was, of course, the years at the school of the *grammaticus*, where the essentials of Latin language and literature, especially poetry, were taught. As Quintilian treats this issue at some length, quite a lot of attention is paid to linguistic correctness.[15] It is here that he proposes a general

---

[9]   See *Thesaurus Linguae Latinae* II, VI, coll. 1213-1234; in fact, the first heading under which the term *auctoritas* is developed in this work is 'in sermone iudiciali'.
[10]   See note 9, col. 1215.
[11]   See note 9, col. 1218.
[12]   See, for instance, *Inst. or.* I.11.12, VIII.3.1, VIII.3.25, IX.4.91, IX.4.108, XII.10.46.
[13]   See, for instance, *Inst. or.* III.2.94, III.5.25, III.8.13, VI.3.30, XII.11.3.
[14]   For a thorough and rich analysis of *auctoritas* in Roman rhetoric, see L. Calboli Montefusco, 'L'*auctoritas* nella dottrina retorica', *Vichiana* 1 (1990) pp. 41-60.
[15]   For Quintilian's sources in these chapters, see J. Cousin, *Études sur Quintilien, I: Contribution à l'étude des sources de l'Institution oratoire*, Paris: Boivin 1935-1936, rpt. Amsterdam: Schippers 1967, pp. 21-107 and M.M. Odgers, 'Quintilian's rhetorical predecessors', *Transactions of the American Philological Association* 66 (1935) pp. 25-36. As Colson points out (see note 2, p. 73), Quintilian's formula on the constitution of language can be found in a parallel form in Varro quoted by Diomedes (Keil I, 439, 15-17): 'Latinitas (...) constat (...), ut adserit Varro, his quattuor, natura analogia consuetudine auctoritate.' Varro also tries to find a balance between analogy (*ratio*) and usage (*consuetudo*) in which the

definition of language and enumerates its elements. Quintilian's text is as follows (I.6.1-3):

> *Sermo constat ratione vetustate auctoritate consuetudine. Rationem praestat praecipue*
> *analogia, nonnumquam etymologia. Vetera maiestas quaedam et, ut sic dixerim, religio*
> *commendat. Auctoritas ab oratoribus vel historicis peti solet (nam poetas metri neces-*
> *sitas excusat, ...): cum summorum in eloquentia virorum iudicium pro ratione, et vel*
> *error honestus est magnos duces sequentibus. Consuetudo vero certissima loquendi*
> *magistra, utendumque plane sermone, ut nummo, cui publica forma est. Omnia tamen*
> *haec exigunt acre iudicium.*
>
> Language is based on reason, antiquity, authority and usage. Reason finds its chief sup-
> port in analogy and sometimes in etymology. As for antiquity it is commended to us by
> the possession of a certain majesty, I might almost say sanctity. Authority as a rule we
> derive from orators and historians (for poets, owing to the necessities of metre, are
> allowed a certain licence...): the judgement of a supreme orator is placed on the same
> level as reason, and even error brings no disgrace, if it result from treading in the foot-
> steps of such distinguished guides. Usage however is the surest pilot in speaking, and
> we should treat language as currency minted with the public stamp. But in all these
> cases we have need of a critical judgement.

The idea of language (*sermo*) presented here by Quintilian coincides almost exactly with what modern linguists call 'norm', which, as E. Coseriu traditionally put it, is a question of choice among the many possibilities that a linguistic system offers to its users.[16] Thus, after having explained at length the possible deviations from the norm, Quintilian presents these four criteria of correctness, of belonging to the norm: *ratio*, *uetustas*, *auctoritas*, and *consuetudo*.[17] Quintilian's preferences, as K. von Fritz pointed out more than fifty years ago,[18] would be the following: analogy (*analogia*, a part of *ratio*) is a good criterion only when usage (*consuetudo*) and authority (*auc-toritas*) do not settle an issue clearly, whether it be because usage presents several possibilities about which authorities do not agree, or because we are before such a strange case that there is not a real *consuetudo* about it. As for *uetustas*, it also depends on authority and usage: archaisms are only tolerable if supported by the usage of some authority. Authority, however, has a limit, for those whom we con-sider as authorities were living in a time which is not ours, so that not all words they

---

latter is considered as more important, and he insists on the value which authority must be granted when several usages concur. On this subject, see R. Amacker, 'Le rôle du sujet parlant dans le *De lingua latina* de Varron', *Cahiers Ferdinand de Saussure* 51 (1998) pp. 39-61. According to H. Nettleship, 'The Study of Latin Grammar among the Romans in the First Century A.D.', *Journal of Philology* 15 (1886) pp. 189ff., Chapters IV.1 to VI.27 could be divided into two main parts: the first one (IV.1 to V.54) would be based upon Remmius Palaemon's *Ars grammatica* and the second one (V.55-VI.27) would follow Pliny the Elder's *De dubio sermone*. See also on the subject, Calboli Montefusco (see note 14), p. 56.
[16]   For the most recent reformulation of Coseriu's conception, see E. Coseriu, 'Die Ebenen der einzel-sprachlichen Kompetenz: System und Norm', in E. Coseriu, *Sprachkompetenz*, Tübingen: Francke 1988, pp. 52-55.
[17]   See K. von Fritz, 'Ancient Instruction in Grammar According to Quintilian', *American Journal of Philology* 70 (1949) pp. 337-366, at pp. 342-343.
[18]   Von Fritz (see note 17), p. 353. On pp. 340ff., he points out several misunderstandings Colson includes in his commentary on Chapters 5 and 6, and also shows (p. 343) how Nettleship's (see note 15) remarks about the lack of unity of this part of the *Institutio* are also based upon a misunderstanding of Quintilian's line of thought.

used are acceptable and may have to be adapted (I.6.42); and sometimes authority is even overcome by usage (I.5.63).[19]

The problem, of course, is whose usage we are talking about, because not every speaker of a language can be taken into account in order to describe its norm. It is here where authority comes again into play and shows a very close link to *consuetudo*, Quintilian's favourite criterion, because only the users endowed with authority can be taken into account. In fact, in the very last paragraph of the chapter, Quintilian makes explicit statements about which language users must be taken into account and whose *consuetudo* is to be followed (I.6.45):

> *Ergo consuetudinem sermonis vocabo consensum eruditorum, sicut vivendi consensum bonorum.*
> I will therefore define usage in speech as the agreed practice of educated men, just as where our way of life is concerned I should define it as the agreed practice of all good men.

On the other hand, we have Quintilian's happy analogy between minted coins and language, which still exists today –we speak about coining both currency and new terms in several European languages. This comparison makes the relationship between usage and authority still clearer. The general analogy is based on the idea of change value: minted coins are guaranteed by a mark that is easy to identify, to which their users grant the appropriate value in order to sell goods or services; much in the same way as a linguistic code is recognised by its users as something shared and which fulfils the group's wish to exchange information. There is also the issue of respect: if there is a means that makes an important exchange possible, it must be preserved in as good a condition as possible, so that such an exchange continues to be attainable. In this context, authority is indeed important for both currency and language: if there is any doubt about whether a coin is a forgery, or about whether some linguistic usage is not legitimate, one must make sure that the coin or the expression comes from the adequate authority.

In this sense, Quintilian is, in a certain way, an anti-essentialist, for the ultimate criterion for linguistic correctness is not directly based upon reason or upon a fixed reference point, but upon the usage of authoritative people. Nevertheless, it must be taken into account that authorities, however well established they are, are always questionable and subject to variation and opinion. Thus, what we find in Quintilian is an effort to avoid any absolute foundation, which is something very closely related to an issue central in every rhetorical principle: the utmost importance granted to the concrete situation, whether it be the speaker, the audience, the time of the day, the subject, and so on.

4. THE IDEAL ORATOR AND AUTHORITY

As we have seen, authority is an important element for the functioning of language, and when Quintilian has to make it explicit where such authority is pre-eminently

---

[19] Quintilian (I.5.65) shows that authority has less importance than usage with the example of the declension of *Calypso*: though Caesar uses *Calypsonem*, his authority has not prevailed over common usage.

located, he has no doubt: in the greatest orators. Nevertheless, the authority the best orators show, cannot be simply linguistic, it must also have a higher quality: it is moral authority[20] and, very closely linked to that, at least in Quintilian's conception, it is also a kind of political authority. This is something Quintilian wants to be clear from the beginning of his work. This is the reason why, very early in the first book of his *Institutio*, he states which his main aim is (I.pr.9):

> *Oratorem autem instituimus illum perfectum, qui esse nisi vir bonus non potest;*
> *ideoque non dicendi modo eximiam in eo facultatem sed omnes animi virtutes exigimus.*
> My aim, then, is the education of the perfect orator. The first essential for such a one is
> that he should be a good man, and consequently we demand him not merely the pos-
> session of exceptional gifts of speech, but of all excellencies of character as well.

Throughout the history of Western civilisation, rhetoric has always been very closely related to politics, whenever the various regimes allowed for it. It is politics, which is the field where the perfect orator can best display his qualities.[21] As Quintilian puts it, the functions that a good orator should ideally perform are (I.pr.10) *regere consiliis urbes, fundare legibus, emendare iudiciis*, that is, 'to guide a state with his counsels, give it a firm basis by his legislation and purge its vices by his decisions as a judge.' There is no need to recall that Quintilian's tripartite formulation of the orator's functions has clear resemblance with the classical division of political powers into the executive, legislative, and judicial branches.[22]

However, the problem Quintilian has to face in order to defend this view is that, in the ancient world, the role he wants to assign to the orator is, though vaguely, more clearly assigned to the figure of the philosopher. That is the reason why, at least in some part, Quintilian has to build the social authority of his ideal orator on an invective against such rivals. Quintilian's argumentation against philosophers' alleged social hegemony focuses on two issues.[23]

First, he presents the issue, we might say, of professional competence: Quintilian underlines the idea that the very matter of philosophy cannot be the object of a technical discipline, but that it is something of general interest and even subject of common conversation. In Quintilian's own words (I.pr.16):

> *Haec autem quae velut propria philosophiae adseruntur, passim tractamus omnes.*
> We all of us frequently handle those themes which philosophy claims for its own.

---

[20]	As M. Winterbottom, 'Quintilian the Moralist', in: T. Albadejo, E. del Río, J.A. Caballero (eds.), *Quintiliano: historia y actualidad de la retórica*, Logroño: Instituto de Estudios Riojanos 1998, pp. 327-328 points out, there is a remarkable likeness between the vocabulary Quintilian uses to deal with moral virtue and the one with which he characterizes linguistic correctness.

[21]	On this subject, see T. Morgan, 'A Good Man Skilled in Politics: Quintilian's Political Theory', in: Y.L. Too - N. Livingstone (eds.), *Pedagogy and Power. Rhetorics of Classical Learning*, Cambridge: Cambridge University Press 1998, pp. 245-262.

[22]	In III.8.13, Quintilian points out that the most important issue in deliberative speeches (which, for him, is the most important of the three genres) 'is the authority of the speaker' (*Valet autem in consiliis auctoritas plurimum*).

[23]	Quintilian's battle is a not so early episode of a long-lasting confrontation in Western culture; for an excellent historical panorama on it, see S. IJsseling, *Rhetoric and Philosophy in Conflict: An Historical Survey*, The Hague: Nijhoff 1976.

However, far more important than that, there is a moral issue:[24] philosophers, as they are found now in society, Quintilian says, cannot be considered as models of conduct, whatever illustrious ancestors they may claim to have (I.pr.15).

> *Ac veterum quidem sapientiae professorum multos et honesta praecepisse et, ut prae-*
> *ceperint, etiam vixisse facile concesserim: nostris vero temporibus sub hoc nomine*
> *maxima in plerisque vitia latuerunt. Non enim virtute ac studiis ut haberentur*
> *philosophi laborabant, sed vultum et tristitiam et dissentientem a ceteris habitum pes-*
> *simis moribus praetendebant.*
> I am ready to admit that many of the old philosophers inculcated the most excellent
> principles and practised what they preached. But in our own day the name of philoso-
> pher has too often been the mask for the worst vices. For their attempt has not been to
> win the name of philosopher by virtue and the earnest search for wisdom; instead they
> have sought to disguise the depravity of their characters by the assumption of a stern
> and austere mien accompanied by the wearing of a garb differing from that of their fel-
> low men.

The character that such philosophers try to conceal is their *êthos*, a Greek word for which Quintilian does not have a completely appropriate Latin translation[25] and which has a technical meaning both in philosophy and in rhetoric. Concretely in rhetoric, *êthos* ('character'), together with *logos* ('reason') and *pathos* ('emotion'), is one of the three traditional means of persuasion. There is some degree of irrationalism implied in Quintilian's position for, among the three, Quintilian trusts most in *êthos*, and persuasion through the orator's *êthos* is inextricably linked to authority, as opposed to persuasion through reason, which would have a more universal and, so to say, philosophical appeal. It is here that we find some contrast within Quintilian's position: on the one hand, he is constantly speaking of the perfect orator-to-be, in whose picture he mixes features taken from Cicero, from an almost Platonic, ideal orator and, one must admit, from Quintilian himself. On the other hand, he is quite conscious of the characteristics that real audiences, not ideal ones, present, and he justifies the appeal to emotion if necessary and, more important, underlines the superior persuasive value of *êthos* and the authority linked to it.

Thus, the authority dealt with is not only that of the orator's *ethos*, an orator who, for Quintilian, is perfect both intellectually and morally and who also cares specifically for contributing to the well-being of his community. On the contrary, there is a certain paradox in the general conception, for acknowledging the need for persuasion, however great the authority behind it, implies that the inevitable limits to such authority are also acknowledged.

5. CONCLUSION

Both the authority that derives from the orator's *êthos* and the authority that linguistic *consuetudo* displays are based, above all, on the audience: they rest upon the consensus of those who grant such authority. In the case of language, it is the *consensus*

---

[24]   On this subject, see the brilliant pages by Winterbottom (see note 20), pp. 317-336.
[25]   See *Inst. or.* VI.2.8: '... *êthos cuius nomine, ut ego quidem sentio, caret sermo Romanus: mores appellantur, atque inde pars quoque illa philosophiae êthikê moralis est dicta.*'

eruditorum. In the case of the person of the orator, it is more a desideratum: it would be the consensus of the people who constitute a society that approaches a certain ideal in the same degree as the orator himself does.

It is a consensus, however, which is being constantly built and which cannot be but the result of a reached agreement, however tacit or unconscious. Anyhow, these agreements, reached through the exercise of a rhetoric where authority plays a relevant role, do not perform the function of avoiding the open confrontation of ideas and proposals. And I would like the following to be my last point: Quintilian's ideal of the orator also implies a desired world, where all matters would be settled through public discussion among well-educated people who are trained in oratory and who would show no ill will in such discussions.

A public space so constituted would not avoid the conflict of opposed views and the holding of passionate debates, in contrast to what we see increasingly frequently in the world around us, where the confrontation of ideas is perceived as something which ought to be avoided. Quintilian's conception of rhetoric, including the role of authority, aims to build an open environment where ideas can be discussed and citizens can take part, precisely through rhetoric, in the decision-making processes which affect their lives.

SERENA QUERZOLI

MATERIA AND *OFFICIA* OF RHETORICAL TEACHING IN BOOK II OF THE *INSTITUTIO ORATORIA*

1. *IUS* IN THE *ENKÝKLIOS PAIDEÍA*

Tracing a sort of ideal circular path, at the beginning and at the end of Book II of Quintilian's handbook, we read the discouraging description of the condition of contemporary rhetoric,[1] deprived of the *officia* or duties rightly belonging to it. Already stressed at the beginning of Book II, with reference to the professions of the rhetoricians and the teachers of grammar,[2] the purpose of recovering the essential components of his art fomented Quintilian's dispute against philosophy, concerning the last part of the book, where the *philosophiae officium* was mentioned.[3] The use of '*officium*' with reference to the duties of the art which Quintilian proclaimed to cultivate, may not be original, as is, for example, shown by Cicero's observations,[4] but it is nevertheless meaningful. The Flavian rhetor, who significantly entitled his book '*Institutio*', aimed at building an educative pattern in which the ethical object was far more important than the technical knowledge.

The *materia* and the *officia* of rhetoric, which Quintilian already discussed in the first part of the handbook, originated from different educative programmes, though the ethical contents were undoubtedly founded on Cicero's theory. The interpreta-

---

[1] In his lost treatise *De causis corruptae eloquentiae* published before the *Institutio oratoria,* Quintilian discussed the reasons of the decline of contemporary oratory, also examined in the handbook (see esp. *Inst. or.* X.1.125-131), ascribed to the diffusion of declamations shaped on Senecan eloquency and on that of his imitators. For the *De causis corruptae eloquentiae,* see G. Kennedy, *The Art of Rhetoric in the Roman World 300 B.C.-A.D. 300,* Princeton: Princeton University Press 1972, pp. 494f., with literature. For the relationship between Quintilian's treatise and the *Dialogus de oratoribus,* see C. O. Brink, 'Quintilian's *De causis corruptae eloquentiae* and Tacitus' *Dialogus De oratoribus',* in *Classical Quarterly* 39 (1989) pp. 472ff. A recent discussion of the debate in ancient culture about the decline of oratory in the first century AD is in A. Cavarzere, *Oratoria a Roma,* Roma: Carocci 2000, pp. 215ff, with literature.
[2] *Inst. or.* II.1.4-6. I use the text edition of L. Radermacher, revised by V. Buchheit, Leipzig: Teubner 1959, rpt. 1965.
[3] *Inst. or.* II.21.12-13.
[4] See esp. Cicero, *De oratore,* I.82, I.213, I.162, I.264, II.64, and II.348; Cicero, *De inventione,* I.6 and I.7-8. About *officium* as a duty of the *orator,* see the historical survey in H. Lausberg, *Handbook of Literary Rhetoric,* foreword by G.E. Kennedy, translated by M.T. Bliss, A.J. Ansen and D.E. Orton, edited by D.E. Orton and R.D. Anderson, Leyden-Boston-Cologne: Brill 1998, esp. §§33, 35, 43, 97, 255, 445, 1078, 1079. 1b, 2b, 3b, 3361. For the importance of rhetoric in Cicero's cultural project in connection with philosophy and politics, see E. Narducci, *Cicerone e l'eloquenza romana. Retorica e progetto culturale,* Roma-Bari: Laterza 1997, with literature. For the use of *officium* by Quintilian, see *Inst. or.* I.pr.21, I.7.1, I.10.47, II.4.29, II.5.4, II.21.19, III.4.6, X.1.3, XII pr.4, and XII.9.1.

tion of Cicero was in some way original, both in the explanatory form and in the choice of the materials and it is greatly influenced by the educational pattern of the *enkýklios paideía* or general education as fitted for the school experience in the Roman world.

It is interesting, in this view, to compare Quintilian's *Institutio,* one of the few surviving Roman handbooks written in Latin mentioning the expression *enkýklios paideía*,[5] with the only other Roman treatise dealing with the education of an *artifex* or 'artist' which explicitly explained the expression *enkýklios paideía*, 'translating' it as *encyclios disciplina*:[6] that of Vitruvius, written in the Augustan age.

Both Vitruvius and Quintilian,[7] in different times, wanted to build a new and complete educational model: Vitruvius claimed for the architect the social prestige

---

[5]   *Inst. or.* I.10.1. For the use of *enkýklios paideía* in the *Institutio oratoria,* see J. Adamietz, 'Quintilians 'Institutio oratoria', in: H. Temporini and W. Haase (eds.), *Aufstieg und Niedergang der römischen Welt* II, 32,4, Berlin-New York: Walter de Gruyter 1986, p. 2238 and note 61, with literature. The expression *enkýklios paideía,* as is well-known, is already in the *Naturalis historia* of Pliny the Elder (*praef.* 14), published in AD 77. This work, thus belonging to the technical writings, cannot be properly defined as a handbook; in contents and purpose it is not similar to those of Vitruvius and Quintilian. In fact, it was addressed to a heterogeneous audience. Pliny's monumental work, dedicated to the emperor, was said by the author, probably 'in chiave di paradosso', [see S. Citroni Marchetti, 'Filosofia e ideologia nella 'Naturalis historia' di Plinio', in: Temporini (see above) II.36.5 (1992) p. 3250] to be written in order to give some knowledge to the *humilis vulgus,* to the *turbae agricolarum* and *opificiorum,* and to the *studiorum otiosi* (*N.H. praef.* 6). For the readers of the *Naturalis historia* see A. Borst, *Das Buch der Naturgeschichte. Plinius und seine Leser im Zeitalter des Pergaments,* Heidelberg: Winter 1994. On the contents of the *epistula* dedicating the work to the emperor, see Th. Köues-Zulauf, 'Die Vorrede der plinianischen 'Naturgeschichte'', *Wiener Studien* 86 (1973) pp. 134ff; G. Pascucci. 'La lettera prefatoria di Plinio alla Naturalis historia' in: *Scritti scelti,* Florence: Univ. Degli Studi. Ist. Filol. Class. 'G. Pasquali' 1983, pp. 921ff.; N. P. Howe, 'In Defence of the Encyclopedic Mode: on Pliny's Preface to the Natural History', *Latomus* 44 (1985) pp. 561ff.
[6]   Vitruvius, *De architectura,* I.1.12 and IV *praef.* 4. For a comparison of Quintilian's *enkýklios paideía* to that of Vitruvius, see I. Hadot, *Arts libéraux et philosophie dans la pensée antique,* Paris: *Études Augustiniennes* 1984, pp. 263ff.
[7]   In Julio-Claudian handbooks, knowledge was 'legitimated', on the one hand, by means of its similarities to philosophy, on the other hand, because of its 'debts' towards rhetoric in content and organisation, as shown by the most ambitious cultural projects. Quoting more or less explicitly Cicero's *De oratore,* many authors of handbooks sought to 'legitimate' their knowledge cultivating the ethical aspects and not simply developing the 'technical' content. Latin manuals, whether addressed to the school or not, - privileged rhetoric, both in purpose and in style - in comparison with other 'sciences' in order to elevate the origin and the learning of the various disciplines. A. Santini and N. Scivoletto, 'Presentazione', in: C. Santini and N. Scivoletto (eds.), *Prefazioni, prologhi, proemi di opere tecnico-scientifiche latine,* I, Roma: Herder 1990, VIII, who think that the constant reference to rhetoric was characteristic of 'quasi tutti gli autori' of Latin handbooks and rightly notice concerning the various *Artes* written in the Augustan age and in the Julio-Claudian Principate, the attempt to give to the 'premesse giustificative del ... lavoro uno 'statuto retorico' evidente in particolare nelle prefazioni o nei proemi'. Purpose and model were similar to those of Cicero, with some important changes. The care in the whole education of the *artifex* and the ethical and social purpose, frequently singled out in *utilitas,* marks the cultural projects proposed. If Quintilian's *Institutio* was somehow a 'Werkfunktion' (therefore it stressed the matter and not the author, like many of these manuals, see C. Santini and N. Scivoletto, 'Presentazione', VII) - with regard to the epistemological status of knowledge, the educational project of the Flavian rhetor was original, as the polemic against philosophy demonstrates. On the progressive separation of *technai* from philosophy, see M. Isnardi Parente, *Techne. Momenti del pensiero greco da Platone a Epicuro,* Florence: La nuova Italia 1966, pp. 203ff. and 287ff.

which was attributed to other *technitai*,[8] and Quintilian aimed at recovering it. Their works, of great moment in the history of the Roman *enkýklios paideía*, were written in times which marked important cultural changes and are consequently connected with consistent and broad projects of reform of the official culture.

It is quite probable, as Romano rightly noted,[9] that Vitruvius' pattern of encyclopedic education reflects Cicero's suggestions about the education of the orator, which also influenced Quintilian's handbook.[10]

Like that of Cicero, Vitruvius' cultural project was, at the same time, functional to the specific training of the *artifex*, and open to all useful knowledge supplied by other *téchnai*, arts. The contents of the art were the product of conjunction and communication with other types of knowledge.[11] Vitruvius, as other authors, for example, Varro the encyclopedist, shaped an *enkýklios paideía* free from rigid definitions which could hinder communication with other *téchnai* and, as regarding social prestige, kept the architect away from the cultivated scholars, whose knowledge was compared to philosophy.[12]

At the beginning of the manual, Vitruvius explained that the architect had to possess the way of reasoning and not the *opus*, the professional training, of those branches of knowledge which were not specific to his work.[13] The lexical preferences reveal that, according to Vitruvius, there was a close relationship between architecture and others disciplines, such as grammar, rhetoric and philosophy, which shared the same theoretical characteristics. As Varro had already done, though without success, Vitruvius tried to include architecture in the official culture.[14] The accuracy of the lexical choice was connected with the system of values announced by Vitruvius in the first part of his manual and which contributed to the shaping of the *artis officium*.[15] The *encyclios disciplina* was constructed out of these parts to form as it were one body.[16] Besides literature, also drawing, geometry, optics, arithmetic, learning *plures historiae*, diligently listening to philosophers, music, medicine, the knowledge of jurists' opinions and, finally, astrology formed part of Vitruvius' ambitious project.[17]

---

[8] See E. Romano, *La capanna e il tempio. Vitruvio o dell'architettura*, Palermo: Palumbo 1990, esp. pp. 81ff.

[9] Romano (see note 8), pp. 69ff. thinks that the 'teoria oratoria' of Cicero seems to show perhaps 'il vero, più importante modello della formazione enciclopedica dell'architetto'. Thus, the 'unità culturale' of *De architectura* is based on the unity of theoretical content and practice of specific knowledge, and was not, as in Cicero's model, first of all functional to a political project.

[10] For a survey of the sources of Quintilian's *Institutio oratoria* with special reference to Cicero, see Adamietz (see note 5), pp. 2332ff. and 2252.

[11] Vitruvius, *De architectura*, I.1.11ff. See Romano (see note 8), pp. 69ff.

[12] See Romano (see note 8), pp. 59ff, 81ff. and 143ff. for the discussion of the ethical values, which philosophy prescribes.

[13] Vitruvius, *De architectura*, I.1.15.

[14] See F. Della Corte, *Enciclopedisti latini*, Genova: Libreria internazionale di Stefano 1946, p. 51, and, for Vitruvius 'inferiority complex' towards literary culture, Romano (see note 8), pp. 84ff.

[15] Vitruvius, *De architectura*, I.1.7. See Romano (see note 8), pp. 143ff.

[16] Vitruvius, *De architectura*, I.1.11f. For a discussion of the importance of the various disciplines in Vitruvius' education of the *artifex*, see Romano (see note 8), pp. 60ff.

[17] Vitruvius, *De architectura*, I.1.1-12.

The list shows the new dignity of some disciplines in the imperial age, also in connection to their importance in the *civitas*.

Vitruvius who, as already noted, may have been the first author of a Latin handbook to stress explicitly the contents of the *encyclios disciplina* was also the first one, as attested by the available sources, to include in the *enkýklios paideía* the law, or better, the *ius* proceeding from the opinions of the jurists. The *iura* also contributed to the foundation of his educational model, being important branches, together with other knowledge, of conjunction and communication which release the architect from the difficulties of rigid, specialistic learning and make it possible to compare him to the philosopher or to the rhetor. The architect who knew the opinions of the jurists had to know only the law necessary for buildings with party walls and other things which are known in these matters and which the *artifices* had to know before building was begun, so that the *patres familiarum* - on completion of the works - were not involved in trials and the *leges* concerning both the employer and the constructor could be written carefully.[18] With the word *leges*, Vitruvius meant the content of the contract, as we can deduce from the use of *cavere* in the continuation of the text, in which he stated that if the conditions were carefully written the parties could get rid of mutual obligations without having to fight it out. Vitruvius' interest in *ius* reveals the prestige of the jurists in the Augustan age, as the anecdote in Justinian's Institutes about codicils testifies,[19] as well as the importance of *ius* in the education of the *artifex*.

The considerations about the importance of *ius* and jurisprudence in Quintilian's *enkýklios paideía* are somewhat similar. As previously Vitruvius, the Flavian rhetor included the *ius* in his handbook, yet allowed the orator a far more important duty in connection with the knowledge of *ius*, or, at least, of parts of it.

In this view, what we can read in Book II about the study of law is extremely significant.

Explaining his attitude towards the old and always lively debate of ancient culture about the importance of education in connection with natural attitude, Quintilian wrote that nobody could dissuade him from the belief that it was necessary to note the individual gifts of each boy. Someone could be better adapted for the study of history, somebody else for poetry, or for law, or, finally, could better practice agriculture.[20] The Flavian rhetor mentioned some of the most important activities in Roman society and culture – also from the point of view of their social prestige, entrusting to the teacher, i. e., to the orator, the choice of what was most suitable for a boy. He compared this sifting of their natural talents to the sifting of the gymnastics master, who had to uncover the physical talents of the boys and to stimulate them to improve their abilities.

The teachers of the various disciplines included in the *enkýklios paideía* were only entrusted with technical instruction, not with the entire education of the boys as well as of the orator and the citizen, without regard to their natural talents. In Quintilian's *enkýklios paideía,* the rhetor as the arbiter of the boys' education was the

---

[18]   Vitruvius, *De architectura*, I.1.10. The list is similar to that of Cicero, *De oratore*, I.173.
[19]   Inst. II.2.5pr.
[20]   *Inst. or.* II.8.6-7.

only keeper of tradition and the guardian of ethical values. Thus he became the pedagogue of the whole community, entrusted at the same time with the education of those who would become political leaders (*principes civitatis*).

2. *LEX*, JURISPRUDENCE, AND RHETORIC

Another striking feature of Book II of the *Institutio oratoria* is the fact that Quintilian, in several ways, connected the *materia* and *officia* of rhetoric with one of the parts of *ius,* i.e., the *lex,* and with jurisprudence.

In the discussion of theses concerned with the comparison of things, in the first part of Book II, he cited as example the comparison of the jurist with the soldier: *iurisperiti an militari viri laus maior?*, which deserves the greatest praise, the lawyer or the solder? He then referred to Cicero's *pro Murena*, which, in his opinion, dealt plentifully with judicial oratory.[21]

The well-known oration in defence of the general L. Licinius Murena also involved in political life, charged with *ambitus* by Cato and the jurist S. Sulpicius Rufus because of his behaviour in order to gain the consulship, was held in special repute by Quintilian, who mentioned it many times in the *Institutio*.[22]

Cicero demonstrated three times the inferiority of the study of law as compared with the art of war and of oratory, even though his criticism did not involve his friend S. Sulpicius Rufus, whom he considered a learned and eminent man.[23] In the comparison of the professions and careers of soldiership and jurisprudence, Cicero skilfully introduced the praise of forensic oratory, which he considered the most important activity in civil life, under the care and protection of valour in war. In Cicero's opinion, the consul's ability in speaking was important and highly regarded, essential to dominate the senate, the people and the jury-class.[24] Therefore, not only military glory had more importance than the formula's and actions of the jurists, but also the experience in speaking exceeded jurisprudence in honour: those who were not able to become orators devoted themselves to the study of law.[25]

---

[21] *Inst. or.* II.4.24.
[22] See also *Inst. or.* IV.1.75, IV.5.12, V.10.99, V.11.11, V.11. 23, V.13.27, VI.1.35, VII.1.51, VII.3.16, VIII.3.22, VIII.3.79, VIII.3.80, VIII.6.30, IX.2.18, IX.2.26, IX.3.32s., IX.3.36, IX.3.82, IX.4.107, and XI.1.69f. For a 'political' analysis of the characteristics and of the contents of the well-known *oratio*, see C. J. Classen, *Recht, Rhetorik, Politik. Untersuchungen zur Ciceros rhetorischer Strategie*, Darmstadt: Wissenschaftliche Buchgesellschaft 1985, pp. 120ff. (=Italian transl., Bologna 1998, pp. 123ff.), with literature.
[23] Cicero, *Pro Murena,*7. For S. Sulpicius Rufus, see R. A. Bauman, *Lawyers in Roman transitional politics. A study of the Roman Jurists in their political setting in the Late Republic and Triumvirate,* Munich: Beck 1985, pp. 4ff., with literature. The extant fragments of his orations are collected by E. Malcovati, *Oratorum Romanorum fragmenta liberae rei publicae,* I, Textus, 4th edition, Turin: Paravia 1976, pp. 376ff., but see also R. Syme, 'A Great Orator Mislaid', in: A.R. Birley (ed.), *Roman Papers,* III, Oxford: Clarendon Press 1984, pp. 1415ff., who thinks that some of them should rather be ascribed to the jurist's son.
[24] Cicero, *Pro Murena,* 24.
[25] Cicero, *Pro Murena,* 29. See also *Inst. or.* XII.3.11-12.

The defence of L. Licinius Murena, comparing the 'civil' qualities of Murena with those of his prosecutor, demonstrated the less prestige of jurisprudence.[26] The science of warfare and forensic oratory shared the same high 'civil' importance, denied to jurisprudence, though the soldier was considered only the bulwark of all the activities of the city, dominated by the orator.

The example chosen by Quintilian in order to explain the theses concerned with the comparison of things was symptomatic of his negative valuation of jurists. Even though we cannot exclude that the Flavian rhetor just wanted to cite a well-known example in Latin oratory, comparing two of the most important civil *officia* of ancient Rome, it has to be considered a violent attack on the supremacy in political life of jurisprudence in the *pro Murena*, functional not only to the glorification of soldiership, but also of oratory.

Obviously together with *De oratore,* Cicero's *pro Murena* set an effective cultural precedent for Quintilian's theory about the relationship between orators and jurists in the *Institutio,* especially in Book XII.

Another example of the connection between law and the *materia* of rhetoric is the fact that the first exercises in rhetoric concerned the praise and denunciation of *leges,* laws. Quintilian examined this subject in Book II, before the discussion about the study of the works of orators and historians necessary for the learning of the rudiments of rhetoric.[27]

Lana rightly noticed that Quintilian's choice of arguments and organisation of the content, which continued the cultural tradition of the *progymnásmata* or exercises, derives from Theon's handbook, written in the first century AD.[28] Several exercises introduced the student of rhetoric to the knowledge of *ius,* before teaching them the most difficult ones.[29]

Probably, like Theon, in the confutation of the *lex,* as he dealt with the praise and denunciation of laws,[30] Quintilian first of all compared the different legal systems of Greeks and Romans. He explained that custom and the law in a state influenced the decision to develop the subject of fault of laws in deliberative or controversial oratory. Then he described the different procedures to approve them, remembering that in Rome it was the custom to urge the acceptance or rejection of a law before the public assembly. In both of them, the arguments advanced in such cases are few of number and of a definite type. Quintilian listed the different branches of *ius: sacrum, publicum, privatum.* He emphasized the utility of this division in the praise of the *leges*: the orator could first of all praise it as a law, then as a public law and, finally, as a law designed for the support of religion. The Flavian rhetor explained that doubts may be raised with regard to the proponent or to the proposal itself, illus-

---

[26] Cicero, *Pro Murena,* 24.
[27] *Inst. or.* II.4.33-42.
[28] I. Lana, *Quintiliano, il 'Sublime' e gli 'esercizi preparatori di Elio Teone',* Turin: Pubbl. Fac. Lettere e Filosofia Univ. Torino 1951, pp. 113ff, for the *laus* and the *vituperatio* of *leges* pp. 146ff and I. Lana, 'Il primo contatto degli studenti romani con la legge alla scuola del retore', in: I. Lana, *Sapere lavoro e potere in Roma antica,* Naples: Jovene 1990, pp. 315ff.
[29] See Lana, 'Il primo contatto' (see note 28), p. 316.
[30] See Lana, 'Il primo contatto' (see note 28), p. 321.

trating his statements with some examples in Roman political and constitutional history. Anyway, these subjects were not pertinent to the first exercises, which were not concerned with persons, times or particular cases.

After this long introduction, Quintilian listed, and briefly described, the various exercises, in his opinion suited - unlike Theon - both to real and fictitious dispute, marking the approach of the future orator to the law.

The fault could concern word or matter: in the first case, it was necessary to examine whether there was something ambiguous or not, while, with reference to the matter, it was necessary to examine whether the law was consistent with itself, or concerned the past or, finally, applied to special individuals. According to Quintilian, the point most commonly discussed was whether a law was *honesta*, right, or *utilis*, expedient.. Although he knew very well that many authors adopted more articulated distinctions, he preferred to include in *honestum* also justice, piety, and religion, and other content similar to these, but he acknowledged that it was impossible to discuss justice separately. The Flavian rhetor considered relevant to the treatment of justice also that of punishment or reward or of the degree of punishment or reward. As to *utilitas*, this was sometimes determined by nature, sometimes by circumstances. It could be debated whether it was actually necessary to observe a law, as famous orators sometimes used to refute it in its entirety or in part. The short discussion of exercises ended with a warning regarding the laws which were not proposed with a view to perpetuity but concerned temporary honours or commands, such as the *lex Manilia*, dealt with by Cicero in an oration of the same name. As these laws did not depend on general characteristics but were marked by special circumstances, he preferred to avoid any advice in this part of his manual.[31]

In the exposition of *progymnásmata*, Quintilian introduced original contents suitable to the constitutional and political situation and to the 'political' project of the Flavian rhetor.

Unlike Theon, he did not differentiate between *anaskeué* and *kataskeué*, in fictitious and real disputes. He dwelled on laws made for special individuals, to which the *progymnásmata* were not suited.[32] The distinction between *honestum* and *iustum*, accepted by Theon, was criticized for not being useful for the orator. Unlike Theon, the Flavian rhetor also mentioned the fact that the *veteres*, ancients, used to call in the assistance of the *dialectici*, logicians, to teach them the theory of argument, as a characteristic of the oratory of the *veteres*, thus marking the difference with his own theory.[33]

The discussion about exercises in the *Institutio* is quite restricted, somewhat fragmentary, and also 'anti-historical', though not unaware of some Roman political and constitutional peculiarities.

---

[31]   The last part of the analysis of *progymnásmata* was dedicated to a short *excursus* on the origin of *ratio argumentandi* and to the comparison of oratory in Greece and Rome: *Inst. or.* II.4.41 and 42.

[32]   See on the expression *leges in singulos homines*, already used by Cicero, *De legibus*, III.44 and *De domo sua*, 43, V. Scarano Ussani, *Le forme del privilegio. Beneficia e privilegia tra Cesare e gli Antonini*, Naples: Loffredo 1992, with literature.

[33]   See Lana, 'Il primo contatto' (see note 28), pp. 320ff.

Quintilian certainly did not ignore that the substantive *lex* did not translate all the meanings of *nómos*, to which the exercises of refutation in *progymnásmata* referred, nevertheless he did not explain and examine the theoretical reasons of the discussion just of *lex* and not of all parts of *ius*. A certain ambiguity characterizes the use indifferently of *lex* and *ius* in the first part of the discussion of *progymnásmata*: after pointing out the peculiarities of praise and denunciation of laws (*leges*) in Rome, the Flavian rhetor listed the various contents in connection not only to the *lex*, but, generally, to the division of *ius* in *sacrum, publicum, privatum*.

It is possible that Quintilian sketched the *progymnásmata* complying with a cultural tradition that he did not approve of unconditionally, though some of the differences between Quintilian's *Institutio* and Theon's handbook seem rather to suggest a theoretical awareness hinting at contents developed in other books of the *Institutio*, especially in Book XII, in the comparison among *artes* with reference to the political tasks of oratory.

Quintilian dwelled upon a source of *ius*, the *lex publica*, which was becoming obsolete during the Principate.[34] At least, in real disputes, the orator had to refute more often jurists' opinions, imperial decisions and senatorial decrees. The *progymnásmata* could in fact be very useful when applied to the decisions of the senators or to the sessions of the *consilium principis*, the council of the emperor to which also important orators will have been admitted.[35]

By restricting the praise and denunciation of *ius* to the *lex*, Quintilian could avoid dangerous discussions about the faults of other contemporary sources of *ius*. First of all the constitutions of the emperors: in important juridical handbooks of the Antonine age they are expressly compared to the *lex* though this may be an older comparison.[36] The Flavian rhetor also carefully avoided naming another important contemporary source of *ius*, i.e., jurisprudence, just when, in the Flavian age, some of its exponents collaborated with the imperial power, entering into competition with the political leaders.[37] Finally, Quintilian deliberately left out decrees of the Senate, for obvious reasons of political opportunity.[38]

---

[34]   See F. de Martino, *Storia della costituzione romana* IV.1, 2nd edition, Naples: Jovene 1974, p. 616 and n.114; M. Bretone, *Tecniche e ideologie dei giuristi romani*, Naples: Edizioni Scientifiche Italiane 1971, rpt. 1984, p. 28; M. Ducos, *Les Romains et la loi. Recherches sur les rapports de la philosophie grecque et de la tradition romaine à la fin de la République*, Paris: Les Belles Lettres 1984, p. 13; V. Scarano Ussani, *L'utilità e la certezza. Compiti e modelli del sapere giuridico in Salvio Giuliano*, Milan: Giuffrè 1987, pp. 67f.; M. Bretone, *Storia del diritto romano*, 4th edition, Roma-Bari: Laterza 1991, rpt. 1995, p. 222.

[35]   For the *consilium principis*, see De Martino (see note 34), pp. 671ff, with literature; F. Amarelli, *Consilia principum*, Naples: Jovene 1983; V. Marotta, *Multa de iure sanxit. Aspetti della politica del diritto di Antonino Pio*, Milan: Giuffrè 1988, pp. 39ff, with literature; F. Millar, *The Emperor in the Roman World (31 BC-AD 337)*, 2nd edition, London: Duckworth 1992, pp. 39, 94ff, 119ff, 230, 234ff.

[36]   Gai. *Inst.* I.5 and D. 1.2.2.11 (Pomp. *l. s. ench.*).

[37]   Celsus, either the father or the son, participated in the plot against Domitian (see Cass. Dio 67.13). Probably, Neratius Priscus, consul in AD 96, 'the year of rewards', was also an opponent of the Flavians; see V. Scarano Ussani, *Empiria e dogmi. La scuola proculiana fra Nerva e Adriano*, Turin: Giappichelli 1989, pp. 22f. The same holds for Titius Aristo, *auditor* of Cassius Longinus and bound up with Neratius Priscus, Celsus *pater*, and Celsus *filius*. See V. Scarano Ussani, 'Il 'probabilismo' di Titius Aristo', *Ostraka* IV.2 (1995) pp. 315-316, with literature.

[38]   For *delatores* in the Julio-Claudian Principate and in the Flavian age in connection with the activity

The task assigned by Quintilian to the orator was to tacitly ignore the changed condition of the Senate in the first century AD, to ignore the faults of the imperial constitutions, and to marginalize jurisprudence as a source of *ius*. This conscious 'anti-historical' perspective of the *Institutio* was functional to the particular political project, and recognizable also in the comparison of honourableness and expediency of *leges*.

Quintilian did not attribute any peculiar characteristic to *iustum*, justice, as a part of *honestum,* which would distinguish it from the other 'ethical' contents of the *lex*. He singled out its sources, not only in nature but also in the concrete circumstances, thereby making it possible to compare it with *utile*, expediency. Justice as well as expediency originated from nature or time. The Flavian rhetor theorized the 'elevation' of expediency to the level of justice and, at the same time, refuted the theories of those who considered justice unchangeable because it was determined only by nature, making it impossible to use *honestum* according to political necessity.

3. *IUSTITIA* AS ART OF GOVERNMENT

There could be a connection between these considerations about *utile* and *honestum* and Quintilian's interpretation of Plato's *Gorgias*, in the discussion of *iustitia* as part of the art of government.

In Book II, the Flavian rhetor dwelled upon the various definitions of rhetoric. None of the traditional answers to the question *quid sit rhetorice* satisfied him.[39] Some had identified rhetoric with *vis* (power), others with science but not with virtue, or with a perversion of art.[40] Quintilian regarded these definitions as awkward attempts to restrict the task of rhetoric to persuasion. He criticized his predecessors because the attitude to persuasion was a feature neither peculiar to the *vir bonus* nor typical of the orator.[41]

Refuting the theories which restricted the *materia* of rhetoric to political subjects, Quintilian examined those who attributed to it the theoretical status of an *ars*.[42] He attacked the superficial and patched-up interpretations of Plato's *Gorgias* and of other dialogues of the Greek philosopher.[43] He argued that the art of rhetoric could not be attained without knowledge of *iustitia*, justice, and cited Plato's *Gorgias* and *Phaedrus*, in which Plato succeeded in refuting the Sophistic definition of rhetoric.[44]

In the *Gorgias*, of uncertain date, the notion of rhetoric was discussed as a tool of persuasion, founded on false opinion and appearance. The polemic answers of Socrates to Gorgias and to his pupil, the otherwise unknown Polus, and to Callicles

---

of the senate, see the literature cited in S. Querzoli, *I testamenta e gli officia pietatis. Tribunale centumvirale, potere imperiale e giuristi tra Augusto e i Severi*, Naples: Loffredo 2000, pp. 71ff.

[39] *Inst. or.* II.15.1.
[40] *Inst. or.* II.15.2.
[41] *Inst. or.* II.15.3.
[42] *Inst. or.* II.15.21.
[43] *Inst. or.* II.15.24-32.
[44] *Inst. or.* II.15.29 about Phaedrus.

concerned the political importance of rhetoric, used to overwhelm and so, exercised in contrast with the human nature, turned to good.[45]

Answering a question of Gorgias, who developed Polus' doubts about the definition of rhetoric as *kolakeía*, Socrates explained that the science of the soul which he also called *téchnê politikê*, the art of government, and which could be divided into *nomothetikê*, legislation, and *dikaiosunê*, justice could be compared with the science of the body (divided into *gymnastikê*, gymnastic, and *iatrikê*, medicine). Like gymnastic strengthened the body, legislation strengthened the soul, and like medicine healed the diseases of the body, the part of politics concerning justice or better the administration of justice healed the illnesses of the soul. He stated that to the two parts of the science of the soul, legislation and justice, corresponded sophistry and rhetoric.[46]

Though Quintilian had undoubtedly read Plato's *Gorgias*, which he cited in the *Institutio*,[47] his interpretation of the relationship between the art of government and justice on the one hand and their 'flatteries' on the other hand differed meaningly from that of Plato.

The Flavian rhetor translated *téchnê politikê* as *ars civilitatis,* art of government, and he divided it into two parts: *corpus*, consisting of medicine and gymnastic, and *animus*, consisting of *pars legalis*, legislation, and *iustitia*, justice. In Quintilian's opinion, the *legalis cavillatrix* was the 'flattery' of legislation, while rhetoric was the 'flattery' of justice.[48] The Flavian rhetor identified *dikaiosunê* with *iustitia*, thereby extending its meaning: in Plato's *Gorgias*, this word referred only to justice in trials. On the other hand, Quintilian limited the 'flattery' of legislation, which he did not identify with the Sophistic movement.

The 'misunderstandings' in the translation of Plato's *Gorgias*, far from being symptomatic of the ignorance of the contents of the dialogue, deliberately aimed at a precise theoretical interpretation by Quintilian.

The art of rhetoric, obviously that of the *vir bonus*, the good man, was no longer the 'flattery' of *dikaiosunê*, and philosophers had to take account of it in politics: rhetoric became a 'civil' art with political tasks independent from philosophy.

Quintilian's contribution to the 'rehabilitation' of rhetoric in the meaning of the art of persuasion in trials was determinant. Since the orator was educated in the ethical virtues of the philosopher and since he, at the same time, embodied the ideal of a *vir bonus,* no one could prevent him from engaging in forensic oratory. His activity was indeed necessary in order to prevent 'bad' orators from dominating the tri-

---

[45]   For an analysis of the *Gorgias* in connection with the concept of justice, see G.B. Kerferd, *The Sophistic Movement*, Cambridge: Cambridge University Press 1981, pp. 125ff. and, in general, about the origin of the concept of justice in Greek culture, see the suggestive hypotheses by E.A. Havelock, *The Greek Concept of Justice from its Shadow in Homer to its Substance in Plato*, Cambridge (Mass.): Harvard University Press 1978.

[46]   Plato, *Gorgias*, 463a – 465e and 466a. The 'flatteries' of the science of the soul are compared to those of the science of the body: *téchnê kommôtikê*, the art of embellishment, for gymnastics and *téchnê opsupoiikê*, the art of cookery, for medicine: Plato, *Gorgias*, 464d – 465b.

[47]   See *Inst. or.* II.15.25-29 with quotations of the following passages: Plato, *Gorgias,* 464b, 500c, 460c, 508c.

[48]   *Inst. or.* II.15.25.

als: a danger for the state and a shame for the art.[49] Quintilian stressed the fact that the object of the polemic in the *Gorgias* was not the 'good' rhetoric, but the rhetoric of Plato's antagonists.[50] In this perspective, the translation of *dikaiosunê* as *iustitia* is meaningful. The Flavian rhetor established a connection between politics and his art, which he judged a 'flattery' only when it was not practised by the *vir bonus*. Rhetoric became the guardian of *iustitia*, and a constituent component of the 'art of government'. In Quintilian's theory, the orator was not only just, but also engaged in propagating *iustitia*, which he practised in leading the *res publica*. Rhetoric was restored in its political tasks, 'stolen' by philosophy, and in the control of ethical values. Quintilian dwelled on the meaning of Plato's words about rhetoric in the *Gorgias*, but seems not to be interested in what he says about legislation and its 'flattery', the *legalis cavillatrix*.

The substantive *cavillatrix*, which, according to the extant sources, we can read only in Quintilian's prose, is also used in Book VII of the *Institutio* in connection with the status of *definitio*.

The Flavian rhetor explained that, because of the great number of objects to define, some authors had included definition under conjecture, while others had preferred to include it under quality, or under legal questions. He added that some did not accept this elaborate and formal method of reasoning employed by dialectics, which he judged more suitable to the acute quibbles over words in philosophical discussions than to the duties of the orator. He agreed with those who stressed that definition was of less use in forensic cases, though he was well aware that definition, limiting the answer of the adversary, could oblige him to be silent or to accept the objections raised.[51]

The word *cavillationes*, sophistical discourses, was used more frequently in the *Institutio oratoria*, both in connection with words and with the blame of aimless verbal debates.[52] According to Quintilian, such discourses also affected *ius*. In the discussion of the quality of an action, in Book VII, he mentioned some examples of legal sophistries: *Quid sit rem publicam laedere*, 'What is the meaning of action contrary to the interests of the state', *laeserit an non profuerit,* 'was the action of the accused injurious or profitable', *ab ipso an propter ipsum laesa est*, 'did the interests of the state suffer at his hands or merely on his account'.[53]

Cicero had 'translated' *sófisma* as *cavillatio*,[54] but the word had already been used by Plautus in the sense of *iocosa calumnatio*, comic insults, mockery, joke.[55]

Quintilian's reference to the *legalis cavillatrix* as the 'flattery' of the *pars legalis* of politics, cannot be identified with the Sophistic movement, as in Plato's *Gorgias*: Quintilian only reffered to the legal aspect of *legalis cavillatrix*, tacitly ignoring the

---

[49] See Hadot (see note 6), pp. 91ff.
[50] *Inst. or.* II.15.27-31.
[51] *Inst. or.* VII.3.14.
[52] See *Inst. or.* I.5.38, I.7.33, II.14.5, II.17.7, II.17.30, VII.4.37, VII.9.4, VIII.6.2, IX.1.16, X.7.14, and XII.2.14.
[53] *Inst. or.* VII.4.37.
[54] See Seneca, *Epistulae,* 111.1-2.
[55] Cf. *Thesaurus Linguae Latinae*.

political role and the philosophical importance of the Sophistic movement. The distinction between *pars legalis* and *iustitia* in politics did not coincide with the Platonic distinction in the *Gorgias*. The rhetoric of the *vir bonus*, the attainment of justice, had the most important political role in the state.

In Plato's *Gorgias*, legislation was the natural field of philosophers, the uncontested leaders of the *polis*. Quintilian restricted law-making to the *pars legalis* and assigned more importance to *iustitia*. He deprived the law-makers of the control of values, the *iustitia*, which was assigned to rhetors. Quintilian separated the technique of legislation from its ethical contents, reducing it to a 'subsidiary' discipline of rhetoric, the only science allowed a leading role in politics.

Quintilian certainly charged the 'bad' orators with *legalis cavillatrix* though it is possible that they were not the only ones. The Flavian rhetor also fulfilled the plan of the 'rehabilitation' of rhetoric with his polemics against jurists. The *prudentes* were certainly skilful makers of *cavillationes iuris* and dangerous antagonists in leading the state.

The assumption that Quintilian identified at least part of jurisprudence with *cavillatrix* is strengthened not only by the way he used *cavillatio* in the *Institutio* but also by the meaning of the adjective *legalis*.

As is well-known, Quintilian used *legalis* not only with reference to *leges*, but also in connection with other sources of *ius*. In Book VII, he explained that, when he wrote about *leges*, he also meant wills, *pacta* (agreements), and stipulations, in short, everything written or expressed orally.[56] He listed here the traditional activities of jurisprudential *cavere* and remembered, in connection with the interpretation of wills, the well-known *causa Curiana* in which Q. Mucius Scaevola and L. Licinius Crassus acted as advocates.[57]

Cicero had already included in legal disputes, except syllogism, the activity of jurisprudence. In his *Topica*, written for his friend, the jurist Trebatius, he stated that controverses of the same kind (that is *controversiae legitimae*) could concern not only *leges*, but also testaments, stipulations, and any other matter which rests on a written document,[58] and in his *De inventione* he mentioned, like Quintilian, the *causa Curiana* in connection with the contrast between letter and intention in *status legales*.[59]

If the interpretation of the relationship between Plato's *Gorgias* and Quintilian's *Institutio* is correct, Quintilian may have been the first to hint, in the explanation of this Platonic dialogue, to *cavillationes* or sophistical discourses in juridical argumentation. His accurate interpretation of the contents and purpose of Plato's dialogues[60] contributed to the formulation of a new relation between rhetoric and jurisprudence aiming at depriving both philosophy and jurisprudence or, at least,

---

[56] *Inst. or.* VII.5.6. For *status legales*, see L. Calboli Montefusco, *La dottrina degli 'status' nella retorica greca e romana*, Hildesheim-Zürich-New York: Olms-Weidmann 1986, pp. 153ff.

[57] *Inst. or.*VII.6.10f. On this text and the *causa Curiana*, see in this book, Jan Willem Tellegen, 'The reliability of Quintilian for Roman law: on the *causa Curiana*', with literature.

[58] Cicero, *Topica*, 96.

[59] See Cicero, *De inventione*, II.122f.

[60] *Inst. or.* II.15.26.

some of the jurists, of theoretical legitimation. Quintilian knew that there could be a very small difference between interpretation of words and sophistical discourses about a point of law: if the philosopher was a dangerous antagonist in the control of ethical values, the jurist could be a skilful adversary in the interpretation of words. The knowledge of the jurist, in trials concerning, for example, a clause in a will, a stipulation, or an agreement was absolutely necessary for the orator. Quintilian wrote that, in some cases of *ius* based on the opinion of a jurist, the orator had to consider the interpretation of words. As he admitted with a certain reluctance, the jurists were qualified, together with the orator, to explain the *vis cuiusque vocis,* the power of every word.[61] Censuring the sophistical discourses of Roman jurists, Quintilian 'anticipated' such a discussion about the definition and the characteristics of *cavillatio.* The verb *cavillor* is used by Celsus *filius,* who, significantly, may have attended Quintilian's lessons.[62] In Book LIV of his Digest, Salvius Iulianus defined the word *cavillatio.*[63] Gaius explained the etymology of *cavillatio.*[64] Cervidius Scaevola used the words *cavillatio iuris,* as Quintilian had previously done.[65] Anyway, *cavillatio,* used in polemics or in skilful disputes, did not meet the favour of all jurists, although it was used by some of them.[66]

Quintilian was well aware of the importance of jurists in the interpretation of words, of which they were the skilful, and sometimes the sole, guardians.[67] Anyway, he tried to depreciate their knowledge, comparing it to *cavillationes iuris.*

His accurate and original interpretation of Plato's *Gorgias* aimed at justifying a hierarchy among arts in which the orator was granted supremacy over philosophers and jurists; after the banishment of the philosophers, the jurists were his only rivals in the struggle for a leading role in politics as counsellors of the imperial power.

The interpretation of the *Gorgias* in the Platonic intellectual tradition during the Principate seems to support the identification of at least part of jurisprudence with Quintilian's notion of *legalis cavillatrix.*

Apuleius, in his *De Platone et eius dogmate,* accepted Quintilian's distinction between 'good' and 'bad' rhetoric, and called the legal profession the 'flattery' of the part which he defined *legalis* in his interpretation of Plato's *Gorgias.*[68] The neg-

---

[61] *Inst. or.* XII.3.7. For the relationship between rhetoric and Roman law in the exegesis of *verba,* see recently G. Calboli, 'Rhétorique et droit romain', *Revue d'Études Latines* 76 (1998) pp. 158ff, with literature.

[62] Cels. D. 34.7.1 For the discussion of the meaning and of the importance of *cavillor* in Celsus *filius'* hermeneutics, see Scarano Ussani, *Empiria* (see note 37), pp. 118ff, with literature, and on Quintilian's influence, pp. 89-90.

[63] Iul. D. 5.17.65. For Julian's definition of *natura cavillationis,* see Scarano Ussani, *L'utilità* (see note 34), esp. pp. 164ff, with literature.

[64] Gai. D. 50.16.233.

[65] Scaev. D. 35.1.85. On *cavillatio* in the extant fragments of the works of the Roman jurists, see also Ulp. D. 50.16.177, reproducing the definition in Julian's *Digesta,* and Ulp. D. 38.17.1.

[66] See Scarano Ussani, *L'utilità* (see note 34), pp. 164ff.

[67] The well-known anecdote on the dispute between Favorinus and Sextus Caecilius Africanus about the XII Tables (Gellius, *Noctes Atticae,* XX.1) is emblematic of the importance of the jurists as the keepers of *verba,* see esp. F. Casavola, *Giuristi adrianei,* Naples: Jovene 1980, pp. 75ff.

[68] Apuleius, *De Platone et eius dogmate,* II.9.232-234. See Hadot (see note 6) pp. 88ff.

ative opinion of Apuleius about jurisprudence, which was considered as 'degeneration' of a political activity and which was deprived of the task of guarding the ethical values, hinted at old disputes about the importance of jurisprudence. The comparison of the epistemological status of philosophy and jurisprudence to that of rhetoric was functional to ensure to the latter supremacy in the official culture. Quintilian's pedagogics propagated ideological theories which were far from neutral.

Quintilian's rhetorical *Institutio* thus proposed a slightly different educational pattern as compared with those of his predecessors, aiming at expelling the orator's antagonists from the establishment, or at least reshuffling them.

If Cicero had already entrusted the orator with the knowledge of the jurists, Quintilian compared the epistemological status of jurisprudence to that of rhetoric in order to legitimate the orator as a political adviser of the emperor. Cicero, who lived in the late Republic, could still describe the struggle among intellectuals for the leading political role in the *civitas*. Quintilian's orator, educated in schools financed by the imperial power, in a subordinate rank, could aim at becoming the privileged adviser of the emperor only if he succeeded in getting rid of his antagonists, apparently first of all the philosophers, who, had already been 'dismissed' by the emperor, anyway, but also the jurists, whose role in political life was a far more complicated and delicate problem for the orator.

TOMÁS ALBALADEJO

THE THREE TYPES OF SPEECHES IN QUINTILIAN, BOOK III

Communicative Aspects of the Political and Legal Features of Rhetorical Discourse

1. INTRODUCTION

Quintilian's *Institutio oratoria* is one of the key rhetorical works in the inherited rhetorical system which I call 'rhetorica recepta', the received rhetoric.[1] Quintilian described the rhetorical tradition as it had come down to him and made antiquity's system of rhetorical knowledge available to future generations.

In Book III of his *Institutio oratoria*, Quintilian studies the components of rhetoric: *quibus constet, quo quaeque in ea modo invenienda atque tractanda sint*, 'its component parts [of rhetoric] and the method to be adopted in handling and forming our conception of each' (III.pr.1).[2] In order to identify these component parts, he mentions a number of aspects relating to rhetorical discourse. First, he states that the art of oratory consists of five parts: *inventio, dispositio, elocutio, memoria,* and *actio* (III.3.1) and he discusses the opinion of other authors on this distinction (III.3.4-15). He does the same with other aspects (causes in III.4; the tasks of the orator in III.5) and notions (questions in III.5; status in III.6). The last part of Book III is dedicated to the three types of causes, the three *genera causarum*: the demonstrative, deliberative, and forensic speeches (III.7-11).

In this essay, I want to discuss the communicative aspects of the political and legal features of rhetorical discourse. These features can be recognised throughout Book III. However, I shall restrict myself to those which are present in the three types of speeches.

2. THE THREE TYPES OF CAUSES AND THEIR COMMUNICATIVE ASPECTS IN GENERAL

Quintilian follows Aristotle's classification of the three types of rhetorical discourses (*tría génê tôn lógôn tôn rhetorikôn*)[3] and also discusses other divisions.[4] The types

---

[1] T. Albaladejo, *Retorica*, Pesaro: Edizioni Europee 1991, pp. 25-26.
[2] I use the text edition by Winterbottom (see 'Introduction' note 26) and the English translation by Butler (see 'Introduction', note 27).
[3] Aristoteles, *Rétorica*, bilingual edition Greek-Spanish by A. Tovar, Madrid: Instituto de Estudios Políticos (Colección Clásicos Políticos) 1971, I.2.1358a 36-1358b 8.
[4] See the systematic presentation of the *genera* in R. Volkmann, *Die Rhetorik von Griecher und Römer*

mentioned in Aristotle's *Rhetoric* are *symbouleutikón*, *dikanikón* and *epideiktikón*, i.e., deliberative, forensic, and epideictic or demonstrative, respectively. These types are already present in Anaximenes' *Rhetorica ad Alexandrum* [5], a work preceding Aristotle's *Rhetoric*. Unlike Aristotle, Anaximenes does not start from the role of the hearer in order to distinguish the types, his presentation of them is linear; he mentions seven *species* besides the three types: suasory, dissuasory, enchomiastic, reprobatory, accusatory, defensive and investigative.

Quintilian thinks that the matter of the types of causes is very large, and that it is difficult to reduce it to these three types.[6] I have the impression, from III.4.4 (*ut mihi in illa vetere persuasione permanenti*, 'as an adherent of the older view'), that he does not agree with *Graecos quosdam* ('certain Greeks') and Cicero (III.4.2) but adheres to the older view presented by Aristotle. He is one of the defenders of antiquity. An important point is the classification of hearers that Quintilian considers from those who deliver discourses of defence (III.4.6).

> *Qui vero defendunt, tria faciunt genera auditorum: unum quod ad delectationem conveniat, alterum quod consilium accipiat, tertium quod de causis iudicet.*
> The defenders of antiquity point out that there are three kinds of audience: one which comes simply for the sake of getting pleasure, a second which meets to receive advice, a third to give judgement on causes.

These kinds of audiences are related to demonstrative, deliberative, and forensic discourses, respectively. This classification of hearers is not very different from the one made by Aristotle. However, the Greek philosopher reaches his classification by applying the criterion of decision: first, he distinguishes two kinds of hearers - those who decide and those who do not decide - and then he divides the former kind into those who decide with regard to the future and those who decide as to the past.

Quintilian gives a reason or principle for a general typology of rhetorical discourses, considering that the functions of a discourse are either in trials or outside trials. In this way, he obtains a first kind, that of forensic discourses. Then, within the discourse which is not related to trials, he distinguishes the type that is related to the past, that is aimed to praise or vituperate (demonstrative type), and the type that is related to future, i.e, the deliberative type (III.4.6-7).

For the author of the *Institutio oratoria*, there are three kinds of cause: laudatory or demonstrative, deliberative, and forensic (III.4.12-15). Within these three types, several species can be distinguished. Quintilian thinks that the three types are a general typology set in a theoretical level, and that concrete discourse contains different species. Elsewhere, I have distinguished between a type of cause and its textual

---

in systematischer Übersicht, Leipzig: Teubner 1885, §2, and H. Lausberg, *Manual de retórica literaria,* 3 Vols, Madrid: Gredos 1966-1968, §§59ff.
[5] Anaximenes, *Ars rhetorica quae uulgo fertur Aristoteles ad Alexandrum,* 1421b 7-14, edited by M. Fuhrmann, Leipzig: Teubner 1966.
[6] J. Cousin, *Études sur Quintilien,* 2 Vols. Paris: Boivin 1935-1936, rpt. Amsterdam: Schippers 1967, pp. 169-171, and D. Pujante, *El hijo de la persuasión. Quintiliano y el estatuto retórico,* 2nd revised and extended edition, Logroño: Instituto de Estudios Riojanos 1999, pp. 76ff.

component parts.[7] Every type of cause has features which can also be found in other types of discourse. Normally, one of these features is so central or predominant that it determines the classification of that particular discourse. I agree with Aron Kibédi-Varga when he argues that the types of rhetorical speeches mainly arise in communicative situations.[8] As Quintilian writes: *nec invenietur ex his ulla in qua non laudare aut vituperare, suadere aut dissuadere, intendere quid vel depellere debeamus*, 'you will not find one in which we have not to praise or blame, to advise or dissuade, to drive or refute a charge' (III.4.15). The types of causes are theoretical constructs and they do not occur purely and exclusively in the reality of discourses; a discourse is placed in a particular type, but it can contain features of other types as well. Quintilian offers a very rich view of the types of rhetorical discourses, by taking the reality of the discourses into account.

Quintilian studies the three traditional types of causes, although he does not give up his idea that the field of discourse is broader than the types.

3. THE EPIDEICTIC SPEECH

Discourses of praise and blame belong to the demonstrative or epideictic kind. This kind of cause became a part of social life. Quintilian rejects the opinion of those who think that rhetorical discourses are always on controversial matters, because the orator of an epideictic discourse can deliver a speech for the praise of gods and heroes (III.7.2-4). It must be borne in mind that, for Aristotle, this is the type of discourse where the hearer is not involved in order to decide, since it is a spectator (*theôrós*), but only to judge the artistic skill of the orator.[9] For Quintilian, the discourses of the epideictic type do not take place in a court of law and they are oriented to the past, where the object of praise or blame is found (III.4.7). These discourses are completely rhetorical, for instance, because they require proof: a discourse of praise in some practical matter must include *probatio*, as does a discourse presented for display only (III.7.4-6). The communicative situation of these discourses makes it necessary that the orator act dialectically by organising his discursive argumentation with a structure of proving and refuting. The exhibition goal of the demonstration of praise is important: Quintilian considers that it is suitable for the orator to amplify and decorate the matter: *Sed proprium laudis est res amplificare et ornare*, 'The proper function however of panegyric is to amplify and embellish its themes' (III.7.6).

Next, Quintilian discusses the objects of praise in an epideictic (or laudatory - from the best of its two goals-) speech. The theme of these speeches is very broad. Quintilian disagrees with the traditional opinion because he thinks the epideictic (or laudatory) kind does not deal with the honest or the good only and the content of this

---

[7]   T. Albaladejo, 'Los géneros retóricos: clases de discurso y constituyentes textuales', in: I. Paraíso (ed.), *Téchne Rhetoriké. Reflexiones actuales sobre la tradición retórica*, Valladolid: Universidad de Valladolid 1999, pp. 55-64.

[8]   A. Kibédi-Varga, *Rhétorique et literature. Études de structures classiques,* Paris: Didier 1970, pp. 24-28, and 'L'histoire de la rhétorique et la rhétorique des genres', *Rhetorica* 3, 3 (1985) pp. 201-221.

[9]   Aristoteles (see note 3), I.2.1358b 6-7.

type of speech concerns mainly the *status qualitatis* (III.4.16; III.7.28). This type of discourse (laudatory speech) is close to the deliberative kind of cause since the objects of praise are objects of advice: *Totum autem habet aliquid simile suasoriis, quia plerumque eadem illic suaderi, hic laudari solent*, 'But *panegyric* is akin to deliberative oratory inasmuch as the same things are usually praised in the former as are advised in the latter' (III.7.28).[10]

Finally, it is important for the orator of an epideictic speech that he takes into account the ideas of the audience he is addressing.[11] Only then will he be able to relate its conception of what is good about the virtues of the person who is the object of his praise, and its idea of what is bad about the vices of the person who is the object of blame (III.7.23-25). Therefore, an adaptation of the speech to the audience is required, of course, within the *aptum*.

The communicative structure of epideictic discourse allows the connection of the orator with the hearers as to principles to be defended in society. The semantic-extensional and the syntactic elements of this communication are organised so that the audience does not decide, but judges the orator's abilities and the speech itself.

4. THE DELIBERATIVE SPEECH

When explaining the deliberative kind of speech, Quintilian does not agree with the idea that this concerns only usefulness. The discourses of this type are connected with the *status qualitatis*, but also with the *status coniecturae* and the *status finitionis* (III.8.1-5). Since the audience of a deliberative speech can (and must) decide, the aim of these speeches is to persuade and to dissuade (III.8.6). Aristotle linked the deliberative kind with hearers who had the role of referees or arbitrators and who, therefore, decided, but their decision was about future things.[12] Quintilian accepts that deliberation relates to the future, but he states that it also deals with the past (III.8.6). Indeed, the decision that the hearers make is related to the future, but, in his discourse, the orator presents to them a set of past events which are important for their decision.

Quintilian offers the semiotic structure of the rhetorical event concerning discourses of deliberative (or suasory) speech as follows (III.8.15-16).

> *Quare in suadendo ac dissuadendo tria primum spectanda erunt: quid sit de quo deliberetur, qui sint qui deliberent, qui sit qui suadeat.*
>
> Consequently there are three points which must be specially borne in mind in advice or dissuasion: first the nature of the subject under discussion, secondly the nature of those who are engaged in the discussion, and thirdly the nature of the speaker who offers them advice

---

[10] For Kibédi-Varga, the epideictic discourse has an indirectly persuasive nature. See A.Kibédi-Varga, 'Rhetoric, a Story or a System? A Challenge to Historians of Renaissance Rhetoric', in: James J. Murphy (ed.), *Renaissance Eloquence. Studies on the Theory and Practice of Renaissance Rhetoric*, Berkeley- Los Angeles-London: University of California Press 1983, pp. 84-91.

[11] As to the adhesion of the audience to the values presented in epideictic discourse, see A. García-Berrio, *A Theory of the Literary Text*, Berlin-New York: De Gruyter 1992, p. 135, and A. López Eire, *Esencia y objeto de la retórica*, México: Universidad Nacional Autónoma de México 1996, p. 177.

[12] Aristoteles (see note 3), I.2.1358b 3.

The matter of the discourse and the discourse itself, the cause, are implied in the first question, which concerns the *status qualitatis*. The hearers (*qui deliberent*) and the orator (*qui suadeat*) are the communicative poles of rhetorical discourse. This semiotic structure, therefore, contains the semantic-extensional, syntactic, and pragmatic[13] domains.

The role of the orator, i.e., the person who tries to persuade, is very important in the discourse of the deliberative kind. The authority (*auctoritas*) of the orator is a decisive element in persuasion. Quintilian thinks that, even more so than in forensic discourses, the orator's morality is very important in deliberative discourses, since advice cannot be separated from the character of the person who gives it (III.8.12-13; III.8.48).

The role of the audience of a deliberative speech is important too because it contains the people who decide. Quintilian states that it is absolutely necessary for the orator to appeal to the emotions of the audience (III.8.12). However, the hearers make up a complex audience. There is an important variety of subjects and hearers. Quintilian states (III.8.15):

> *Nobis maior in re videtur varietas; nam et consultantium et consiliorum plura sunt genera.*
> This type of oratory seems to me to offer a more varied field for eloquence, since both those who ask for advice and the answers given to them may easily present the greatest diversity.

The variety of hearers is determined by the number and diversity of hearers of a speech. I have proposed the concept of polyacroasis (*polyakróasis*, from *poly* and *akróasis*), which means plural hearing, plural interpretation of an oral discourse; it refers to the diversity of hearers of rhetorical discourses.[14] Quintilian offers a consideration on the diversity of the hearers of discourse of the deliberative speech (III. 8.37).

> *Nam consultant aut plures aut singuli, sed in utrisque differentia, quia et in pluribus multum interest senatus sit an populus, Romani an Fidenates, Graeci an barbari, et in singulis Catoni petendos honores suadeamus an C. Mario, de ratione belli Scipio prior an Fabius deliberet.*
> For those who ask us for advice are either single individuals or a number, and in both cases the factors may be different. For when advice is asked by a number of persons it makes a considerable difference whether they are the senate or the people, the citizens of Rome or Fidenae, Greeks or barbarians, and in the case of single individuals, whether we are urging Cato or Gaius Marius to stand for office, whether it is the elder Scipio or Fabius who is deliberating on his plan of campaign.

---

[13] The pragmatic domain of rhetoric is a domain which contains the semantic-extensional and the syntactic domains. For the pragmatic aspects of rhetoric, see D. Breuer, *Einführung in die pragmatischer Texttheorie*, Munich: Fink 1974, pp. 140-209; F. Chico Rico, *Pragmática y construcción literaria. Discurso retórica y discurso narrative*, Alicante: Universidad de Alicante 1987; J.A. Hernández Guerrero, 'Hacia un planteamiento pragmático de los procedimientes retóricos', *Theoría/Crítica*, 5 *Retórica hoy* (1998) pp. 403-425, and T. Albaladejo, 'The Pragmatic Nature of Discourse-Building Rhetorical Operations', *Koiné*, III (1993) pp. 5-13.

[14] T. Albaladejo, 'Polyacroasis in Rhetorical Discourse', *The Canadian Journal of Rhetorical Studies / La Revue Canadienne d'Études Rhétoriques* 9 (1998) pp. 155-167.

In Quintilian's view, a deliberative speech can have an introduction (*proemium*) but it should be short. The statement of facts (*narratio*) is never required in a speech on private subjects, but it may be useful in speeches on public matters. In addressing a public assembly, it will often be necessary for the orator to set forth the order of the points which have to be treated (III.8.10-11). Indeed, it is very important to give complete information to the hearers, so that they can decide on the basis of their knowledge of the matter.

The honest and the useful are the matters of the deliberative kind for Quintilian, who thinks that the necessary is not its matter: *Partes suadendi quidam putaverunt honestum utile necessarium. Ego non invenio huic tertiae locum*, 'Some have held that the three main considerations in an advisory speech are honour, expediency and necessity. I can find no place for the last' (III.8.22). For Quintilian, deliberative speeches always deal with subjects which allow different opinions. If there is a necessary decision, deliberative speech has no function: *Itaque mihi ne consilium quidem videtur ubi necessitas est, non magis quam ubi constat quid fieri non posse: omnis enim deliberatio de dubiis est*, 'It appears to me, therefore, that where necessity exists, there is no room for deliberation, any more than where it is clear that a thing is not feasible. For deliberation is always concerned with questions where some doubt exists'(III.8.25).

The hearers are advised by the orator as to their decision, in such a way that there is a comparison between different decisions: *Ita fere omnis suasoria nihil est aliud quam comparatio*, 'Consequently as a rule all *deliberative* speeches are based simply on comparison' (III.8.34). The orator compares the different possibilities and tries to convince the hearers to follow his advice.

The communicative structure is very important for explaining the deliberative kind of speech. It is mainly political discourses that belong to this category. The orator tries to persuade the hearers and they have the faculty or the power to decide on the matter of discourse and on the proposals that the different orators offer them. The linguistic action taken by the orator has a response not only in the decision of the audience, but also in the discourses that the other orators deliver. In this connection, it is interesting to mention the notion of polyphony, introduced by Michail Bachtin for the literary genre of the novel.[15] He uses this term to indicate speeches which constitute the verbal element and represent the ideological element through the ethical element inside the novel.[16] Elsewhere, I have suggested that this notion can also be applied to parliamentary communication when several speeches are delivered.[17]

---

[15] M. Bachtin, *Dostoevskij. Poetica e stilistica*, Turin: Einaudi 1968, pp. 11-63; H. Beristáin, *Diccionario de Retórica y Póetica*, 8th edition, 1st revised and extended edition, Mexico: Porrùa 1997, pp. 401-403; O. Ducrot, *El decir y lo dicho, Polifonía de la enunciación*, Barcelona: Paidós 1986; M.M. Garcia Negroni, M. Tordesillas Colado, *La enunciación en la lengua. De la deixis a la polifonía*, Madrid: Gredos 2001.

[16] M. Bachtin, *Teoría y estética de la novela*, Madrid: Taurus 1989, pp. 30-47.

[17] T. Albaladejo, 'Polifonía y poliacroasis en la oratoria política. Propuestas para una retórica bajtiniana', in: Francisco Cortés Gabaudan, Gregorio Hinojo Andrés, Antonio López Eire (eds.), *Retórica, Política e Ideología. Desde la Antigüedad hasta nuestros días*, Vol. III, Salamanca: Logo 2000, pp. 11-21.

The deliberative discourses, by means of the advice for the future given by the orators, constitute proposals of reality. These proposals are offered to the hearers, who can contribute to their transformation into effective reality if they vote in favour of what one of the orators proposes.

5. THE FORENSIC SPEECH

Quintilian begins by mentioning the five parts in which a forensic speech usually is divided: *Cuius partes, ut plurimis auctoribus placuit, quinque sunt: prohoemium narratio probatio refutatio peroratio*, 'Most authorities divide the forensic speech into five parts: the *exordium*, the statement of facts, the proof, the refutation, and the peroration' (III.9.1). Quintilian holds the view that the refutation is independent from the argumentation. An interesting idea developed by Quintilian is that of the reach of arrangement as well as of invention and style (III.9.2).

> *Partitio vero dispositionis est species, ipsa dispositio pars rhetorices et per omnis materias totumque earum corpus aequaliter fusa, sicut inventio elocutio,*
> Partition on the other hand is merely one aspect of *arrangement*, and *arrangement* is a part of rhetoric itself, and is equally distributed through every theme of oratory and their whole body, just as are *invention* and *style*.

This conception of arrangement, invention, and style as unfolded in the whole discourse is very important for the idea of discourse as a coherent and articulated text. The parts of rhetorical discourse are an important element of textual macrostructure.[18]

In forensic discourses, there are only two duties to be performed:[19] prosecution and defence (i.e., rejection of prosecution): *Nunc de iudiciali genere, quod est praecipue multiplex sed officiis constat duobus, intentionis ac depulsionis*, 'I now come to the forensic kind of oratory, which presents the utmost variety, but whose duties are no more than two, the bringing and rebutting of charges' (III.9.1).

The object of forensic discourses is a controversy on one question (*causa simplex*) or on several questions (*causa coniuncta*) (III.10.1). According to Quintilian, in forensic speeches, the status of the cause is very important: *Cum apparuerit genus cause, tum intuebimur negeturne factum quod intenditur, an defendatur, an alio nomine appelletur, an a genere actionis repellatur: unde sunt status*, 'As soon as we are clear as to the kind of cause on which we are engaged, we must then consider whether the act that forms the basis of the charge is denied or defended, or given another name or excepted from that class of action. Thus we determine the *basis* of each one'(III.10.5).

The question (*quaestio*), the reasoning (*ratio*), the main issue of a dispute (*continens* or *firmamentum*), and the sentence (*iudicatio*) constitute the basic structure of

---

[18] A. García-Berrio, T. Albaladejo, 'Compositional Structure. Macrostructures', in: János S. Petöfi (ed.), *Text and Discourse Constitution. Empirical Aspects, Theoretical Approaches*, Berlin-New York: De Gruyter 1988, pp. 170-211.
[19] O. Tellegen-Couperus, *A Short History of Roman Law*, London: Routledge 1993, pp. 50ff., pp. 128ff.; A. Fernández de Buján, *Derecho Público y Recepción del Derecho Romano en Europa*, 3rd edition, Madrid: Civitas 1998, pp. 167ff.

the cause of the forensic discourse. The reasoning consists in the grounds upon which the existence of a fact is defended. The *continens* or *firmamentum* is the main argument of the defence, its foundation. The *iudicatio* is the judge's sentence (III.11.1-17). The connection between the main issue and the sentence is very important for the forensic discourse and has a communicative support: the *status* is the main issue and the sentence. The forensic discourse delivered by the orator and the judge's decision are linguistic constructions that have (or can have) a meeting point in the status, where the main issue of the forensic discourse and the sentence meet. The identity of cause and question and the object of the decision (*quae omnia idem sunt*, 'these three being identical') means a communicative coherence in the rhetorical event centred in the rhetorical discourse. As Quintilian writes (III.11.24):

> Nam et de eo quaestio est quod in controversiam venit, et de eo iudicatur de quo quaestio est.
> For the *question* is concerned with the matter in dispute and the *decision of the judge* is given on the point involved in the *question*.

The forensic discourse is addressed to the judge as the person who has the competence of deciding in the trial. His decision, which is expressed in the judgment, is oriented to the same semantic-extensional and syntactic construction that is the question of discourse. The basic structure of a forensic speech is a communicative one, in which the orator and the hearer are connected by the semantic-extensional basis of discourse, its referent, and by means of the syntactic (textual) dynamic object that is discourse.

6. CONCLUSION

Rhetoric offers a communicative framework for political and legal components of speeches and it contributes decisively to make them understandable and, hence, communicatively efficient. In this sense, rhetoric is a tool which gives speech form to different political and legal features. The orator and the audience are connected by rhetorical speech as to political and legal questions. The different ways of connection are linked to the kinds of speeches dealt with by Quintilian in Book III of the *Institutio oratoria*.[20]

---

[20]   I thank Olga Tellegen-Couperus very much for her suggestions with regard to this paper.

OLIVIA ROBINSON

QUINTILIAN (BOOK III) AND HIS USE OF ROMAN LAW

1. OUTLINE OF BOOK III

The third book of Quintilian's *Institutio oratoria* moves on from the outline of a young man's education with which Quintilian's work began, and the discussion of the nature and purpose of oratory, which formed the subject matter of the second book. This third book embarks on technical or practical matters, but begins with a brief survey of the origins of oratory. Quintilian lists the writers of textbooks after Empedocles (c.493-33 BC), with a dismissive glance at Pericles; he seems to view Aristotle and Isocrates as the start of a new era.[1] He then moves through later Greek teachers of rhetoric to Marcus Cato, probably the earliest Roman writer on oratory, and then to Cicero - *unicum apud nos specimen orandi docendique oratorias artes* ('for he stands alone among Romans as combining the gift of actual eloquence with that of teaching the art'); finally he mentions contemporaries of his own, such as the Elder Pliny. He points out that oratory springs naturally from the use of speech for persuasion.[2] The constituent parts of oratory are deciding what needs saying (*inventio*), establishing the order of the arguments (*dispositio*), choosing the words needed to express most eloquently the orator's thoughts (*elocutio*), which requires memory (*memoria*), and then delivering the message (*pronuntiatio*). These five parts were settled on by Cicero in his *Partitiones oratoriae*, and Quintilian is in full agreement that all these and no more are wanted, and that this is the preferred order.[3] Next he points out that there are rather three kinds of causes, laudatory (or alternatively condemnatory), political, and forensic, than three kinds of oratory. Some writers have held that there are more than three, but Quintilian appeals to the authority of Aristotle for the three-fold division, although he also remarks that it is possible to distinguish between forensic and other oratory.[4] Of course, in his time forensic oratory, speeches in the courts, will have been the most practical and the most practised branch; indeed, in the early mediaeval world, before the establishment of law schools, the teaching of law, insofar as it existed, was as a branch of rhetoric, predominantly Cicero's rhetoric.

---

[1] *Inst. or.* III.1.13. Unless indicated otherwise, I use the edition and translation in the Loeb Classical Library by Butler (see 'Introduction', note 27).
[2] *Inst. or.* III.2.
[3] *Inst. or.* III.3.
[4] *Inst. or.* III.4.

His discussion from here onwards is largely concerned with the precise definition of technical terms, and is indeed, as he warned in his introduction to the book, dry and unattractive. Questions are the most important subject of forensic oratory, those concerned with what is written being questions of law, those with what is unwritten questions of fact.[5] Questions can be seen as causes, and he spends considerable time in discussing the status or basis of causes.[6] He then returns to a review of the three kinds of causes, laudatory or panegyric, political or deliberative, and forensic.[7] The last two chapters are concerned with whether a cause is multiple or simple, and with lines of defence, such as justification, with refining the point for the decision of the judge, and putting forward the foundation (*firmamentum*), the moral or legal ground on which the orator is resting his arguments.[8] Within my topical divisions I shall deal with the legal issues mentioned in the order of Quintilian's treatment.

2. THE NEED FOR CAUTION

The third book is a good illustration of how useful Quintilian can be as a source of law, and also how dangerous. It must be stressed at the start that what we have in the *Institutio oratoria* is a textbook, a book aimed at encouraging students in virtue and at perfecting their rhetorical technique. (In similar vein Vitruvius' *de architectura* assumes the identity between the architect and the virtuous man, whereas Fronto's letters reveal that the truly virtuous man is the philosopher.) Therefore, although legal issues are important, they are important in the context of oratory not jurisprudence. In this way Quintilian as a source for our knowledge of Roman law is quite different from either Cicero or Pliny, whose speeches and letters deal with real cases in which they were taking a part. Quintilian practised as an advocate, and must have known his law, but in this elementary work he often uses dramatic illustrations rather than worrying about current details; for example, when he turns to the interrelationship of Orestes, Clytemnestra and Agamemnon. In fact his use of the Atridae is less dangerous than some other references to the Greek past because he is here overtly moving from a real Roman case to a mythical one.[9] Later we get an explicit statement of his approach: 'Why should we not use the same example as nearly everyone else has done. Orestes has killed his mother; the fact is admitted; he pleads justification,' because she had killed her husband, his father. The question is whether even a guilty mother should be killed by her son.[10] Similarly, it is asked whether Horatius had been justified in killing his sister (in the Roman regal period), when she could be held to be a traitor for mourning the death of a *hostis*.[11]

---

[5]   *Inst. or.* III.5.4.
[6]   *Inst. or.* III.6.
[7]   *Inst. or.* III.7-9.
[8]   *Inst. or.* III.10-11.
[9]   *Inst. or.* III.5.10-11. There are more glaring exemples: for instance, in V.10.114-115 an apparently informative discussion of rights over property captured in war turns out to be set in ancient Delphi, justified by a comparison of the Amphictyonic council with the centumviral court.
[10] *Inst. or.* III.11.4 & 11ff. Cf. Marci. D. 48.9.5, on the *pater* killing his son without due form.
[11] *Inst. or.* III.6.76. The legal answer must surely be no, since the *paterfamilias* was around to take action.

Many of Quintilian's examples are drawn from Cicero, whom he greatly admired,[12] but when he discusses the speeches that Cicero had made, one must remember that these speeches might not necessarily reflect either the law or the style of more than a century later, in the new imperial age. For example, Cicero's defence of Milo was based on the ground, which needed proving, that Clodius had lain in wait to ambush him[13] - later described as conjecture[14] - and Cicero argued that we have the right to kill someone lying in wait for us, that it is self defence[15] - later described as a matter of quality.[16] Now self-defence will regularly be pleaded in criminal courts of all periods, and not surprisingly was dealt with by the jurists;[17] it was a justification, but only if minimum force were used - totally repugnant to the law would be Brutus' rejoicing that a bad citizen had been killed.[18] Such conduct as the brawling of Clodius and Milo might have seemed unreal to the Roman aristocracy of nearly one hundred and fifty years later, and the Senate as a court not minded to accept it,[19] but Quintilian keeps referring back to the case rather than to general arguments concerning self-defence; presumably a particular case, being more dramatic, was likely to make a deeper impression on his students.[20]

Further, when Quintilian is considering political or deliberative oratory, his model Cicero undoubtedly made speeches to the popular assemblies, and wrote about the art, but Quintilian's pupils will hardly have done so;[21] references to the *comitia*, or their *contiones*, are anachronistic. Similarly, whether the Senate should vote pay for the troops, or deliver the Fabii to the Gauls could hardly be relevant issues in the later first century AD.[22] These, like Julius Caesar's deliberation on whether he should persist with his invasion of Germany,[23] were, of course, merely exercises in declamation, but there is no chance of the reader being misled while the author is dealing with the political area. The case of the man forbidden to address the

---

[12] Particularly when dealing with abstract questions, cf. *Inst. or.* III.5.15.

[13] *Inst. or.* III.6.12.

[14] *Inst. or.* III.11.15 & 17

[15] *Inst. or.* III.5.15; cf. Cicero, *Pro Milone*, 10-11.

[16] *Inst. or.* III.11.15 & 17.

[17] E.g. Ulp. D. 9.2.5pr. 'Sed et si quemcumque alium ferro se petentem quis occiderit, non videbitur iniuria occidisse' ('If someone kills anyone else who is trying to go for him with a sword, he will not be deemed to have killed unlawfully'); Ulp. D. 48.8.9 'Furem nocturnum si quis occiderit, ita demum impune feret, si parcere ei sine periculo suo non potuit' ('If anyone kills a thief by night, he shall do so unpunished if and only if he could not have spared the man['s life] without risk to his own'); Paul. D. 9.2.45.4 'Qui cum aliter tueri se non possent, damni culpam dederint, innoxii sunt; vim enim vi defendere omnes leges omniaque iura permittunt' ('Those who do damage because they cannot otherwise defend themselves are blameless; for all laws and all legal systems allow one to use force to defend oneself against violence'). I use the translation in A. Watson (ed.), *The Digest of Justinian*, Vols. 1 and 4, Philadelphia: University of Pennsylvania Press 1985.

[18] *Inst. or.* III.6.93.

[19] Nor, of course, was the actual court which heard the case.

[20] *Inst. or.* III.5.10; III.6.12; III.6.93; III.11.12, 15, 17. *Pro Rabirio* too was not concerned with current law, cf. *Inst. or.* III.6.11.

[21] *Inst. or.* III.8.2; III.8.7, 11, 14.

[22] *Inst. or.* III.8.18, 19.

[23] *Inst. or.* III.8.19-21.

assembly because he had used up his patrimony seems similar.[24] Admittedly, in private law a prodigal's agnatic family could demand the appointment of a curator for him, and a known prodigal would be unlikely to be called on by the presiding magistrate in a *contio*, but the notion of such a legal prohibition seems fantastic.

Sometimes Quintilian explicitly says he will treat of a stock theme of the rhetorical schools.[25] But a modern reader looking for information about the first century AD may not know what are stock themes, or even the story of Orestes. Cicero too as an orator used such stock themes; it was the normal currency of the ancient world, but he is very sparing of their use in his forensic speeches. But Cicero and Quintilian could rely upon their audience knowing the difference between Greek myth and contemporary law. Readers some two thousand years later are not soaked in the literary background, and lack precise knowledge of the Roman law of the 70s BC or AD. Trying to distinguish is not necessarily easy for them, and this is why Quintilian is particularly dangerous. Cicero's speeches were delivered at actual trials,[26] and the arguments have to be tied reasonably closely to reality. We do not have such speeches from Quintilian, only what he thought of as suitable exercises for his budding orators.

3. TEXTS THAT CONFIRM OR INCREASE OUR KNOWLEDGE

However, when Quintilian asks: *an tormentis credendum*? *Testibus an argumentis maior fides habenda*?[27] we know that the effectiveness of torture was a problem which did concern the Roman authorities. The emperor Augustus had laid down that torture was not to be the first resort in investigating crime, and that too much reliance should not be placed upon its results.[28] Again, Quintilian reasonably points out that: 'Even if I did it, I was justified, but I did not do it' is a fair defence, but that the denial is stronger.[29]

Quintilian can also be informative, but without giving us quite enough. Somebody who has been a professional actor (*qui artem ludicram exercuerit*) is never entitled to sit in the fourteen front rows at the theatre reserved for equestrians. Someone who has performed before the praetor in his private gardens but never appeared publicly on a stage, takes his seat in the fourteen rows. The man seeking to deny him this privilege alleges he has been an actor (*nempe intentio est: 'artem ludicram exercuisti'; depulsio: 'non exercui artem ludicram'*). So what does 'appearing as an

---

[24] *Inst. or.* III.11.13: 'Qui bona paterna consumpserit ne contionetur' ('He who has spent his patrimony, is not allowed to address the people'); the defence was: 'In opera publica consumpsit' ('But he spent it on public works').

[25] *Inst. or.* III.6.96ff. It is very complex, most suitable for students.

[26] Well, not *Pro Milone* of course, or not in its published form.

[27] *Inst. or.* III.5.10: 'Should one believe evidence given under torture? Do witnesses or logic have greater credibility?'

[28] Ulp. D. 48.18.1pr.; there are further warnings from other emperors in the rest of the fragment.

[29] *Inst. or.* III.6.10; cf. III.6.49. Cf. the fourteenth century York defendant who claimed that no promise of marriage could have been made because he was in another village on the day in question, but if he had been present he had only been jesting; see R.H. Helmholz, *Marriage Litigation in Medieval England*, Cambridge: Cambridge University Press 1974, p. 126.

actor' mean? If the alleged amateur is accused under the *lex Roscia* of 67 BC (*accusabitur theatrali lege*), the *depulsio* [not quite the burden of proof] lies on him. But if he has been thrown out of the theatre and consequently raises an *actio iniuriarum*, the *depulsio* is on his accuser.[30] We have learned a little about the workings of the *lex Roscia*, but there is a problem springing from the technical language; an *intentio* is a civil term whereas *accusare* is criminal. The language suggests that there was an *actio popularis*, and that the breach of the *lex Roscia* fell into the class of acts administratively repressed, like the potentially dangerous placing of something over the streets,[31] but we are left in some doubt as to the procedure followed.

Quintilian's remarks concerning sacrilege seem correct for the law of his day; the crime did not comprise the stealing from a temple, but the stealing of property dedicated to the gods.[32] Definition again lies behind the defences: *Sustuli sed non furtum feci*; *Percussi, sed non iniuriam feci*.[33] Similarly, his discussion of the competence of the forum seems entirely exact. It involved such questions as: did the party have the right to raise the action, and to raise it against the other party; did it fall under the statute alleged; was the court competent; was there some dilatory exception, and other similar issues.[34] Further, his comment that the consul had a jurisdiction over larger sums than the praetor in cases involving *fideicommissa* is our main source of knowledge of their relative jurisdictions in the later first century.[35] A reference to disinheritance is unfamiliar to the modern textbooks, but seems accurate, when he puts forward the argument that somebody who has lost through infamy (*ignominia*) the right to partake in formal legal transactions is not able to disinherit.[36] This would presumably be true even for the praetorian law of succession, in that an infamous person was denied the right to formal witnesses; disherison was not in itself a formal legal transaction but it could not be done other than through a will, which was. Quintilian remarks a little later that there are some things which are not naturally laudable but which are permitted by law, and he cites the obscure passage in the Twelve Tables authorising the body of a debtor to be divided among the creditors.[37]

---

[30] *Inst. or.* III.6.18-19; see also Jul. D. 3.2.1.
[31] Inst. IV.5.1; see also O.F. Robinson, 'Justinian's Institutional Classification and the Class of Quasi-Delict', *Journal of Legal History* 19 (1998), p. 245.
[32] *Inst. or.* III.6.33, 38, 41. See F. Gnoli, 'Rem privatam de sacro surripere', *Studia et Documenta Historiae et Iuris* 40 (1974), p. 401; O.F. Robinson, 'Blasphemy and Sacrilege', *The Irish Jurist* 8 (1973), p. 356.
[33] *Inst. or.* III.6.49: 'I took it, but did not steal it; I struck him, but did not commit an assault'.
[34] *Inst. or.* III.6.69ff.
[35] *Inst. or.* III.6.70; Gai. *Inst.* 2.278 confirms that they both had jurisdiction. Incidentally, this is grossly mistranslated by Butler (see 'Introduction' note 27), I 445 and also by Russell in the more recent Loeb edition (see 'Introduction', note 27) II 85. The English should run: 'You ought not to sue on the *fideicommissum* (trust) before the praetor but before the consuls, for the sum is too large for the jurisdiction of the praetor [*fideicommissarius*].' Noted by R. Röhle, 'Praetor fideicommissarius,' *Revue Internationale des Droits de l'Antiquité* 15 (1968) p. 399, at p. 427.
[36] *Inst. or.* III.6.77.
[37] The problem here is the issue of what the Twelve Tables had actually meant; *Inst. or.* III.6.84; cf. Gai. *Inst.* 4.81, but there are no literary records of such a bizarre course of action.

And when in a later chapter Quintilian points out that it is not possible to bring accusations of different crimes before the same *quaestio perpetua*, and yet that this practice is common before the Senate or the emperor (and had also been common in the days of *iudicia populi*), he is making a simple comment on contemporary as well as earlier law.[38] Our chief interest here lies in what, unfortunately, he does not specify: how many jury courts still operated in his time. He then refers to the many and diverse private suits tried by formula before a single *iudex*.[39] The formulary system is confirmed to have been in full operation in the first century AD. Again, Pliny the Younger amply confirms the continued jurisdiction of the centumviral court over actions concerning succession, a matter referred to by Quintilian in passing.[40] Another passing reference is to the *divinatio*, the procedure to decide which of several claimants should be the chief prosecutor, of which the most famous example was Cicero's *divinatio in Caecilium*.[41]

4. TEXTS THAT ARE MISLEADING

Other issues, however, raised by Quintilian were certainly not appropriate to his day – or not appropriate as legal issues. To ask whether a man should marry, and whether an old man should marry,[42] were questions, legally speaking, covered by Augustus' legislation (*lex Iulia de maritandis ordinibus* and *lex Papia Poppaea*), requiring, on pain of various civil losses, all men between 25 and 60 (and women between 20 and 50) to be married. Admittedly, the context makes clear that it is a rhetorical trope, but it also emphasises that Quintilian raises the traditional question or *causa* regardless of the real legal world.

Another example, or group of examples, of where it would be misleading to take Quintilian literally concerns adultery. An accuser charges somebody with homicide; the accused can deny the charge, or plead justification in that he killed an adulterer: *Quid si confitetur, sed iure a se adulterum dicit occisum? Nempe legem esse certum est quae permittat.*[43] As a general statement of the law in the first century AD this is wrong. Augustus legislated on adultery in the *lex Iulia de adulteriis coercendis* of 18 BC, and one of his purposes seems to have been to restrict the *ius occidendi*, the right to kill the adulterous woman and her paramour. The *lex Julia*, in its second section, laid down that it was permitted to a *paterfamilias* to kill with his own hand his daughter, together with her lover, no matter what his status, if they were taken in the act of adultery in his own house or that of his son-in-law; he was also specifically allowed to beat up the paramour. But there were severe limitations in that while this

---

[38] *Inst. or.* III.10.1.
[39] *Inst. or.* III.10.1: '…; privata quoque iudicia saepe unum iudicem habere multis et diversis formulis solent' ('Private suits again are often tried by one judge, who may have to determine many different points of law'). He does not mention the use of *recuperatores*, but in his context there was no need.
[40] *Inst. or.* III.10.3; e.g. Pliny, *Epistulae*, II.14 or VI.33.
[41] *Inst. or.* III.10.3.
[42] *Inst. or.* III.5.16.
[43] *Inst. or.* III.6.17: 'Or again, if he admits that he has killed a man, but states that the victim was an adulterer and justifiably killed (and we know that the law permits homicide under these circumstances)'.

applied to an adoptive as well as a natural father, it did not apply if the natural father were himself still in paternal power, nor where the *paterfamilias* was not also the father.[44] If the *pater* were to exercise his right to kill he must kill both, together or as nearly so as was possible, or be liable for homicide in regard to the paramour.[45] The husband was permitted under the statute (perhaps the fifth chapter) to kill the paramour if, and only if, he was caught in the husband's own house and if he fell into the class of degraded persons, such as slaves or actors.[46] The husband was not permitted to kill his wife.[47] These restrictions on the *ius occidendi* cannot easily be made to fit with Quintilian's statement. It is just possible that he is talking of the *paterfamilias*, but in the absence of a specific statement to this effect, I would hold that when one meets an unspecified man in relation to *adulter* and *adultera* the normal rules of interpretation suggest that he is the husband. However, as we have just seen, the law hardly ever permitted the husband's killing the adulterer. Quintilian's statement is made as a generalisation, which would seem to have been true in Cicero's day but was certainly no longer so for his own.

Adultery, viewed from the patriarchal perspective rather than legally, recurs when Quintilian is dealing with the treatment of an adulterer, presumably caught in the act, who is scourged, or starved to death;[48] starving a man to death was never a lawful act,[49] and, looking at the matter practically, it would seem impossible in the 20 hours allowed for the interrogation under Augustus' *lex Julia*. For the purposes of instruction Quintilian preferred a dramatic rather than a realistic example as being of more effect.

Again, the case of the slaying of the adulteress caught in the act and the hot pursuit of her paramour, ending in his slaying in the forum, would be good law for the *paterfamilias* who caught them in his own house or his son-in-law's, but in no other case, yet Quintilian presents it as a generalisation, and the natural grammatical interpretation would again be that the subject of the verb is the husband.[50] It remains, of course possible that there were more husbands with *manus* in the late first century AD than is commonly reckoned, but in this case it is surprising that he never raises the issue of whether a marriage was with *manus* or free.

A final example: when Quintilian is considering the effect of number on the orator's treatment of a question, he prefers to ask whether the state owes Thrasybulus thirty rewards for ridding it of thirty tyrants (in fourth century BC Athens), rather

---

[44] Pap. D. 48.5.21 which denies the power to a father himself in power; cf. Ulp. h.t. 22; Pap. h.t. 23.pr & 2-3; Ulp. h.t. 24.2-3; *Pauli Sententiae*, 2.26.1.

[45] Ulp. D. 48.5.24.4; Mac. h.t.33.pr.

[46] Mac. D. 48.5.25.pr; Sev. Alex. C. 9.9.4; *Pauli Sententiae*, 2.26.4,7.

[47] Pap. D. 48.5.23.4; *Collatio*, 4.10.1, although presumably there would be a strong plea in mitigation; D. 48.5.39.8, Papinian citing Marcus Aurelius.

[48] *Inst. or.* III.6.27. Cf. A.D. Manfredini, 'Galba negabat', in J.W. Cairns - O.F. Robinson (eds.), *Critical Studies in Roman Law, Comparative Law and Legal History in honour of Alan Watson*, Oxford: Hart 2001, p. 93.

[49] Cf. Ulp. D. 48.19.8.1.

[50] *Inst. or.* III.11.7: 'qui cum adulteram deprehensam occidisset, adulterum qui tum effugerat postea in foro occidit' ('when the husband caught his wife in adultery and slew her and later slew the adulterer, who had escaped, in the market place').

than, for example, to refer to the humbler fact that rustling was distinguished from theft by the number of animals stolen.[51]

5. CONCLUSIONS

Much of the material in Quintilian's *Institutio oratoria* was traditional in the rhetorical schools, dealing with classical Greek tragedy. Other material, rhetorical and legal, was drawn from Cicero in the Late Republic; this can fill in gaps in our knowledge of Cicero's writings, but is not necessarily helpful for the law of Quintilian's day. Obviously Quintilian was well acquainted with current law, but at the same time he is in his summation explicitly dismissive of jurists in comparison with orators. Jurists had their place as legal experts, but were to be classed as harmless drudges (as one might say) when they did not also fall, as did Marcus Cato, Q. Mucius Scaevola and Servius Sulpicius, into the category of orator.[52] He remarks that Cicero's legal knowledge was sufficient for his pleading, and sufficient for him to begin a book on the subject.[53] In his general introduction, he maintains that education in rhetoric as well as philosophy produces the virtuous man, capable of playing his part as a citizen in both public and private affairs;[54] there is no mention at all of jurists, let alone as priests of justice.[55] Quintilian's surviving work is a valuable source, not to be ignored, but it must be used with caution for discovering the substantive law or procedure of his own day; it is certainly not a juridical source in the sense that Cicero's speeches and Pliny's letters can be so described.

---

[51] *Inst. or.* III.6.26. Cf. Claudius Saturninus D. 48.19.16.1 & 7. This fragment in the Digest is similarly concerned with the issues of person, time, place, number, quality, motive and outcome; the jurists had all had some training in oratory as the normal higher education in ancient Rome.

[52] *Inst. or.* XII.3.9: 'If the class of legal experts is as a rule drawn from those who in despair of making successful pleaders have taken refuge with the law, how easy it must be for an orator to learn what has been learned by those who by their own confession are incapable of becoming orators'.

[53] *Inst. or.* XII.3.10. Cicero's claim (*Pro Murena*, 28) that he could become a jurist in three days if he set his mind to it is not to be taken seriously, nor in that context are his other jibes at lawyers. On the other hand, in *De oratore*, I.235-237, Cicero makes clear that, while jurisprudence is a noble art, 'ita est tibi iuris consultus ipse per se nihil nisi leguleius quidam cautus et acutus...' ('so by your account the learned lawyer, in and by himself, is nothing but a circumspect and sharp kind of pettifogger, ...'), and it is hard to see Quintilian disagreeing with his hero on this.

[54] *Inst. or.* I.pr.10: 'Neque enim hoc concesserim rationem rectae honestaeque vitae (ut quidam putaverunt) ad philosophos relegandam, cum vir ille vere civilis et publicarum privatarumque rerum administrationi accommodatus, qui regere consiliis urbes, fundare legibus, emendare iudiciis possit, non alius sit profecto quam orator' ('For I will not admit that the principles of upright and honourable living should, as some have held, be regarded as the peculiar concern of philosophy. The man who can really play his part as a citizen and is capable of meeting the demands both of public and private business, the man who can guide a state by his counsels, give it a firm basis by his legislation and purge its vices by his decisions as a judge, is assuredly no other than the orator of our quest').

[55] Ulp. D. 1.1.1: 'Cuius [ius] merito quis nos sacerdotes appellet; iustitiam namque colimus et boni et aequi notitiam profitemur, ... veram nisi fallor philosophiam, non simulatam affectantes' ('Of that art we [jurists] are deservedly called the priests. For we cultivate the virtue of justice and claim awareness of what is good and fair, ... and affecting a philosophy which, if I am not deceived, is genuine, not a sham').

IDA MASTROROSA

QUINTILIAN AND THE JUDGES

Rhetorical Rules and Psychological Strategies in the 4ᵗʰ Book of the Institutio oratoria [1]

1. THE JUDICIAL PERSPECTIVE OF BOOK IV

Among the various aspects that make the *Institutio oratoria* a significant and, in some way, original work, far from being a simple container of precepts extracted from antecedent treatises, are the many and precise observations on the use of oratory in court. It is in this field, that was definitely not considered a secondary one by previous writers either (e.g. Cicero), that this work reveals the most interesting indications of the practice acquired by Quintilian through the legal profession[2] which, as we know, he exercised in the period prior to accepting and holding, for twenty years, the chair of rhetoric established by Vespasian in 69 AD.[3] In particular, proof of the great importance that the experience gained by the author in youth played when writing this work is also found, in my opinion, in the specifically technical nature of several lexical choices pertaining to the juridical world[4] and in the many suggestions aimed at influencing the judge most of all.[5]

---

[1] Throughout this paper, I will quote Quintilian's *Institutio oratoria* from Michael Winterbottom's text (see 'Introduction', note 26). The English translation is from Butler (see 'Introduction', note 27).

[2] As regards this subject, see Th. Froment, 'Quintilien avocat', *Annales de la Faculté des Lettres de Bordeaux* 2 (1880), pp. 224-240; J. Cousin, *Études sur Quintilien, I: Contribution à la recherche des sources de l' 'Institution oratoire'; II: Vocabulaire grec de la terminologie rhétorique dans l' 'Institution oratoire'*, Paris: Boivin 1935-1936, rpt. Amsterdam: Schippers 1967, Vol. II, Chapt. 1: 'L'orientation juridique', pp. 685-732; G. Kennedy, *Quintilian*, New York: Twayne Publishers 1969, pp. 20-22; J.A. Crook, *Legal Advocacy in the Roman World*, London: Duckworth 1995, p. 120; O.E. Tellegen-Couperus, 'Quintilian and Roman Law', *Revue Internationale des Droits de l'Antiquité* 47 (2000), pp. 167-177.

[3] Cf. *Inst. or.* I.pr.1; Suetonius *Vespasianus* 18; Hieronymus, *Chronicon*, in Migne, PL XXVII, col. 460; in general, for the interventions of the first of the *Flavii* in the world of culture, see M.A. Levi, *Gli studi superiori nella politica di Vespasiano (A proposito di un nuovo documento epigrafico)*, repr. in M.A. Levi, *Il tribunato della plebe e altri scritti su istituzioni pubbliche romane*, Milan: Cisalpino - La Goliardica 1978, pp. 203-208. Useful insights into this theme are found also in C. Barbagallo, *Lo stato e l'istruzione pubblica nell'Impero romano*, Catania: Battiato 1911, pp. 81-99; M.St.A. Woodside, 'Vespasian's Patronage of Education and the Arts', *Transactions of the American Philological Association* 73 (1942) pp. 123-129; P. Desideri, *Dione di Prusa. Un intellettuale greco nell'impero romano*, Messina-Florence: D'Anna 1978, pp. 61-67; I. Lana, 'La politica culturale dei Flavi', in: *Atti del Congresso Internazionale di Studi Vespasianei*, Rieti: Centro di Studi Varroniani Editore 1981, I, pp. 85-103.

[4] In this context, see the remarks in I. Mastrorosa, 'Appunti per un lessico giudiziario in Quintiliano', in: P. Radici Colace (ed.), *Atti del II Seminario Internazionale di Studi sui Lessici Tecnici Greci e Latini*, Naples-Messina: ESI 1997, pp. 233-243.

[5] The peculiar role and aspects of the figure of the judge in the *Institutio oratoria* have never before

The latter, although interspersed throughout the *Institutio oratoria*, are more significantly and organically expressed starting from its 4th book. At the beginning, the author appears not only eager to educate to the best of his abilities the young descendants of the imperial family assigned to him by Domitian (IV.pr.2-4),[6] but equally concerned about the possible criticism of his readers, to whom he confesses the particular difficulty of the topic he intends to discuss (IV.pr.6). Indeed, this book, that was completed around 92 AD,[7] introduces a part of the work explicitly dedicated to the order to be followed in forensic causes, which, according to Quintilian, were of the utmost complication and variety. It focuses on arguments deemed much more complicated and arduous than the ones treated in the previous books (for example, the function of the *exordium*, the technique for stating the facts, the weight of the proof brought to confirm one's own assertions or to refute those of the opponent, the aim and the purpose of the final peroration). As concerns these arguments, Quintilian proposes to provide a systematic and coherent treatise, thus distancing himself from those authors who preferred to discuss each part separately (IV.pr.7).[8]

On the basis of these explicit premises, it is no surprise then that, starting from Book IV, certainly abounding in reminiscences taken from pre-existing literature,[9] the interest in the figure of the judge starts to grow progressively, as indicated by the many annotations that constitute the main theme of this paper. Indeed, they indicate the objectively central role attributed by Quintilian to the person called on to give judgment in the final phase, and they underline the fact that this person is the actual target of the orator's speech. In the second book of the *Institutio oratoria*, Quintilian refutes the thesis of those who hold that the aim of rhetoric is to persuade (II.15.11). He names among others Apollodorus of Pergamum, the rhetor concerned foremost

---

been the subject of in-depth study; it has been touched upon only in G. Melzani, 'L'attenzione di Quintiliano per la psicologia', in P.V. Cova, R. Gazich, G.E. Manzoni, and G. Melzani, *Aspetti della 'paideia' di Quintiliano*, Milan: Vita e Pensiero 1990, pp. 173-230, at pp. 200-203.

[6] Further remarks on this subject can be found in J. Giet, 'Quintilien et les jeunes Flaviens I', *Revue des Sciences Religieuses* 32 (1958), pp. 321-334; Id., 'Quintilien et les jeunes Flaviens II', *Revue des Sciences Religieuses* 33 (1959) pp. 1-17; J. Adamietz, 'Quintilians 'Institutio oratoria'', in: H. Temporini and W. Haase (eds.), *Aufstieg und Niedergang der römischen Welt* 2, 32, 4 (1986), pp. 2226-71, at p. 2230.

[7] As regards the overall dating of the work, see the debate through the various proposals put forward by scholars offered in I. Lana, 'Quando fu scritta l'*Institutio oratoria* di Quintiliano', *Atti dell'Accademia delle Scienze di Torino. Classe di Scienze Morali, Storiche e Filosofiche* 85 (1950) pp. 55-68 (= Id., *La teorizzazione della collaborazione degli intellettuali con il potere politico in Quintiliano, Institutio oratoria, Libro XII*, Turin: Giappichelli 1973, pp. 5-18); B. Zucchelli, 'Quintiliano e i Flavi', in: *Atti Vespasianei* (see note 3), II, pp. 571-591 at p. 583, n. 58-59; Id., 'Sulla data di pubblicazione dell'Institutio oratoria di Quintiliano', in: *Filologia e forme letterarie. Studi offerti a Francesco Della Corte*, Urbino: Università di Urbino 1987, IV, pp. 47-60; with special reference to the dating of the 4th book, *ibidem* pp. 51-54; Adamietz (see note 6), pp. 2245-49.

[8] As regards this passage, see also J.D. O'Banion, 'Narration and Argumentation: Quintilian on Narratio as the Heart of Rhetorical Thinking', *Rhetorica* 5 (1987) pp. 325-351, at p. 327, who underlines: 'In the Preface to Book IV, he pointed out the key functions of each stage of the oration, which are easy to list, but he also declared that they cannot be adequately explained in separate treatises.... A crucial result of his decision to 'treat them altogether' was his synthetic perspective, which led him to declare that proof and narration are twin arts, the means by which rhetorical 'generalship' is possible'.

[9] The importance of antecedent technical sources in Book IV of the *Institutio oratoria* is highlighted already in Cousin (see note 2), p. 252.

with legal aspects (III.1.1) who states that the peculiarity of the *oratio iudicialis* is that of convincing the judge.[10] Despite this fact, I believe no one could argue that, in many places in Book IV, as well as in the following ones, the figure of the judge, with his conduct and moods, dominates the author's attention. Although the dialectics of the case accurately discussed throughout the work sees the alternation of both the defending counsel and of the prosecution, the *iudex* is evidently the arbiter called to watch the entire game and assign victory to the party who best supported his position, that is to say, by means of a speech based on rhetorical and emotional strategies and techniques so knowledgeably and cautiously dosed both in terms of structure and of form as to prove the most persuasive.

This pragmatic outlook, that also appears at the beginning of the second book of Aristotle's *Rhetoric*,[11] sheds light on the many precepts supplied by Quintilian in his other books (V to IX), where the possibility and indeed the necessity to influence the decision of the judge continues to represent the more or less constant final objective. This objective requires great care in setting up and presenting the proofs and the arguments, in analysing the cases in hand according to the doctrine of the *status*, as well as in choosing the words and style with which they are laid out, stated, and pronounced. In short, the *inventio* and the *dispositio* of the various parts of the speech, as well as the speaker's *elocutio*, become useful tools in conditioning the judge.

2. CONVINCING THE JUDGE IN THE VARIOUS PARTS OF THE SPEECH

The first concrete proof of this is found, first of all, in several passages of Book IV of the *Institutio oratoria*. They give the impression that, according to Quintilian, each phase of the *oratio*,[12] and thus not only the commencement (the *exordium* or, in Greek, *prohoimion*), but also the more central and important one (the *narratio*), or the more marginal one (the *egressio*), constitutes a useful occasion for winning the good-will of the judge. His decisions seem to rest on the capability of the orator to build his case on criteria orchestrated, according to need, either on an emotional level or on a rational one, starting from the very first words of the *exordium*. Noteworthy, to this end, is the passage in *Inst. or.* IV.1.3, where the author specifies that the term *prohoemium* indicates 'the portion of the speech addressed to the *iudex* before he has begun to consider the actual case'. No less noteworthy is the acute observation that follows immediately afterwards, where he underlines once again[13]

---

[10] See *Inst. or.* II.15.12, where Quintilian criticises the opinion of Apollodorus, stating that it conditioned the orator's function to the result. Cf. R. Granatelli (ed), *Apollodori Pergameni ac Theodori Gadarei testimonia et fragmenta*, Roma: L'Erma' di Bretschneider 1991, *frg.* 1, p. 4.

[11] Cf. *Rhetorica*, II.1.1377b 20-24.

[12] As regards the theories found in technical treatises concerning the various parts of the *oratio*, see especially L. Montefusco Calboli, *Exordium, narratio, epilogus. Studi sulla teoria retorica greca e romana delle parti del discorso*, Bologna: Clueb 1988.

[13] In this regard, consider also what the author has to say in *Inst. or.* II.10.8 when referring to the fictitious nature of school exercises in which even the presence of the judge is simulated for realistic purposes: 'nam si foro non praeparat, aut scenicae ostentationi aut furiosae vociferationi simillimum est. Quid enim attinet iudicem praeparare qui nullus est...' ('For if declamation is not a preparation for the actual work of the courts, it can only be compared to the rant of an actor or the raving of a lunatic. For

the difference that exists between actual practice in court and the fictitious one imagined in school, stating that the practice adopted in schools of preparing the *exordia* by assuming that the judge is already acquainted with the case does not prepare for reality in court, as it arises from the fact that a preliminary sketch of the case is always given in declamatory exercises (IV.1.3-4):

> *Certe prohoemium est quod apud iudicem dici prius quam causam cognoverit[14] possit, vitioseque in scholis facimus quod exordio semper sic utimur quasi causam iudex iam noverit. (4) Cuius rei licentia ex hoc est, quod ante declamationem illa velut imago litis exponitur.*
> But in any case there can be no doubt that by proem we mean the portion of a speech addressed to the judge before he has begun to consider the actual case. And it is a mistaken practice which we adopt in the schools of always assuming in our exordia that the judge is already acquainted with the case. (4) This form of licence arises from the fact that a sketch of the case is always given before actual declamation.

On the other hand, the attention paid by Quintilian to the gap that divides these two worlds sheds light on the methods used in his time. In fact, he explains that, in real court cases, *exordia* without detailed information on the case are used 'when a case comes on for the second time', and only rarely in the first hearing, unless the judge 'has knowledge of the case from some other source' (IV.1.4). Basically, the *exordium* is the first good occasion for preparing the judge psychologically (IV.1.5), so as to secure his good-will (*benivolentia*) as was traditionally done (IV.1.6) or yet again to obtain his compassion using tact and restraint (IV.1.28). During this phase, the *iudex* remains passive but constantly vigilant and therefore needs to be treated with great caution and care. This explains the meaning of Quintilian's advice to avoid any open or even hinted attack on the judge (IV.1.11), but instead to praise him in various ways, as most appropriate, by appealing to his dignity in favour of the honest, to his sense of justice in favour of the humble, to his pity in favour of the unfortunate, to his severity in favour of 'victims of wrong' (IV.1.16), and also to harness his emotions in the service of one's cause (IV.1.17). However, in Quintilian's view, the judge is not solely to be the object of flattering praise and persuasion. In fact, the author admits that the orator may sometimes find it necessary to amicably 'frighten' the judge by reminding him of the possibility of the displeasure of the people or even of indictment, as actually foreseen by Roman law,[15] or, as a last

---

what is the use of attempting to conciliate a non-existent judge …'). However, references to the real gap between scholastic fiction and reality in court occur throughout the work: see, e.g., *Inst. or.* V.13.44 and VI.1.42-4. On this subject, see also S.F. Bonner, *Roman Declamation in the Late Republic and Early Empire*, Liverpool: University Press of Liverpool 1949; I. Lana, 'Il primo approccio degli studenti romani con la legge alla scuola del retore', *Klio* 61 (1979) pp. 89-95 (= Id., *Sapere, lavoro e potere in Roma antica*, Naples: Liguori 1990, pp. 311-325); M. Winterbottom, 'Quintilian and Declamation', in: *Hommages a Jean Cousin. Rencontres avec l'Antiquité classique*, Paris: Les Belles Lettres 1983, pp. 225-235.
[14]   Of interest here is the use of the verb in its technical-legal meaning; for further examples, see *Inst. or.* IV.4.9; VIII.3.62; XI.1.77.
[15]   In this regard, see, e.g., Cicero, *In Verrem actio*, I.8: '… sed nos non tenebimus iudicia diutius; etenim quis poterit Verre absoluto de transferendis iudiciis recusare?' ('… but the law-courts will be in our keeping no longer; for who can possibly hesitate about transferring them to other hands, if Verres is acquitted?' Text and translation by L.H.G. Greenwood, in *Cicero. The Verrine Orations*, London - Cambridge (Mass.): Loeb Classical Library 1928, rpt. 1978, at pp. 88-89.

resort, to aggressively threaten him with prosecution for bribery (IV.1.21). Once again, these last suggestions show, next to the author's psychological acumen, his expertise in technical juridical matters. Suffice it to consider the specific remark he makes immediately afterwards (IV.1.22):

> *Quod si necessitas exiget, non erit iam ex arte oratoria, non magis quam appellare, eti-amsi id quoque saepe utile est, aut antequam pronuntiet reum facere; nam et minari et deferre etiam non orator potest*
> But if necessity should drive us to such a course, we must remember that such threats do not come under the art of oratory, any more than appeals from the judgment of the court (though that is often useful), or the indictment of the judge before he gives his decision. For even one who is no orator can threaten or lay an information.

Thus, according to Quintilian's suggestions, the orator may resort to intimidation by using a whole set of technical-procedural means actually set out in the Roman legal system only to find a solution in cases when the trial was not carried out in the right way. One of these means is the *appellatio*,[16] mentioned in the text through the use of the technical verb *appellare*, and notoriously applicable within the judicial context of the *cognitio extra ordinem*. In this regard, Quintilian specifically[17] stresses that these means do not require rhetorical skills, since any citizen may question the actions of a judge. Conversely, I have no doubt that the suggestions provided in the text implicitly refer to the problem of the not always morally irreproachable behaviour of the *iudex*. However, as also indicated in two subsequent points where the possibility that a judge may be prejudiced before coming into court is hinted at,[18] the fact that Quintilian mentions a case in which the judge was partial to the opposing party (IV.1.18) is certainly significant. Here, too, the orator is urged to exercise great caution, since it is not rare for biased judges to pass judgment against their friends and in favour of their rivals only because they wish to appear impartial. In this manner, Quintilian does not merely covertly point out the tendency of the judge to partiality. It was actually so much a part of the judicial context as to appear at the beginning of Aristotle's *Rhetoric* among the aspects that deviate judgment and call for a limitation of the judge's powers (I.1.1354 a 24-25; 31-33; b 8-15) and to be considered further on (I.12.1372a 20-21). Therefore, Quintilian also urges the orator, based

---

[16] As regards this subject, see E. Perrot, *L'appel dans la procédure de l'ordo iudiciorum*, Paris: Rousseau 1907; M. Lauria, 'Sull''appellatio''', *Archivio Giuridico* 97 (1927) pp. 228-234; C. Sanfilippo, *Contributi esegetici alla storia dell'appellatio. I. Sull'appello contro la sentenza del giudice formulare nell'impero*, Spoleto: Arti Grafiche Panetto & Petrelli 1934; R. Orestano, *L'appello civile in diritto romano. Corso di diritto romano*, 2nd edition, Turin: Giappichelli 1953; Id., 'Appello (Diritto romano)', in: *Enciclopedia del diritto*, Milan: Giuffrè 1958, II, pp. 708-714; R. Villers, 'Appel devant le prince et appel devant le senat au premier siècle de l'empire', in: *Studi in onore di Pietro De Francisci*, Milan: Giuffrè 1956, I, pp. 373-391.

[17] In this context, I do not see as problematical but rather as quite precise the reference to the *appellatio* offered by the technical use of the verb *appellare* that has been commented on as 'of inconsequence' by M. Winterbottom, *Problems in Quintilian* (= *Bulletin of the Institute of Classical Studies*, Suppl. 25), London: University of London. Institute of Classical Studies 1970, p. 79, according to whom the verb used in *Inst. or.* IV.1.22 does not have the technical meaning of 'to appeal', otherwise known to Quintilian who, as the scholar states, uses it in *Inst. or.* XI.1.76, but rather that of 'to accuse'.

[18] Cf. *Inst. or.* IV.1.20; IV.2.80.

on his own senior experience in the field, to keep an eye open for the stratagems used by the judge to hide such partiality.

Nonetheless, the fact remains that, during the *exordium* phase, the person who is called upon to pass judgment is destined to be the target of strategies mainly applied to the sphere of his emotions. In my opinion, we must consider the contents of *Inst. or.* IV.1.24 in detail. In this text, Quintilian discusses the opinion of writers such as Theodorus of Gadara,[19] who unconditionally accept that the *prohoemium* should anticipate the main issues of the case. However, in Quintilian's view, this would force the orator to give a detailed account of the facts, therefore inappropriately anticipating what is more specifically suited for the *narratio*, and most of all would burden the psychologically unprepared judge with the whole case in all its complexity. This observation shows once again how, according to the author, the purpose of the *exordium* is to subject the judge to strategies aimed at influencing his emotions. It is a tool used by the orator to secure the judge's favour by taking advantage of the judge's insufficient knowledge of the facts of the case. In this context, it remains a distinct phase of the speech in any case. Its purpose should not overlap that of the *narratio*, as we have just seen, or that of the other phases of the *oratio*, as indicated in the concise statements of *Inst. or.* IV.1.60 and in a precise statement made further on in *Inst. or.* IV.2.24. Nevertheless, such a rigid distinction of functions that should be put forth without sudden and obscure jumps of the speech from one phase to another (IV.1.79) can be followed only in a general way, as significantly observed by the author as early as in *Inst. or.* IV.1.73. Here Quintilian shows his extensive experience in legal practice and quite appropriately explains that, in certain circumstances, the functions of the *exordium* may be applied in other parts of the speech, for example, at a later time in the proceedings when seeking to obtain from the judge his utmost attention and good-will in the *narratio* or during the phase dedicated to the *argumenta*.

3. CONVINCING THE JUDGE BY ARTIFICE, TRICKERY, AND FALSEHOOD

Going back to the author's view of the importance, in court, of the judge's sensitivity, one cannot overlook the very real argument introduced in *Inst. or.* IV.1.33. This text is interesting because here Quintilian sketches the profile of the typical *iudex* who allows himself to be led or impressed by the novelty or the atrocity of the case, who is affected by what may concern the *res publica*, or his own public role, who is stirred by hope or even by fear, who reacts to admonition or to entreaty, according to a tendency already noted by Aristotle[20] and indicated by Antonius in Cicero's *De oratore* II.178. Far from being only a rule of theory, the use of emotions, as considered here, can be compared with the possibility for the orator to resort to falsehood

---

[19]   As regards Theodorus of Gadara and his theories on rhetoric, cf. the observations collected by R. Granatelli, 'Per un ripensamento sulle radici culturali di Apollodoro di Pergamo e Teodoro di Gadara', *Annali dell'Istituto Universitario Orientale di Napoli = Seminario di studi del mondo classico. Sezione filologico-letteraria* II-III (1980-1981) pp. 75-109; as regards this passage in particular, see also M. Schanz, 'Die Apollodoreer und die Theodoreer', *Hermes* 25 (1890) pp. 36-54, at p. 39.
[20]   See Aristoteles, *Rhetorica* II.1.1377b 30-1378a 5.

if necessary. This strategy obviously poses the problem of how Quintilian can reconcile the idea of cheating the judge with the orator's need to stand up to moral and ethical values. An answer to this question, albeit thwarted by the author's overall and very real faith in the definition of an *orator* as being not only a *dicendi peritus* but also a *vir bonus* (II.15.1; XII.1.1) in terms of ethics and morals,[21] can perhaps be found in several detailed opinions in Book II of the *Institutio*, that should be considered presuppositions of what he states later on in the work. It is useful to outline first of all the fundamental meaning that Quintilian attributes to the individual faculty of using rhetoric correctly and of putting it to good use (II.16.1-10). Rhetoric cannot be considered evil per se, nor can it be accused of being a tool for unlawful purposes, such as the protection of criminals from rightful punishment or the condemnation of innocent people (II.16.2). The most significant considerations supporting the point of view stated in this paper are found in a subsequent passage (II.17.26). There Quintilian opposes those who accuse rhetoric of turning to illicit means, namely, the use of falsehood and the stirring up of passions, by stating that one should look at the *bona ratio* generating such means. Most importantly, what emerges from the words of the author is that the need to emotionally steer the judge stems from the impossibility of inducing him in any other way to pass judgment according to reason and that the need to resort to tricks is often the only way to prevent unskilled judges from falling into error (II.17.27). In other words, it seems that Quintilian believes that 'the end', i.e., the best possible judgment, shall we say 'justifies' the 'means', i.e., tricking the judge when necessary.

As regards this argument, that is obviously critical in other parts of the *Institutio oratoria*, too, another passage, found in Book VI, deserves to be mentioned (VI.2.5):

> *Ubi vero animis iudicum vis adferenda est et ab ipsa veri contemplatione abducenda mens, ibi proprium oratoris opus est.*
> But the peculiar task of the orator arises when the minds of the judges require force to move them, and their thoughts have actually to be led away from the contemplation of the truth.

In this case, the author specifically points out the orator's precise task of leading the judge's mind away from the contemplation of truth.[22] This obviously does not mean that Quintilian ignores the fact that the suggestion of tricking the *iudex*, although called for, may appear questionable in terms of ethics and of deontology. Actually,

---

[21] As regards the expression and its many implications, see M. Winterbottom, 'Quintilian and the Vir Bonus', *Journal of Roman Studies* 54 (1964) pp. 90-97; A. Brinton, 'Quintilian, Plato and the Vir Bonus', *Philosophy & Rhetoric* 16 (1983) pp. 167-183; B. Cassin, 'Philosophia enim simulari potest, eloquentia non potest, ou: le masque et l'effet', *Rhetorica* 13 (1995) pp. 105-124, at pp. 117-119; M. Winterbottom, 'Quintilian the Moralist', in: T. Albaladejo, E. Del Río, and J.A. Caballero (eds.) *Quintiliano: Historia y Actualidad de la Retórica*, Logroño: Instituto de Estudios Riojanos 1998, I, pp. 317-334, at p. 320 ff.; P. García Castillo, 'Influencias filosóficas en la definición del *vir bonus* de Quintiliano', *ibidem*, II, pp. 891-898.

[22] The meaningfulness of this passage is also underlined by S. Gély, "Bona voluntas'. Vouloir, pouvoir et devoir dire chez Quintilien (*Inst. or.* XII. 11. 31)', *Bulletin de l'Association Guillaume Budé* (1997) pp. 58-66, at p. 60; see also A. Manzo, '*Manente honesta voluntate* (Quint. *Inst. or.* XII.1.46). Tra ideologia e retorica', in: *Atti Vespasianei* (see note 3), II, pp. 443-457; S. Gély, 'L'*Institution oratoire*, une éthique de l'attention', in: Albaladejo (see note 21), II, pp. 899-906.

in an extremely interesting passage in the last book of the *Institutio oratoria*, the author admits that the statement that the *vir bonus* should sometimes keep truth from the judge is objectionable and hastens to explain, inviting anyone who marvels at his statement, that is after all supported by the greatest teachers of the past, to consider that many situations are made more or less morally correct not by their intrinsic nature but by the causes that motivate them (XII.1.36). In short, what is interesting, in my view, is that for Quintilian, the end, i.e., the best verdict, and the presuppositions, i.e., the *causae* of the controversy, are determining factors in reconciling the idea of a morally irreproachable orator with the use of rhetorical and psychological strategies based on deceit, allowed for on various points in the 4th book of the *Institutio oratoria*.

In this book, that is the main subject of this paper, special attention should also be paid to the suggestion that the orator deflate, in his *narratio*, the seriousness of the facts being discussed, in other words, that he alter the facts somewhat (IV.2.62). Even more interesting in this regard is what can be inferred by the reasoning that follows immediately afterwards (IV.2.64-65). Here Quintilian pauses to consider the *evidentia*, certainly a quality that is desirable in a speech, even though, according to some, it can come in the way of the need, in some cases, of partially obscuring the truth. Against such a contention, Quintilian argues that, precisely in such cases, the need to obscure the truth leads the orator to state what is false in place of the truth, and to strive to present the facts *quam evidentissima*. Here, once again,[23] the author provides us with an indirect albeit significant confirmation that the problem of the modification of the truth exists and is intrinsically linked to the use of oratory in court. This problem was relevant not only in the ancient practice: it exists also in the trial procedures of modern times where it represents a risk that is not totally avoidable, although bound to compliance with professional ethics and deontology. Despite this, he does not hesitate to touch upon the topic again immediately after (IV.2.66), where, with a truly pragmatic approach, he considers the case in which the orator is faced with facts that are against his client, namely, when he has to defend someone who does not deserve to be defended. Even in such an event, Quintilian does not admit the possibility of omitting the statement of facts, since the orator's silence would be too eloquent and would surely bring on an unfavourable decision by the judge. Obviously, no judge would give a decision in favour of a case whose facts have been withheld from him, unless he is totally dense (IV.2.66). Thus, in this text, too, the advice not to stay totally silent in a bad case, and to omit only the least suitable facts (IV.2.67) shows that, according to Quintilian's typically judicial viewpoint, the orator should never throw in the towel, not even when the situation is at its worst, but should rather give what we could call a 'censored version' of the facts, with the aim of winning the favour of the judge.

Another interesting consideration regarding this issue is found in *Inst. or.* IV.2.126 where Quintilian exhorts the orator to avoid appearing artful, in order not to lead the judge to suspect, as is often the case during the *narratio*, that the speech is fictitious, deriving from the art of oratory rather than being the natural result of the

---

[23]   See also, e.g., the author's arguments in *Inst. or.* II.17.19; 20.

case itself. A statement in the same vein seems to be made by the author in a subsequent passage in Chapter 5 of the same book, dedicated to the *partitio*,[24] i.e., the enumeration in the order of the *propositiones* of both parties. In this case, after criticising the indiscriminate use of this logical-rhetorical tool that, at times, threatens to make an argument look like it was specifically prepared beforehand and therefore less attractive because deemed not spontaneous, Quintilian admits that the orator may, if necessary, use various artifices to make the judge believe that the orator's aim is other than what it really is (IV.5.4-5). By comparing the judge who fears what he knows is about to be said because he knows it in advance with the patient who shrinks from the surgeon's knife before the operation,[25] the author hints at the possible dangerous consequences of the *partitio*. In short, what Quintilian wishes to point out is that an inconsiderate use of the partition may make the judge suspicious and therefore less willing to give credence than when subjected to artful concealment strategies. In other words, in the light of this reasoning, I believe the *partitio* may be said to limit somewhat the orator's possibility of speaking more freely by providing beforehand the layout of the speech and thus of concealing whatever manoeuvre or artifice that may ultimately alter the truth.

In conclusion, it is quite evident, in my opinion, that the considerations offered in the passages analysed so far imply the author's awareness of an habitual and almost normal tendency of orators to alter the truth during a trial. Moreover, they also seem to demonstrate, yet again, how according to the mechanisms in use in courts at the end of the 1st century AD, the need and real possibility of manipulating the decision of the judge would take precedence over the observance of pure truth. This is further confirmed by what seems at first glance to be a minor observation in *Inst. or.* IV.2.76, that indicates that the *narratio* represents a truly fundamental occasion for influencing the judge. To pass up such a chance by not providing one's own version of the facts means to induce the judge to reach a decision based only on the opponent's speech and thus to indirectly provide the latter with greater chances of victory:

> *Expectat naturaliter iudex quid narretur a nobis. Si nihil exponimus, illa esse quae adversarius dixit et talia qualia dixit credat necesse est.*
> The judge naturally waits to hear what we can state in our behalf. If we make no statement, he cannot help believing that our opponent's assertions are correct and that their tone represents the truth.

The lawfulness of resorting to falsehood during the *narratio* in some cases is openly admitted, as in *Inst. or.* IV.2.91 where the use of fiction in lieu of the truth does not seem to be in question, whereas it is deemed dangerous for the orator only in the case that he does not remember the fiction he has used and that he therefore runs the risk of contradicting himself.

Basically, Quintilian holds that the task of the orator is to interact with the judge, turning to his advantage the personal inclinations of the latter. In this context, it is

---

[24]   As regards its function and characteristics, see L. Calboli Montefusco, 'La funzione della 'partitio' nel discorso oratorio', in: *Studi di retorica oggi in Italia*, Bologna: Pitagora 1987, pp. 69-85.
[25]   For an analysis of the passage, see I. Mastrorosa, 'Medicina e retorica nell'*Institutio Oratoria* di Quintiliano', *Sileno* 22 (1996) pp. 229-80, at pp. 254-256.

interesting to consider another text where he explains that, before starting to speak, the orator should take into consideration what the judge is likely to be preoccupied with (IV.1.52). Equally indicative of the importance that seems to have been attributed in the courts of the 1st century AD, to the psychology of the judge, to whom the *cognitio extra ordinem* system progressively gave increasing decision-making power,[26] is Quintilian's advice in a subsequent passage (IV.1.57) to provide the judge with formally polished speeches:

> *Sed ipsum istud evitare summae artis est. Nam id sine dubio ab omnibus, et quidem optime, praeceptum est, verum aliquatenus temporum condicione mutatur, quia iam quibusdam in iudiciis, maximeque capitalibus aut apud centumviros,[27] ipsi iudices exigunt sollicitas et accuratas actiones, contemnique se nisi in dicendo etiam diligentia appareat credunt, nec doceri tantum sed etiam delectari volunt.*
>
> But to avoid all display of art in itself requires consummate art: this admirable canon has been insisted on by all writers, though its force has been somewhat impaired by present conditions, since in certain trials, more especially those brought on capital charges or in the centumviral court, the judges themselves demand the most finished and elaborate speeches, think themselves insulted, unless the orator shows signs of having exercised the utmost diligence in the preparation of his speech, and desire not merely to be instructed, but to be charmed.

Further proof of the judge's natural attraction to a stylistically flawless speech is found in *Inst. or.* IV.2.119 where, according to the author, the judge may be so charmed by it as to trust its contents. Other passages that highlight this concept are found in Book VIII that is dedicated more specifically to the *elocutio*.[28]

4. INFLUENCING THE JUDGE ON THE LOGICAL-RATIONAL LEVEL

In addition to the suggestions useful for understanding the value attributed by Quintilian to the use of psychological strategies most suited to win the indulgence and good-will of the judge, as we have seen, especially in the *exordium* phase of an orator's speech, Book IV of the *Institutio oratoria* also contains advice for making the judge well-disposed through the use of rhetorical techniques. These techniques are

---

[26] As regards this topic, useful comments are found in G. Scherillo, *Lezioni sul processo. Introduzione alla 'cognitio extra ordinem'*, Milan: La Goliardica 1961; M. Lemosse, *Cognitio. Étude sur le role du juge dans l'instruction du procès civil antique*, Roma: L'Erma' di Bretschneider 1971 (rpt. ed. 1944); I. Buti, 'La 'cognitio extra ordinem': da Augusto a Diocleziano', in: *Aufstieg und Niedergang* (see note 6), 2.14 (1982), pp. 29-59, at p. 46; B. Santalucia, *Diritto e processo penale nell'antica Roma*, Milan: Giuffrè 1989, pp. 91-133.

[27] On this type of proceedings, see F. Gayet, 'Centumviri', in: Ch. Daremberg - E. Saglio, *Dictionnaire des Antiquités Grecques et Romaines*, 1.2, Paris: Librairie Hachette 1877, rpt. Graz: Akademische Druck u. Verlaganstalt 1969, pp. 1013-1015; M. Wlassak, 'Centumviri', in: *Paulys Realencyclopädie der classischen Altertumswissenschaft*, III.2, Stuttgart: Druckenmüller 1899, rpt. 1970, coll. 1935-1952; W. Kunkel, *Untersuchungen zur Entwicklung des römischen Kriminalverfahrens in vorsullanischer Zeit*, München: Bayerische Akademie der Wissenschaften 1962, pp. 115ff.; M. Kaser and K. Hackl, *Das römische Zivilprozessrecht*, 2nd edition, Munich: Beck 1996, p. 46; pp. 52-55; E.P. Parks, *The Roman Rhetorical Schools as a Preparation for the Courts under the Early Empire*, Baltimore: The Johns Hopkins Press 1945, pp. 50ff.

[28] Cf., e.g., *Inst. or.* VIII.2.13; VIII.2.23, VIII.3.62; VIII.5.32.

not exclusively based on an appeal to the emotions, which however are never totally banned (IV.2.111; 115; 120), but prevailingly on the possibility of directing and influencing the judge's will on the logical and rational level. In this context, especially interesting are several considerations concerning the layout of the *narratio*. This part of the speech is not introduced solely to instruct the judge about the facts, but also to win his approval. When the orator wishes not to inform the judge but only to influence him, he must preface his statement of the facts with a sort of *praeparatio*, as, for example, a speech capable of cajoling the judge into listening to the narration of how the facts, with which he is probably already familiar, occurred (IV.2.21). It is obviously a phase in which the true subject of the trial tends to acquire increasingly greater importance and represents the grounds on which the orator, urged never to neglect the judge in any way (IV.2.103: *ne avertatur a iudice sermo*), must concentrate his efforts in a more concrete fashion. Further proof of this seems to be the advice that the *narratio* should be as short as possible (IV.2.40): [29]

> *Brevis erit narratio ante omnia si inde coeperimus rem exponere unde ad iudicem pertinet, deinde si nihil extra causam dixerimus, tum etiam si reciderimus omnia quibus sublatis neque cognitioni quicquam neque utilitati detrahatur.*
>
> The statement of facts will be brief, if in the first place we start at that point of the case at which it begins to concern the judge, secondly avoid irrelevance, and finally cut out everything the removal of which neither hampers the activities of the judge nor harms our own case.

Notice how, at this point, Quintilian does not stop at providing a rule dictated by the ancient literature, but goes on to explain how a short statement of the facts starts at that point of the case where it begins to concern the judge, leaving out everything that is irrelevant and the removal of which does not hamper the proceedings or the orator's case. To this end, he also explains shortly afterwards that, with the word *brevitas*, he means not saying less but rather not saying more than what is convenient to the case (IV.2.43). In short, the orator is to narrate succinctly, avoiding not only the excessively lengthy speech but the excessively short one as well, not for aesthetical reasons, but for reasons directly linked to the best understanding of the facts of the case.

This is further expounded by Quintilian's description of the difference between the learned reader, capable of understanding even what is expressed in too concise a manner, and the average judge who is often a countryman and not too cultivated, called upon to give a decision only on what he understands and who must therefore be addressed, according to the highly pragmatic reasoning of the author, by saying only what is necessary and not more than what is sufficient (IV.2.45). This clearly practical approach explains why, in given circumstances, the orator should also use those rhetorical stratagems aimed at lifting from the judge the sensation of having to listen to an excessively long speech. To this end, he can use the *partitio*, i.e., he can briefly mention in order all the points that he will discuss, or the *commonitio*, i.e., he can give a short summary in the final phase of the *narratio* (IV.2.49-51). These precise instructions on how to make the statement of facts as functional as possible

---

[29] As regards this passage and the meaning of *brevitas* as concerns the *narratio*, see also J.D. O'Banion (see note 8), p. 347.

clearly point to the fact that it is considered a fundamental phase, the correct rendition of which favourably prepares the judge for what follows.

This point is proven by the reasoning given in *Inst. or.* IV.2.86, where the *narratio* is outlined as an essential introduction to the proof phase.[30] Here, in fact, Quintilian states that each individual point cannot be proved or refuted, unless the judge has already been presented with a detailed account of the facts of the case. Notice how, at this point, we witness the advice taken from the author's personal experience as an orator in court, namely, suggestions deriving from actual practice. Indeed, Quintilian states in this passage that he has personally followed this rule when acting as counsel and that, as a result, he has obtained the approval of learned persons and of the judges. It is therefore my opinion that, in this passage, the author wishes to stress that the order indicated for the succession of the various phases stems not from abstract rules but from practical requirements that he has directly experienced in the field. By following this order, the orator makes sure that each phase of the speech performs its peculiar function and satisfies the expectations of the judge who remains the constant and real target of the orator's efforts. From this standpoint, the remark about the judge who is in a hurry to hear the *probatio* immediately after hearing the facts set forth in order, so as to confirm his impressions as soon as possible with hard facts (IV.3.8), seems to be a telling example. Once again, Quintilian suggests adapting the layout and the succession of the speech after carefully observing the person who will be called upon to give judgment.[31]

In conclusion, given his role, the judge is the constant focal point of the orator-counsel who must attempt to spark his interest and hold his attention using quick admonitions (IV.4.9) or through the clever use of the *partitio*. More specifically, the orator must avoid an excessive fragmentation of the speech (IV.5.6) since, by concentrating the main facts of a case into a single point, he could induce the *iudex* to consider whatever comes afterwards as superfluous and thus make him impatient (IV.5.8). It must also be taken into account that the judge will wish to reach the most important point as soon as possible, and will, in a more or less urbane manner, show his impatience (IV.5.10).

Thus, from Quintilian's perspective, the *partitio* is a rhetorical tool by which the orator can arrange the various parts of the speech to his advantage in an ordered and, shall we say, rational manner, introducing its general subdivision to the audience so as to help it follow his case (IV.5.22). However, it can also become, if necessary, a tool for modulating the expectations of the judge, which should be observed and studied for tactical purposes as the trial proceeds. In this context, an interesting concept is defined in *Inst. or.* IV.5.18-19, where the author boldly states that, most of all

---

[30]   As regards the close link between the statement of facts (*narratio*) and the proofs phase specifically concerning the presentation of proof in favour of what has been stated (*confirmatio*), see also *Inst. or.* IV.3.1-2 where Quintilian speaks against those who, between the two phases, interpose digressions with the aim to show off.

[31]   Significant, in this context, is also *Inst. or.* XII.10.56 where Quintilian refers to an unknown passage by Cicero to remind the orator that the face of the judge should be the speaker's constant guide: 'Nam id quoque plurimum refert, quo modo audire iudex velit, atque "eius vultus saepe ipse rector est dicentis"' ('For it is most important that we should know how the judge is disposed to listen, and his face will often (as Cicero reminds us) serve as a guide to the speaker').

in special cases, for example, those concerning the sphere of morality (*de pudore*), it is possible to use the *partitio* to interact with the judge, i.e., to take his preferences into account to such an extent that, should he suspect that the judge desires proof other than that being offered, the orator may promise that he will be soon satisfied on that point.

The possibility and opportunity of following and of acting 'in real time' on the moods and expectations of those called upon to give judgment are also referred to in the author's suggestions concerning the use of several specific types of *egressiones* (IV.3.10). After the *narratio* and prior to the *quaestio*, the orator would do best to use a form of digression such as the *praeparatio* with a view to exciting or mollifying the *iudex* or to disposing him to follow more readily the rest of the speech, while reminding his reader that it is not easy to persuade someone who does not wish to be persuaded. In this case, too, the orator's choice of strategy must not be exclusively based on the emotional aspect, although this remains fundamental,[32] but must remain strongly pragmatic in nature. According to Quintilian, the *praeparatio* is an excellent occasion for studying the disposition of the judge, namely, for understanding whether he prefers equity or a strict interpretation of the law: *iuri magis an aequo sit adpositus* (IV.3.11).

In other words, the tactical application of an apparently secondary phase of the logical-judicial *iter* allows to acquire an element that is truly fundamental for the purposes of the rest of the case that evidently pivots on the *modus operandi* of the *iudex*, in that it all depends on the judge's propensity to decide according to *ius* or according to *aequum*.[33] It is obvious that this is not a captious explanation or a minor detail. Indeed, the remark stresses once again the author's juridical acumen and illustrates his consideration for a court practice increasingly willing, starting from the 1st century AD, to give way to the power of the *iudex's* discernment. Aware of the contrast between law and equity, already detected by Cicero[34] and, prior to him, clearly indicated by Aristotle,[35] Quintilian quite appropriately exhorts the orator to closely observe the inclinations of the judge in order to understand the judgment criterion he will apply.

---

[32] Cf., e.g., *Inst. or.* IV.3.16: 'Sed plurima sunt quae rebus nihil secum cohaerentibus inseruntur, quibus iudex reficitur admonetur placatur rogatur laudatur' ('There are however a number of topics which are inserted in the midst of matter which has no connexion with them, when for example we strive to excite, admonish, appease, entreat or praise the judge').

[33] As regards this topic, with special reference to Quintilian, see J. Cousin, 'Quintilien et la notion d'aequum', in: J. Bibauw (ed.), *Hommages à Marcel Renard*, Bruxelles: Latomus 1969, I, p. 260-267; M. Ducos, 'Philosophie, littérature et droit à Rome sous le Principat', in: *Aufstieg und Niedergang* (see note 6), 2,36,7 (1994), pp. 5134-80, at p. 5156, n. 121.

[34] *Part. orat.* 98; 130

[35] Consider what Aristotle says in *Rhetorica* I.13.1374a 26-28: 'For that which is equitable seems to be just, and equity is justice that goes beyond the written law' (*Aristotle. The Art of Rhetoric*, translated by J. H. Freese, London-Cambridge (Mass.): Loeb Classical Library 1926, rpt. 1959, p. 145) and also in the *Nicomachean Ethics* 1137b 11-13 where 'equity, though just, is not legal justice, but a rectification of legal justice' (*Aristotle. The Nicomachean Ethics*, translated by H. Rackham, London- Cambridge (Mass.): Loeb Classical Library 1934, rpt. 1982, p. 315). Due to the natural limitations of the law, the judge is forced to pronounce judgment in a general statement without considering the detail, cf. *Rhetorica* I.13.1374a 28-34; *Nicomachean Ethics* 1137b 13-17.

In conclusion, by teaching the orator to learn the combined use of the rhetorical rules with the psychological strategies for studying the judge's inclination, Quintilian urges his reader to never stop observing the person who evidently plays the decisive role in settling the case.

GIOVANNI ROSSI

RHETORICAL ROLE MODELS FOR 16TH TO 18TH CENTURY LAWYERS

1. QUINTILIAN'S SUCCESS IN THE RENAISSANCE

Quintilian's work was known and used in the Middle Ages,[1] but it is from the beginning of the 15th century that this author started to enjoy special favour.[2] Poggio Bracciolini, the eminent hunter of manuscripts containing classical works, among others rediscovered the *Institutio oratoria*,[3] while Lorenzo Valla, from the height of his scholarly authority, set Quintilian's style as absolute model, such as to match Cicero's Latin.[4]

As a result of this return to fame, reference to the *Institutio oratoria* was not restricted to the works of the humanists as an *auctoritas* invoked to support their erudite disputes or to act as the main subject of such debates and sometimes of criticism.[5] This is actually not surprising. The intellectuals who tackled with renewed spirit and knowledge the novel approach to the study of the *humanae litterae*[6] were

---

[1] Abundant literature now exists on this topic; among others, see above all J.O. Ward, *'Artificiosa eloquentia' in the Middle Ages: The Study of Cicero's 'De inventione', the 'Ad Herennium' and Quintilian's 'De institutione oratoria' from the Early Middle Ages to the Thirteenth Century, with Special Reference to the Schools of Northern France*, 2 Vols., Ph.D. Diss., Toronto: Toronto University 1972, *passim*; J. Cousin, *Recherches sur Quintilien: Manuscrits et éditions*, Paris: Les Belles Lettres 1975, pp. 1-38; see also P. Lehmann, 'Die Institutio oratoria des Quintilianus im Mittelalter', *Philologus* 89 (1934), pp. 349-383, now in Id., *Erforschung des Mittelalters*, II, Stuttgart: Hiersemann 1959, pp. 1-28; A. Mollard, 'La diffusion de l'Institution oratoire au XIIe siècle', *Le Moyen Age* 44 = 3rd series 5 (1934), pp. 161-175 and 45 = 3rd series 6 (1935), pp. 1-9; P.S. Boskoff, 'Quintilian in the Late Middle Ages', *Speculum* 27 (1952), pp. 71-78.

[2] However, Petrarch had already read Quintilian closely, and had copiously annotated (mutilated, actually) the manuscript of the *Institutio oratoria* given him by Lapo da Castiglionchio the Elder in 1350: cf. M. Accame Lanzillotta, 'Le postille del Petrarca a Quintiliano (Cod. Parigino lat. 7720)', *Quaderni petrarcheschi* 5 (1988) pp. 1-201.

[3] Cf. M. Winterbottom, 'Fifteenth-Century Manuscripts of Quintilian', *Classical Quarterly* n.s. 17 (1967), pp. 339-369; Cousin (see note 1), especially pp. 50-69; F. Murru, 'Poggio Bracciolini e la riscoperta dell'Institutio oratoria di Quintiliano (1416)', *Critica Storica* 20 (1983) pp. 621-626.

[4] Cousin (see note 1), pp. 125-146; quite significant are Valla's notes to Quintilian's work: L. Valla, *Le postille all''Institutio oratoria' di Quintiliano*, edizione critica a cura di L. Cesarini Martinelli e A. Perosa, Padova: Antenore 1996. In this regard, see also J. Fernández López, *Retórica, humanismo y filología: Quintiliano y Lorenzo Valla*, Logroño: Instituto de Estudios Riojanos 1999.

[5] See, e.g., J. Monfasani, 'Episodes of Anti-Quintilianism in the Italian Renaissance: Quarrels on the Orator as a Vir Bonus and Rhetoric as the Scientia Bene Dicendi', *Rhetorica* 10 (1992) pp. 119-138.

[6] J.O. Ward, 'Quintilian and the Rhetorical Revolution of the Middle Ages', *Rhetorica* 13 (1995) pp. 231-284; C.J. Classen, 'Quintilian and the Revival of Learning in Italy', *Humanistica Lovaniensia* 43 (1994) pp. 77-98.

necessarily also interested by dint of *ratione materiae* in an *institutio* entirely dedicated to the explanation of oratorical techniques. The majority of them were, after all, scholars and professional teachers,[7] experts in grammar, rhetoric and philosophy, who dominated as *magistri* the respective chairs in Italian universities or ran famous private schools,[8] where the *studia humanitatis* that were the core of education at the time were mostly embodied in these same disciplines.

2. THE REVIVAL OF CLASSICAL RHETORIC IN THE BAROQUE AGE: DE LUCA'S TREATISE 'DELLO STILE LEGALE'

The wealth of rhetorical knowledge accumulated by the *culti* jurists during the Renaissance did not vanish, however. On the contrary, the truly vast amount of reading material and the steady expansion of the canon of works (even if not always concerning law) considered important somehow for a thorough education, necessary for the jurist as well, gave results that were absorbed by later generations of scholars.

The truly Quintilian-style approach, that blends scholarship with real-life forensic experience as a means to the complete education in rhetoric of the court orator, was therefore destined to re-emerge in more modern times, when it was rediscovered and fully appreciated. This was due to the intense production of works dedicated to the forensic art, which took root in the public's imagination as an *ars*. It was seen as a set of rules and precepts forming a unitary *corpus* that could be transmitted by teaching, a prerogative of a compact social class protected by rigid limitations to membership, easily recognisable from the outside and with a strong group self-conscience. In this context, the most field-proven rhetorical techniques for obtaining victory in court were obviously given priority. Of course, when compared to juridical knowledge, these techniques remained mere tools but they were never marginal or negligible in the training of a lawyer.

Perhaps the archetype of Italian juridical treatises in this field may be considered *Dello stile legale*, dated 1674 and written by Giovan Battista De Luca,[9] a fairly important legal practitioner in Rome in the second half of the 17th century. The treatise includes an in-depth reflection 'about the way of writing and speaking' in

---

[7] As regards the previous period, see M. Curry Woods, 'Quintilian and Medieval Teaching', in: T. Albaladejo, E. Del Río, and J.A. Caballero (eds.), *Quintiliano: historia y actualidad de la retórica*, Logroño: Instituto de Estudios Riojanos 1998, pp. 1531-1540.

[8] Famous are those in the Veneto area, run by eminent names such as Gasparino Barzizza, Guarino Veronese and Vittorino da Feltre; in this regard, E. Garin, *L'educazione in Europa 1400/1600. Problemi e programmi*, 2nd edition, Bari: Laterza 1966, especially pp. 123-137 is noteworthy; see also P.F. Grendler, *Schooling in Renaissance Italy: Literacy and Learning, 1300-1600*, Baltimore & London: The John Hopkins University Press 1989, pp. 125-132.

[9] For detailed information on the life and works of De Luca, see A. Mazzacane, 'De Luca, Giovanni Battista', *Dizionario Biografico degli Italiani*, Rome: Istituto della Enciclopedia Italiana 1990, XXXVIII, pp. 340-347, with additional references, as well as a brief curriculum vitae in A. Lauro, *Il cardinale Giovan Battista de Luca. Diritto e riforme nello Stato della Chiesa (1676-1683)*, Naples: Jovene 1991, pp. XXXV-LXII. Finally, also see I. Birocchi, *Alla ricerca dell'ordine. Fonti e cultura giuridica nell'età moderna*, Turin: Giappichelli 2002, pp. 297-315.

court,[10] even though the work does not focus solely on the lawyers but discusses in turn the actions of all actors in a court case, starting with the judge:

> ... mainly will be discussed, in this work, the manner in which the judges and the magistrates, or their assessors, and also the lawyers and attorneys and other jurisconsults, are expected to form their votes, or motivations, or decisions, and their counsel, or information and assertions respectively, and also how the defenders, or reporters of the cases, must speak when they are called upon to play those parts, as was done by the ancient orators.[11]

Without considering problems purely concerning the form, grammar, or linguistic style of the language used, De Luca's sole purpose was to:

> ... discuss the legal style of the forum, namely, how to put forth the motivations and the reasons, and the authorities, by which to justify present or future judgments more in one way than in another, so as to better prove what is the truth and the justice of that cause.[12]

A true prince of lawyers, on the pinnacle of his wide experience gained in 30 years of working in Roman courts, at the end of a truly successful career that qualified him as a great expert in the procedures in force at the time, the author did not stop at examining the speeches of lawyers. He knew that in most cases, as we have already seen, a real oral debate in front of the judge is usually replaced by a legal battle fought with barrages of written documents, where the rules can change and different problems arise as a consequence of the peculiar judgment procedures of the *ius commune*.[13] What does emerge, from the very beginning, is that the fundamental rule to be applied is that of brevity, both in speaking and in writing:

> ... style in writing and in speaking on legal subjects, will be all the better, and more estimable, the shorter and the more substantial, concise, and penetrating, it is, otherwise

---

[10]   Therefore, the term 'style' in the title of De Luca's book is used in a non-technical context, as underlined by the author, because 'with jurists, the same word has many and diverse meanings; it mainly indicates the usage, or the custom, that elsewhere is also called *rite*, so in the gracious subjects in the secretariats, in the princes' chanceries, in the Datary, in the Apostolic Chancery [...]; as in the cases of litigation and of judgment, in which the issue of style of the courts and magistrates is more frequent'. Cf. G.B. De Luca, *Dello stile legale cioè Del modo, col quale i professori della facoltà legale, così avvocati, e procuratori, come giudici, e consiglieri, ed anche i cattedratici, o lettori, debbano trattare in iscritto, ed in voce delle materie giuridiche, giudiziali, ed estragiudiziali*, as appendix to Id., *Il dottor volgare ...*, Vol. VI, Colonia: a opera di Modesto Fenzo stampatore 1740, Chapt. II, pp. 441-442, n. 2. The translations of the Italian texts in this essay are my own.

[11]   De Luca (see note 10), Chapt. II, p. 442, n. 3.

[12]   De Luca (see note 10), Chapt. II, p. 443, n. 5.

[13]   Among the essential problems tackled by De Luca, noteworthy is first of all that of the choice of language, namely, whether to continue to use Latin or to adopt the vernacular. Another equally delicate problem that was debated at length involved the appropriateness of indicating in the defending counsel's written briefs references to the *auctoritates* and to the *communes opiniones* for each single item litigated and the value to be attributed to such *receptae sententiae*: in this regard, see G. Rossi, 'Del modo di deferire all'autorità de' dottori': scienza giuridica e *communis opinio doctorum* nel pensiero di Giovan Battista De Luca', in: I. Birocchi, M. Caravale, E. Conte and U. Petronio (eds.), *A Ennio Cortese*, Rome: Il Cigno 2001, Vol. III, pp. 176-203.

with useless digressions, and with the superfluous beyond what is necessary, it will be a jousting lance and not a stiletto.[14]

With the wise pragmatism that permeates all of his statements, De Luca starts by saying how it is necessary to avoid laying down general and rigid regulations in a field in which flexibility and the capability of adjusting to any situation arising from the case itself are mandatory qualities.[15] This point of view is quite similar to that of Quintilian, who introduced the topic in Book IV of his *Institutio oratoria*. He underlines the objective difficulty of setting up a preceptive speech when faced with the greatest variety of causes, and how important it always is to attempt to do this in any case: 'for my next task is to explain the order to be followed in forensic causes, which present the utmost complication and variety'.[16] Both the Roman rhetor and the baroque jurist have experienced the *varietas et multiplicitas* of forensic cases, and they accept the idea of having to change with humility, when necessary, the behavioural models suggested by the art of rhetoric that, as such, cannot proceed along the rigid lines of an exact science. Conversely, the late 17th century lawyer cannot hope to blindly follow in the footsteps of the ancient rhetoricians, not even in those cases that allow for the oral exposition of the parties' motives. The ordered sequence of the speech, namely, *exordium, narratio, argumentatio, peroratio*, and the diligent application of the precepts concerning each part of the speech, certainly provides a useful guide but can be changed and rearranged to suit the case.

And so one must administer food enough for and in proportion to the stomachs, and one should not go on indifferently with the very boring and damnable style, used by students when reciting the master's lesson, of wanting to say everything that was said in the information, without leaving out even a comma, as some do.[17]

There were many occasions for pronouncing a speech before a judge, although the general rule was exchanging written documents, especially in the active courts of Rome.[18] For this reason, in Chapter 14, the author illustrates the behaviour of the

---

[14] De Luca (see note 10), Chapt. II, p. 443, n. 6. The author here plays on the different meanings of the word 'style', which, in ancient times, designated the sharp writing tool (*stylus*) used to engrave waxed tablets and in De Luca's time, a knife that was 'all the better and estimable if it was short, sharp and penetrating' ('tanto più è buona, e stimabile, quanto che sia breve, aguzza e penetrante').

[15] 'The rules and precepts of good style [...] resemble a lantern, or the torch the traveller uses to make light, that he may walk along the good road and not fall into the brambles. In the same way, as this lantern may do nothing for the traveller if he is blind, or if he walks inadvertently, without looking where he sets foot; thus nothing, or very little, may these rules benefit without due study and the application for putting them into practice, lacking which they remain useless theory, as practice should not be always the same in every case': De Luca (see note 10), Chapt. I, p. 440, n. 16.

[16] 'Sequitur enim, ut iudicialium causarum, quae sunt maxime variae atque multiplices, ordo explicetur': *Inst. or.* IV pr.6. Throughout this paper I will quote Quintilian's *Institutio oratoria* from Michael Winterbottom's text (see 'Introduction', note 26). The English translation is from Butler (see 'Introduction', note 27).

[17] De Luca (see note 10), Chapt. XIV, p. 520, n. 18.

[18] De Luca's perfect familiarity with the courts of justice of baroque Rome is evident in his detailed treatises regarding the matter: G.B. De Luca, *Il dottor volgare...*, Roma: nella stamperia di Giuseppe Corvo 1673, Libro XV, parte I, *Delli giudizii civili, e della loro Pratica nella Curia Romana* and Jo. Baptista de Luca Venusinus, *Theatrum veritatis et iustitiae...*, Romae: Typis Haeredum Corbelletti 1673, Lib. XV, Pars II, *Relatio Curiae romanae forensis eiusque Tribunalium et Congregationum*. For a diachronic

lawyer called upon to speak in court and more specifically in those proceedings based on an adversary system.

> The third function, which is the most common, and the most suitable for all parts of the world, more so among lawyers than among attorneys, namely, orating for their clients before the judges in public debate with the lawyers, and the attorney of the adversary, which is very rare, in proportion to the cases, and the negotiations, is practised in the Roman Court.[19]

Right at the beginning of his treatise, De Luca gives proof of being intimately familiar with rhetorical precepts. He mentions the teachings of the Roman sources as an example and makes reference to the '[...] orators and declaimers of ancient Rome, who learned the rules and methods of oratory from the Greeks, as indicated in the orations and declamations by Cicero, Seneca, Quintilian, and such others [...]'. He quite briefly but accurately sums up the methods and aims of the rhetorical strategies applied in a forensic cause, from the function of the *exordium* to the arrangement of the arguments in the *narratio*, to the importance of giving a statement of facts made more interesting and captivating through the use of emphasis and of the appropriate gestures in the *actio*.[20]

> The style of those of the first species [the orators] is in step with the rules and with the precepts of rhetoric and of the art of oratory; that is, that with the *proemii et apparati*, they catch the attention of the audience for what is about to be said, and then, starting from the motivations, and from the weaker things, make sure that the oration proceeds in crescendo, until they conclude with the motivations, and the best and most conclusive reasons, even by overstating a little, and repeating the same thing more than once [...]. Considering that those orations or declamations, that we read in the ancient authors mentioned above, and in others similarly, and also in their modern imitators [...] were recited out loud, accompanied by emphasis, by gestures and by other parts [...].[21]

First of all, De Luca underlines the enormous gap between the Roman trial model and that of his own times, and consequently the difference between ancient orators and modern lawyers. Secondly, thus showing sound historical knowledge of the

---

description of the governmental and jurisdictional system in force in Pontifical Rome, see N. Del Re, *La Curia Romana. Lineamenti storico-giuridici*, 4th edition, Città del Vaticano: Libreria Editrice Vaticana 1998, especially pp. 197-242 on courts.

[19] De Luca (see note 10), Chapt. XIV, pp. 512-513, n. 2. De Luca carefully distinguishes between the various cases: 'Four types of speaking function, therefore, are used by the lawyers, attorneys, and other professors of the forum of the Curia, for the defence and for directing the cases, respectively: the first, used in the Congregations of lawyers, attorneys, and other operators of one of the parties for the direction and for the good preparation of the case [...]; another used in public hearings before the judge, who in the truly judicial format, in his capacity as court judge, hears the clerk read the summons and rules on them. The third is used in the public cross-examinations before the judge with lawyers and defenders of the other party; and the fourth is used for informing the judges privately in their chambers, without the opposing party [...] There is also another type of function [...], namely, that used by the new auditors of the Rota, and by the new Consistorial lawyers in public disputes, with the intervention of the Sacred College': De Luca (see note 10), Chapt. XIV, p. 510, n. 2.

[20] Quintilian himself, based on his own experience as a forensic orator and faithful to his intention of providing instructions that could be applied in practice, paid great attention to such aspects; cf. P. Wülfing, 'Antike und moderne Redegestik. Quintilians Theorie der Körpersprache', *Der altsprachliche Unterricht* 36 (1994) pp. 45-63.

[21] De Luca (see note 10), Chapt. IV, p. 456, n. 2, and 458, n. 9.

Roman court system as inferred by ancient literature that refers to the simultaneous presence of many different actors, i.e. the orator, the lawyer, the *patronus*, and the legal counsel,[22] he highlights the fact that, both in ancient Rome and in papal Rome, it was necessary to distinguish between various different active professional classes having different roles in the proceedings, based on specialised functions and on their different rhetorical and juridical skills. In this manner, he can refute the accusation coming from the classical literature against the *rabole forensi*, the Roman representatives, so different from the rhetors and the jurists and not comparable to the lawyers of his own time.

> And therefore there follows the manifest mistake of those who having dabbled in the reading of Seneca's works, and of other ancient writers, want to apply to the lawyers, and to today's representatives, and especially to those of the Roman court, what was attributed to the orators and declaimers and representatives of those times, that is, to sell or rent out the words, the clamour, the cries, the sighs, the laughter, the jokes, the gestures and the gags, and such stuff, while nothing of all this is practised.
>
> Equally clear is the mistake of the same dabblers in thinking that the orators and ancient declaimers are the same as the modern lawyers; or that whatever is said in contempt of the representatives and of the pettifogging laywers can be equally said of the lawyers and attorneys and men of law of our times. Considering that, in ancient times some were the orators, the declaimers, and others the lawyers, and others again the masters of the cases; and others still those of lower classes, that are called by the generic name of representatives, they being distinguished as if in different spheres. In the same way, today we have different types, or classes, of lawyers, attorneys, and solicitors. And these too are distinguished according to their qualities and styles of the courts [...] So that those representatives, contemptuously spoken of by Martial and by other ancient writers, were precisely those who in Rome today are called 'mozzorecchi' (pettifoggers); and this is proven by Martial when he speaks of the representative Postumo, who in a penal trial informed the judge of the theft of just a few goats (which shows what sort of a representative he was).[23]

In those trials in which an opportunity for using eloquence to convince the judge and win the case does indeed arise,[24] one makes use of '[...] the rules and precepts that are usually to be observed in this form of oratory, or during the information phase in public debates, so as to apply them in the correct proportion according to the customs of each country, or court, pursuant to which one must mainly act'.[25] The true distinction depends on the type of *iudex* (it matters little whether he sits alone or with a jury), and whether we are dealing with an individual devoid of professional legal experience or with expert and experienced magistrates. In the first case, the use of an energetic rhetorical technique for the lawyer's speech will be highly effective,

---

[22] On these closely resembling but different figures, see W. Neuhauser, *Patronus und Orator. Eine Geschichte der Begriffe von ihren Anfängen bis in die augusteische Zeit*, Innsbruck: Universitätsverlag Wagner 1958.

[23] De Luca (see note 10), Chapt. XIV, pp. 513-514, n. 7.

[24] A small minority of trials was conducted before Roman courts: '[...] And even if this custom is practised before some individual judges, and most frequently in the court of the auditor of the House, it is seen only in the congregation of barons, as an image of solemn public cross-examination, in the senate or a superior court. However, they resemble more a kind of family debate than those solemn and fearful cross-examinations, that may resemble the ancient forms of oration, or of declamation in public following the rules and formal precepts of the art of oratory': De Luca (see note 10), Chapt. XIV, p. 513, n. 6.

[25] De Luca (see note 10), Chapt. XIV, p. 514, n. 9.

since the judgment will be given above all on the basis of the common sense and the feelings of the person judging rather than of statutory laws and sophisticated technical interpretations based on doctrine. He who is capable of presenting his arguments in the most convincing of manners may prevail, after winning the attention, sympathy, and trust of the judge, finally managing to condition his persuasions.

> ...or it is a question of speaking before the judges and magistrates, who legally do not qualify as scholars, and whom we vulgarly call idiots, or 'pectorals', according to the common practice in those cities that are governed as republics or that are not so now but once were, and therefore still retain the ancient customs; and in this case, one must imitate as much as possible the style of ancient orators and declaimers with the rules of the art of oratory, using the proemia, and the display to capture the attention of the audience, and starting with the weaker arguments, so that the oration develops in crescendo and finally concludes with the stronger and more compelling arguments, so that the gradually opened mind stays open, in which one must reach the decision, exaggerating, and once again magnifying the arguments and the reasons by repeating them over and over again, so that they may be more impressive; and even by embellishing the speech with erudition and jokes and gestures and actions so as to render the speaking graceful and to keep the audience attentive and uplifted, while speaking about the case's arguments alone would bore them. Using other ancient tricks still, such as putting forth the arguments for compassion, accompanying them with tears and sighs, or exaggerating the merits of the litigant for the public, and such things, even if extraneous to the context of the dispute, according to what is taught by the orations and the declaimers of Cicero, Seneca, Quintilian, and others [...].[26]

In such a situation, the orator is justified in employing all of the means which the art places at his disposal in order to emphasise the arguments in favour and to convince the judges of the triviality of the arguments against, to move and emotionally involve them, to win their pity and take advantage of their emotional involvement, excluding none of the rhetorical ruses, illustrious examples of which can be found in the classics. Hence a judge who is not a jurist, who does not know how to conduct the case on technical grounds and to interpret the laws to be applied, represents the ideal subject for an attempt to influence him by means of eloquence:

> The reason for the difference between these two forms of style is clear: in the first case, one addresses non-legal people, who must at that very time without other preparation pass judgment using only natural understanding and speech, namely, only with their practice and experience in transactions, so that they are more susceptible to the art of oratory and to the orator's capability of persuasion, which is why they are called 'pectoral judges', in that the resolution arises from their chest, namely, from natural speech; in the other case one addresses people who, in hearing that information, are prepared for future study, namely, for a better understanding of the things already studied, must pass judgment founded on arguments and their justifications, so in fact, as in law [...].[27]

Conversely, the modern jurist may be immune to the expedients described and suggested by Quintilian and by the other rhetoric treatises so well-known to De Luca, for the simple reason that he is governed by more severe limitations to his *arbitrium*. The legal rules, both procedural and substantive, that he is obliged to observe con-

---

[26] De Luca (see note 10), Chapt. XIV, pp. 514-515, n. 9.
[27] De Luca (see note 10), Chapt. XIV, p. 516, n. 10.

dition him heavily and allow him only in very specific cases to resort to a free
assessment of the elements of the case.

In fact, De Luca states how Roman jurists had already understood and theorised
the various rhetorical strategies to be used according to the type of judge hearing the
case.

> This difference, for the same reason, was also known and practised by the ancient
> Romans, as witnessed by Quintilian and by other writers of those times. What was very
> different was the style of the orating in the times of the Republic when, even for the
> decision of the cases, one orated before an audience, namely, in a Senate, or in the cen-
> tumviral Court or to the tribune of the people, and the more modern style under the
> emperors after the introduction of the courts composed by the jurists, the responses of
> whom formed the laws of the Digest, or of the Pandects […].[28]

It is obvious that the humanistic lesson of Budé and of Alciatus fell on fertile
ground. The knowledge of history was considered fundamental even beyond the
closed circuit of university professors, and became a part of the cultural foundation
of every good jurist.

3. THE LAWYER'S ROLE IN VENICE: THE EXPERIENCE OF CARLO GOLDONI

The Venetian system excludes application of the *ius commune* and represents one of
the most relevant exceptions.[29] This system envisages a much less formalised type of
procedure conducted by persons (the judge as well as the counsels of the parties)
who were not required to have a law degree (a requirement that was not introduced
until the 18th century[30]) and were not allowed to apply the doctrinal knowledge at the
heart of the *ius commune*. De Luca is quite clear on this subject and inserts this
peculiarity within the context of the very special constitutional order established in
Venice.[31] He even presents the republican institutions of the Serenissima as almost
an ideal continuation of those of ancient Rome, making reference to Venetian publi-
cists who loved to emphasise this analogy, though at the same time they forbade the
use of Roman law in the lagoon republic since it was Imperial law:

> Nor do we today have the ancient order, or the class of orators, of declaimers, of whom
> but a few images remain in the city of Venice called 'avvogadori', as opposed to the
> 'avvocati' (lawyers). Considering this, just as that Republic retains somewhat the dig-
> nity of the ancient freedom of Italy, and of the majesty of the ancient Roman Republic,
> so it preserves many styles.[32]

---

[28] De Luca (see note 10), Chapt. XIV, p. 517, n.11.
[29] For an outline of its configuration, from a diachronic viewpoint, see G. Zordan, *L'ordinamento giuridico veneziano. Lezioni di storia del diritto veneziano*, Padua: CLEUP 1980.
[30] In this manner, although the distinction illustrated above between trials held before Venetian magis-
trates and trials held in the subject cities of the Terraferma (or continent) still remained, the contrast
between the two systems inevitably started to fade.
[31] There is a vast literature concerning the historical vicissitudes of the lagoon city; I mention one: R.
Cessi, *Storia della Repubblica di Venezia*, 2nd edition, Florence: Giunti-Martello 1981.
[32] De Luca (see note 10), Chapt. XIV, p. 514, n. 8.

So, in contrast with what was happening in the rest of the Italian peninsula as well as in many European countries, trials in the Republic of San Marco preserved the distinction between experts of law and court orators, introducing the *avvogadore*, together with a generalised use of oral deliberation. In fact, unlike their 'terra firma' colleagues, Venetian lawyers did not prepare written statements, but rather dissertations which were proclaimed before a court made up of judges taken from among the city's noblemen, experts in customary Venetian law and in native statutes, called upon to deliver judgment in the name of justice, but purposely ignorant of the *ius commune*.[33]

A useful guide for our purpose is found in the treatise consisting of five books in dialogue form, *L'avvocato* (1554), by Francesco Sansovino,[34] a Venetian humanist and polygraph writer who studied law in Padua and then graduated in civil law in Bologna in 1543.[35] It describes the treatment of a case in the Venetian court by bad lawyers who were only interested in personal gain and lacked moral principles and solid theoretical training. In the following passage, a crafty lawyer gives a piece of dreadful advice to a young and inexperienced colleague.

> Marino: '[...] As for the plea, use all those formulas that are in the mouths of everyone in the Palazzo all day long [...] for the rest do not worry about what you say: but talk at random. Shout as much as you can, perspire and get all heated up: because as many drops of sweat drip from your brow, just as many coins will drop in your purse, because the audience, in hearing how heart-felt is your defence, will run to your home to see you; and by acting thus, in a state of confusion, you can fit in bad things about the other party, or about the adversary lawyer, and having dragged the case beyond its limits, exclaim, laugh, cry, and finally swear as much as you can, so that the judges will be on your side; and should you have to answer your adversary, confute everything and you won't be far wrong'.[36]

However, according to Sansovino, the training of a good lawyer requires the study of law and history and the dedicated application of the art of oratory (together with the reading and analysis of ancient orators such as Demosthenes and Cicero), all of which is verified by practice in the forum. The result will be a case treated according to a 'reasoned order' ('ordinato ragionamento'), essential for convincing the judge and for winning the trial: the tool required to obtain this result is the use of the

---

[33] As regards the sources in Venice, subject of a heated historiographic debate, see also G. Cassandro, 'Concetto caratteri e struttura dello Stato veneziano', *Rivista di storia del diritto italiano* 36 (1963), pp. 23-49; G. Cracco, 'La cultura giuridico-politica nella Venezia della 'serrata'', in: G. Folena *et al.* (eds), *Storia della cultura veneta. Il Trecento*, Vicenza: Neri Pozza 1976, pp. 238-271; G. Cozzi, 'La politica del diritto nella Repubblica di Venezia', in Id. (ed.), *Stato società e giustizia nella repubblica veneta (sec. XV-XVIII)*, Rome: Jouvence 1980, pp. 15-152; see also V. Crescenzi, 'Il problema delle fonti nell'esperienza giuridica della Repubblica di Venezia. Lo statuto e la sua interpretatio', in: *A Ennio Cortese* (see note 13), vol. I, pp. 364-389.

[34] F. Sansovino, *L'avvocato, dialogo nel quale si discorre tutta l'autorità che hanno i magistrati di Venezia. Con la pratica delle cose giudiciali del Palazzo*, Vinegia: appresso Lelio Barileto e fratelli 1566. This work describes the Venetian judicial order: the lawyer's tasks, the various persons participating in a trial, the magistrates, the order to be followed in a trial. It also has a sort of glossary of Venetian law terms.

[35] Cf. E. Bonora, *Ricerche su Francesco Sansovino imprenditore libraio e letterato*, Venice: Istituto Veneto di Scienze, Lettere e Arti 1994, especially pp. 11-62.

[36] Sansovino (see note 34), f. 7r.

'art', namely, of the techniques of rhetoric laid down by the classical authors. This art produces a profitable 'order in speaking' ('ordinatione di parlamento'), as opposed to the rambling chaos of speaking 'according to nature' that is based solely on the use and, often enough, on the worst customs of vulgar practice. Such application of the rules of rhetoric not only satisfies the aesthetic sense of harmony so dear to humanists, that 'nature' must be enhanced and sublimated through the *'ars'*, according to a typically Renaissance code, but also brings excellent practical results for winning the case. Then Sansovino makes one of the other participants in the dialogue give proper advice to his young colleague:

> Lorenzo: 'You shall thus place the narration in its proper place, and shall lightly touch upon the qualities of the adversary with all of the parts of the art that makes you a maestro, you will begin to read the scriptures and meditate on them in the passages that suit you best. You will then establish the confirmation of your case, in which you will state your reasons, derived from the main body of the trial as from your own. And then you will read bylaws, customs, laws and similar things. And then you will indicate cases and trials similar to yours. And you will debate the adversary's reasons, in the epilogue you will briefly repeat your reasons reading several significant passages here and there to confirm them, and you will end [...] By observing this order, and others that you know, it will never happen that you have in front of you someone who knows nothing, or that your audience will not more gladly listen to you rather than to the other, since the occult devices infinitely operate on men every time, because the devices are based on the oratory of an eloquent orator'.[37]

This passage contains the subtle recall of the sequence of the *narratio - confirmatio - peroratio*. Especially important is the final statement regarding the infallible effectiveness of the rhetorical devices, when used with due skill: they allow the orator who is capable of using them to convince the audience and therefore to surely obtain a victory. In this case also, Quintilian's influence is evident and is confirmed by the treatise produced by Sansovino on the education that the youth destined for a legal career should receive, an evident reference to the precepts given in the 1st book of the *Institutio oratoria*, and by strongly underlining the lawyer's duties, binding him to observe the rigid ethical rules that forbid him to take on unjust cases and obligating him to use the art of oratory to the exclusive advantage of the triumph of truth:

> Lorenzo: '[...] use any industry virtuously, and any device to gain a victory, but every time make sure you are right and do not defend what is wrong: defend the innocence of the poor man against the insolence of the rich man. Put peace and love where there is war and dispute. Before accepting the cases, consider whether you should accept; after accepting them, do not neglect anything that is their due'.[38]

The reference to the prescripts of Book XII of Quintilian's treatise is undeniable and is used to make even clearer the contrast between an offhand practice and a tradition of theory that made credible the model of the *vir bonus dicendi peritus*, postulating the vital link between technical expertise and ethical tension in the work of the judicial orator. Not all lawyers observed the same ethical standards, as appears from the following quotation from Sansovino: 'I have met some who would do anything to obtain any case, whether just or unjust making no difference, and having obtained

---

[37]   Sansovino (see note 34), f. 15v.
[38]   Sansovino (see note 34), f. 16v.

them eloquently showed one thing or another to the judge [...]'.[39] He considers this sophistical attitude as an unequivocal sign of indifference and moral laxity, which must be banished from the legal profession and excluded from the options available to the forensic rhetor.

Moving ahead by about two centuries, but remaining in Venice, we can borrow a few words and concepts from a fictitious but entirely probable plea that Carlo Goldoni inserted in one of his comedies. A Venetian lawyer, called in to rebut the arguments of a 'doctor' from Bologna, feels the need to set out beforehand a kind of brief overview of the sources of law of the Venetian system:

> I will reply with my Venetian style, according to the practice of our forum, namely with our native idiom, the terms and expressions of which are equivalent to those of the more cultivated and cleanest (idioms) of the world. I will reply with the law at hand, with the law of our Statute, that is equivalent to the entire code and to the digests of Justinian, since it is based on the justice of nature, from which derive all of the laws of the world [...] But I will leave aside the imperial text, because we have our Venetian text that is abundant, clear and instructive and, lacking this, in some cases, among the infinite cases that are possible in the world, not foreseen or not judged by the Statute, natural reason is the fundamental basis on which quietly rests the soul of the very learned judge; we have the pending cases, the cases judged, the special laws of the magistrates, equity, the consideration of the circumstances, all of which are things that are infinitely more valid than all of the doctrines of legal authors. For the most part, these are used to confuse the matter, to stretch reasoning and to distress the judge who, no longer capable of judging, binds himself and submits to the opinion of the doctors, who were men just like him, and who could have ruled thus for some private reason.[40]

Goldoni's words illustrate how the peculiarity of the procedure followed in the courts of the Serenissima was widely known and emphasized. The return to a system of alternative legislative sources in lieu of those of the *ius commune* and the refusal to use the technical tools created by juridical science resulted in a quite original type of trial, with a chain of consequences that affected every aspect of the procedure. Indeed, among the more obvious and easily perceived effects, we can count the lawyer's different approach, the result of his being forced to become an orator as well as a professional lawyer, exactly because of the nature of the judges before whom he had to plead his client's cause.

There is certainly no lack of 18th century treatises dedicated to the practise of the law according to Venetian procedures. Suffice it to mention here Leone Ongarini's work written in the second half of the 18th century,[41] and *Il foro all'esame* by Giovanni Antonio Querini.[42] This Venetian lawyer was famous for the controversial reply[43] which he gave (in 1743) to the provocative observations compiled by Muratori for a debate among jurists and politicians in his *Dei difetti della giurisprudenza*

---

[39]   Sansovino (see note 34), f. 17r.
[40]   C. Goldoni, *L'avvocato veneziano*, in Id., *Tutte le opere*, a cura di G. Ortolani, II: *Commedie*, Milan: Mondadori 1936, pp. 705-795, at p. 777.
[41]   L. Ongarini, *Istruzioni utili e necessarie ad un veneto interveniente*, Venice 1775.
[42]   G.A. Querini, *Il foro all'esame. Considerazioni utili, dilettevoli, erudite, morali per li giudici, avvocati, clienti ed altri*, Venice: Pitteri 1737.
[43]   G.A. Querini, *La giurisprudenza senza difetti che da sé medesima si difende contro il trattato del signor Ludovico Antonio Muratori*, Venice: Mora 1743.

(1742). In his treatise about the different actors in a trial (the judge, the lawyer, the client), Querini underlines the importance of the role played by the lawyer[44] and about how difficult it is to do his job well: 'The art of speaking well requires inborn qualities, and acquired qualities, acute intelligence, ready judgment, easy recall, charming grace and enchanting pronunciation'.[45] This treatise also included an annotated compendium of rhetoric rules to be used when practising law, precisely because of the popular practice in the Republic of San Marco of defending a client's interests orally.

However, also in the Veneto area, where *ius commune* was peaceably applied, despite subordination to the Republic that refused to implement it, the writers of treatises on legal profession were not loath to showing off their higher skills in rhetoric.[46] Domenico Micheli, for example, a Veronese lawyer,[47] wrote in 1735 *L'avvocato*, a work that includes five speeches dedicated to the forensic profession (the role and social status, the cultural training, the deontological rules, the counselling and pleading activities).[48] It goes without saying that Quintilian appears among the technical sources of rhetoric mentioned. Above all, Micheli offers the implicit but easily recognisable pattern for addressing the issue of judicial oratory that, contrary to what happens in the other activities of the legal world, shows evident continuity of content and form when compared to Roman forensic practice. Suffice it to read the indications relating to the *narratio*:

> Having attracted the attention of the judge using the vague exordium, it is then immediately necessary to pass on to the narration, or exhaustive information, extending from the beginning to the end of the facts demonstrated by the documentation. The narration must be clear, sincere and well-ordered, so as not to give rise to any confusion whatsoever, or to any suspicion of being open to attack. It would be quite difficult to put it in order, should the lawyer not have the faculty, unlike with historians, to stray from the chronological order and start either in the middle, or at the end, and then pick up again the remote things, and unite them all [...] Therefore the exposition of the facts, requiring a good order that gradually descends, must in any case be embellished with nice words and suitable style figures, and, excluding any digression or superfluity, should reach its conclusion by showing in a natural manner the true points to which the debate must refer.[49]

---

[44] 'Lawyers are necessary, vital even, to the good constitution of civil life, just as the heart is necessary to man for natural life. No method is better for knowing the truth than the knowledge of the lawyer [...] [He] divides truth from falsehood, reason from deception, and illuminates justice [...]': Querini (see note 42), pp. 187-188.

[45] Querini (see note 42), p. 177.

[46] For an analysis of the forensic issue in the Veneto area, see L. Tedoldi, *Del difendere. Avvocati, procuratori e giudici a Brescia e Verona tra la Repubblica di Venezia e l'età napoleonica*, Milan: Franco Angeli 1999, especially pp. 86-109.

[47] His expertise in the things of the forum and in the practice of the legal profession emerges in another of his works, dedicated to the detailed description of the judicial procedure in force in Verona in the 18th century: Domenico Micheli avvocato veronese, *L'ordine del procedere nei giudicj civili del foro di Verona*, Verona: Ramanzini 1733.

[48] D. Micheli, *L'avvocato*, Verona: Ramanzini 1735. The titles of the speeches (*discorsi*) are: *Nobiltà dell'avvocato, Scienze dell'avvocato, L'avvocato nel consigliare, L'avvocato nell'arringare*, and *Morale dell'avvocato*, respectively.

[49] Micheli (see note 48), pp. 46-47.

Actually, every part of the oration is repeated and briefly described using classical notions, evident despite the use of the Italian language instead of the Latin: the defences are listed after the *narratio*; then 'the lawyer is led by the need to persuade and, to this end, produce evidence'; then the exposition of the objections and their confutation; finally, 'the smooth but impressive beginning of the peroration to move the emotions, almost as if to use them to point out to the judge the desired decision'.[50]

In describing the situation existing in the 18th century in Veneto, the clear words of Carlo Goldoni may be helpful. He majored in law in Padua[51] and for a time practised law in Venice.[52] In 1749-50, the playwright, still fresh from his experience as a lawyer, and as a way of honouring the community of lawyers in his city, wrote *L'avvocato veneziano*. In this play, the protagonist is a lawyer called on to conduct a case in Rovigo, a place in fact where Roman law was practised, and whose adversary is a lawyer from Bologna (engaged apparently as the quintessence of a legal model alternative to the Venetian one, as a means of highlighting the difference between the two judicial systems). In order to point out such technical contents which perhaps were not familiar to the public, Goldoni feels the need at the beginning of the comedy to underline the customs in force in Venice and their 'originality' by having Alberto (the Venetian lawyer) hold a small lesson on the topic:

> Alberto: 'The heat of the dispute does not allow for distraction. The lawyer who pleads is using all his powers. His eyes are careful to follow the movements of the judge, to guess from external signs in what direction he is leaning. His ears are on the alert in order to hear whether the adversary grumbles while he speaks, to detect on what arguments [the adversary] may base the objections to fortify his position, so that he can foresee where the adversary's target will be and therefore react with greater emphasis. His whole mind must be focused on weaving a good speech that is clear, concise, and convincing, distributed into three essential parts: narration, which informs; reasoning, which proves; epilogue, which convinces [...]'.

---

[50]   Micheli (see note 48), p. 52.

[51]   Venetian lawyers were under the obligation to graduate in jurisprudence anyhow (usually in Padua, seat to the only *Studium* in the territories of the Serenissima, particularly famous precisely for its Faculty of Law). Witness to this is Goldoni himself, who puts the following words in the mouth of the Venetian lawyer: 'I can surely reply to the doctrines of the adversary, as those texts or those legal authors are known to me, because we too, before receiving our degree, and even after, study *ius commune*, so as to be fully informed about that too, and to hear the various opinions of the doctors on jurisprudential precepts' (Goldoni, see note 40, p. 777). Goldoni, after all, practised law in Pisa too, and therefore certainly applied the rules of *ius commune* in the forum of that Tuscan city; cf. what he himself tells the reader in the exordium to the comedy (Goldoni, see note 40, p. 709).

[52]   As regards Goldoni's juridical training, repeatedly object of study, see B. Brugi, *La laurea in legge di Carlo Goldoni*, in Id., *Per la storia della giurisprudenza e delle università italiane. Saggi*, Turin: UTET 1915, pp. 198-213; *L'avvocato veneto Carlo Goldoni (1707-1762)*, in: N. Messina (ed.), *Carlo Goldoni vita, opere, attualità*, Rome: Viviani 1993; M.A. Cattaneo, *Carlo Goldoni e Alessandro Manzoni. Illuminismo e diritto penale*, Milan: Giuffrè 1991, especially pp. 15-36 (where he recalls and critically analyses the previous literature on the issue) and 55-76; G. Cozzi, *Note su Carlo Goldoni, la società veneziana e il suo diritto*, now in Id., *La società veneta e il suo diritto. Saggi su questioni matrimoniali, giustizia penale, politica del diritto, sopravvivenza del diritto veneto nell'Ottocento*, Venezia: Marsilio 2000, pp. 3-17; and especially, G. Zordan, 'Il dottorato padovano di Carlo Goldoni tra fonti documentarie ed autorappresentazione', *Quaderni per la storia dell'Università di Padova* 30 (1997) pp. 19-56.

Lelio: 'I don't know how Doctor Balanzoni, your adversary, will understand this manner of dispute. He is from Bologna, and you are from Venice: in Bologna they write,
they do not talk'.
Alberto: 'Very well. He will write, and I will talk [...] He can come in with his written
allegations, studies, revised and corrected as much as he likes, and I will reply by
improvising. *This is the special manner of us Venetian lawyers, that imitates the style
and customs of the ancient Roman orators'*.[53]

However, it can be said that in almost every important Italian court of law, above all
in the 18th century, a local tradition of writings explicitly dedicated to the practice of
law was established, construed also, but not exclusively, in the sense in which it has
been examined here, i.e., of a conscious salvaging of an ancient but still valid tradition of rhetorical precepts useful for presenting one's arguments in the best possible
manner to both capture the attention of the judge and win his sympathy, in order to
persuade him of the truth of one's arguments. In this context lies the indisputable success of Quintilian's *Institutio oratoria*, still used as an effective guide for the work of
modern lawyers, whose formation is deeply rooted in the classical works on rhetoric.

By way of an example, the Tuscan production of such works between the 18th
and the 19th centuries is noteworthy. It includes several especially significant treatises[54] still governed by the trial system of the *Ancien Régime* that survived for an
exceptionally long time in the Grand Duchy of Tuscany, until the union of Italy in
1860.

As can be inferred from the titles of these works, that contain suspiciously insis-
tent repeated references to judicial eloquence, we have here a very specialised
reflection on the oratory techniques to be applied in court. They are dedicated to
enhancing the positive results of the merge of rhetoric, considered in its *genus iudi-
ciale* aspect, the rules of procedure by which the lawyer acts, and the rules of substantive law, on the basis of which the judge decides in favour of one of the parties
in a case or considers the defendant's behaviour as lawful or unlawful. Such literature, on the one hand, is actually technically interesting because of the scholarly
sources and the expertise of the suggestions offered to the orators, but, on the other
hand, it is not very original.

The final result is the confirmation of the full vitality and importance, even in the
19th century, although with the difference in accent typical of the various juridical
traditions of Italy's regions, of these precepts, mainly intended for the world of practice. They continued to nourish the forensic world, their privileged recipient, that
recognised their concrete utility in training a good lawyer. It did not want to miss the
opportunity of acquiring the tools for forming a good forensic orator, firmly convinced that eloquence played a decisive role in ensuring victory in court.

---

[53] Goldoni (see note 40), pp. 716-717 (the italics are mine). The meaning of this passage, with the
evocative charge of the parallel drawn between the Venetian pleadings and Roman judicial oratory
attracted the attention of Zanardelli; cf. G. Zanardelli, *L'avvocatura. Discorsi*, Florence: Barbèra 1879, at
p. 42.
[54] Among others, cf. F. Rossi, *De procuratoribus dialogus*, Florentiae: 1781; G. Bertieri, *Avvertimenti
sulla maniera di scrivere nelle materie forensi*, Florence 1797; G. Carmignani, *Escursione storico-
giuridica sulle vicende della eloquenza giudiziaria antica e moderna*, in Id., *Cause celebri da lui dis-
cusse*, Pisa: Nistri 1843, pp. 1-40; G. Pellegrini, *Della eloquenza forense*, Florence: Pezzati 1838.

BELÉN SAIZ NOEDA

PROOFS, ARGUMENTS, PLACES: ARGUMENTATION AND RHETORICAL THEORY IN THE *INSTITUTIO ORATORIA*, BOOK V

1. INTRODUCTION

Book V of Quintilian's *Institutio oratoria* is concerned with the *probatio* and the *refutatio*, the main parts of the forensic genre of rhetorical discourse, since 'an orator's peculiar and foremost task is to strengthen his case with proofs and refute those of his opponent' (V.pr.2).[1] According to the rhetorical system, the *probatio* and the *refutatio* are the two parts, positive and negative, respectively, making up the *argumentatio*.[2] Quintilian considers the *probatio* (or *confirmatio*) and the *refutatio* as two different parts with their own identities within the discourse as a whole, following the tradition set in the *Rhetorica ad Alexandrum*, the *Rhetorica ad Herennium,* and also by Cicero, a view that departs from the Aristotelian *pistis*.[3] In practice, both parts of the discourse are closely related and neither could exist without the other. Proofs constitute the central element, hence the interchangeable role of the *argumentatio* and the *probatio* in the theory of rhetoric.[4]

After seeking to make the judge 'benevolent, attentive and receptive' (IV.1.5), insofar that it is won to his cause in the *proem* or *exordium*, and after 'stating before the judge the facts regarding which he will have to issue a final decision' (IV.2.1), in the *narratio*, the orator will have to provide solid foundations for the matter previously presented, including the refutation of the case put forward by the opponent. The importance of the proof is such that the aim of both previous parts of the discourse is solely to engender receptiveness in the judge for this stage of the discourse[5]

---

[1]   All the quotations in Latin are taken from Winterbottom's edition (see 'Introduction', note 26). I have used the original Latin text for all the translations and I have also checked the editions of Butler and Cousin (see 'Introduction', note 27), and the editions by J. M. Casas i Homs (ed.), M. Fabi Quintilià. *Institució oratòria*, Vols. I-II, Barcelona: Fundació Bernat Metge 1975-1980; A. Ortega Carmona (ed.), Marco Fabio Quintiliano. *Sobre la formación del orador. Obra completa*, 3 Vols., Salamanca: Universidad Pontificia 1997-1999; I. Rodríguez & P. Sandier (eds.), M. Fabio Quintiliano. *Instituciones Oratorias*, 2 Vols., Madrid: Imprenta de Perlado Páez y Compañia 1916.
[2]   Cf. H. Lausberg, *Handbuch der literarischen Rhetorik. Eine Grundlegung der Literaturwissenschaft*, 2 Vols., Munich: Max Hueber Verlag 1960; English translation: *Handbook of Literary Rhetoric: A Foundation for Literary Study*, Leiden-Boston: Brill 1998, §430.
[3]   Cf. Lausberg (see note 2), §262.
[4]   Cf. T. Albaladejo, *Retórica,* Madrid: Síntesis 1989, p. 93.
[5]   In various passages of Book IV, Quintilian points out the close relationship which exists between the *narratio* and the *probatio* (IV.2.48; IV.2.55); after all, 'Is there any difference between the proof and the

and it is not until then that the bases of causes (*status*) attain their *raison d'être*. This is the only essential part: without proof, there can be no suit (V.pr.5).

The presentation of the arguments is the core of rhetorical discourse, which is, by its very nature, a convincing device: it shares in the essence of rhetoric as the agent ('artisan') of persuasion.[6] In the *argumentatio*, persuasion basically follows the intellectual course of *docere*, as the first degree of *persuadere*,[7] related to the teaching process (V.pr.1). The proof requires intense reflection, subtle intelligence forged by instruction and developed by experience, the intelligent use of the method (*ars*), which involves 'finding' beyond it, actually transcending it. Quintilian echoes but does not share the view held by those early teachers of rhetoric, who excluded the stirring up of emotions in the hearers from the orator's main tasks on the grounds that such an undertaking was barren, superfluous, and almost improper when coming off victorious with the truth is at stake (V.pr.1). He accepts the obvious rational nature of this part of a speech, but he does not forget *delectare* and *movere*; he appeals both to the delight and to the emotions to enliven the arguments and thus succeed in persuading the audience (V.13.57). Quintilian does not yield to the idea of leaving all feeling aside, even in the most technical parts of the discourse; for him, there is always room for emotions, in all phases of the speech (VI.1.51). If an orator who masters 'invention' and succeeds in presenting the best proofs in the best possible way is considered a good orator, the best one would be the orator who manages to impress the judge, to move at will his heart. Herein lies the majesty of eloquence: *hic eloquentia regnat* (VI.2.3-4).

Refutation is the main task of the counsel for the defence; besides, all statements made by the opponent must also be refuted, in the defence or in the prosecution (V.13.1). However, it is by no means possible to establish clear-cut limits between the task of refutation and that of proof, since the very act of proof implies, above all, the action of refuting, and refutation is nothing but tearing to pieces the opponent's arguments (proofs). Although, according to Quintilian, refutation calls for more variety, is more subtle and devious (V.13.2), the method followed in both instances is quite similar: in refutation and confirmation, the arguments must be drawn from the same sources; this is also the case as regards the nature of the words, phrases, and figures used in the refutation. On the one hand, it is possible to take the proof in a general sense which includes refutation as a way of proving by negation; on the other, refutation attains its own relevance and tries to define its peculiar features, as defending is more complicated than accusing, just as healing is more difficult than inflicting the injury (V.13.3).

2. PROOFS AND ARGUMENTATION: *INVENTIO* AND *DISPOSITIO*

The contents of the *probatio*, viz., the proofs (Greek: *písteis,* Latin: *probationes*), which includes the arguments (*argumenta*), constitute the conceptual centre of the

---

narration, if only that the narration be a continuous statement of the proof, and the proof, in turn, be nothing but a confirmation in accordance with the narration?' (IV.2.79).

[6] Cf. J. Cousin, *Études sur Quintilien,* 2 Vols., Paris: Boivin 1935-1936, rpt. Amsterdam: Schippers 1975-1980, p. 39.

[7] Cf. Lausberg (see note 2), §257.

argumentation and, given the central role of the latter, the overall topic of the oration concentrates in the proofs.[8] Quintilian does not intend to exhaust the subject related to the proofs, which is in itself inexhaustible; rather, his aim is to suggest a certain way of action and method so that the orator may master them, thus being capable of 'inventing' similar resources in accordance with the nature of each case (V.1.3). Here we enter the scope of the *inventio* (*heúresis*), the first part of rhetoric or the first phase of the composition of the speech, carried out in the order dictated by tradition. To the *inventio* phase corresponds 'the thing signified' (III.3.1), or *res*, the subject matter of the discourse, in the form of a *quaestio* or point of controversy. This is the process whereby the orator collects the materials for his oration, much in the same way as the builder gathers stones, timber, and other useful elements to erect a building (VII.pr.1); this is the method used to find and treat these materials, it is the search and finding of ideas,[9] i.e., proofs, arguments. The theoretical complexity of the *inventio*, as pointed out in Book V of the *Institutio oratoria*, is two-fold. Firstly, it is to be found in its location, between reality (extra-discursive, extra-textual) and the discourse (the text). Secondly, this complexity lies in the necessary meeting point, arising from the *inventio*, of the 'accepted', that is, the standard precepts of the art, and the new elements required by each different case; i.e., it lies at the balanced point of contact existing between the art, *ars*, and the natural capacity, *ingenium*.

The first aspect is a reflection on the boundaries between extra-textual reality and discourse reality (or 'fiction'), which concerns the principle of probability, the basis upon which rhetoric stands from its origins. The *inventio* is the search for true (or probable) arguments that make our case credible.[10] Rhetorical discourse uses factual reality, events of the court case to which the speech refers, as its point of departure and the basis upon which to create its own referent, which must appear to be the reality.[11] The matter of the cause being perceived from both parties' partial standpoints is 'created' by means of the oration. Initially, the truth is not clear (there arises the controversy) and it will be (re)constructed in the oration, mainly through the argumentation stage; once it is clarified in the oration, it will be projected outside the discourse.[12] The truth is thus discursive truth, that which is constructed by and in the discourse and that which the judge validates by his decision if he considers it as *the* truth, that is, if it sounds credible. Therefore, what is true is not as important as what appears to be true, since, in the teachings of Quintilian, an orator is allowed to suppress, ignore, or even deny the obvious: he must do so if the *utilitas*, according to the partial perception of his case, requires it of him. The ethics of

---

[8]   Cf. Lausberg (see note 2), §348 and 349.
[9]   Cf. Lausberg (see note 2), §260.
[10]   Cf. Cicero, *De inventione*, I.9; *Rhetorica ad Herennium*, I.3.
[11]   The facts and objects of reality may translate into proofs, which the orator obtains from the case itself and not as the results of the art; this is what Quintilian labels as non-artificial proofs [see section 3.1]. In this connection, Alfonso Reyes defines artificial or technical proofs as those created in the oration, as opposed to non-artistic or extra-technical proofs, which are all the 'certainties'. Cf. A. Reyes, *La crítica en la edad ateniense. La antigua retórica* (*Obras Completas*, XIII), Mexico: F.C.E. 1961, p. 506.
[12]   Cf. D. Pujante, *El hijo de la persuasión. Quintiliano y el estatuto retórico*, 2nd edition, Logroño: Instituto de Estudios Riojanos 1999, p. 79-80.

the orator, who is a 'good man' (*vir bonus dicendi peritus*),[13] justifies all his devi-
ousness, as his only aims are (and must be) truth and justice.

These insights into the *inventio* and probability of rhetorical discourse necessarily lead us to the *dispositio*, the second rhetorical operation, consisting of a useful
distribution of the ideas and various parts of the speech (VII.1.1). The discovery of
truth, or, in a more rhetorical wording, the construction of a proving mechanism
capable of persuading (that is, credible), depends not only on the ideas found, but
also on their being properly arranged and distributed in the oration. As Quintilian
puts it, the *probatio* (and also the *refutatio*) requires finding and arranging, i.e., it
requires both *inventio* and *dispositio*, which cannot be separated. Since the same
material may be useful for both parties to defend their opposing stances, the way of
connecting them and their arrangement, always guided by *utilitas*, prove to be decisive factors that must be borne in mind when processing the materials suitably and
efficiently. The *dispositio* without the *inventio* is useless, Quintilian states bluntly, as
an abundance of data would prove fruitless without a proper distribution and close
connections between them (VII.pr.1). In addition to treating the arrangement of the
proofs and the arguments in several instances throughout Book V, the *probatio* and
refutatio, as parts of the oration, constitute arrangement categories or ordering structures themselves.[14] The role of the *inventio* is therefore oriented toward the arrangement dictated by the parts of the speech, which is shown as a paradigm in forensic
discourse, the kind of oratory focused on by Quintilian, but also in the deliberative
and epideictic genres. Then, the study of the *inventio* is undertaken from the standpoint of the parts of the speech, the general structure of the *dispositio*, which represents a traditional meeting point for both.[15]

As regards the combination of art (*ars*) and talent (*ingenium*), Quintilian
painstakingly conveys the traditional precepts of rhetorical theory seasoned, as it
were, with his extensive experience as an advocate and educator, since an orator
must know the principles of the art and practice their application to carry out the task
of invention. However, the matter of rhetoric is infinite and the ultimate key to the
success of the demonstration lies in the particular case. Consequently, the orator

---

[13]   *Inst. or.* I.pr. 9: '[…] that perfect orator, […] cannot achieve such a degree of excellence, save he be
an honest man, and it is for this reason that we do not only require of him an extraordinary talent in the
art of speaking, but also that his character be adorned by all the virtues of the soul'.

[14]   Cf. Lausberg (see note 2), §261.

[15]   Using theoretical semiotic and textual assumptions, within the framework of a General Rhetoric (see
A. García Berrio, 'Retórica como ciencia de la expresividad (presupeustos para una Retórica General)',
Estudios de Lingüística 2 (1984), pp. 7-59), Tomás Albaladejo (see note 4), pp. 46-47, has established a
difference between an extensional *res* and an intensional *res*. The nature of the former is semantic and
extensional, and is related to the *inventio*; the nature of the latter is syntactical and intensional and concerns the *dispositio*, where the parts of the oration are located. From this point of view, we could say that
the *inventio* and the *dispositio* are in the intensional *res*, the space where Quintilian's treatise is. Extensional elements (the source of the material for non-artificial proofs) are also approached from the discursive standpoint of the construction of the proofs, as the material originating from the case and the partiality dictated by *utilitas*. As David Pujante has said (see note 12), p. 79, Quintilian does not differentiate
between the extensional and intensional aspects of the *res*; likewise it remains unclear what the concepts
of constructed meaning (i.e., the reality fashioned after discursive construction) and preliminary content
mean for him.

must be able to find similar resources to those he has already learned (V.1.3) and even to open new ways where there are currently none (V.14.30). Thus, the *inventio* implies the process of selection, finding, discovery, creation[16] by means of the *ingenium* guided by *ars* and safeguarded by good judgment (*consilium*).

Of the *inventio*, it may be said that it comprises a certain assessment that, according to some minor rhetoricians, preceded the *inventio* and belonged to the *intellectio*. The determination of the cause's *status*, so closely related to the proofs, of the *genus* and the degree of defensibility would be part of this preliminary task of the orator, a precondition of the *inventio*.[17] Quintilian follows in the footsteps of the great rhetoricians as he does not include this sixth phase along with the other rhetorical parts; all he does is to include it under the category of *iudicium*, not as a preliminary step, but mingled with *inventio*, *dispositio*, and *elocutio*.[18]

3. CLASSIFICATION OF THE PROOFS

There are three key terms to define the corpus of evidence in forensic discourse: *proofs*, *arguments*, and *places*, that support the rhetorical system of argumentation. In some chapters (V.8, V.12), the proof and the arguments seem interchangeable or appear to be referring to the same concept, perhaps by way of metonymy, naming the part (the argument) for the whole (the artificial proof). For Quintilian, however, proofs (*probationes*) is the most general concept, the corpus including all pieces of evidence. At the same time, he uses the term *argumentum* to refer to a particular type, the most important, of artificial proof. Places are the basis for arguments.

In keeping with the rhetorical tradition initiated by Aristotle, Quintilian classifies proofs in two main categories: *átechnoi* or non-artificial proofs (i.e., all proofs extraneous to the art), and *éntechnoi* or artificial proofs, namely, the proofs which emanate from the principles of the art in connection with the case.

3.1 Non-Artificial Proofs

Non-artificial proofs (V.2-7) are not obtained by the orator, since they already exist.[19] They are not a part of the art itself, but they must be counteracted with the best resources of eloquence in the sense of the *utilitas* of the particular case. Accordingly, Quintilian focuses on how to refute them, resulting in an ongoing intertwining of proof and refutation, which shows, not only that *probatio* is also *refutatio* and vice versa, but also that, given the 'objective' nature of these proofs, what really

---

[16]   Cf. Lausberg (see note 2), §260.
[17]   Cf. Lausberg (see note 2), §97.
[18]   Quintilian mentions a sixth part of rhetoric, which was added by others to the invention phase, i.e., judgement (*iudicium*); according to him, it cannot be separated from the *inventio*, the *dispositio,* and the *elocutio* (III.3.5-6). On the relationship between the *ingenium*, the *iudicium*, and the *consilium*, on the one hand, and the *intellectio*, on the other, in the *Institutio oratoria*, see F. Chico Rico, 'La *intellectio* en la *Institutio oratoria* de Quintiliano: *ingenium, iudicium, consilium y partes artis*', in: T. Albaladejo, E. del Río and J.A. Caballero (eds.), *Quintiliano: historia y actualidad de la retórica*, Vol. 2, Logroño: Instituto de Estudios Riojanos 1998, pp. 493-502.
[19]   Cf. Aristoteles, *Rhetorica*, I. 1.1355b 35.

matters is how to 'artistically' handle that which can be difficult or impossible to deny, that is, how to play down or inspire doubts regarding that which is evident. It is possible to say that Quintilian is creating a *téchne* or *ars* of non-artificial proof, as a system or method obtained from experience and oriented toward practice,[20] also linked with teaching, a linking which has characterized rhetoric from its inception.[21] This suggests an interesting approach to the idea of the *ars* itself, the boundaries of which are blurred or moved, resulting in an enlargement of the concept. Thus, non-artificial proofs are not dismissed from rhetorical art.

The first of the non-artificial proofs are the previous judgments (*praeiudicia*) (V.2), or judgments that have been given in similar cases or previous court decisions issued on the case being heard or decisions issued with reference to the same case. Previous decisions rest on two fundamental principles: similarity and authority. By virtue of the first, they remain linked to the examples, which are considered as artificial proof;[22] by virtue of the second, they are connected with another type of artistic proof brought from outside the case, which is authority (see section 3.2).

Fame (V.3) is a public testimony for some, a vague rumour born of mischief for others. Confessions obtained through torture (V.4) are also subject to a two-fold approach: as an infallible tool to gain knowledge of the truth and as a way of forcing a confession regarding something that never happened. It can be said that in some of these types of evidence a sort of *topica* is created, i.e., a catalogue of 'places' where arguments reside (see section 5). Examples of such places would be, in the case of torture: who requests it, from whom, against whom, the reasons for it; or who inflected the torments, how, to whom, etc. Likewise, in the case of documentary evidence (V.5), which is often rejected, places concerned with the individual or the set of circumstances are normally used so as to find arguments against its validity.

Oaths (V.6) and testimonies by the witnesses (V.7) make up the list of non-artificial proofs available to the orator. Both require a certain degree of credibility on the part of the witness making the oath or delivering the testimony. The witnesses provide common ground for both parties, the commonplace (see section 5) 'for or against the witnesses': while one of the parties stresses the fact that the strongest evidence is that supported on people's knowledge, the other will list all the possible ways of asserting falsehoods (V.7.3-4). The lawyer has to master the skill of examination so as to carry the witness through the chosen course to the chosen point, to the centre of the case, to his own ground. We cannot leave out the kind of proof known as divine evidence (*divina testimonia*, V.7.35), based on prophecies, oracles, and predictions, which require a great deal of effort in the reasoning to corroborate or reject them.

---

[20] Cf. Lausberg (see note 2), §3.

[21] See H.-I. Marrou, *Histoire de l'éducation dans l'antiquité*, Paris: Edition du Seuil 1948, 7th edition 1971 (English translation: *A History of Education in Antiquity*, Madison, Wis.: University of Wisconsin Press 1982, 1st edition 1956); C. Naval, *Educación, Retórica y Poética. Tratado de la educación en Aristóteles*, Pamplona: Eunsa 1992.

[22] In fact, Quintilian points out that the first manifestation of previous decisions, those issued in similar cases, should more correctly be labelled 'examples' (V.2.1).

The proofs interweave and interrelate, and the art penetrates the non-artificial proofs. The argumentation constitutes an edifice of proofs, which are closely linked and support one another, and the arguments, as a method of reasoning, are the foundation upon which that structure rests.

3.2. Artificial proofs

The source of artificial proofs is the rhetorical art. Its method is therefore based on its technical (rational) means to awaken credibility. The orator's natural ability must know how to 'find' them and use them when the case permits. The most important type in this group of proofs is that of the arguments; they constitute a kind of scaffolding that supports the oration. The other proofs serve as a corporeal shell for the oration; in other words, they support it and adorn it (V.8.2). The delightful and the emotive remains subordinated to the rational understanding of the case. Artificial proofs are not intended for an easy ovation; however, in it lies the key to forensic victory, since it is through artificial evidence that the judge will come to know fully all the facts of the case, as the orator sees fit (IV.2.20), since it is a partially oriented knowledge according to the *utilitas*.

All kinds of proof have certain elements in common (V.8.4-7). Every matter concerns humans or things, and therefore arguments can only find their grounds (places) in the circumstances surrounding humans or things (V.8.4), which are usually considered for themselves or in connection with other things. Likewise, all proof derives from consequent or opposite things and this is a question that must be dealt with from the standpoint of the past, the precise moment when the event took place or the subsequent time. All things must be proven in connection to other things, which must be greater, equal, or lesser. Arguments are to be found in the questions raised by the case regardless of the circumstances surrounding an individual or a thing (of a general, infinite nature); they are also found in the case itself (finite in nature). In addition, proofs can be divided into four categories, connected with four forms of reasoning: (a) 'because one thing is, another is not' ('it is daytime, so it is not night time'); (b) 'because one thing is, another thing is' ('The sun is high in the sky, so it is daytime'); (c) 'one thing is not, so another is' ('It is not night time, so it is daytime'); (d) 'one thing is not, so another is not either' ('he is not a reasoning being, so he is not a man'). As regards the degree of credibility, all are necessary or credible or not impossible.

Artificial proofs consist of indications, arguments, and examples.

Indications or signs (V.9), called *sémeîon* in Greek, and *signum*, *indicium* or *vestigium* in Latin, are perceptible signs (e.g., a bloodstained garment, a cry, injuries or similar signs), which allow us to infer that something has taken place. This kind of proof is not found by the orator through his careful reasoning. Rather, it originates in the case itself, hence its close connection to non-artificial proofs. If indications do not give rise to doubts, they cannot serve as arguments; conversely, they are not arguments either if there are doubts concerning them, but they need arguments to support them. In this point originates Quintilian's two-fold classification of indications: necessary indications (*tekméria*), which are irrefutable indications *(ályta sémeîa)*, and the indications called *eikóta* ('probabilities') by the Greeks, which do

not necessarily imply a conclusion. When Quintilian offers a definition of this second type, he uses the general term *séméîon*, thereby introducing a sense of probability into the very essence of the indications.[23]

Examples (V.11) constitute another category of artificial or extrinsic proof, that
is, brought to the case 'from the outside', or, in other words, arising from the *ars*.
Examples constitute rhetorical induction (*inductio, rhetorikè epagôgê*)[24] in addition
to deduction or deductive reasoning. These are the two parts or types of argumentation or proof. Even though Quintilian identifies the *exemplum* as a generic concept
in his initial terminological exposition, when he combines it with the *similitudo*,
examples really act as a particular instance of similarity. Examples rest on similar,
dissimilar, or contrary things and consist in adducing a real, or allegedly real, fact,
which is useful to persuade the audience according to the orator's objectives. It is
impossible to separate a major part of Quintilian's thoughts on examples from the
doctrine of places as the foundation of the arguments (see section 5), particularly
regarding that of similarity, dissimilarity and the contrary, with which they share the
same method, i.e., induction (V.10.73).

Quintilian also considers authority (Greek: *kríseis*, Latin: *iudicia*, 'judgments', and *iudicationes,* 'adjudications') as a type of proof closely related to
examples; it conveys the thinking of nations, peoples, wise men, popular citizens,
and famous poets, as well as general opinions and the convictions held by society. These judgments are in a way 'testimonies' of great strength as they are
extraneous to the case and are delivered by minds free of prejudice or influence.
They are closely connected to previous decisions, non-artificial proof which, contrary to authority, arise from the case itself. The authority of the gods, which is
manifested in the answer provided by the oracles, is also to be considered in this
category (V.11.42). If these oracles are part of the background of the case before
the court, they are called divine evidence and are used as non-artificial proofs (see
section 3.1).

Artificial and non-artificial proofs are so closely related that they sometimes
overlap. That is why certain rhetoricians considered examples and authority as non-
artificial proofs. To support this view, they argued that those elements are not discovered ('invented') by the orator, but that he rather receives them, e.g., the witnesses and other similar means. On the other hand, that which is taken from outside

---

[23]   In a narrow sense, from the standpoint of Aristotelian *Rhetoric*, I.2.1357b 5, signs connected through
a non-necessary type of relationship 'lack a designation', as Aristotle distinguishes between that which is
probable, *eikós* (what takes place in general; that which, though dealing with things that can be otherwise,
is related to that in respect of which it is probable, as the universal relates to the particular; 1357a 35),
and indications, *séméîon* (some bear the same relation to that of which they are signs as the individual in
connection to the universal, and others bear the same relation as the universal in connection to the particular; 1357b). Of all the indications, 'conclusive arguments' (*tekméria*) are the necessary ones, which are
the basis for syllogisms (Aristoteles, *Rhetorica*, I.2.1357b). Cicero, as he distinguishes between necessary
and probable argumentation, seems to be bringing Aristotle's *eikós* and *séméîon* into the second category
(Cicero, *De Inventione*, I.44). In this connection, Quintilian would be following Cicero's classification.
Cousin points out a mistake on the part of Quintilian, as he seems to consider *eikós* and *séméîon* as syn-
onyms (Cf. Cousin, see note 5, III, p. 232, n. IX, 8).
[24]   Cf. Aristoteles, *Rhetorica*, I.2.1356b 5; Cicero, *De Inventione*, I.51.

the case (taken from rhetorical art) has no value whatsoever in itself unless the orator has the talent to somehow render them useful to support his analysis.

4. ARGUMENTS

Arguments are central to artificial proofs and the proof mechanism in its entirety. The umbrella term *argument* includes *enthymemes, epicheiremes,* and *apodeixis,* terms which, according to Quintilian, have more or less the same meaning, despite the differences existing between them. The Greeks refer to all these forms of argument as *písteis,* which, though the literal translation is *fides* ('credibility, a warrant of credibility'), is more clearly rendered as *probatio* ('proof'). The three forms, in their role of arguments, constitute a method for the inspiration of credibility.

Arguments are, then, a form of reasoning that provides proof whereby one thing can be inferred from another, and also confirms uncertainties by means of facts which are certain, which are beyond any kind of doubt (V.10.11), according to the pattern set in the following example: 'Since the world is governed by Providence, the State must be administered; hence, it can be inferred that the State must be administered, if it is manifest that the world is governed by Providence' (V.10.14).

Therefore it is essential, in all kinds of litigation, to have something that does not need to be proved, whereby we can prove something; something being or appearing to be true, something to make credible that which is dubious. The following things are regarded as certain: (a) those things that are perceptible through the senses; what we see and hear, like indications; (b) that about which universal agreement exists, like the existence of the gods or that parents should be loved; (c) everything established by law or that has become a part of custom, if not of all men, at least of the State or the nation where the proceedings are taking place; (d) that regarding which there is agreement between both parties; (e) proven things, or (f) matters unanswered by the opponent (V.10.12-13). Credibility, i.e., that which is taken as certain, as truth, has three degrees: the highest degree of credibility is granted to what usually happens (e.g., Parents love their children); secondly, that which is highly probable (e.g., A healthy person will probably live till tomorrow); the third degree of credibility is found where there is nothing to fully contradict an assertion (e.g., The robbery in the house was committed by someone who was in the house).

Consequently, credibility and plausibility are key concepts of argumentative theory; they are the real foundation of the *probatio* and of rhetoric itself.

From among the parts or ideas which are by their nature related to the probable, Quintilian mentions the appeal to the emotions, which already is associated to probability in the *Rhetorica ad Alexandrum* (1428a). The study of the character and emotions of man may assist in discovering why, and consequently how, emotions awake; in Quintilian's own words: 'what things and persons are naturally adverse or friendly to other things or persons' (V.10.17). Quintilian includes in the proofs the pathetic or emotional proofs (*probationes ductas ex adfectibus,* V.12.9), which are taken from an individual's emotions and habits (*êthos*). Thus the arguments, rational processes, are connected to the flow of emotions, an essential ingredient of persuasion, making room for a 'rhetoric of emotions', that appeals to the orator's character and the emotions of the hearer, and also must take into consideration the character of the judge, since there is no stronger proof than that offered to an individual taking into account his/her own character (V.12.13).

The first type of argument is the enthymeme (*enthýméma*, the Latin *commentum*, 'thought-fiction', or *commentatio*, 'reflection'). The enthymeme is a proposition based upon a reason, and, more accurately, a sure conclusion of an argument deduced from necessary consequences or from what is contradictory (V.10.1-2). Thus, the enthymeme, term designating both the argument in itself (i.e., the matter being presented to prove another) and its utterance, is expressed in two conclusive ways: it can either be an enthymeme of consequents (arising from necessary consequences), which is called epicheireme by some rhetoricians and which consists of a proposition (*propositio*) immediately followed by its proof or reason (*ratio*), without a conclusion (V.14.1);[25] it can also be an enthymeme drawn from incompatibles (based upon incompatible terms), which many rhetoricians consider as the only real form of enthymeme, and consequently a much stronger proof (V.14.2).[26]

The enthymeme is the 'rhetorical syllogism' (V.10.3), or 'oratorical syllogism' (V.14.24), which, as has been said above, is an 'incomplete syllogism' (V.10.3; V.14.1), as its parts are not clearly distinguishable and neither it has as many as a regular syllogism.[27] In this connection, it is also considered as a part of the syllogism.

Unlike the enthymeme, the term epicheireme, (*epicheiréma*, in Latin *adgressio*, 'attack', 'attempt'), in Quintilian's view, should not be used to refer to the way of dealing with a subject, but to the subject itself, to the very thing being undertaken (or 'attacked'); in other words, the argument whereby a person seeks to argue something and which is already formed in the mind, even though it has not been put into words yet (V.10.4). However, some see it not as a merely projected or commenced proof, but as proof fully fashioned in its ultimate form; in harmony with which the epicheireme designates, in the proper and more common sense of the word, a definite conception of some thought made up of at least three parts (V.10.5).

Cicero calls the epicheireme *ratiocinatio*, a Latin term which, in a broader sense, corresponds to the Greek *syllogism*, as far as it is the 'perfect' form of the *ratiocinatio* (V.14.25).[28] According to Quintilian, whose terms remind us of what was said by Aristotle regarding the enthymeme, the epicheireme differs from syllogism in that the latter takes on multiple forms and is used to deduct one truth from another,

---

[25]   For instance: 'Virtue is a good thing because no one can put it to a bad use' (V.14.25).

[26]   For instance: 'Can money be a good thing, when it is possible to put it to a bad use?' (V.14.25). In *Rhetorica ad Herennium*, IV.25, reasoning from contraries (*contrarium*) (cf. *Inst. or.* V.10.3) is not considered an argument, but rather a rhetorical figure, i.e., it falls within the *elocutio*.

[27]   For Aristotle, the enthymeme is the highest form of argument: it is the rhetorical demonstration, which constitutes the most effective proof by persuasion (*Rhetorica*, I.1.1355a 5). The Aristotelian enthymeme is a rhetorical syllogism, understood as a syllogism arising from probabilities and signs, where two types of enthymeme find their source (*Rhetorica*, I.2.1357a 30). Whilst syllogisms are made of necessary propositions, the enthymeme concerns 'those things which oftentimes can be otherwise' (I. 1357a 15). The idea of an enthymeme being an incomplete syllogism can be found in Aristoteles, *Rhetorica*, I.2.1357a 15.

[28]   Cf. Lausberg (see note 2), §371.

whilst the epicheireme is used more frequently about the credible (V.14.14).[29] Quintilian takes part in the discussion on the number of constituents of an epicheireme. Cicero's thesis[30] was that it consists of no more than five parts, viz., the major premise (*propositio*) and its reason (*ratio*), the minor premise (*adsumptio*) and its proof or demonstration (*probatio*), and, fifth, the conclusion (*complexio*).[31] Quintilian joins the majority of authors, who accept the existence of three parts at most (V.14.6), though in a variable way (V.14.10-13), since, according to the very nature of reasoning, there has to be (and its sole presence suffices) something to support the formulation of the question, the principle (*intentio*), and something to provide the proof (*adsumptio*). To these can be added a third element, resulting from the agreement between the previous parts: the connection (*conexio*). The other parts, viz., confirmation, development, or adornment of the premises, can be considered as included where they belong.

The last type of argument, the *apodeixis* or demonstration (*apodeíxeis*), is an evident proof. On the one hand, Quintilian refers to it as an incomplete epicheireme (just like an enthymeme is an incomplete syllogism); on the other, he considers it a part of the epicheireme, the part which provides its confirmation (V.10.7).

5. PLACES

In the field of the *inventio*, it is essential to study the 'places of arguments' (*tópoi*, *loci argumentorum*). If the *inventio* is a search and finding of ideas, the rhetorical art does not leave the orator to chance (*túchê, casus*), but rather empowers him with a rational method of research (*téchnê, ars*) with which he can find ideas suitable for the matter and the *utilitas* of the case. For Quintilian, places of arguments are the 'seating', the foundation of arguments; they are the places where arguments reside, where they are concealed, and from which they must be drawn forth.[32] They are 'reservoirs of ideas',[33] slots or 'cells' where the arguments are stored. The theory of places or *topica* thus becomes a powerful instrument for the orator's *ingenium*, which is essential in his learning stages. Nevertheless, not all the arguments have their origin in all places; that is, not all the places may be a source in every case.

---

[29] However, when Cicero uses the term *ratiocinatio* (cf. *De Inventione*, I.51 and 57ff.), he is referring to the strictly rhetorical syllogism or epicheireme, taken as a complex form of deductive reasoning whose scope, as in the case of the enthymeme, is that which is probable. The *Rhetorica ad Herennium*, II.28, also touches upon the *epicheiremata* or rhetorical reasoning in similar terms to those used in *De Inventione*. In this connection, it can be said that the epicheireme is, in Roman rhetorical theory, the equivalent of the enthymeme in Greek rhetoric, although the epicheireme is a more complex form of enthymeme.

[30] Cf. Cicero, *De Inventione*, I.67.

[31] *Inst. or.* V.14.7-9: [Main premise:] Things governed by reason are better governed than those which are not. [Reasons which prove the initial proposition:] A house governed by reason is better equipped and supplied in all aspects than a house carelessly administered without intelligence. The same applies to an army or to navigation. [Minor premise:] But nothing among existing things is better administered than the universe. [Proof for the minor premise:] True, the rise and fall of heavenly bodies is subject to a well-defined order; the change of seasons, the succession of day and night... [Conclusion:] Therefore the universe is governed by reason (Quintilian takes this example from *De Inventione*, I.58ff.).

[32] *Inst. or.* V.10.20: 'Locos appello [...] sedes argumentorum, in quibus latent, ex quibus sunt petenda'.

[33] Cf. Lausberg (see note 2), §260.

Although places have a general content, they must be adapted to the case in hand; the circumstances surrounding the case finally determine the search.

Quintilian's theory of *tópoi* has an evident oratorical and practical character, which places it close to Cicero's view and therefore detaches it from the Aristotelian *topica*, which is more theoretical and philosophical.[34] Quintilian seeks to develop as complete a catalogue of places as possible but, at the same time, as simple as possible, from a pedagogical point of view, whereby the prospective orator is able to obtain the best results and deliver effective speeches. Quintilian's theory is a practical approach in an appealing balance between a painstaking attempt to embrace the multiplicity of situations and difficulties that can be encountered in the practice of advocacy at law, and the impossibility, accepted by definition, of systematizing the infinite number of different features of each particular case. The material is, in any case, infinite, as 'most of the proofs are interwoven to the very structure of controversial cases' (V.10.103). Consequently, in spite of the painstaking efforts shown by Quintilian, any classification can be but a mere attempt.

The doctrine of places, which is basically developed in the argumentation,[35] spreads to the other parts of discourse, even to other parts of rhetoric. Despite the fact of being tailored for forensic oratory, the doctrine of places is also applicable to the other genres of discourse (e.g., the causes of future events (V.10.33), the element of time (V.10.42), and possibilities (V.10.50) are important places in deliberative discourse; or the place of time is also present in the three *genera* of discourse, V.10.43); having said that, he approaches the subject of places throughout his work.[36]

Quintilian distinguishes between places of arguments (*loci argumentorum*) and commonplaces (*loci communes*), the study of which he considers an impossible and superfluous task (V.12.15-16). The *loci communes* he refers to (also in II.1.9-11; II.4.22; V.1.3; V.10.20) are those places that allow the orator to speak without being bound to any particular person or thing. This definition reminds of Cicero's *loci communes*, in their role as arguments of a more common nature, which can be adapted to suit all or most cases of the same type.[37] In contrast with the places of arguments, which are a sort of moulds or empty spaces that the orator fills with the particular contents favourable to his case, according to *utilitas* (his opponent might use the same place with a different content, from an opposing viewpoint), commonplaces have turned into recurring themes by common usage (because it is the custom

---

[34]   For an analysis of the *topica* in Aristotle and Cicero, see Th. Viehweg, *Topik und Jurisprudenz: ein Beitrag zur rechtswissenschaftlichen Grundlagenforschung*, Munich: Beck 1953 (5th edition 1974); English translation: *Topics and Law: A Contribution to Basic Research in Law*, Frankfurt am Main/Berlin/New York: Peter Lang 1993.

[35]   Cf. Lausberg (see note 2), §260.

[36]   On a wide interpretation of the concept of *topica* in the *Institutio oratoria*, see B. Saiz Noeda, '*Inventio y dispositio*; Retórica y Lingüística del texto. *Loci argumentorum* y 'estructuras tópicas' en la *Institutio Oratoria* de Quintiliano', in: Albaladejo (see note 18), II, pp. 733-741.

[37]   Aristotle defined the *koinoì tópoi*, firstly, as those that did not belong to any particular discipline, but rather to a knowledge or usage common to all men (*Rhetorica*, I.2.1358a 11ff.). Commonplaces are proper to dialectical and rethorical syllogismus, opposed to the specific conclusions (*ídiai*), which are inferences related to a specific subject (I.2.1358a 17ff.). Secondly, *koinoì tópoi* are those that are useful for any kind of rhetorical discourse, i.e., common to the three rhetorical genres (*Rhetorica*, II.19.1392a 8-1393a 20).

to speak of them), for instance, speaking against lust, adultery, or similar things (II.4.22; V.10.20). Quintilian also refers to them as resources shared by both parties: commonplaces regarding witnesses, documentary evidence, etc. (V.7.4), (see section 3.1). In contrast to the commonplaces, specific places (*loci proprii*) are those which are particular to each case, connected therefore with each party's particular point of view (they are used to praise or regret an action, to show it fair or unfair, more or less important, more or less harsh, V.13.57).

There is another element of the doctrine that stands out: the close connection existing between places and the three *bases* of the cause.[38] Both the proof and the refutation support their research and method in what constitutes the very beginning of the rhetorical process: the *status*, since in both parts it is either examined, by means of conjecture, whether the thing is true, or by means of definition, whether it is relevant for the trial, or finally, by means of quality, whether it is disgraceful, unfair, evil, inhuman, etc. (V.13.19). *Status* and *argumenta* interweave and interact.[39] Thus, the matters of the definition depend at times on the motives; for instance, 'Is a man a tyrannicide if he kills a tyrant who found him committing adultery?' (V.10.36). The circumstance of place is relevant, not only to prove 'whether something is' (*status coniecturae*), but also for the exact determination or the legal classification of the action (*status finitionis* and *status qualitatis*): it matters whether the place is private or public, sacred or secular, one's own or someone else's, just like it matters, regarding individuals, whether somebody is an official of the State, a father or a foreigner; and not all places are equally worthy and modest (V.10.38-40). Time is essential to distinguish actions from a qualitative perspective and is especially useful for cases of conjecture; for instance, when a person, who is accused of the commission of some crime, had not been born when he allegedly committed the crime (V.10.44). The question of whether someone had the intention (*an voluerit*) or the possibility (*an potuerit*), deriving from the *status coniecturae*, is to be found in the place of possibilities, and they have a great deal of influence as regards the credibility of the case (V.10.50). Manner concerns the three bases of the cause (V.10.52). Etc.

Quintilian's theory of *loci argumentorum* is briefly as follows.

Regarding persons (*loci a persona*), the places where arguments are obtained are (V.10.23-31): birth (*genus*): generally children look like their parents; nationality (*natio*): each nation has its own habits and not everything has the same value as far as persuasion is concerned; country (*patria*): laws, institutions, and opinions differ from one state to the next; sex (*sexus*): for instance, 'a man is more likely to commit a robbery, a woman to poison'; age (*aetas*): different things are more suitable

---

[38] For Quintilian, the *status* or basis is the main point or general question (arisen from the first conflict) of the cause (III.6.2-5). As question, he connects it with the ten Aristotelian categories, which he distributes among the bases of the cause and the places of arguments (III.6.23-24), although they cannot make the *status* sufficiently clear and not all places are covered (III.6.28). Questions may have several *status*, but there is only one *status causae*, being the main point upon which the case is based (III.6.9). In addition to the three questions formulated in every case, Quintilian mentions a forth *status*, the *status translationis*, which concerns *competence*, and whose value as *status* is not always acknowledged (III.6.68-75). These questions comprise the foundations of all cases (*genus iudicale*), both with reference to the rational part (*genus rationale*) and to the legal part (*genus legale*) (III.6.67, 82, 86ff.).

[39] Cf. Lausberg (see note 2), §374.

for a certain age than for another; education and instruction (*educatio et disciplina*): who has taught a person and how; bodily constitution (*habitus corporis*): for example, beauty is often used as an argument for lust, physical strength for insolence, etc.; fortune (*fortuna*): as regards money, relatives, friends, or persons in his care; condition (*condicio*): is a man famous or unknown, a magistrate or a private individual, father or son, a citizen or a foreigner, a free man or a slave, married or single, etc.; natural disposition (*animi natura*): is he covetous, irascible, merciful, cruel, severe; way of living: is he a lover of luxury, sober, sordid; occupation (*studia*): is he a peasant, advocate, merchant, soldier, etc.; personal ambitions: whether the individual wants to appear as rich or eloquent, fair or powerful; past life and previous utterances: the present can be inferred from the past; passion (*commotio, animi motum*): sudden emotions like anger, terror; also intentions referring to the past, present, or future, and the disposition of mind; the name seldom turns into an argument, sometimes the by-name: the Wise, Magnus, Pius.

The systematization causes more difficulties in the case of places of things, not only due to its greater richness and diversity, but also due to the close link which exists between some places and others; this makes more difficult to establish well-defined 'cells', which do not exist in reality. Regarding things (*loci a re*, V.10.32-118), actions are the most closely related to persons. Since the questions deriving from all actions are: why, where, when, how, and by what means, the first circumstances to be taken into consideration are the causes or motives (*a causa*, in the sense of psychological causes)[40] (V.10.33-36). Both future and past *causes* can be the source of arguments. The materials for these causes are divided in two genres and four species, as usually the motive behind an action is the desire to achieve, to increase, to preserve, and to use some good, or to avoid, to free, to mitigate, and to endure evils.

Place (*a loco*, V.10.37-41) is another circumstance from which arguments can be drawn (whether it is mountainous or flat, near the coast or inland, cultivated or uncultivated, inhabited or deserted, close or distant, advantageous or disadvantageous for plans).

Time (*a tempore*, V.10.42-48) has a double meaning: general and specific (*tempus vs. tempora*); the first meaning suggests time-related circumstances of a more general nature ('now', 'yesteryear', 'in the reign of Alexander', and simply past, present, or future); the second sense makes reference to more established periods in time ('in summer', 'in winter', 'by night', 'by day') and temporary circumstances ('in time of war', 'during a banquet'). Time is divided in three parts: preceding, simultaneous, and subsequent.

The place of possibilities (*a facultate*, V.10.49-50) makes reference to the circumstances that favour the accomplishment of the action. The place of instrument (*a instrumento*, V.10.51) must be added to possibilities.

Manner (*a modo*, V.10.52-53) concerns the question regarding the way in which something happened.

Arguments can be derived from the definition of the thing (*a finitione* or *a finis*, V.10.54), covering the whole thing or dividing it into smaller parts (what Cicero

---

[40]   Cf. Lausberg (see note 2), §379.

called 'definitions by partition'). A thing is defined by its contents or its etymology. The concepts of genus, species, properties, and differences are especially joined to the definition (V.10.55). Properties are used to confirm the definition, differences destroy it; the loss of a property renders the definition void and not all the properties of a thing make it valid. Cicero[41] separates genus and species, which he calls 'form', from the definition and subordinates them to relation (V.10.62). Furthermore, Cicero argues that the division (*divisio*, i.e., the classification of genus in different species) supports the definition[42] and he also distinguishes division from partition (*partitio*), which divides the whole into parts (V.10.63). Division takes on multiple forms and constitutes a genre of arguments by elimination (called *enumeratio* by Cicero[43]), by means of which one can prove that something is entirely false or that the remaining things are true (V.10.66).

The orderly and gradual unfolding of events in three stages, beginning (*initium*), growth (*incrementum*), and consummation (*summam*), plays a main role in the finding of arguments that support each other, since by means of certain principles a climax is inferred and vice versa, or the development can serve as the foundation for either the beginning or the end (V.10.71-72).

Similarities are another source of arguments (*a simile*, V.10.73). This belongs to the way of demonstration called 'induction', which is therefore inseparably connected with examples (see section 3.2). In combination with similarities, arguments derive from dissimilarities (*ex dissimilibus*), from opposites (*ex contrariis*), or from contradictions (*ex pugnantibus*) (V.10.74); others originate in necessary consequences (*ex consequentibus*) or in which is implicit in them (*ex adiunctis*). By *consequens* (consequential), Quintilian means 'that which follows, that which can be deduced from something' (V.10.76;78), therefore, what the Greeks called *akóloutha* (*consequentia*, 'consequent phenomena') is included in this group, just as the *parepómena* (*insequentia*, 'that which follows immediately after or that will ensue in the future'). Likewise, a type of arguments derived from facts that stand by each other, arguments of things mutually related (V.10.78), are included among the consequential arguments, also those in which the reciprocal relationship is established between opposing terms (V.10.79). An argument called 'from causes' (*genus a causis*, V.10.80) or argument of effect (in the sense of physical or metaphysical cause)[44] is very similar; it consists of the inference of facts from their efficient causes, and vice versa. Others call them *ekbáseis*, 'result'; in short, that which derives from an action (V.10.86). Cicero's conjugate argument belongs to this group ('Those who perform a just act, act justly').[45]

Apposition or comparison (*a comparatione*, V.10.87-93) is the source of arguments that prove major things by means of minor things, minor things by means of major things, and similar things by means of equal things, i.e., unlike the *locus a simile*, it connects dissimilar elements. Thus it is also related to the example.

---

41 Cf. Cicero, *Topica*, 13.
42 Cf. Cicero, *Topica*, 17.
43 Cf. Cicero, *De Inventione*, I.45.
44 Cf. Lausberg (see note 2), §381.
45 Cicero, *Topica*, 12.

Places of fiction (*a fictione*, V.10.95) are at the basis of arguments that are deduced not from admitted events, but from fictitiously supposed facts. They must be connected to the facts of the case being studied; in other words, their analogical relationship must be made clear. They are therefore also linked with examples.

The arguments taken from the circumstances (*a circumstantia*, V.10.103-109), viz., from that which corresponds to each particular case, are the most valuable proof. They are facts not included in a particular way, at least not in their distinctive complexity, among the traditional *loci*. From them, the orator must create new places;[46] in Quintilian's words, [...] *quia communia ex praeceptis accepimus, propria invenienda sunt* (V.10.103).

6. CONCLUSION

After the long and exhausting path that has been trodden, the mysteries of the art are finally revealed. However, the last word is up to the individual orator and the particular case. The orator must make good use of this comprehensive corpus of precepts taken from rhetorical theory, always following the dictates of the *utilitas* most favourable to his cause and obeying also the ordering principle of *decorum*. Each argument has its own function and must have a clear aim. He must avoid overloading the discourse with enthymemes and epicheiremes that would prove to be overwhelming and tiring even for the judge, since rhetorical orations are not dialectic inquiries. To this end, the orator can apply the powerful resources of eloquence, which are not in conflict with clarity at all. There is no *res* without *verba*, and furthermore, the *res* would be ineffective without appealing *verba*. Accordingly, it behoves the orator to cover the rational strength of his arguments (*docere*) with the virtues of *elocutio*, with a rich, colourful, and impressive 'corporeal' mantle (*delectare*), following the natural flow of eloquence. It is also necessary that his discourse is not weak or full of artifice, but rather full of strength, and spirit, capable of delighting, enthusing, and *moving* the judge and the audience (*movere*) so as to attain the victory of truth and justice.

Quintilian finds inappropriate weakened eloquence, seeking only the pleasure of entertainment, both in the Forum and in the School. The young man being trained in rhetoric must prepare himself to deal with the 'imitation of the truth'. Quintilan's teaching is useful for real life, for the forensic profession, and its aim is to expose and remedy the futility of rhetoric in his day.

Method is the instrument to develop *ingenium*, to broaden intelligence. It must seek to foster and not to hinder the orator's innate talents. The success of rhetorical discourse depends on sound and well-connected proof, on a clear, accurate, and suitable speech, on the correct measure of adornment to season the dryness of the subject matter, on enthusiasm, confidence, and authority in the manner of delivery. All these must be governed by temperance and by good judgment. Therein lies the true secret of a perfect discourse, of a perfect orator.

---

[46] Cf. Lausberg (see note 2), §399.

ANDREW LEWIS

'SECUNDUM LEGEM' IN *INSTITUTIO ORATORIA* V.13.7.

Apud iudices quidem secundum legem dicturos sententiam de confessis praecipere ridiculum est.[1]

My purposes in this paper are twofold. Firstly to suggest a workable translation of the phrase *secundum legem* in the context of Quintilian's discussion in Book V.13 and secondly to use this understanding of the sentence in which it occurs to advance some remarks upon Quintilian's understanding of the legal procedures of his day. To anticipate, my conclusion is that the words *secundum legem* should here be translated 'according to rule'.

In this part of Book V Quintilian is considering replies to arguments on the other side, and whether they are intrinsic to the case or not. In the former case he suggests we have only three choices: we can deny the facts upon which our opponent's argument is based, we can attempt to justify despite the facts, or in the last resort else seek to have the case referred elsewhere. This last plea to the jurisdiction is the least interesting response and I propose to say nothing more about it here.

To refer to the two earlier responses listed by Quintilian, the English Common law has a comprehensive and useful language: the first is a 'traverse' or denial of the facts, the second a 'plea of confession and avoidance', in which we confess or accept the facts as alleged by the other side but seek to avoid their conclusion by colouring them in some way so as to justify our conduct.

The classic illustration of this distinction (and incidentally of another important English procedural rule) is the schoolboy accused of throwing a stone at window. He replies: 'I did not do it and in any case it was an accident'. This is to advance two defences, firstly a traverse of the accusation, a denial that he did it, and then secondly a plea of confession and avoidance, admitting that he did it but that it was not done deliberately. In the courtroom, though perhaps not in the schoolyard, this is an improper 'double plea'.

When both traverse and confession and avoidance are unavailable – where there is no doubt of who broke the window - we are left only with the only other avenue open when all else fails, the plea for mercy. Of this last Quintilian rightly observes that it is only ever of use, and not necessarily then, when the court is one of plenary jurisdiction and not, as most Roman civil tribunals, limited in the judgments it can give. To emphasise this distinction Quintilian classifies the first type of tribunal, that before which a plea of mercy is admissible, as one which can do as it pleases *utrum*

---

[1] *Inst. or.* V.13.7. A translation is postponed to the argument that follows.

velit liceat. Before such a court, making such a plea, he observes, we use ordinary persuasive, deliberative, argument, not particularly juristic arguments. For we seek to persuade the judge to exercise mercy rather than pursue the course of justice and retribution.

All other courts are those where the judges must give judgment *secundum legem.* Because they are bound to give only appropriate judgments we can only use forensic arguments leading to these and cannot hope to use ordinary, non-juristic, arguments appealing to their clemency. Before such ordinary courts such a course is ridiculous.

What are the limitations on these tribunals and how do they arise? The question is an important one as it raises acutely a significant distinction between classical Roman judicature and modern courts. Most modern courts, although their decisions are subject to some form of appeal process in which those decisions can be scrutinised and if necessary overturned, nevertheless possess initially a broad intrinsic jurisdiction to hear and determine the case before them. Although procedure does not, in modern practice, have such a compelling role as in classical Rome (and in most early modern European jurisdictions) there is still room for defensive arguments which seek to deny or traverse or failing that avoid the those of the opponent. But if all else fails there can be an appeal to mercy, for the court is, in Quintilian's phrase cited earlier, 'allowed to do as it wishes'.[2]

Not so the typical Roman civil tribunal. This is not the occasion for a detailed account of the development of civil judicature in Rome but some rough account is necessary.

We need go back no further than the introduction, probably during the course of the second century BC, of the procedure known as the formulary procedure. This was dependant for its efficacy upon the jurisdiction of the urban praetor, the main jurisdictional magistrate. In his edict, which each magistrate published yearly on coming into office, the praetor offered a range of juridical remedies to those who felt that their legal rights had been infringed. Each lawsuit, in the modern world today as much as in Rome, is likely to turn on either a matter of fact or a matter of law. If you are stopped for going through a red traffic light you may defend yourself by saying either the light was green or that you were taking someone to hospital. If you succeed in the former case then it is because of a difference of fact between you and the prosecutor: the policeman said that it was red. If you succeed in the latter case it will be because the rule about stopping at red lights does not apply, as a matter of law, in emergencies.

The question whether the light was red or green is a question of fact, answerable by anyone capable of assessing the relevant information. In English terms it is a question for the jury and, in the Roman formulary system, a question for the lay judge chosen, often by the parties themselves, for his capacity and good judgment.

---

[2] A good, though controversial, example is the capacity of the jury in most Anglo-American jurisdictions to return a verdict of acquittal against the evidence. Where no appeal against acquittal is permitted such jury-nullification is irremediable. The classic account is M.R. Kadish and S.H. Kadish, *Discretion to disobey*, Stanford, California: Stanford University Press 1973.

The question whether the rule about stopping at a red light applies in an emergency is not a question of fact. It is a question about the law: what exactly is the rule?

Now in most modern Western states most of the law is set out, in greater or less detail, in the form of legislation. The modern judge's, and modern lawyer's, task, is to understand and interpret the written rule and apply it. Although laymen may quite properly have views on the meaning of a particular legal provision they would be wise not to rely upon it unless the view is endorsed by a good lawyer. As Chief Justice Coke said in at the beginning of the seventeenth century when King James I proposed to come and give judgment in person in court, the craft of law requires the application of not of ordinary but of artificial reason, in which it requires long study to become proficient.[3]

The position in Republican Rome was not so clear cut. Many issues of law were necessarily subsumed within the various remedies offered by the praetor in his edict. If the edict contained a remedy for those who claimed to have suffered loss as a result of another's physical act of damage to their property, as it did in the form of an action on the *lex Aquilia* relating to loss, then this was because the praetor, and the lawyers advising him, took the view that such loss was in principle remediable. The main issue in any case brought under its terms would be whether any such loss as was claimed had occurred. But although the general proposition that damage of this sort was compensatable was beyond question there was plenty of scope for legal argument about the exact interpretation of the remedy. Was someone who lightly beat your slave for his rudeness within the scope of the remedy? Could the piercing and stringing of pearls, which increased their value, be a loss to one who preferred them in a natural state?[4]

I shall return briefly at the end to the problem posed by these types of question for our understanding of the Roman scheme. First I should like to turn to the fundamental distinction between the legal issue about whether a remedy is available and the factual questions relating to its application. The first of these questions is, as we have seen, one for the lay judge: it is precisely for this purpose that the formulary system utilised the divided procedure of the Roman civil trial, relieving the praetor of the necessity of hearing argument on the factual details of cases and thus allowing him to concentrate on the questions of availability of remedies. It was not that the praetor felt unable or unqualified to find facts: where it was thought proper to do so the praetor announced that he would only grant a remedy *causa cognita*, when he had run through the facts of the case. Doubtless his purpose was limited to establishing that there was a *prima facie* case in these circumstances, as the matter was

---

[3] 'Then the king said that he thought the law was founded upon reason, and that he and others had reason as well as the judges. To which it was answered by me that true it was that God had endowed his majesty with excellent science and great endowments of nature; but his majesty was not learned in the laws of his realm of England, and causes which concern the life or inheritance or goods or fortunes of his subjects are not to be decided by natural reason, but by the artificial reason and judgment of law — which law is an act which requires long study and experience, before that a man can attain to the cognizance of it — and that the law was the golden metwand and measure to try the causes of the subjects, and which protected his majesty in safety and peace.' *The Case of Prohibitions* (1607) 12 Reports 64.
[4] These examples are taken from Ulp. Dig. 9.2.27.17, 30.

still sent for trial before a judge, but this would frequently include the demonstration of certain facts, for example the exact family relationships of the parties concerned.

Broadly then, and subject to some later remarks, issues of law, of availability of the remedy, were for the praetor at the stage *in iure* where the formula was debated and established, issues of fact, whether in this instance the plaintiff was entitled to recover for what had happened, were for the judge, *apud iudicem*. The judge's role is thus subordinate to the praetor: his task is to carry out an investigation of the facts relevant to the remedy being pursued and his judgment is restricted to this determination. How was this achieved in practice?

Before the praetor the plaintiff had to choose a remedy from those offered by the praetor in his edict. This in effect required him to state his main claim against the defendant in language drawn from the edict. So if the complaint was about goods he had purchased not being up to standard the plaintiff would have to frame his complaint in language appropriate to the action on sale, *actio empti*; if the complaint were about a broken formal undertaking, a stipulation, then the claim would be made in language appropriate to the *condictio,* the general action for simple debts.

Suppose the latter case. The plaintiff's case is that the defendant promised to pay him a sum of 1,000 sesterces by 1st September and has not done so. He cannot make his claim *in iure*, before the praetor, in so many words; rather he must adopt the language of the *condictio* and say that the defendant owes him 1,000 sesterces. The defendant must now either admit or deny the debt. If he admits *in iure* then there is no need to go to trial before the judge, for there is need of trial only where there is a dispute. If he denies he may do so in either of the ways outlined earlier by Quintilian, he may simply traverse the plaintiff's claim: 'I do not owe the plaintiff 1,000 sesterces'; or he may plead by confession and avoidance, that is, he may admit the facts upon which the plaintiff's claim rests, but colour them or set up other facts, proof of which leads to his exculpation. He may for example say, 'The plaintiff said that I did not have to pay the debt'.

Now, although this appears to be a simple claim of fact – that at some point the plaintiff offered to let the defendant off paying his debt, the question it raises is quite momentous. The general rule in early Roman law was that formal debts were only discharged by payment or formal release (I set aside here discussion as whether even payment sufficed in the earliest times without a formal release). Mere informal agreements, pacts, of the type alleged by the defendant in our case were insufficient to release the debtor.

Suppose our debtor, badly or not at all legally advised, chooses to deny that he owes anything, relying upon the plaintiff's informal undertaking not to claim. He announces: 'I do not owe the plaintiff 1,000 sesterces'. The praetor now has drawn up the *formula* for this case. It will read as follows:

> If it appears that the defendant owes the plaintiff 1,000 sesterces
> Then, judge, condemn the defendant to pay the plaintiff 1,000 sesterces
> If it does not appear, absolve (him).[5]

---

[5]   This is, of course, a translation of a supposed Latin original but precisely because it is supposed and not directly attested in so many words I only present the translation. Examples of actual *formulae* can be

The case is now passed to the judge, before whom the plaintiff will have to lead evidence in support of his claim that the debt is owed. This done the defendant may counter with evidence that the debt is not outstanding. The only evidence he can offer is that the plaintiff said that he would not pursue the debt. The judge now has to give judgment. His is not a plenary jurisdiction, He is appointed to give a decision in this one case and on the basis of this formula. What does it say? If the defendant owes condemn, if he does not absolve. So does the defendant owe? Seemingly, yes. In the first place the defendant's case rests upon an admission that the money was once owed: this is not a case of mistaken identity or straightforward lying by the plaintiff. In the second, if the judge has any doubts which lead him to consult a lawyer he will be told as a matter of law that such informal undertakings are not sufficient to discharge the defendant of his debt. Appeals to the judge's mercy, as indicated by Quintilian, are ridiculous and otiose, as the judge is empowered only to give judgment in accordance with the *formula* and cannot step out of this function in order to satisfy appeals to his humanity.

Suppose however a different sequence. Suppose that *in iure,* before the praetor, the defendant had countered the plaintiff by not merely traversing the claim but rather telling his story about the plaintiff's undertaking not to pursue the claim. As it happens the praetor's edict contained a provision enabling those who thought that they had been taken advantage of in this way, to place in the formula a clause, an *exceptio,* stating that it had been agreed between the parties that the money would not be claimed. The justification for this clause in the edict appears to have been the praetor's unwillingness to allow the law to be used as an instrument of fraud and wrong by permitting plaintiffs to resile from undertakings freely entered into. The old rule, insisting that debtors obtain a formal release, could not be directly changed save by legislation, but it could be circumvented by allowing defendants to set up informal releases as a defence.

The *formula* in our case now reads:

> If it appears that the defendant owes the plaintiff 1,000 sesterces
> Then, unless there has been an agreement between the parties that the money should not be claimed,
> Judge, condemn the defendant to pay the plaintiff 1,000 sesterces
> If it does not appear, absolve (him).

As before the judge has to be satisfied of the truth of the plaintiff's case – it must be made to appear that the defendant owes in principle. Once this is established by the plaintiff, the question arises whether or not there has been an informal undertaking not to claim. On this the defendant leads his evidence and, we may suppose, succeeds in convincing the judge. As a result the judge has no option but to absolve the defendant.

Let us briefly consider a third factor. Suppose that the plaintiff had been induced to release his debtor by some untruth: the debtor claimed that he had lost his job or

found, for example, in the legal papyri from Pompeii: G. Camodeca, *Tabulae Pompeianae Sulpiciorum,* Roma: Edizioni Quasar 1999.

had become very ill, neither of which were true. It was the discovery of the fraud that induced the plaintiff to go back upon his undertaking and sue for the debt. He will in vain urge the judge to consider the iniquity of discharging the defendant in these circumstances. Just as the defendant's appeal to mercy in the first scenario were ridiculous in the context of that *formula*, just so are the plaintiff's in the fact of this *formula* which directs the judge to absolve if he finds the agreement not to sue proved. In each case the judge is not a free agent able to give judgment at large, *utrum velit liceat*, but rather only according to the *formula*.

What then? The wise plaintiff, knowing the whole state of affairs, will ensure before the praetor that once the defendant has obtained the insertion of the clause, the *exceptio pacti,* directing absolution he argues for and obtains the insertion of a further clause, a replication, directing the judge to investigate whether or not fraud was involved in the making of the agreement or in subsequent proceedings. Now when the matter comes before the judge and the debt is proved and the agreement established, the plaintiff can invite the judge to assess the value of his assertion that the defendant was acting fraudulently. If the judge is convinced he will be able to give judgment for the plaintiff, requiring payment of the debt.

In all this the fundamental point about the formula is that it strictly determines and defines the Roman judge's role. The term judge can be a misleading translation of *iudex* precisely because the modern judge has a much wider discretion in deciding cases than any Roman *iudex* had.

To return to our Quintilian passage, having observed that in plenary tribunals, *utrum velit liceat*, we may seek to persuade to clemency by reasons:

> Apud iudices quidem secundum legem dicturos sententiam de confessis praecipere ridiculum est.
> However, it is ridiculous to urge arguments in the case of those who admit liability before judges who are required to give judgment according to rule.

The rule, *lex*, which binds the judge is the *formula* by which alone is he empowered to give judgment and which determines exactly what he may do. In such circumstances using general arguments to persuade him to some course other than one regulated by the *formula* is so much wasted breath. Those who can neither traverse the claim nor seek to confess and avoid it are in a hopeless case before such a tribunal and there is no room for oratory.

The frequent translation 'according to law' (for example in the Loeb translation of H.E. Butler)[6] is not so much wrong as lacking in precision. Even judges of plenary jurisdictions give judgment according to law, albeit that the measure of their discretion is very wide. The specific characteristics of the Roman civil trial are what lie behind Quintilian's observation here that, where the judge's freedom of action is constrained by the rules of the *formula*, arguments which step outside this framework are a waste of time. In this Quintilian is shown to be very alive to the subtleties of the Roman civil judicature system.

---

[6] See above, *'Introduction'*, note 27; at p. 315, he translates: 'in accordance with the prescriptions of law'.

AFTERWORD

The picture I have sketched of the Roman formulary process is one that is familiar from the textbooks. Dr Tellegen-Couperus and Dr Tellegen have severally argued recently that it is too schematic an account and that it is, in at least one major particular, wrong and misleading.[341]

The Roman civil judge was indeed chosen *ad hoc* by the parties from amongst their fellow-citizens. Nevertheless there is evidence that in Rome, at least, parties tried to choose judges with some knowledge of the law. Moreover the assumption that the praetors, who were themselves rarely legal specialists, acted wholly or mainly on the advice of jurists is not well supported by the direct evidence. It must not be assumed that the *in iure* stage of the process was all about law and the procedure before the judge wholly evidential.

The point can be strengthened from a more technical direction. The scheme of rules of law which can be observed in the writings of the classical jurists preserved in the Digest was the product of a long course of development which was itself constrained by the procedural technicalities of the *formula*. The legal rules followed and did not precede the formulation of the praetors' remedies in the edict and were the product of juristic reflection upon real cases which had had to be decided before the legal rules were at all clearly set out. The judges of the Republican and early Imperial eras therefore would have had to deal with many cases in which the criteria of judgment were by no means fixed. It could not be assumed that in a case of technical difficulty they could simply turn to the jurists for unambiguous advice. A good illustration of this can be found in Cicero's speech *pro Roscio* from which it appears that the definitions of debt with which we have become familiar in the writings of subsequent jurists were not universally accepted in the last century of the Republic.[342] In this light the curious spectacle of Aulus Gellius, as judge, consulting a philosopher for advice on his judgment in a case of debt, appears less problematic.[343]

From this it follows that we cannot draw too rigid a distinction between issues of fact and issues of law and assume that the role of judge was confined to determining the former. Nevertheless there remains a very important distinction to be made between those matters, which clearly include the receipt and evaluation of evidence presented by the parties, which lie exclusively within the judge's competence and are largely unconstrained, and those matters which are pre-determined by the *formula*, including the possible judgments to be given. It is as regards these latter that the judge has no discretion not given him by the terms of the *formula* itself and in respect of which he must give judgment *secundum legem* 'according to rule'.

---

[7]   See O. E. Tellegen-Couperus, 'The Role of the Judge in the Formulary Procedure,' *Journal of Legal History* 22 (2001) pp. 1-13; J.W. Tellegen, '*Oratores, iuripudentes*, and the '*causa Curiana*'', *Revue Internationale des Droits de l'Antiquité* 30 (1983) pp. 293-311 and the same author's contribution to this volume 'The Reliability of Quintilian for Roman law: On the *Causa Curiana*,' see also Tellegen-Couperus & Tellegen, 'Law and Rhetoric in the *causa Curiana*,' *Orbis Juris Romani* 6 (2000) pp. 171-203.

[8]   It is, of course, possible that Cicero is deliberately obscuring the legal position to assist his client but the picture he paints seems nevertheless far from the position stated, say, in Gaius, *Institutes*.

[9]   Aulus Gellius, *Noctes Atticae*, XIV.12. For further discussion of this text in this connexion, see A. Lewis, 'The Autonomy of Roman Law' in: Peter Coss (ed.), *The Moral World of the Law*, Cambridge: Cambridge University Press 2000, pp. 37-47.

MARIA SILVANA CELENTANO

BOOK VI OF QUINTILIAN'S *INSTITUTIO ORATORIA*: THE TRANSMISSION OF KNOWLEDGE, HISTORICAL AND CULTURAL TOPICALITIES, AND AUTOBIOGRAPHIC EXPERIENCE[1]

1. INTRODUCTION

The transmission of rhetorical knowledge in Greek and Latin civilization was marked by a constant pragmatic adaptation of techniques and persuasive precepts, along with changes in the ways of production and reception of discourse. Among our sources, the manuals of rhetoric bear witness to this long, uninterrupted process of transformation and adaptation of the art of rhetoric. Together with the precepts and the exemplifications linked with historical topicalities, they collaborate to give us an idea of the tradition and transmission of the specialized knowledge of rhetoric, which extended its sphere of influence from the well-defined bounds of persuasive techniques to all types of discourse. Even if rhetoric originated as the art of persuasion, it soon became an overall art of communication (verbal and non-verbal), with explicitly pedagogic aims and with special reference to the fields of linguistics and discourse. Of course, this also implies a gradual transformation of the role of the master of rhetoric: initially, he was a theorist of effective language, who transferred technical notions to others, but subsequently he became an educator, responsible for the training of young people through the teaching of the conscious use of discourse.

2. THE *INSTITUTIO ORATORIA* AS A COMPLETE MANUAL OF RHETORIC

As regards the forms that the manual of rhetoric assumed during the course of the centuries, we may recall that, while in 5th century BC, presumably only compendia of types of arguments adaptable to the various circumstances and different kinds of discourse were in circulation, during the imperial age, the theories and rhetorical

[1] The following reflections form a revised and updated part of my paper on the Sixth book of Quintilian's *Institutio oratoria*: 'Il sesto libro dell'*Institutio oratoria* di Quintiliano: la trasmissione del sapere, l'attualità storica, l'esperienza autobiografica', in: L. Calboli Montefusco (ed.), *Papers on Rhetoric* III, Bologna: Clueb 2000, pp. 61-74. Cf. also M.S. Celentano, 'Quintilian's *Institutio oratoria* Book VI (Italian translation and commentary)', in: A. Pennacini (ed.), *Quintiliano*. Institutio oratoria. *Edizione con testo a fronte*. Traduzioni, sommari e note di: T. Piscitelli, R. Granatelli, A. Pennacini, D. Vottero, V. Viparelli, M.S. Celentano, M. Squillante, F. Parodi Scotti, A. Falco, A.M. Milazzo, M. Vallozza, and R. Valenti, Turin: Einaudi 2001, I, pp. 685-795; 1053-1087.

precepts were collected and listed in an orderly, detailed fashion, in complete manuals, essential for preparing the new generations for public life, in which the opportunities to make speeches were very frequent.[2]

The reading of ancient manuals of rhetoric makes it possible to draw useful indications from the constant manifestations of the specific pragmatics of rhetoric, with its continual adaptations and the different forms it takes in relation to the cultural transformations of the various ages. Quintilian's *Institutio oratoria* may be considered to be a case in point in illustrating this process. And more than that. We may think, for example, of Quintilian's frequent personal reflections about the ways and forms of communication and of his original innovations or additions within a long-consolidated system of rhetoric destined for scholastic use. We notice, first of all, that the title of the work, *The Orator's Education*, is reductive with respect to the actual discussion of the subject in the collection of twelve books. More than of the young aspiring orator, Quintilian seems to be thinking constantly of the individual who, in every different period, needs to acquire knowledge and experience useful for the creation and construction of discourse. In this sense, what Quintilian proposes is to use a terminology dear to the politicians and bureaucrats presently in charge of the different stages of education, lifelong or continuing education, which does not set any age limits for learning, and goes on, so to speak, from the cradle to the grave. Hence the historical topicalities, or the re-interpretation of those traditional precepts that no longer responded to the new requirements of the historical and cultural con-

---

[2] As regards the different phases of the historical development of rhetoric, the formulation and the progressive transformation of manuals for scholastic use, and the role of the master of rhetoric, see: G. Kennedy, *The Art of Persuasion in Greece*, Princeton: Princeton University Press 1963; Id., *Quintilian*, New York: Twayne Publishers 1969; Id., *The Art of Rhetoric in the Roman World*, Princeton: Princeton University Press 1972; R. Barthes, *La retorica antica*, tr. it., Milan: Bompiani 1994 (=1970), especially pp. 13-30; J. Adamietz, 'Quintilians Institutio oratoria', in: H. Temporoni and W. Haase (eds.), *Aufstieg und Niedergang der Römischen Welt* 32.4 (1984) pp. 2226-2271; Th. Cole, 'Le origini della retorica', *Quaderni Urbinati di Cultura Classica* n.s. 23 (52) (1986) pp. 7-21; Id., *The Origins of Rhetoric in Ancient Greece*, Baltimore-London: The Johns Hopkins University Press 1991; A. Pennacini, 'L'arte della parola', in: G. Cavallo, P. Fedeli and A. Giardina (eds.), *Lo spazio letterario di Roma antica*, II. *La circolazione del testo*, Roma: Salerno Editrice 1989, pp. 215-267; K. Welch, 'Writing Instructions in Ancient Athens, after 450 B.C.', in: J.J. Murphy (ed.), *A Short History of Writing Instruction. From Ancient Greece to Twentieth-Century America*, Davis: Hermagoras Press 1990, pp. 1-17; J.J. Murphy, 'Roman Writing Instruction as Described by Quintilian', in: Murphy (see above), pp. 19-76; F.H. Robling, 'Ars', in: G. Ueding (ed.), *Historisches Wörterbuch der Rhetorik*, 1, Tübingen: Niemeyer 1992, pp. 1009-1030, especially pp. 1009-1020; J.J. Murphy and R.A. Katula (and F.I. Hill, D.J. Ochs and P.A. Meador), *A Synoptic History of Classical Rhetoric*, II, Davis: Hermagoras Press 1994[2]; D.M. Schenkeveld, 'Scholarship and Grammar', in: F. Montanari (ed.), *La philologie grecque à l'époque hellenistique et romaine*, (= Entretiens sur l'antiquité classique, Tome XL), Vandoeuvres-Genève: Fondation Hardt 1994, pp. 263-301, especially pp. 263-269; C.J. Classen, 'Rhetorik und Literarkritik', in: Montanari (see above), pp. 307-352, especially pp. 327-329; I. Worthington (ed.), *Persuasion. Greek Rhetoric in Action*, London-New York: Routledge 1994; M.L. Clarke, *Rhetoric at Rome. A Historical Survey*, revised and with a new introduction by D.H. Berry, London-New York: Routledge 1996; B. Mortara Garavelli, *Manuale di retorica*, Milan: Bompiani 1997 (= 1988), pp. 17-39; T. Morgan, *Literate Education in the Hellenistic and Roman Worlds*, Cambridge: Cambridge University Press 1998, pp. 226-239; M.S. Celentano, 'Le regole della comunicazione: pragmatica e antichi manuali di retorica', in: P. Radici Colace and A. Zumbo (eds.), *Atti del Seminario Internazionale di Studi 'Letteratura scientifica e tecnica greca e latina'* (Messina, 29-31 ottobre 1997), Messina: Edas 2000, pp. 263-274.

text. The *Institutio oratoria* is, in a word, a complete manual of training in discourse, pervaded by the constant desire to update the reader, and to adapt the traditional rules of persuasive discourse to new uses. Quintilian often explicitly adds his own personal baggage of professional and human experience. Also in the sixth book, these characteristics are clearly visible.

3. A FEW CHARACTERISTICS OF BOOK VI

Even the discussion of certain arguments, which is omitted by others, or placed at a different point, depending on its close relationship with practice, is an element of clear innovation in the structure of the work. See the case of *altercatio*, which is the subject of the fourth chapter (VI.4.1):

> The place to outline the rules of Altercation might seem to be after I had finished dealing with everything related to the set speech, for the use of Altercation comes last. However, since Altercation is entirely a matter of Invention, cannot involve Disposition, has no great need of the ornaments of Elocution, and has no problems with Memory or Delivery, it seems reasonable to treat this topic, which depends wholly on the first part of Rhetoric, before proceeding to the second. Other writers have left it alone, perhaps because they thought they had taken care of it sufficiently by their other precepts.[3]

Furthermore, the sixth book is a book of transition. It is the volume that closes the first half of the work. It is the volume that concludes the discussion of the *partes orationis*: the first chapter deals with the *peroratio*. It is also the volume that marks the passage from *inventio* to the other rhetorical sections, starting from *dispositio*, and thus we find arguments here which, in reality, are connected with the parts of rhetoric as a whole, and not just *inventio*. However, a failure to describe them would have aroused a suspicion of incompleteness in the *Institutio oratoria* (VI.5.1):

> Having dealt with these matters to the best of my ability, I should have had no hesitation about proceeding at once to Disposition, which comes next in order, were I not afraid that, as some scholars have included Judgement under Invention, I might be thought by some to have left this out. My own view is that it is so inextricably involved in every part of our work that it cannot be separated from the study of individual thoughts and even single words; and it can no more be taught by art than taste or a sense of smell.[4]

---

[3] 'Altercationis praecepta poterant videri tunc inchoanda cum omnia quae ad continuam orationem pertinent peregissem: nam est usus eius ordine ultimus; sed cum sit posita in sola inventione neque habere dispositionem possit nec elocutionis ornamenta magnopere desideret aut circa memoriam et pronuntiationem laboret, prius quam secundam quinque partium hanc quae tota ex prima pendet tractaturus non alieno loco videor. Quam scriptores alii fortasse ideo reliquerunt quia satis ceteris praeceptis in hanc quoque videbatur esse prospectum.' I use the text edition and translation by Russell (see 'Introduction', note 27).

[4] 'His pro nostra facultate tractatis non dubitassem transire protinus ad dispositionem, quae ordine ipso sequitur, nisi vererer ne, quoniam fuerunt qui iudicium inventioni subiungerent, praeterisse hunc locum quibusdam viderer: qui mea quidem opinione adeo partibus operis huius omnibus conexus ac mixtus est ut ne a sententiis quidem aut verbis saltem singulis possit separari, nec magis arte traditur quam gustus aut odor.'

The presence of a chapter on the *peroratio*, a part which usually presents a clearly pathetic character, brings with it the discussion of the arousing of feelings (Chapter 2), which displays a parallel and antithetic correspondence to the long, detailed examination of the phenomenon of laughter, how it may be provoked, and with what effects (Chapter 3). In particular, with reference to the latter chapter, I have already pointed out elsewhere[5] that it is immediately possible to perceive Quintilian's need to complete his exposition of precepts, already largely known from a long, authoritative tradition, with some sections specifically dedicated to *urbanitas* or elegance. At the same time, he needed to update, so to say, his discourse on the comical, i.e., to make it pragmatically easier to exploit, thus entering into the merits of an argument that was still the subject of a lively debate in his times: what relationship exists, if any, between humour and elegance. Aspiring orators could find elements of reflection on a theme that was the subject of an actual, real discussion among contemporary rhetors; the history of rhetorical studies was enriched by Quintilian's detailed discussion of the problem of *urbanitas*. It is well known that he was a rigorous scholar of the theory and the history of the orator's art, as well as being aware of the responsibilities that he assumed as a teacher of rhetoric.

4. THE PREFACE TO BOOK VI

Besides combining tradition and innovation in the specific discussion of the technical aspects, which occupies Chapters 1-5, I believe that, in order to understand fully the precise configuration that Quintilian wanted for his manual - and not only for the sixth book or for the second half of the work - the proem or preface (VI pr.1-16) is particularly illuminating:

> 1. I began this work, Marcellus[6] Vitorius, principally at your desire, but also in the hope of making some useful information available to deserving students; latterly, too, my efforts have been stimulated by the almost imperative demands of the duty which has been entrusted to me. All the time, however, I was considering also my own pleasure, because I hoped to leave this, as the best part of his inheritance, to my own son, whose outstanding abilities justified even obsessive care on a father's part. I intended that, if fate cut me off - and this would have been fair and greatly to be wished - he would still have his father as his teacher. 2. Day and night I worked at it, hastened by the fear of my own mortality, until Fortune so laid me low in an instant that the fruit of my labours came to matter to no one less than to me. Bereavement struck me a second time; I lost the child of whom I had such expectations, and in whom I rested the sole hope of my old age. 3. What am I to do now? What service am I to think that I can still do when

---

[5] M.S. Celentano, 'Umorismo, *urbanitas* e polemiche retoriche', in: E. Degani, G. Gnoli, S. Mariotti and L. Munzi (eds.), *MOUSA. Scritti in onore di G. Morelli*, Bologna: Pàtron 1997, pp. 323-330. The need to make a manual of rhetoric more complete and up-to-date by dealing with subjects not usually included in the typical structure of the manual, is confirmed by writers after Quintilian as well. See the case of the *Ars rhetorica* by Julius Victor (4th cent.), cf. Celentano (see note 2), pp. 268-274; Ead., 'Retorica e bon ton', *Storia e Dossier* 43 (settembre 1990) pp. 16-19.; Ead., 'Un galateo della conversazione nell' *Ars Rhetorica* di Giulio Vittore', *Vichiana* 3a serie 1 (1990) pp. 245-253; Ead., 'La codificazione retorica della comunicazione epistolare nell' *Ars rhetorica* di Giulio Vittore', *Rivista di Filologia e di Istruzione Classica* 122 (1994) pp. 422-435.

[6] *Marcus* Russell. See comm. *ad loc.*

the gods so fight against me? For it happened that I had been struck by a like blow when I began to write my book on the "Causes of the Decadence of Eloquence". Only one right course remained: to cast this ill-fated work and whatever wretched learning I have upon that untimely pyre whose flames were to consume the issue of my loins, and not to aggravate by fresh labours the offence of my continuance in life. 4. What good parent could forgive me for finding the strength to go on with my studies? Who would not feel disgust at my insensitivity, if I could find any use for my voice except to blame the gods for letting me survive all those I loved, and to bear witness that no Providence looks down on earth? My own destiny may indeed not give rise to any such thoughts (for my only crime is that I am still alive) but the fate of those condemned undeservedly to a premature death most surely does. I had lost their mother first: before even her nineteenth year had passed, having borne two sons, she was snatched away by a cruel and untimely fate. Yet she did not die unhappy; 5. it was I who was so laid low just by this one misfortune that no subsequent chance could make me happy. Not only did her death bring her husband incurable grief, for she possessed every virtue that woman can have, but also, given her age (especially compared with mine), her loss too could be thought of as like the loss of a child. 6. Yet, since her children survived her and I was in good health - it was very wrong, but it was what she herself prayed for - her premature end saved her from terrible afflictions. My younger son, just past his fifth year, went first, and took away one of the two lights of my life. 7. I have no desire to flaunt my troubles or exaggerate the causes of my tears: I only wish there were some way of making them less! But how can I conceal what beauty he showed in his face, what charm in his talk, what flashes of intellect, what solid possession of a calm and even at that age almost unbelievably lofty mind? This was a child who would have deserved love, even if he had been another's. 8. It was a further trick of Fortune, meant to torment me even more, that this delightful child preferred me to his nurses, preferred me to the grandmother who brought him up, preferred me to all those who commonly win the affections of little children. 9. This is why I have reason to be grateful for the grief I had suffered, a few months before, in the death of his excellent mother, who was indeed beyond all praise. I have, you see, less cause for weeping on my own account than for feeling glad on hers. Henceforward, I depended entirely on the hopes and delights given to me by my little Quintilian. He could be comfort enough. 10. He had shown not just promising flowers, like his brother, but, by the time he entered his tenth year, sure and well-formed fruits. I swear by my own troubles, by the misery that my heart knows, by those spirits of the departed who are the gods of my grief, that I saw in him excellences not only of natural capacity for learning (and I never saw anything more outstanding in all my experience) and of application, which even at that age needed no compulsion (as his teachers know), but also of honesty, piety, humanity, and generosity, such that one might indeed have found in them cause to fear the lightning stroke; for it has often been observed that early ripening means a quicker fall, and that there is some envious power that cuts short great promise, presumably to prevent our blessings being prolonged beyond what man is allowed to enjoy. 11. He had all the fortuitous advantages too: a clear and pleasant voice, a sweetness of speech, and an exact pronunciation of every letter in either of the two languages, as though it was the one he was born to. All this was still only promise: he had other qualities already ripe - constancy, dignity, strength to face even pain and fear. With what courage, with what admiration on the part of his doctors, did he bear his eight months of illness! How he comforted me in his last hours! How, when he was failing and no longer part of our world, did the wanderings of his delirium dwell on school and on his studies! 12. O my unfulfilled hope, did I indeed see your fading eyes, your fleeting breath? Did I have strength to embrace your cold and lifeless body, to receive your last breath, and still myself breathe the common air, I who deserve to bear these torments and to think these thoughts? 13. <Have I then lost> you, when your recent adoption into a consular family brought you nearer to hopes of the highest offices, when you were destined to be the son-in-law and nephew of a praetor, when you were a candidate for your grandfather's eloquence - I, your father, who live on only to suffer? May my endurance of life - not indeed my wish for it - make reparation to you for the rest of my days! It is in vain that we shift all our troubles on to Fortune. No one mourns long save by his own fault. 14. But I live on, and I must find some reason for living, and must believe those learned men who have held that literature is our only solace in trouble. Yet, if ever my present emotions subside enough to allow other thoughts to find a place amid all these griefs, I should have some justification for asking pardon for my delay. For who could be surprised at the postponement of a work when the wonder is that it was not broken off altogether? 15. And if some parts of it are less finished than the parts that I had begun when my afflictions were less, let this be set down to the tyranny of Fortune, who has at any rate weakened, even if she has not extinguished, whatever modest powers my talents had. It is hard to bear Fortune, but easy to despise her; and this is yet another reason why I should show more defiance, and pull myself to my feet. She has left herself nothing more to do to me; indeed, out of these troubles, she has brought me an unhappy, but completely certain, freedom from anxiety. 16. It is only fair that my labours should be well thought of, if only because I persevere in them for no useful purpose of my own. All this effort is directed to the service of others - if, that is, there is anything serviceable in what I write. Like my estate, this is something I shall leave to others than those for whom I was getting it ready.[7]

---

[7] 'Haec, Marcelle *(Marce* Russell*)* Vitori, ex tua voluntate maxime ingressus, tum si qua ex nobis ad iuvenes bonos pervenire posset utilitas, novissime paene etiam necessitate quadam officii delegati mihi sedulo laborabam, respiciens tamen illam curam meae voluptatis, quod filio, cuius eminens ingenium sollicitam quoque parentis diligentiam merebatur, hanc optimam partem relicturus hereditatis videbar, ut, si me, quod aecum et optabile fuit, fata intercepissent, praeceptore tamen patre uteretur. 2 At me fortuna id agentem diebus ac noctibus festinantemque metu meae mortalitatis ita subito orbavit ut laboris mei fructus ad neminem minus quam ad me pertineret. Illum enim de quo summa conceperam et in quo spem unicam senectutis reponebam, repetito vulnere orbitatis amisi. 3 Quid nunc agam? aut quem ultra esse usum mei dis repugnantibus credam? Nam ita forte accidit ut eum quoque librum quem de causis corruptae eloquentiae emisi iam scribere adgressus ictu simili ferirer. Unum igitur optimum fuit, infaustum opus et quidquid hoc est in me infelicium litterarum super inmaturum funus consumpturis viscera mea flammis inicere neque hanc impiam vivacitatem novis insuper curis fatigare. 4 Quis enim mihi bonus parens ignoscat si studere amplius possum, ac non oderit hanc animi mei firmitatem si quis in me alius usus uocis quam ut incusem deos superstes omnium meorum, nullam in terras despicere providentiam tester? si non meo casu, cui tamen nihil obici nisi quod vivam potest, at illorum certe quos utique inmeritos mors acerba damnavit, erepta prius mihi matre eorundem, quae nondum expleto aetatis undevicesimo anno duos enixa filios, quamvis acerbissimis rapta fatis, <non> infelix decessit. 5 Ego vel hoc uno malo sic eram adflictus ut me iam nulla fortuna posset efficere felicem. Nam cum, omni virtute quae in feminas cadit functa, insanabilem attulit marito dolorem, tum aetate tam puellari, praesertim meae comparata, potest et ipsa numerari inter vulnera orbitatis. 6 Liberis tamen superstitibus et - quod nefas erat [sera] sed optabat ipsa - me salvo, maximos cruciatus praecipiti via effugit. Mihi filius minor quintum egressus annum prior alterum ex duobus eruit lumen. 7 Non sum ambitiosus in malis nec augere lacrimarum causas uolo, utinamque esset ratio minuendi: sed dissimulare qui possum quid ille gratiae in vultu, quid iucunditatis in sermone, quos ingenii igniculos, quam substantiam placidae et (quod scio vix posse credi) iam tum altae mentis ostenderit. Qualis amorem quicumque alienus infans mereretur. 8 Illud vero insidiantis quo me validius cruciaret fortunae fuit, ut ille mihi blandissimus me suis nutricibus, me aviae educanti, me omnibus qui sollicitare illas aetates solent anteferret. 9 Quapropter illi dolori quem ex matre optima atque omnem laudem supergressa paucos ante menses ceperam gratulor. Minus enim est quod flendum meo nomine quam quod illius gaudendum est. Una post haec Quintiliani mei spe ac voluptate nitebar, et poterat sufficere solacio. 10 Non enim flosculos, sicut prior, sed iam decimum aetatis ingressus annum certos ac deformatos fructus ostenderat. Iuro per mala mea, per infelicem conscientiam, per illos manes, numina mei doloris, has me in illo vidisse virtutes, non ingenii modo ad percipiendas disciplinas, quo nihil praestantius cognovi plurima expertus, studiique iam tum non coacti (sciunt praeceptores), sed probitatis pietatis humanitatis liberalitatis, ut prorsus posset hinc esse tanti fulminis metus, quod observatum fere est celerius occidere festinatam maturitatem, et esse nescio quam quae spes tantas decerpat invidiam, ne videlicet ultra quam homini datum est nostra provehantur. 11 Etiam illa fortuita

If literary categories are applied, we shall immediately find in this proem the combined presence of a descriptive and a programmatic proem, together with *laudatio*,
consolatio,[8] and autobiography. The work is concluded by some reflections of a
philosophical nature, and the explicit final testamentary instructions.[9]

---

aderant omnia, vocis iucunditas claritasque, oris suavitas et in utracumque lingua, tamquam ad eam
demum natus esset, expressa proprietas omnium litterarum. Sed hae spes adhuc: illa matura, constantia,
gravitas, contra dolores etiam ac metus robur. Nam quo ille animo, qua medicorum admiratione mensum
octo ualetudinem tulit! Ut me in supremis consolatus est! Quam etiam deficiens iamque non noster ipsum
illum alienatae mentis errorem circa scholas, litteras habuit! 12 Tuosne ego, o meae spes inanes, labentis
oculos, tuum fugientem spiritum vidi? Tuum corpus frigidum exsangue complexus, animam recipere
auramque communem haurire amplius potui, dignus his cruciatibus quos fero, dignus his cogitationibus?
13 Tene consulari nuper adoptione ad omnium spes honorum propius admotum, te avunculo praetori
generum destinatum, te [omnium spes] avitae eloquentiae candidatum, superstes parens tantum <in> poe-
nas: et si non cupido lucis, certe patientia vindicet te reliqua mea aetate; nam frustra mala omnia ad
crimen fortunae relegamus. Nemo nisi sua culpa diu dolet. 14 Sed vivimus et aliqua vivendi ratio
quaerenda est, credendumque doctissimis hominibus, qui unicum adversorum solacium litteras
putaverunt. Si quando tamen ita resederit praesens impetus ut aliqua tot luctibus alia cogitatio inseri possit, non iniuste petierim morae veniam. Quis enim dilata studia miretur quae potius non abrupta esse
mirandum est? 15 Tum si qua fuerint minus effecta iis quae levius adhuc adflicti coeperamus, imperitanti
fortunae remittantur, quae si quid mediocrium alioqui in nostro ingenio virium fuit, ut non extinxerit,
debilitavit tamen. Sed vel propter hoc nos contumacius erigamus, quod illam ut perferre nobis difficile
est, ita facile contemnere. Nihil enim sibi adversus me reliquit, et infelicem quidem sed certissimam
tamen attulit mihi ex his malis securitatem. 16 Boni autem consulere nostrum laborem vel propter hoc
aecum est, quod in nullum iam proprium usum perseveramus, sed omnis haec cura alienas utilitates, si
modo quid utile scribimus, spectat. Nos miseri sicut facultates patrimonii nostri, ita hoc opus aliis
praeparabamus, aliis relinquemus'.

8   On *laudatio* and *consolatio* cf. R. Lattimore, *Themes in Greek and Latin Epitaphs*, Urbana: The
University of Illinois Press 1942; R. Kassel, *Untersuchungen zur griechischen und römischen Konso-
lation-literatur* (= Zetemata Heft 18), Munich: Beck 1958; H.Th. Johann, *Trauer und Trost*, Munich:
Fink 1968; J. Soffel, *Die Regeln Menanders für die Leichenrede. In ihrer Tradition dargestellt, herausgegeben, übersetzt und kommentiert*, Meisenheim am Glan: Hain 1974; M.G. Ciani, 'La *consolatio*
nei tragici greci', *Bollettino dell'Istituto di Filologia Greca dell'Università di Padova* 2 (1975) pp. 89-
129; A. Traina, *Lucio Anneo Seneca, Le consolazioni. A Marcia-Alla Madre Elvia-A Polibio*, Introduzione, traduzione e note di A. Traina, Milan: Rizzoli 1987, pp. 9-39; L. Pernot, *La rhétorique de
l'éloge dans le monde gréco-romain*, Paris: Institut d'Etudes Augustiniennes 1993, pp. 106ff.; 600ff.;
Id., *La rhétorique dans l'antiquité*, Paris: Le Livre de Poche 2000, pp. 261ff.; M. Vallozza, 'Laudatio'
(Antike), in: G. Ueding (ed.), *Historisches Wörterbuch der Rhetorik* 5, Tübingen: Niemeyer 2001,
pp. 50-56.

9   On this and the other proems of the *Institutio oratoria* is again useful T. Janson, *Latin Prose Prefaces.
Studies in Literary Conventions* (= Acta Universitatis Stockholmiensis. Studia Latina Stockholmiensia
XIII), Stockholm-Göteborg-Uppsala: Almqvist & Wiksell 1964, especially pp. 50-60. As regards the
rhetorical functions of proems in the ancient technical tradition, see L. Calboli Montefusco, *Exordium
Narratio Epilogus. Studi sulla teoria retorica greca e romana delle parti del discorso*, Bologna: Clueb
1988, pp. 1-32. More generally, it would appear to be appropriate to underline the present renewed interest of scholars in the opening and closing parts of ancient works. Cf. recently P. Castronuovo, E. D'An-
gelo, L. Spina and M. Squillante, *La fine dell'inizio. Una riflessione e quattro studi su* incipit *ed* explicit
nella letteratura latina. A cura di L. Spina, Naples: Pubblicazioni del Dipartimento di Filologia Classica
"F. Arnaldi" dell'Università degli Studi di Napoli Federico II, 17, 1999; Fr.M. Dunn and Th. Cole (eds.),
Beginnings in Classical Literature, Cambridge: Cambridge University Press 1992; C. Santini and N.
Scivoletto (eds.), *Prefazioni, prologhi, proemi di opere tecnico-scientifiche latine*, I-II, Rome: Herder
1990-1992; C. Santini, N. Scivoletto and L. Zurli (eds.), *Prefazioni, prologhi, proemi di opere tecnico-
scientifiche latine*, III, Roma: Herder 1998.

In itself, the proem does not display a close thematic connection with the subject discussed in the sixth book, except for one significant aspect to which I will return below. The primary reason for the composition of this proem was that Quintilian felt the need to communicate that, after the death of his only surviving son, the natural heir of his material and spiritual wealth, his expectations, his attitude to his studies and his profession, and even his attitude to life, had radically changed. The present mourning and grief, which is added to the past suffering, with the resulting inevitable sense of abandonment, and the loss of the only hope of a continuity on the family and intellectual levels, had determined an emotional upset, which Quintilian elaborated, expressing it and transforming it into something else.

Like the proem to the fourth book, this proem is justified by an event which is external to the composition of the work. In the former case, it was a question of recalling and celebrating the official appointment of Quintilian as educator of the imperial heirs, whereas in this case, it was an event of his private life.

The manifestation of joy for the position obtained, and the deference paid to the sovereign required an invocation to the gods, which he had never included before, that they would assist him in the continuation of his studies and his work. Of course, the first divinity whose benevolent aid he invoked was Domitian himself (IV.pr.4f.).

> 4. No one is surprised that the frequent practice of the greatest poets was to invoke the Muses not only at the beginning of their works, but also later on, when they came to some particularly important passage, to repeat their vows and as it were offer up fresh prayers; 5. surely then I may be pardoned for doing what I omitted to do when I first began this work, and calling on all the gods to help me, and in the first place on that God than whom no other power gives such present help or looks with more favour on learning; may he inspire me with genius equal to the new expectations he has aroused for me, may he be favourable to me and come willingly to my aid, and make me what he has believed me to be![10]

Essentially, the honour granted by the emperor recognised such merits in Quintilian, which were to be displayed even more from then on, in the composition of the *Institutio* and, consequently, this honour warranted a new ritual beginning of the work. The affinity with literary and poetic compositions is mentioned by Quintilian himself (pr.4). The awareness of the literary nature of this form of proem, rather than its rhetorical nature, allows us to interpret also the proem of the sixth book better. Although it does not appear at the beginning of the second section of the work, this proem is placed at the end of the first one, and clearly assumes the status of a 'central proem', like some central proems of Ennius (*Annales*, VII.213-219 V.[2]), perhaps Lucretius (*De rerum natura*, IV.1-25), and Virgil (*Georgica*, IV.3.1-22; *Aeneis*, VII.37-45)[11]. It is a proem that is at the same time expository (of the subject dis-

---

[10] 4. Quod si nemo miratur poetas maximos saepe fecisse ut non solum initiis operum suorum Musas invocarent, sed provecti quoque longius, cum ad aliquem graviorem venissent locum, repeterent vota et velut nova precatione uterentur, 5. mihi quoque profecto poterit ignosci si, quod initio quo primum hanc materiam inchoavi non feceram, nunc omnis in auxilium deos ipsumque in primis quo neque praesentius aliud nec studiis magis propitium numen est invocem, ut, quantum nobis expectationis adiecit, tantum ingenii adspiret dexterque ac volens adsit et me qualem esse credidit faciat.

[11] I adopt the term 'central proem' here, following G.B. Conte, *Virgilio. Il genere e i suoi confini*, Milan: Garzanti 1984, pp. 121ff.

cussed) and programmatic (dealing with the modalities of the discussion, and the conscious use of the intervention of the author, following a very strict tradition).

The subject under examination is combined with the point of view from which it is examined, thus creating an opposition between the subject of the song (in poetry), the illustration (in prose), and how the song or the illustration is presented. The result is something new which maintains a respect for traditional elements, but also expresses highly original aspects, strongly motivated by a new cultural and literary context, together with, especially in poetry, the inequivocable explicitation of the self. In particular, in the proem to the sixth book, Quintilian clearly underlines the passage from one part of the work to the other, reconstructing the events that determined the composition of the *Institutio oratoria*, confessing that he had always hoped to leave this possession, more than any other, to his son (VI.pr.1), and questioning himself about the attitude to be assumed from this moment on (VI.pr.3). But nobody suffers for long, unless it is his own fault (VI.pr.13), and as we are alive, we must find a new reason for living. Perhaps his studies can be the only comfort, at least this is what men of greater culture and wisdom have suggested (VI.pr.14). His decision to press on undauntedly with the composition of the work gives him some faint hope for the future: if destiny does not continue to torment him, Quintilian will go on with his work, and if there is a delay in its publication, he trusts he will be excused. Indeed, realising that those who have suffered the hardest blows of destiny, and the greatest grief, become stronger than others, and can even despise fortune because they have nothing more to fear from it, he confirms his decision to continue his work. He is certain that nobody will be able to accuse him of any personal interest in it, because the *Institutio oratoria* will be directed to others, and not to his adored son, seeing that others will be the heirs of his fortune (VI.pr.14-16). The proem is expository in the parts in which he describes the work already performed and what still remains to be done; the rest of it is programmatic.

The authorial 'I' is at the centre of the new undertaking, and is situated inside the work.[12] The master, the intellectual with all his technical baggage, and all his professional and human experience, establishes a new relationship with his own work; he analyses himself, proposes himself as a model of behaviour for possible readers, in the name of his studies. This procedure also makes use of the long digression about his sad private affairs, culminating in the funeral oration for his late son, and then for his other son and his young wife, who had also died prematurely (VI.pr.3-13). The consolation, or better, self-consolation that derives from this is based on the sublimation of grief in writing. The final result is that future orators will have at their disposal not only the technical teachings and the professional experience of the mas-

---

[12]   I do not intend to discuss here the complex problem of the relationship between biography, autobiography and literary work (see, e.g., the recent publications by G. Arrighetti and F. Montanari (eds.), *La componente autobiografica nella poesia greca e latina fra realtà e artificio letterario. Atti del Convegno (Pisa, 16-17 maggio 1991)*, Pisa: Giardini 1993 and I. Gallo and L. Nicastri (eds.), *Biografia e autobiografia degli antichi e dei moderni. Atti delle «Prime Giornate Filologiche Salernitane» (Salerno-Fisciano, 2-4 maggio 1994)* (= Pubblicazioni dell'Università degli Studi di Salerno - Sezione Atti Convegni, Miscellanee, 45), Naples: Edizioni Scientifiche Italiane 1995). However, as I believe it may be of interest to evaluate in this perspective the autobiographical, or at least personal, details mentioned in the *Institutio oratoria*, I will deal with them on another occasion.

ter. In him, in his person, they will also have a model of behaviour: Quintilian's grief and the possibility to overcome it with the help of rhetorical studies[13] are highly effective pedagogic instruments. The technical knowledge is thus enriched by personal experience; autobiographic reflection becomes a pedagogic precept.

5. CONCLUSION

In conclusion, I would like to return to the very close thematic link between proem and subject discussed in the sixth book, making this one consideration: Quintilian speaks of his suffering, and reveals his emotions and his despair in mournful tones in the proem of the same book in which he introduces the 'pathetic' *peroratio* (Chapter 1) and deals with the arousing of feelings (Chapter 2); in the latter, he describes the images that the mind creates by means of imagination and translates into words by means of the creative power of *enárgeia*.[357] Everything would appear to display a harmonious correspondence: the distressing personal experience and the evocation from the depths of suffering expressed in the proem are reflected in the different chapters of the book in the description of specific technical subjects of rhetoric, and become effective, exemplary discourse.

---

[13] The 'therapy' of the word, which follows confession - a 'diagnosis' of the state of pathological suffering caused by bereavement, brings us back to the homology between the doctor and the orator, between the art of medicine and that of rhetoric. On this subject, see the recent, extremely useful contribution of I. Mastrorosa, 'Medicina e retorica nell'*Institutio oratoria* di Quintiliano', *Sileno* 22 (1996) pp. 229-280.
[14] *Inst. or.* VI.2.29-33. On *phantasía* and *enárgeia*, cf. H. Lausberg, *Elementi di retorica*, tr. it., Bologna: Il Mulino 1969 (= 1949), pp.197-198; Id., *Handbuch der Literarischen Rhetorik*, Stuttgart: Steiner 1990³ (= 1960), pp. 399f.; B. Mortara Garavelli, *Le figure retoriche. Effetti speciali della lingua*, Milan: Bompiani 1993, pp. 120-121; Ead. (see note 2), p. 238; B. Cassin, 'Procédures sophistiques pour construire l'évidence', in: C. Lévy and L. Pernot (eds.), *Dire l'évidence (Philosophie et rhétorique antiques)* (= Cahiers de philosophie de l'Université de Paris XII-Val de Marne, 2), Paris-Montréal: l'Harmattan 1997, pp. 15-29; R. Webb, 'Mémoire et imagination: les limites de l'*enargeia* dans la théorie rhétorique grecque', in: Lévy-Pernot (see above), pp. 229-248; A. Manieri, *L'immagine poetica nella teoria degli antichi. Phantasia ed enargeia*, Pisa-Rome: Istituti Editoriali e Poligrafici Internazionali 1998, especially pp. 123-154.

J.A.E. BONS & R.T. LANE

QUINTILIAN VI.2: ON EMOTION

1. TRANSLATION (BONS & LANE)

[1] Even though this part of judicial speeches consists first and foremost of appeals to the emotions and I have of necessity spoken of this subject before, I was not yet able – nor was there compelling reason for me to do so – to bring this topic to an end in and by itself. Therefore now the task remains, which is most important to obtain what we desire but at the same time more difficult than anything previously considered: to stir the minds of the judges and to mould or, as it were, transform them into the state which we intend. [2] Where required by the subject-matter I did already say a few things on this, while my purpose was rather to show what ought to be done rather than to set forth the means by which we can attain it. Now it is time for a more profound and systematic treatment of the subject as a whole.

1.1 Significance of the emotions

[3] As we have already said, each and every part of a speech offers room for emotions. Their nature is complicated and should not be dealt with in passing, since there is nothing that contributes more to the impact of speaking. It may be that a slight and limited vein of talent, with the help of instruction and experience, is capable of producing and bringing to a certain fruition other tasks: certainly there is and always was a considerable number of speakers of adequate skill to be able to recover useful material for proofs. I for one do not look down on them, but in my opinion they have limited usefulness: they can provide the judge with information that is lacking and (to tell you frankly how I feel) they are well suited to instruct talented speakers about the facts of the case at hand. But the man who is able to rob away a judge's self control and to bring him into the intended state of mind, and whose words can bring about an irresistible urge to weep or be angry, such a man has always been the exception.

[4] Yet this is what dominates in the courts, in this respect Lady Eloquence reigns! More often than not arguments arise from the case itself and a larger number is always available on behalf of the better case. Thus, who wins the trial because of them knows this at least, that his advocate did not fail him. [5] However, when it is necessary to bring forceful pressure to bear on the minds of the judges and to draw away their attention from the very contemplation of the facts, then the task proper of the orator comes into play. No instruction from the litigant provides this, and neither can one find it in the official records of the case. For it is indeed by proofs that judges can be made to believe that our case is the stronger, but the emotions make them even

to want to believe: and what they want, they also do believe. [6] For when they begin to feel anger, good will, enmity or pity, they look upon the case as their own. Like somebody who is in love can not be the judge of beauty, because his mind directs his sense of sight, in the same way a judge loses every rational capacity to discern the facts when he is beset by emotions. He is carried away by the tide and as it were surrenders himself to the rushing stream. [7] Thus it is the verdict which shows what the arguments and evidence succeeded in doing, but when a judge has been moved by the orator, how he feels can be observed while he still sits and listens. When those tears flow – which most perorations aim to accomplish –, is that not a verdict for all to see? It is to this, therefore, that the orator must apply himself, 'there lie the task and toil', and without it all the rest is bare, barren, weak and unattractive: so such an extent is, as it were, the living force and soul of his work in the emotions.

1.2 Definition and typology of the emotions

[8] Now, if we follow ancient tradition, of the emotions there are two kinds: the first the Greeks call *pathos*, which we render correctly and appropriately with the word 'emotion'; the second is *êthos*, for which in my view the Latin language lacks a term. 'Morals' is in use, and hence that part of philosophy known as *êthikê* is called *philosophia moralis*. [9] But on close inspection of the character of the subject by itself, it seems to me that it is not so much 'morals' which is referred to, but rather a certain particular feature of morals: for the term 'morals' includes every state of mind. In a more cautious approach it has been attempted to grasp the sense of the term rather than to translate words: *pathos* is said to be the excited emotions, *ethos* the calm and gentle ones; the former are the strongly aroused, the latter the subdued; hence, the first ones command and serve to cause disturbance, the second persuade and create goodwill.

[10] Some add that *ethos* is continuous, *pathos* momentary. While I admit that this indeed happens in many cases, I do believe that there are quite a few subjects demanding continuous emotion. The more gentle emotions, however, demand no less technical skill and experience, even if not the same level of force and vehemence. In fact they are present in a majority of cases, and even in a certain sense in all. [11] For if one can say that no subject treated by an orator does not belong to the domain of ethics, anything he says on the honourable and useful, or on action to undertake or avoid, can be termed *ethos*. In the opinion of some recommending and excusing are the particular elements of this task, and I do not deny that they belong to it, but I do not agree that they are the only ones. [12] I'd rather add the following: *pathos* and *ethos* sometimes are of the same nature, in the sense that the one is a stronger variant of the other, as love is a *pathos* and affection an *ethos*. At other moments they differ, as in perorations: there usually *ethos* is used to calm down what *pathos* has excited.

1.3 The nature of ethos

However, I have to provide an explanation of this word accurately, because it seems to me that the term itself is not sufficiently clear in its meaning.

[13] Let *ethos* as I understand it and as I demand it from speakers be defined thus: it commends itself before all else by goodness, and is not only mild and calm, but especially also friendly, civil, and attractive and pleasant to an audience. Its expression has as its most important quality that everything seems to flow naturally from the circumstances and persons involved and that the speaker's moral attitude is revealed by his words and can somehow be recognized.

[14] Without a doubt this happens first and foremost between persons intimately connected, whenever we tolerate, forgive, offer satisfaction or give warning, while anger or hate are absent. Still, one has to differentiate on the one hand between the moderation shown by a father towards his son, a teacher towards his student, and a husband towards his wife (they let the affection for the persons who have done them wrong come first and they do not induce dislike against them except by expressing their love), and on the other hand when an old man is insulted by a young man unrelated to him, or a man of high rank by somebody of lower position. In the latter case outrage is called for, in the former also being deeply moved. [15] Also the following are of the same nature, albeit less moving: to ask a pardon because of youthfulness or to apologize for infatuation. Sometimes a gentle mockery of somebody else's state of excitement is a result of this type, but not from these sources alone.

Much more appropriate to this has always been the quality of pretence, the *eironeia* in giving satisfaction or asking questions, which aims at understanding something different from what is said. [16] From the same source that even stronger emotion directed towards stirring hatred originates, when the very fact of our yielding to our opponents is understood as a silent reproach of lacking self-restraint. For precisely by this yielding of ours they stand out as troublesome and unbearable persons, and they fail to see in their tendency for abuse or their affectation for boldness that making someone the object of ill-will is more effective than insult: ill-will creates ill-will against our opponents, insult against ourselves.

[17] A kind of in-between position is taken by the emotion that stems from love and from the desire for friends and relatives: it is stronger than *êthos* and weaker than *pathos*. And we have good reason to have called *êthê* those school exercises in which we portray boorish, superstitious, greedy and cowardly persons according to the theme given. For if we can say that *êthê* are moral attitudes, then we use those as a source for our speech if we represent them.

[18] Finally every *êthos* demands a good and friendly man. While the orator should, if possible, make these qualities evident in his client, he should also have them himself or should seem to have them. This will be especially useful in cases where he will produce trustworthiness on the basis of his goodness. Who in speaking gives the impression of being a bad man, actually is a bad speaker, because his words do not come across as right: otherwise his *êthos* would have become apparent. [19] That is the reason why the manner of speaking here should be calm and mild: haughtiness and especially self-elevation and loftiness are out of the question. To use fitting, pleasant and convincing words is sufficient, and therefore the middle style of speaking is most appropriate.

1.4 Pathos and the Dramatic

[20] To be distinguished from this is so-called *pathos*, for which we correctly use the word emotion. To indicate the distinction between both as closely as possible, *êthos* rather resembles comedy, *pathos* tragedy. Here one is practically entirely concerned with hatred, fear, ill-will and pity. From which sources to derive these is evident to all and has been stated by us in the treatment of the Introduction and the Peroration. [21] Fear, by the way, I prefer to see as of two kinds, the fear we feel and the fear we cause. The same goes for ill-will, for it can cause feeling of ill-will or being the object of ill-will. The first refers to persons, the second to facts, in which case there is even more work involved for the speech. For some facts are considered grave by themselves, like parricide, murder and poisoning, but others have to made such. [22] This happens when it is made clear that what we have suffered is of a more grave nature than what is elsewhere considered an evil, as for example in Vergil: *O blessed, before all other maidens, daughter of Priam / at your enemy's tomb under the high walls of Troy / doomed to die* (for how miserable is the fate of Andromache, if compared to her Polyxena is said to be blessed). [23] Another example is when we intensify the injustice done to us by saying that what is a far less evil is impossible to bear: 'if you had struck him, you would have had no defence: but you have wounded him.' We will consider this in more detail later when we speak of amplification. For the moment suffice it to note that to excite emotion not only aims at presenting what actually is grievous and lamentable, but also at making what is usually taken to be endurable seem more grave. This happens when we say that insult is a more serious injustice than assault, or that disgrace is a more serious punishment than death. [24] It is here that the force of eloquence is to be found: not only is the judge inescapably led towards the point where the nature of the case itself would have brought him, but also that a previously non existent state of emotion is effected or an already existent one is intensified. This is what is called *deinosis* or 'intensification': the speech gives additional impact to what is shameful, hard to bear or causing ill-will. In this quality more than in all others Demosthenes was most accomplished.

1.5 Methodology

[25] If I were satisfied to just repeat the traditional rules, I would have said enough on this subject by leaving out nothing of what I read or was taught, inasmuch, that is, as it was sound. But I have a mind to bring to light what lies hidden and to open up the very deepest secrets of this topic, which I have learned not by any tradition of some kind, but from my own experience and nature. [26] The most important thing in stirring the emotions is – and this is how I feel about this – to be moved oneself. To simulate grief, anger or indignation can sometimes become ridiculous, when we have only adapted our words and facial expression accordingly, but not our state of mind. What other reason is there when people in grief, particularly when their sorrow is recent, seem most eloquent in what they say, or when anger sometimes lends eloquence to the uneducated, but this: that the power of thought and the authenticity of their moral attitude is upon them. [27] Therefore, if our intention is to come

across as authentic, we must become like people who actually are affected by emotion and our speech must originate from the same state of mind as we wish the judge to have. Will he become sad when he hears me speak with that intention but without feeling sadness myself? Will he become angry if the one who stirs anger and demands it is lacking any like passion? Will he shed tears when the speaker's eyes are dry? Impossible. [28] Only flame can cause a fire, only moisture can make us wet, and only what has colour itself can transfer it to another thing. The first requirement is, in conclusion, that what we wish to be strongly present with the judge, must be strongly present with ourselves, and that we ourselves are emotionally moved before we attempt to move others.

[29] But how can we stir these emotions in ourselves? We are, after all, not master of our own emotions. Nevertheless I will try to say something about this. There exist what the Greeks call *phantasiai* – which we can perfectly well call 'visions' – by which images of things absent are presented to our mind in such as way that we get the impression to see them with our eyes and take them for actually there. [30] The man who has apprehended these well will be emotionally most effective. Some call the man who can imagine most realistically things, words and actions *euphantasiôtos*. We can easily succeed at it too, if we want. When our mind relaxes, when we entertain vain hopes and have what one could call day-dreams, do not these visions about which I speak occur to us, so that we imagine to be travelling, sailing on a ship, taking part in battle, speaking to crowds, having at our disposal wealth we do not posses? Can we not turn these illusions into something useful? [31] Let's say I make a complaint before court for the murder of a man. Shall I not have before my eyes everything which in the actual case would presumably have happened? Will not the murderer suddenly make his move? Will not the victim tremble in fear, cry for help, ask for mercy or try to escape? Will I not see the fatal blow, the man falling? Will not the blood, the face's paleness, the groans of agony and finally the last breath be engraved in my mind?

[32] This results in *enargeia*, which Cicero calls 'illustratio' or vividness and 'evidentia' or distinctness, which seems to depict rather than to give an account, and the emotions will follow just as if we were part of the events themselves. Do not the following lines originate from such visions: 'suddenly the shuttle flies from her hands, spilled is a day's worth spinning' or 'the wound splitting open his smooth chest' [33] or that horse at the funeral of Pallas 'stripped from trappings'? Well, and has the same poet not fully apprehended the scene of the moment of dying to be able to say 'and in death he remembers sweet home Argos'. [34] When it is pity we must arouse, we must believe that what we complain about has befallen ourselves and of this we must convince our mind. We ourselves must be the ones whose grave, undeserved and sad fates we lament, and we must not treat the case as somebody else's, but we must for the moment identify with their sorrow. Then we will speak the words as we would have used them ourselves being in a similar predicament. [35] Many times I have seen actors in tragedy and comedy after having put down their mask at the end of a rather intense performance leaving still in tears. If the mere delivery in what others have written can cause such excitement by fictitious emotion, what will we be able to achieve who have to call these words to mind in order

to be moved as being in the place of those in jeopardy. [36] But also in school it is fitting to be moved by facts themselves and to imagine them to be true, all the more so because there we more often speak as litigants than as advocates. We impersonate an orphan, a shipwrecked man, a man in grave danger: what use would it be to play their roles, unless we also assume the emotion?

I considered it necessary not to conceal these things, by which, I believe, I have come to acquire a certain name for my talent, inasmuch as I possess it now or once possessed it. Many times I was indeed moved: then not only my tears were the signs, but also my paleness and grief, as if it were real.

2. COMMENTARY (BONS)

Quintilian's account of the role of the emotions in rhetoric, as he presents it in his *Institutio oratoria* VI.2, has been qualified as confusing and muddled. Among the criticisms directed against it is his supposed lack of precision, which manifests itself by a lack of clear definitions of the notions involved, a conflation of precedent traditions and discussions, and a failure to distinguish between the role and function of the advocate and his client.[1] More recently, Chr. Gill has argued that Quintilian's account is less muddled than it seems and that it essentially is a development of Cicero's ideas as set forth in his *De oratore* and *Orator*.[2] As in other cases, here too Quintilian seems to prove himself to be an admirer and follower of the great man of Roman rhetorical theory and practice.

In what follows, I offer a close reading of this passage and I suggest that the peculiarities of the treatment can be explained by the fact that Quintilian had a leading, basic notion throughout his exposé: the analogy of stage and courtroom, and of orator and actor. Furthermore, as some features of Quintilian's treatment indicate, it seems reasonable to assume that he is not only following Cicero, but that in form of presentation, treatment, and content he also relies on the Aristotelian tradition.

2.1 The significance of emotions

The second chapter of Book VI of the *Institutio oratoria* is explicitly characterized as a separate and general treatment of the emotions: it seeks to give an account of the conscious manipulation by the speaker of the feelings and passions of the judges. In the first two paragraphs this manipulation is qualified as the 'most powerful means of obtaining what we desire' and 'more difficult than any topic previously considered' (*opus...ad obtinenda quae volumus potissimum,...supradictis multo difficilius*). The aim of this task of the rhetorician, i.e. the teacher of rhetoric and the future orator, is to 'move the feelings of the judges, and of moulding and transform-

---

[1]   See F. Solmsen, 'Aristotle and Cicero on the ortaor's playing upon the feelings', *Classical Philology* 33 (1938), pp. 390ff; F. Zucker, *'Anêthopoiêtos*. Eine semasiologische Untersuchung aus der antiken Rhetorik und Ethik', in: Id., *Semantica, Rhetorica, Ethica*, Berlin: Akademie Verlag, 1963; E. Keuls, *Plato and Greek Painting*, Leiden: Brill, 1978.
[2]   Chr. Gill, 'The *Ethos/Pathos* distinction in rhetorical and literary criticism', *Classical Quarterly* 34 (1984), pp. 149-166.

ing them to the disposition we desire' (*movendi iudicum animos atque in eum quem volumus habitum formandi et velut transfigurandi*). It is important to note that Quintilian aims for a systematic treatment of this subject. Thus far, his remarks on emotions had been made in passing and related to another subject, but now he takes a step further. Previously, he had only made remarks on *what* (*quid oporteret fieri*) ought to be done with regard to the emotions, now he wants to show *in what manner* (*quo... modo consequi possemus*) they can be manipulated. In short, what he will offer is a systematic treatment of the complete subject (*omnis rei... ratio*).

The systematic method (*ratio*) Quintilian is using is comparable to what is known as the Aristotelian dialectical method of investigation. In principle, this method consists of three stages: first, to record and collect the existing accepted opinions on the issue, in Aristotelian terms the *endoxa* or *phainomena* (the stage, therefore, of 'observation'); secondly, to critically evaluate these opinions and to point out difficulties and problems that arise from this evaluation; and finally, to present a solution by the formulation of an improved perspective on the issue, on the basis of the results of the preceding stages and of one's own conceptualization. This method, devised to tackle theoretical problems, Aristotle also adapts for 'practical' issues like the field of ethics.[3] Thus the results of the investigation are adapted to a didactical purpose. Like Aristotle, Quintilian has a similar didactic purpose: his investigation of the emotions is not a strictly theoretical analysis, but provides valid focal points from which to examine the issue and thus practical information for the student of rhetoric. As he already states in the proemium to Book I (c. 23): his purpose is 'to instruct pupils with scientific knowledge' (*scientia studiosos instruere*) and 'to feed their capacity for speaking and strengthen their powers of eloquence' (*facundiam alere et vires eloquentiae augere*). In this passage Quintilian follows the Aristotelian method: the 'movements' of his discussion in 8-13 are (1) to treat the accepted tradition (8: *antiquitus traditum*), (2) to evaluate them (9: *spectanti mihi*), (3) to provide discussion of difficulties (10: *adiciunt quidam*), (4) to offer his own perspective (12: *quin illud adhuc adiicio*) and finally to present a new definition (13: *'ethos' id erit*).

Also in accordance with Aristotle's method as applied to practical issues, Quintilian's discussion is as precise as the subject matter allows, and the subject being a rhetorical one, it has less scientific precision than a theoretical discussion. As Aristotle formulated on the treatment of ethics (*Ethica Nichomachea* 1094b 11-13): 'our discussion will be sufficient if a degree of clarity is achieved that befits the subject matter at hand; for one should not demand the same levels of precision on all issues.' (*legoito d' an hikanôs ei kata tên hupokeimenên hulên diasaphêtheiê: to gar akribes ouch homoiôs en hapasi logois epizêteteon*). This point Quintilian explicitly makes in XII.2.11, where he talks about the use an orator makes of philosophical disciplines: 'in speeches one should use these not as precise and detailed as in philosophical discussions, because the speaker must not only instruct his audience, but also move and please it.' (*ea non tam est minute atque concise in actionibus uten-*

---

[3] On Aristotle's dialectical method as applied to a practical issue see his *Ethica Nichomachea*, 1145 b 2-7; in general, see J. Barnes, 'Aristotle and the Method of Ethics', *Revue Internationale de Philosophie* 34 (1980), pp. 490-511; from the Aristotelian perspective, rhetoric too is a practical science.

dum quam in disputationibus, quia non docere modo sed movere etiam ac delectare audientis debet orator). The main reason for this is that, in rhetoric, the audience usually does not consist of intellectuals and philosophically trained people, but of ordinary people without higher education.[4]

At the outset of his discussion, in VI.2.2, Quintilian emphasizes the crucial importance of the emotions (*affectus*) to rhetoric:

> *Nam per totam, ut diximus, causam locus est adfectibus, et eorum non simplex natura nec in transitu tractanda, quo nihil adferre maius vis orandi potest.*
> As we said before, in every part of a speech there is room for emotions. Their nature is complicated and should not be treated cursory, because the power of speech can bring to bear nothing stronger than this.

All the other techniques of rhetoric even a mediocre student can master to a satisfactory degree, so that he is able to find adequate arguments and provide information to a speaker of real eloquence. But precisely in the ability to move the judge emotionally, to have an emotional impact (*vis*), lies the mark of a truly talented speaker (VI.2.3-4):

> *Qui vero iudicem rapere et in quem vellet habitum animi posset perducere, quo dicente flendum irascendumve esset, rarus fuit. Atqui hoc est quod dominetur in iudiciis, haec eloquentia regnat.*
> The man able to sweep the judge with him and bring him to adopt the disposition of mind which he desires, whose words make him irresistibly weep or angry, has always been rare. Still it is this that dominates in the courts, here eloquence reigns.

The case at hand will always provide the orator with arguments, and if the orator finds them he will not have failed as an advocate, a legal advisor, to his client.[5] But when it becomes necessary to have an impact on the judge's mind (*animis iudicum vis adferenda est*) and to distract his attention from the facts (*ab ipsa veri contemplatione abducenda mens*),[6] then the proper task of the orator comes into play. It is true that arguments can convince a judge that one's case is stronger, but the emotions will have the further effect that the judge also wants to believe you: 'and what they wish, they also believe' (*id quod volunt, credunt quoque*,VI.2.5).[7] Thus, the capacity to manipulate the emotions is a talent to be developed rather than an acquired skill, as Quintilian emphasizes again later (c. 25) when he speaks of his own capabilities in this respect (*natura ipsa mihi*).

---

[4] Cf. XII.2.15-20 on the relevance of ethics to the orator; on the nature of the 'rhetorical' audience, see V.14.28-29: 'in those disputes the learned amongst the learned are looking for truth: they scrutinize everything in detail and minutely, and continue to do so until there is clarity and agreement...but a speech must be composed by us to be judged by others, and quite often we have to speak amongst utterly ignorant people who certainly are unacquainted with that learning' (*namque in illis homines docti et inter doctos verum quaerentes minutius et scrupolosius scrutantur omnia et ad liquidum confessumque perducunt...nobis ad aliorum iudicia componenda est oratio et saepius apud omnino imperitos atque illarum certe ignaros litterarum loquendum est*).

[5] On the preparatory stage consisting in the production of a 'memo' listing the main points of a case to be used as the basis of a courtroom-speech see Juvenalis, *Satura*, VI. 244-245, Suetonius, *Julius*, 56 and J. Cousin, *Quintilien. Institution Oratoire*, Tome VI, Paris 1977, p. 24 & n. 2.

[6] I translate *verum* with 'the facts', i.e. the evident state of affairs: on this interpretation of *verum*, see P. Wülfing, 'Verus, verum und veritas', *Glotta* 46 (1968), pp. 278-293.

Quintilian offers a psychological explanation for this phenomenon. If a judge begins to feel anger, or a favourabe disposition, or hate, or pity (*irasci, favere, odisse, misereri*), then from that moment he will think that it is his own case which is tried. Quintilian's words are: *agi iam rem suam existimant*, which makes it clear that the judge, under these circumstances, will identify with the orator's client and regard him, as it were, as a friend.[8] Using the analogy of lovers, Quintilian describes the effect of the emotional impact: just as lovers lose the capacity to form a reasonable judgment (*iudicare*) on the other's outward appearance as a result of the fact that their mind tells them what to see (*sensum oculorum praecipit animus*),[9] so will a judge, being under the sway of emotions, lose his capacity of rationally investigating the facts (*omnem veritatis inquirendae rationem iudex omittit occupatus adfectibus*). A comparable observation is made by Aristotle in his Rhetoric at the beginning of his treatment of the emotions:

> ...*chrêsimôteron...to de diakeisthai pôs ton akroatên eis tas dikas: ou gar tauta phainetai philousi kai misousin, oud' orgizomenois kai praôs echousin, all' ê to parapan hetera ê kata to megethos hetera: tôi men gar philounti, peri hou poieitai tên krisin, ê ouk adikein ê mikra dokei adikein, tôi de misounti tounantion.*
> It is more useful...in forensic cases that the hearer be disposed in a certain way: the same thing does not appear the same to men when they are friendly and when they hate, nor when they are angry and when they are in gentle mood; rather, they will appear either wholly different in kind or different as to magnitude. To the friendly hearer, the person about whom he is making a judgment will seem either to be innocent or guilty of only a minor crime, to the inimical hearer just the opposite.[10]

Both Aristotle and Quintilian point to the effect the emotions have on the hearer/judge: his capacity of judgment is influenced by his emotional disposition, either positively or negatively. It is important to note that Aristotle's analysis of emotional appeal constitutes a new perspective on emotion in the context of persuasion. The traditional idea, as exemplified by Gorgias (e.g. *Palamedes*, 33) and also by the Platonic Socrates (*Apologia* 35b 9 - c 2),[11] holds that emotion is opposed to reason. Seen in terms of affliction and even enchantment, the emotional state impairs or even disables the capacity for rational thought or cognition. The contribution Aristotle made was to show that to respond in an emotional way does not exclude reasoning. To be angered, according to Aristotle, is to respond in accordance with the thought of unjust insult: 'their belief may be erroneous and their anger unrea-

---

[7]   Cf. Caesar, *Bellum Gallicum*, III.8.6: *et quod fere libenter homines id quod volunt credunt*; *Bellum Civile*, II.27.2; and also Demosthenes, *Olynthiacus*, III. 19: *ho gar bouletai, touth' hekastos kai oietai.*

[8]   See also c. 14 where commonplaces *inter coniunctas personas* are given; for Aristotle's notion of friendship as a kind of association or community (*koinônia, oikeiotês*), see *Ethica Nichomachea*, 1171 b 33 f., and on its application in rhetoric, see *Rhetorica*, II.1.1381a 8-11 and 1386a 19-25. It is noteworthy that the parallels in Cicero adduced by J. Cousin, *Études sur Quintilien*, Tome 1, Paris 1935 *ad loc.* (i.e. *Brutus*, 188; *Orator*, 131) only mention the effect of the stirring of emotions and do not contain the phraseology of the notion of friendship.

[9]   On the blindness of love, cf. Plato, *Respublica*, 474 d; Theocritus, X.19 (*tuphlos...d' Erôs*); Lucretius, *De Rerum Natura*, IV.1153 ff.; Horatius, *Saturae*, I.3.38; Propertius, II.14.18.

[10]   Aristoteles, *Rhetorica*, II.1.1377b 31-1378a 2. Translation adapted from L. Cooper, *The Rhetoric of Aristotle*, New York 1960 (= 1932).

[11]   See also Gorgias, *Helena*, 10.14.19; Plato, *Phaedrus*, 267c 7 - d 1.

.

sonable, but their behaviour is intelligent and cognitive in the sense that it is grounded upon a belief which may be criticized and even altered by argumentation.' This viewpoint opened the way for a role of the emotions in all parts of the speech, and not just in the proemium and peroration.[12] Quintilian seems to follow Aristotle in emphasizing that emotion is relevant to all parts of the speech (c. 3). He seems more to adhere to the traditional view when he says that emotion can impart a judge's capacity for rational judgment (c. 5-6).

2.2 Definition and typology of ethos and pathos

Quintilian then proceeds (VI.2.8-9) to discuss the different kinds (species) of emotions, starting with terminology. He identifies two kinds, in accordance with tradition:
- the first is what the Greeks call pathos, which in Latin has the proper equivalent in adfectus;
- the second is êthos, for which there does not exist, says Quintilian, an equivalent Latin word, but which is referred to by mores. Not satisfied by this, he suggests another, more correct equivalent, which is closer to the nature of the matter: morum quaedam proprietas 'a certain special kind of morals'.[13] This more specific, albeit somewhat periphrastic, phrase is preferable, because mores can refer to any and every disposition of the mind.

Then he turns to a discussion of the interpretation of these kinds and remarks that 'more cautious writers' have preferred to use the sense of these terms (voluntas) rather than the actual terms themselves (nomina).[14] According to these writers, the first species of pathos refers to the more violent emotions (concitatos, vehementer commotos) that command and disturb (imperare, ad perturbationem praevalere); ethos, on the other hand, refers to emotions that are more calm, gentle and subdued (mites atque compositos, lenes), and persuade and induce goodwill (persuadere, ad benevolentiam praevalere). Quintilian mentions, furthermore, that some have added that while pathos is a momentary emotion (temporale), ethos is continuous (perpetuum). He expresses a general agreement with this view, but also he feels the need to formulate some nuances. First, also the strong emotions can in some cases be necessarily continuous, if the subject requires it. Secondly, even if the more gentle emotions imply less force and impetus, they require no less art and experience (ars aut usus), and are generally in demand in a majority of cases, if not in all.

---

[12]   Thus W. W. Fortenbaugh, Aristotle on Emotion, London: Duckworth 2002, p. 17; see further his excellent discussion of Aristotle's views on emotion with respect to persuasion, pp. 16-18, 103-113.

[13]   On moralis as a neologism, cf. Cicero, De fato, I.1: quia pertinet ad mores, quod êthos illi vocant, nos eam partem philosophiae de moribus appellare solemus, sed decet augentem linguam latinam nominem moralem.

[14]   Quintilian prefers to be a 'translator' rather than an 'interpres' in looking for the sensus in stead of a verbatim rendering: for Roman theorizing on the principles of translation cf. Cicero, De optimo genere oratorum, 14; Horatius, Ars Poetica, 133-4; and see A. Seele, Römische Übersetzer. Nöte, Freiheiten, Absichten, Darmstadt: Wissenschaftliche Buchgesellschaft 1995, pp. 93-101.

After this discussion of the viewpoint of others,[15] Quintilian discusses his own view on the matter (VI.2.12 f.: *quin illud adhuc adiicio*): both types are sometimes of the same nature (*pathos atque êthos esse interdum ex eadem natura*) and the one is a stronger variant of the other (*ut illud maius sit, hoc minus*), an example being 'love' (*amor*, stronger) and 'affection' (*caritas*, weaker). The difference between the two is therefore not one of species, but of degree.[16]

Not satisfied with this, Quintilian then says he must elaborate further on *êthos*, because the term itself (*appellatio*) is not sufficiently clear. He offers now his own definition: *êthos...id erit*, 'let ethos be defined as'.[17] The required 'ethos' needs to meet a number of criteria: first, that it commends itself before anything else by 'goodness' (*bonitate*),[18] which can manifest itself not only as mildness and calmness (*mite ac placidum*), but also as friendliness, civility, and attractiveness and pleasantness to the audience (*blandum et humanum et audientibus amabile atque iucundum*). Then Quintilian formulates a crucial rule (VI.2.13):

> ..., *in quo exprimendo summa virtus ea est, ut fluere omnia ex natura rerum hominumque videantur utque mores dicentis ex oratione perluceant et quodammodo agnoscantur.*
> The expression of these (sc. attitudes) has as its most important quality that everything seems flow naturally from the circumstances and persons involved, and that the character of the speaker is revealed in his words and can somehow be recognized.

Quintilian distinguishes between two constituents in formulating this general and crucial rule. The first constituent in the technique of expressing ethos regards the *materia* of the case: the facts, circumstances and parties involved, as they constitute the commonplaces or topics of this type of case (note the phraseology *fluere ex*): actions (*res/pragmata*) and persons (*homines/anthrôpoi*).[19] What is said in the speech must not seem to conflict with what is naturally assumed about these particulars and what is known about them. Such conflict would make the acceptance of what is said impossible and therefore the speech ineffective. The second constituent is about the speaker himself *qua* speaker: his character, or *persona* defined as the whole of the character-traits given to him as speaker in this particular speech (see below), must reveal itself from his words and must be recognizable in one way or another. This constituent, too, has to do with requirements of acceptance: the audience must be able to acquire an impression of what kind of man the speaker is and

---

[15] On these, cf. Cicero, *De Oratore*, II.178, 185, 189ff., 206ff.; see also Cousin (see n. 8), *ad loc.*; Gill (see note 2), 149-166; W.W. Fortenbaugh, 'Quintilian 6.2.8-9: *Ethos* and *Pathos* and the ancient tradition', in: W.W. Fortenbaugh – D.C. Mirhady (eds.), *Peripatetic Rhetoric after Aristotle, R.U.S.C.H. VI*, New Brunswick: Rutgers University Press 1994, pp. 183-191; see also Anonymus Seguerianus, 128, and Julius Victor, *Rhetores Latini Minores*, 439.32; 36.
[16] On the probability of a Peripatetic background to this concept of graduality, see Fortenbaugh (see n. 15), pp. 186-188, Zucker (see n. 1), p. 43.
[17] On the Aristotelian phraseology of proposing a definition, cf. the recurrent *estô dê* ('let...be defined as') in his *Rhetoric*, I.2.1360b 14; 1362a 21; 1363b 7-8; 1368b 6; II.1.1378a 31; 1380a 7; 1381b 35; 1382a 21; 1383b 13; 1385a 17; 1385b 13. See also W.M.A. Grimaldi SJ, *Aristotle. Rhetoric I. A Commentary*, New York: Fordham University Press 1980, *ad* 1360 b 14; Fortenbaugh (see n. 12), p. 16 n. 2.
[18] On *bonitas*, cf. V.10.75 and XII.1.24.
[19] See also the technical use of *locus* in 15: *his non ex locis tantum*; and for this use of *ex*, cf. 17: *ex amoribus et ex desideriis*.

it must be able to develop good feelings towards him, in order to want to believe him.[20] Quintilian does not distinguish explicitly here between the character portrayal of the advocate and of the client, as he is discussing this technique in general, but see also below.

This general statement is followed by a series of examples of the dispositions and attitudes Quintilian has in mind (VI.2.14-17). First he names the dispositions which people intimately connected have towards each other, such as tolerance, forgiveness, offering satisfaction or gentle reproof (*quotiens ferimus, ignoscimus, satisfacimus, monemus*), provided that the strong emotions of anger and hate are absent. A further class consists in the moderation (*moderatio*) shown by a father to his son, a guardian to his ward or a husband to his wife: they let their affection for the persons who have done them wrong come first and they do not induce dislike (*invisos...faciunt*) against them except by expressing their love. This second class is distinguished as the class of friendship between unequals, in which one of the parties in volved is in some way superior over the other. Also Aristotle notes this type of friendship in *Ethica Nichomachea*, 1158b 10-28: it includes the categories father-son, older man-younger man, man-wife and any type of ruler-subordinate (*archonti pros archomenon*) relation. In Roman terms their relationship is based on affection (*caritas*) or mutual fondness and commitment, and includes the relationship of *clientela* and also the relationship of teacher-student.[21] This is different from the disposition of an old man being insulted by a young man unrelated to him or a man of high standing by somebody of a lower position. The contrast is intended by Quintilian to clarify the effect of the disposition he is talking about: the latter cases will provoke a response of outrage (*concitari*: the judges will feel outrage because of a socially unacceptable action), the former of being deeply moved (*adfici*: the judge will be emotionally affected because he can identify and hence feel the emotion of the party involved, because the *caritas* implies shared emotion).[22] The list of examples is continued by dispositions of less impact, such as the willingness to ask pardon for youthful error or infatuation, and gentle forms of derision and irony.[23] Finally he points to the dispositions of love and desire between friends and relatives (*adfectus...ex amoribus et ex desideriis amicorum et necessariorum*) as an intermediate class between ethos and pathos.

Significantly Quintilian rounds off his list of dispositions with a reference to a particular school exercise, appropriately called *êthê* ('character-portrayals'), in VI.2.17:

---

[20] Cf. *êthos* and *doxa tou legontos* (portrayal of character) in Aristoteles, *Rhetorica*, I.2.1356a 1-20 (and compare Plato, *Gorgias*, 513 c); II.1.1377 b 21-78a 5; *Rhetorica ad Alexandrum* (Anaximenes), 1430a 28-29.

[21] Cf. Cicero, *Laelius de amicitia*, 19-20; see D. Konstan, *Friendship in the Classical World*, Cambridge: Cambridge University Press 1997, pp. 135-137.

[22] Reading *debet* (with A) in stead of *dedecet* (Winterbottom).

[23] VI.2.16 contains a short digression on irony, the discussion of which necessarily goes beyond the scope of this paper. Suffice it to say that Quintilian relegates the use of irony to the techniques of provoking hatred (*odium*), not only towards the opponent: there is a danger that excessive use of it will turn against the speaker and make himself disliked; see Cousin (see n. 5), p. 193.

quibus plerumque rusticos, superstitiosos, avaros, timidos secundum condicionem propositionum effingimus. Nam si êthê mores sunt cum hos imitamur, ex his ducimus orationem.
in which we usually portray people of a rustic, superstitious, greedy or timid character in accordance with the requirement of the proposed theme. For if 'characters' are dispositions, we take them as the starting point of our speech if we imitate them.

This school exercise, also known as *êthologia*[24], involves the imitation or life-like copying of certain patterns of behaviour, based on a certain disposition. As the phraseo-logy used (*effingimus; imitari*) makes clear, the exercise consists of role playing, whereby the required character or *persona* is represented, very much like a theatrical representation of characters on stage. With this, Quintilian introduces an analogy between the orator and the actor: both must be able to present a believable character on stage and thereby convey emotion to their audience. The point is that they are capable of making the audience believe that their character is real and therefore acceptable as such. That is why Quintilian in the conclusion of this section (VI.2.18) insists that the orator must be able to convince his audience that he is a good and courteous man: he must possess these qualities in reality or, at least, must be thought to possess them (*aut habeat aut habere credatur*). Here Quintilian focuses on the impression the speaker/advocate wants to make on his audience, his self-representation as a morally good man. This 'subjective character portrayal' differs from the representation of his client as a certain type of man ('objective character portrayal'), a distinction not yet present in the Greek tradition of conceptualization, as representation of a client before law is a part of Roman legal procedure and is absent in Greece.[25]

2.3. Dramatic performance, identification and emotion

The analogy orator/actor and dramatic performance in general remains on Quintilian's mind, also in his treatment of the second type of emotion, pathos, or *adfectus* (VI.2.20-24; see also above on VI.2.8 f.). To illustrate the difference with ethos, he says that pathos is rather like tragedy, ethos like comedy.

Then, in VI.2.25, Quintilian continues by providing the future orator additional treatment of the emotions, which he derives from personal experience and 'following nature' (*experimento meo et natura ipsa duce*[26] *accepi*): in this final part of his treatment he wishes to go beyond what tradition has to offer on the subject (VI.2.25-

---

[24]   Thus I.9.3: the exercise belongs to the propaedeutic stage of the study of rhetoric, the *progymnasmata*, as they are taught by the *grammaticus*. For *ethologi* as 'actors in farces', see Cicero, *De oratore*, II.242: they imitate character-types. The orator uses this technique surreptitiously: by hinting at a certain type, e.g. by imitating a typical tone of voice, he makes the audience think of it, rather than giving a full performance of the type (*orator surripiat oportet imitationem, ut is, qui audiet, cogitet plura quam videat*); see also 'Ethologia' in *Historisches Wörterbuch der Rhetorik*, Bd. II, pp. 1512-1516 [G. Naschert].

[25]   On subjective *ethos*, see above; on objective *ethos*, cf. *Rhetorica ad Herennium*, IV.63-65; Cicero, *Orator*, 128; *De oratore*, II.178-184.

[26]   On *natura* as as an important motif for Quintilian, cf. IV.5.3; IX.1.40 and 120; X.7.6 etc.; see Fr. R. Varwig, *Der rhetorische Naturbegriff bei Quintilian. Studien zu einem Argumentationstopos in der rhetorischen Bildung der Antike*, Heidelberg: Winter 1976, pp. 81-92.

36).[27] The secret behind a successful manipulation of emotions in others is, according to Quintilian, to be moved oneself (VI.2.26). This is a crucial prerequisite (VI.2.28):

> Primum est igitur, ut apud nos valeant ea quae valere apud iudicem volumus, adficiamurque antequam adficere conemur.
> The first demand is, therefore, that those (sc. feelings) we wish to be strongly present in the judge, are strongly present in ourselves, and that we are moved before we attempt to move (sc. others).

In order to be capable of stirring emotions in himself, Quintilian says, the orator has at his disposition the technique of *visiones* or 'mental representations', which the Greeks call *phantasiai*. This entails the representation of things absent in the mind, in such a way that one has the impression to see them with the eyes, as if they were present. These representations are comparable to daydreams (*velut somnia quaedam vigilantium*) or hallucination (*animi vitium*), but they can be put to practical use for the orator. If he is able to construct such a mental representation, for instance of a man murdered – whereby the orator imagines all the circumstances likely to occur in such a case, such as the murderer jumping his victim, the victim trembling and crying for help, begging for mercy, trying to escape, the fatal blow, the victim falling, his groans of agony, his last breath –, he can use this impression as the material to provide the audience with a vivid description or *enargeia* (VI.2.32):[28]

> ..., quae non tam dicere videtur quam ostendere, et adfectus non aliter quam si rebus ipsis intersimus sequentur.
> which seems to put before the eyes rather than to speak, and the emotions will follow as if we are present at the actual occurrences.

It seems plausible that this passage is connected to, if not an elaboration of, ch. 17 of Aristotle's *Poetics*, which discusses the role of imagination in the process of dramatic composition:

> Dei de tous muthous sunistanai kai têi lexei sunapergazesthai hoti malista pro ommatôn tithemenon: houtô gar an enargestata [ho] horôn hôsper par' autois gignomenos tois prattomenois heuriskoi to prepon kai hêkista an lanthanoi [to] ta hupenantia.
> A poet ought to imagine his material to the fullest possible extent while composing his plot-structures and elaborating them in language: by seeing them as vividly as possible in this way – as if present at the very occurrence of the events – he is likely to discover what is appropriate, and least likely to miss contradictions.[29]

The situation Aristotle has in mind is the one of the theatre, and especially the relationship between the poet and the audience. The poet will visualize the scene and the representation of the characters in that scene, so as to realize a dramaturgically efficient spectacle that conforms to the requirements of plausibility and appropriateness. Crucial part of this is the emotional impact on the audience: they must be able to

---

[27] On the personal commitment with which Quintilian treats this subject see Cousin (see n. 5), p. 194: 'Q. parle de son *ars* avec une ferveur religieuze, et il tient à en révéler les mystères comme un *vates*.'
[28] On *enargeia*, see Cousin (see n.5), pp. 194-195.
[29] Aristoteles, *Poetica*, 1455a 22-26. Translation S. Halliwell, *The Poetics of Aristotle. Translation and Commentary*, Chapel Hill: University of North Carolina Press 1987, p. 50.

believe in the character represented, and in his emotional state. This the poet can bring about by his capacity for emotional self-involvement.[30]

Like the poet/playwright with his dramatic character, so the orator should, according to Quintilian, identify with his client and imagine himself in his situation and circumstances (VI.2.34):

> *nos illi simus, quos gravia, indigna, tristia passos queremur, nec agamus rem quasi alienam, sed adsumamus parumper illum dolorem.*
>
> We must ourselves be these people of whom we bewail their suffering of grievous, unmerited and sad fates, and we must not treat their case as if it related to somebody else, but we must for a hort while make their suffering our own.

This point is illustrated by Quintilian by a direct return to the analogy of orator and actor. He mentions how he has often observed actors both in tragedy and comedy (*histriones atque comoedos*) leave the theatre still moved to tears, even after they had stepped out of their role in a moving play (*cum ex aliquo graviore actu personam deposuissent*). The relevance of this for the orator is accentuated by an argument a fortiori, which takes the orator/actor analogy into account (35). The theatre is a place where make-believe reigns and the competent audience knows that the story, actions and scenes they see on stage performed by actors are an illusion, which they can accept and go along with temporarily. If the sole performance of what others, i.e. the third party of the playwright, have written can bring about such strong emotional reactions, even if they are fictional and illusionary (*falsis...adfectibus*), then the impact of the facts of the client's case, based in reality, becomes clear. The orator speaks for his client and wants to achieve through his words the same effect on his audience: the judge.[31]

At this point (36) Quintilian returns to the school-exercises of the *êthê*, already mentioned in 17 (see above, with n. 23), which allows the student to train himself in the capacity of identification. The educational value of these exercises goes even further: if the speaker in such an exercise is taking on a specific role or persona, the distinction between advocate and client is collapsed (*ut litigatores loquimur frequentius quam ut advocati*). If a student is to impersonate an orphan, shipwrecked man or a man in grave danger (*orbum agimus et naufragum et periclitantem*), then the only way to do this succesfully is to take on their emotional state as well.

The significance of dramatic techniques, both tragic and comic, to rhetoric as indicated by Quintilian becomes apparent both from rhetorical theory and from analysis of oratory in general. As a source for typology the Theophrastean *Characters* was used in rhetorical education, and also the *Rhetorica ad Herennium* IV, 66

---

[30] I follow closely Gill (see n. 14), pp. 152-3; see also Halliwell (see n. 29), pp. 145-8; this passage of the *Poetics* also seems to have informed Horace, *Ars Poetica*, 101 ff. (*si vis me flere, dolendum est primum ipsi tibi*); Cicero, *De oratore*, II.188-97, *Orator*, 132; and Longinus, *De sublimitate*, 15; see also P. H. Schrijvers, 'Invention, imagination, et théorie des émotions chez Cicéron et Quintilien', in: B. Vickers (ed.), *Rhetoric Revalued. Papers from the International Society for the History of Rhetoric*, Binghamton, NY: Center for Medieval and Early Renaissance Studies 1982, pp. 47-58.

[31] On imagination and the emotions, see Schrijvers (see n. 30).

offers clear evidence of this practice.[32] Speeches such as Lysias, or. 24 *On the invalid* and Cicero, *Pro Marco Caelio* offer exemplary cases of oratory inspired by the dramatic.[33]

---

[32] On Theophrastus, see O. Immisch, 'Über Theophrasts *Charaktere*', *Philologus* 87 (1989), pp. 193-212 and W.W. Fortenbaugh, 'Theophrastus, the *Characters*, and Rhetoric', in: Fortenbaugh - Mirhady (see n. 15), pp. 15-35; cf. also Tacitus, *Dialogus de oratoribus*, 20, 26, 39, 40 on theatricality and rhetorical practice; on trials as theatre cf. Quintilian VI.1.38; 45; 47; 2.35; 3.29; one may also think of Herodas, *Mimes*; see in general S. Gastaldi, 'Il teatro delle passioni. *Pathos* nella retorica antica', *Elenchos* 1 (1995), pp. 59-82.

[33] On Lysias, see J.A.E. Bons, 'Geen been om op te staan. Lysias' De zaak van de invalide (or. 24)', *Lampas* 34 (2001), pp. 207-219, and S. Usher, *Greek Oratory. Tradition and Originality*, Oxford: Oxford University Press 1999, pp.106-110; on Cicero, see K.A. Geffcken, *Comedy in the Pro Caelio*, Leiden: Brill, 1973.

RICHARD A. KATULA

EMOTION IN THE COURTROOM

Quintilian's Judge —Then and Now

1. QUINTILIAN ON THE PLACE AND VALUE OF EMOTION IN A COURTROOM

She was the most beautiful of the Athenian courtesans, a goddess of love. Her statue in gold stood at Delphi. Men paid great sums for her services, and so she was also rich. She was a woman of power; she was Phryne of Thespiae, and she was in trouble.

Brought to trial in 340 BC for profaning the Eleusinian mysteries, Phryne faced capital punishment. Her advocate, the orator Hyperides, sensing that the trial was not going well, tore the garments from his client. As she stood bare-bosomed before the tribunal, Hyperides implored the judges to gaze upon her and show pity. The image of Phryne, her reputation, and Hyperides' piteous lamentation, moved the judges to fear this handmaid of Aphrodite, and so, indulging their feelings for the vision before them, they voted to acquit. So scandalous was the verdict that Euthias, who brought the charge, never pleaded again before the courts, and, as we are told in Athenaeus' *The Deipnosophists*, 'a decree was passed that no person speaking on a defendant's behalf should indulge in lamentation, nor should the accused man or woman be bared for all to see.'[1]

That Quintilian would mention this episode near the beginning of his treatise on emotion in the *Institutio oratoria*[2] is not surprising. It was well within the scope of his *vir bonus dicendi peritus* that the orator should know all the tricks of the trade, and, should circumstances warrant, defend a worthy cause or a hopeful client using the panoply of the rhetorical arts.[3] Judges are, above all else, human beings. Quintilian grants to the philosophers their preeminent curricular focus on logic; he understands that the good judge should resist emotion and focus on the factual arguments in hearing a case. And yet Quintilian, and for that matter Hyperides and all the orators of the ancient world, understood how difficult that is to do; in fact, how primal and connected is emotion to reason and to persuasion.

---

[1]   Athenaeus, *The Deipnosophists*, trans. Charles Burton Gulick, Cambridge, Mass.: Harvard University Press 1950, VI, xiii, p. 590.

[2]   *Inst. or.* VI.1.7. In this essay, I will use the text edition of Winterbottom and the translation by Butler (see 'Introduction', notes 26 and 27 resp.).

[3]   M.L. Clarke, *Rhetoric at Rome: A Historical Survey*, 3rd edition, London-New York: Routledge 1996, p. 117.

In Quintilian's Rome, as in ancient Greece, the courtroom was a spectacle of emotional fervor and display. Quintilian himself was known for occasional outbursts of passion. In our day, courtroom etiquette requires a more decorous and 'civilized' style of communication. Not that they always succeed, but judges are expected to present a 'judicially proper' look: serious, dispassionate, overtly objective.[4] They speak most properly in the impersonal voice, best described, perhaps, as a single-octave monotone that suggests a conscious 'down-regulating' of the affect. Even the black judicial robes symbolize their disdain for displays of emotion. And yet we also know that there is a man or a woman inside those robes; we know our judge 'feels.' The question in this essay is whether Quintilian's teaching on emotional display remains valuable today, especially given a rhetorical situation that seeks to suppress it.

In this essay, we synthesize Quintilian's teaching on the use of emotional proof throughout a trial. Reviewing Book VI, primarily Chapters 2 and 3, we define emotional proof, note the rules for its use, and discuss how it is to be employed strategically. We then turn to contemporary research on emotion, asking whether it might reinforce or add to Quintilian's advice, and whether it might assist us in understanding how emotion affects the fact-finding and decision-making functions of the judge in the contemporary courtroom. In this essay, we look at emotional proof from the judge's perspective, and we interrogate the courtroom as a rhetorical site as well as a legal one.

Following his reference to Phryne, Quintilian explains when to use emotion in the peroration, the closing argument. Normally, he says, the peroration should be a recapitulation of the key arguments, and modern evidence supports this strategy when delivered properly.[5] Quintilian urges the use of emotional appeal, however, '...if there are no other means for securing the victory of truth, justice, and the public interest.'[6] In such cases, perhaps when both sides have argued reasonably and when the verdict hangs in the balance, vivid, intense emotional displays, both in word and gesture, may turn the tide in one's favor. He encourages appeals to pity and even, should circumstances warrant, suggests that the accused throw himself on the ground and embrace the knees of the judge.[7] He advocates the use of theatrics as well as emotionally charged words that might have been spoken during the commission of the crime: the waving of bloody garments, the appearance of shattered family members and victims, invocations of the gods; in short, any technique that will reduce the judge to tears. In the peroration, urges Quintilian, 'we must let loose the whole torrent of our eloquence'.[8]

In Chapters 2 and 3, Quintilian expands on his theory of emotion from its use in the peroration to its use throughout the trial. 'We have still, therefore,' he says, 'to discuss a task which forms the most powerful means of obtaining what we desire, and

[4] Peter David Blanck, 'Off the Record: Nonverbal Communication in the Courtroom,' *Stanford Lawyer*, Spring (1987) pp. 21-22.
[5] Richard D. Rieke and Randall K. Stutman, *Communication in Legal Advocacy,* Columbia, SC: University of South Carolina Press 1990, pp. 205, 209-211.
[6] *Inst. or.* VI.1.7 *in fine.*
[7] *Inst. or.* VI.1.34.
[8] *Inst. or.* VI.1.51.

is also more difficult than any of those which we have previously considered, namely, that of stirring the emotions of the judges and of molding and transforming them to the attitude which we desire.'[9] He then proceeds to discourse on the complete range of rhetorical techniques used to arouse emotion: from anger to laughter, from the witty and urbane to the sarcastic and coarse.

Quintilian believes that with training any good advocate can arrange facts to prove a point. That is, one does not need an orator to help the judge 'to know' a case. But since each side has its advocate mustering the facts, the judge may be led through the fact-finding process only to indecision. Facts are frequently arrayed equally for and against. The peculiar task of the orator, the reason he has been hired, begins after the arguments have been discovered. As he struggles to win the judge's mind, the advocate knows that he must also win the judge's heart. He must know how to deliver emotional appeals and when to use them most persuasively. The rhetorical side of the judicial process, Quintilian urges,

> *Hoc opus eius, hic labor est,*
> There lie the task and toil.[10]

In its power to sway the emotions lies the life and soul of oratory. For Quintilian's orator, Kennedy notes, 'his greatest achievement is a tear in the eye of a judge.'[11]

Quintilian divides the emotions into two types: *êthos* and *páthos*. Pathos is the *affectus* or emotion while ethos refers, for want of a better term, to moral behavior or character.[12] Pathos describes the stronger and sometimes 'darker' emotions, ethos the milder. Pathos is love, ethos is affection. Pathos is anger aroused by hatred; ethos is anger tempered with understanding. Emotional appeals based on ethos are those coming from the qualities of a person's character, the sincerity the orator and/or his client show during a trial. Emotional appeals based on pathos derive from the psychological states through which a judge may pass impulsively during the course of a trial: the anger, hatred, fear, envy, joy, sympathy, or pity an orator may invoke at the appropriate moment.

The orator's task lies in arousing the judges' emotions at critical points in the trial. Facts help a judge 'know,' but emotions make him 'feel.' A judge moved by emotion begins to wish one side right, and what the judge wishes, Quintilian argues, he begins to believe. The flooding over of reason by the emotions is particularly crucial when the facts are arrayed against one's client, since only emotion has the power to lead the judge away from the contemplation of the truth. His experience as a passionate advocate has taught Quintilian that, '…just as lovers are incapable of forming a reasoned judgment on the beauty of the object of their affections because passion forestalls the sense of sight, so the judge, when overcome by his emotions, abandons all attempt to inquire into the truth of the arguments and is swept along by the tide of passion, yielding himself unquestioning to the torrent.'[13]

---

9   *Inst. or.* VI.2.1.
10 *Inst. or.* VI.2.7.
11 George Kennedy, *Quintilian*, New York: Twayne Publishers Inc. 1969, p. 74.
12 *Inst. or.* VI.2.8.
13 *Inst. or.* VI.2.6.

2. QUINTILIAN ON THE ART OF MAKING AN EMOTIONAL APPEAL AND USING IT STRATEGICALLY[14]

The purpose of emotional proof, then, is that it may persuade when the facts alone do not. But how does one deliver an emotional appeal? Quintilian's advice on how to deliver an emotional appeal may be condensed into six rules. 'Quintilian's Rules' are as follows:

Rule One is that the advocate must know the emotions. He must know what 'fear' is, what 'envy' is, what 'hatred' is, and he must practice making each emotion. He must know the difference between his own fears and those he may arouse in the judge for the case at hand. He must know whether an act will naturally arouse hatred, or whether he will have to make the connection for the judge. He must know when a joke that seems funny to him will also seem funny to the decision-makers. In short, the advocate must be 'emotionally literate.'

Rule Two for evoking pathos is to feel the emotions one is invoking. Sincerity counts. Signs of feigned emotion rebound against one's client. 'If we wish to give our words the appearance of sincerity,' Quintilian says, 'we must assimilate ourselves to the emotions of those who are genuinely so affected, and our eloquence must spring from the same feeling that we desire to produce in the mind of the judge.'[15] A sincere emotional appeal is one that comes from the advocate's heart. If he is to move the judge, he must be moved himself.

Rule Three states that the advocate must express in tone and gesture the emotional state he wishes to arouse in the judge. The advocate achieves this state himself by imagining the scene as he describes it (*visiones*). He must see the murderer move from behind the bushes. He must see the raised dagger, gleaming for the briefest moment in the moonlight. He must feel the fatal blow, and hear the stricken victim pleading for mercy. The advocate must envision the crime itself; and speak and act as though it were happening again. Quintilian says, 'We must identify ourselves with the persons for whom we complain... and must... for a brief space feel their suffering as though it were our own, while our words must be such as we should use if we stood in their shoes.'[16]

Rule Four asserts that the advocate must awaken emotions that do not naturally arise from the case. Quintilian uses the word *deínôsis* to capture this quality.[17] *Deínôsis* involves turning events that might seem tolerable to a judge into unendurable agony for the victim through the use of vivid language and exaggerated descriptions. A judge who is a veteran of war may have survived his experience without psychological damage, while an advocate's client may have suffered post-traumatic stress from the same experience. The advocate must help the judge feel his client's pain through language that changes the judge's perception of the same experience.

---

[14]   This section of the essay is reprinted from an article published in *Rhetoric Review*, January, 2003.
[15]   *Inst. or.* VI.2.27.
[16]   *Inst. or.* VI.2.34.
[17]   *Inst. or.* VI 2.24.

Rule Five for an effective emotional appeal states that the advocate's client must mimic his lawyer's emotions. Sometimes, says Quintilian, 'our appeal falls flat owing to the ignorance, indifference or uncouthness of our client, and it is consequently most important that the advocate should take all necessary precautions in this connection.'[18] By synchronizing their affective displays, the advocate and his client (and whomever else they can get to join in), create in the courtroom an emotional climate that they hope will become contagious.

Rule Six asserts that, in his training, the orator should speak, not in his own voice but in the voice of his client. 'Even in the schools,' Quintilian notes, 'it is desirable that the student should be moved by his theme, and should imagine it to be true; indeed, it is all the more desirable, then, since, as a rule in scholastic declamations, the speaker more often appears as the actual litigant than as his advocate.'[19] The goal of Rule Six is to arouse the appropriate sympathetic emotions in the judge, and then persuade the judge to transfer those feelings, not to him, but to his client. Having learned the rules for presenting an emotional appeal, the orator must also know *when* to use it. Our focus shifts here from emotional display to their strategic placement. Most importantly, the advocate must study the judge since some judges are more susceptible to emotional appeal than others. 'There is a type of judge,' says Quintilian, for instance, 'whose temperament is too serious to allow him to tolerate laughter.'[20] We should know whether a witty barb aimed at our witness might not also wound the judge. We should know when the judge is angry with our witness, perhaps in a case of child abuse or rape, and avoid fueling that anger with our own emotional displays.

Similarly, emotional appeals work best when they activate something the judge knows or has experienced him or herself: emotion must be connected to cognition. For instance, a judge who is himself a veteran of war would be more likely to empathize with a defendant accused of murder whose defense is trauma resulting from combat (post-traumatic stress syndrome). Thus, it is not simply emotional appeals, but emotional appeals that are appropriately timed to the case, the judge, and the client.

In fact, underlying all use of emotional appeal is an understanding of its value as strategy. While in its undertaking an emotional appeal must appear spontaneous and sincere, in its planning it must be considered as strategically as the arrangement of one's case. The advocate must know who might and who might not be offended. The witty remark or jest, timed properly, persuades; timed poorly, may cause offense and require apology.[21] The outburst of anger occurring at exactly the right moment persuades; anger unhinged to one's case or the judge's experience may appear as merely petulance. The advocate must know when to move by emotional proof and when to remain silent. He must know when a remark, a sarcastic one, for instance, might reflect on his own integrity more than the person's to whom it is directed. The advocate must situate him or herself within the rhythm and movement of the trial;

[18]   *Inst. or.* VI.1.37.
[19]   *Inst. or.* VI.2.36.
[20]   *Inst. or.* VI.3.31-32.
[21]   *Inst. or.* VI.3.34-35.

and even while immersed in it, must remain sensitive to the deep-seated premises underlying his case. This quality Quintilian calls 'sagacity.' It is not given to general rules, but he considers it the heart, the genius, of eloquence.[22]

If we were to summarize Quintilian's theory of emotion in contemporary terms, it might be stated as follows. A well-trained advocate understands that emotions are impulsive feelings. These feelings are expressed nonverbally through tone of voice, bodily postures, and gestures; and verbally through vivid descriptions of the crime. Through these channels the advocate seeks to create an emotional climate in the courtroom leading to the 'catching' of those emotions by others including the judge.[23] Once the advocate has the judge feeling the right way, he must transfer those feelings to his client, not to himself. Finally, emotional appeals must be well thought out and used as strategically as questions and arguments. If these rules are followed, emotional proof may spell the difference in a forensic situation, especially when the arguments are arrayed equally on both sides of the case. Quintilian's advice reminds us of the contemporary aphorism: A good lawyer knows the case; a great lawyer knows the judge.

3. QUINTILIAN'S THEORY OF EMOTIONAL DISPLAY AND THE COURTROOM TODAY

Very little of import has been written since the *Institutio oratoria* about the purpose, presentation, and strategic use of emotion in forensic rhetoric. Indeed, as Kennedy notes, one reason for the resurgence of interest in the Institutes in the 14th century and again in the 20th is the result of his treatment of both principles and practice, part of what Kennedy calls the 'fullness of the rhetorical system which he expounds.'[24] We profit from Quintilian's wisdom and experience, then, simply as advice on how and when to use emotional proof. At the same time, we might legitimately ask whether emotional proof as Quintilian describes it is as persuasive a strategy with our judges, those judicially proper magistrates described earlier, as it was in the highly charged courtrooms of ancient Rome. The answer may be surprising.

Courtrooms today are much different from the Roman courts of the 1st century. There is greater ambivalence today about the place of emotional display in the court-room, owing to both enlightenment and positivist traditions that have sought to sep-arate reason from emotion. Today, most judges believe that they must acquire knowledge of the case through logic and the separate and distinct cognitive domain. A trial has evolved into a rule-governed process, one that emphasizes fact-finding and the application of those facts to a law. Emotion is based on feelings, and giving way to one's feelings is often seen today as a sign of weakness, or bias, or loss of control - all impediments to one's thinking or knowing. Emotional display, except perhaps in the opening and closing arguments, often strikes negatively at the

---

[22]   *Inst. or.* VI.5.3.

[23]   Elaine Hatfield, John Cacioppo, and Richard Rapson, *Emotional Contagion*, New York: Cambridge University Press 1994, p. 4.

[24]   Kennedy (see note 11), pp. 140-141.

speaker's credibility. 'Counsel should refrain from harassing the witness' or 'We'll recess for 15 minutes to give the defendant time to regain her composure' are commonplaces in courtroom proceedings today. For this reason, both the western tradition of law and the rules established for proper courtroom procedure seek to segregate the world of emotion and assign it an inferior place in judicial pleading; in short, to eschew its significance as 'fact' or its utility in decision-making.

Perhaps because the emotions are now seen as antithetical to the judicial process, there is little empirical or social scientific research available concerning the persuasiveness of emotional display in the courtroom when the judge, as opposed to a jury, is the fact-finder and decision-maker. A study by Blanck revealed that judges inadvertently 'leak' their feelings, beliefs, or expectations to jurors about defendants through nonverbal channels, but the study did not determine whether such emotional leakage affected the jury's decisions.[25] Research by Bower, and by Gregory, Caldini, and Carpenter supports Quintilian's rule about the use of vivacity in unlocking the imagination, but only in the closing argument and only when the decision-making agency is a jury rather than a judge.[26] That is, causing jurors to imagine an event through vivid description increases the viability and memorability of a story but not necessarily the jury's decision. As for humorous emotional appeals, there is no conclusive evidence that a humorous message is more persuasive than a non-humorous message, all else being held constant, or that humor increases a jury's recall and comprehension of a message.[27] We also know that there is a 'beauty bias' that operates with jurors, and that has, in experimental conditions, affected their decisions.[28] Unfortunately, there is no experimental or empirical data compiled from judges themselves regarding their attitudes toward emotional display and the effect they perceive emotion to have on them during the course of a trial.

Toward the end of gathering information from bench-trial judges about emotional display, we conducted a survey of magistrates from across America, asking them about their perceptions of the role emotion plays in their fact-finding and decision-making.[29] These judges reported, as we hypothesized, a generally negative attitude toward emotional display but a surprising degree of ambivalence about its impact on a trial.

In support of the enlightenment and positivist traditions noted above, and in defiance of Quintilian's First Rule, the judges we surveyed noted overwhelmingly that they received no training in emotion while in law school or college. Judges (and attorneys by extension), while predominantly individuals of high intelligence, admit that they are not 'emotionally literate.' Judges today see emotion and reason as separate faculties of the mind, and they are ambivalent about whether an emotional reaction is a form of intelligence. For reasons such as these, 95% of the judges we

---

[25]   Blanck (see note 4), p. 22.

[26]   Rieke and Stutman (see note 5), p. 209.

[27]   Rieke and Stutman (see note 5), pp. 69-70.

[28]   John Stossel, 'Your Looks/ Beauty Bias', *20/20 ABC Network*, June 16, 1995. Tape available from the author.

[29]   Richard A. Katula and Scotty Hargrove, 'A Survey on Emotion', paper presented at Eastern Communication Association Convention, Washington D.C., April 2003. Available upon request of author.

surveyed reported that they seek to block out, or 'down-regulate,' their own emotions during a trial. They expressed a near unanimous belief that their emotions are neither useful nor appropriate guides during a trial as it pertains to their decision-making; thus, they report speaking in proper judicial tones, suppressing emotional display, and calling a recess when emotions flare. Quintilian's ideal condition, a tear in the eye of the judge, may not be a realistic goal with today's magistrates.

With regard to using emotion as a guide to determining cases that are equal on the facts, the judges we surveyed suggested that this might be appropriate and about half said they had done so; the more common principle to be applied, however, would be the 'burden of proof' standard. They were adamant about not allowing an emotional appeal to turn their decision against a case that is stronger on the facts. Finally, while a small number of judges reported basing a decision on a reaction to a person (such as an attractive defendant or plaintiff, or an abused child), most reported that they have not, or at least 'hope' that they have not.

Judges responding to our survey did report that an emotional display might strike positively or negatively at the credibility of a witness or defendant depending upon how sincere the emotion appears to be. As Quintilian suggests in Rule Two, sincerity counts. Thus, while the courtroom today is more heavily governed by rules, procedures, and a general philosophy of law that militates against emotion, Quintilian's Rule Four is partly upheld in our survey; that is, emotion may be 'probative,' but probably not 'dispositive.'

Are the judges we surveyed, like so many of us who are educated in the western tradition, unaware of their own emotional reactions? Neuroscientific research tells us conclusively that emotions are present in all that we do. Panksepp notes, for instance that, 'Emotional and cognitive processes interact in untold ways. Emotions appear able to both guide and disrupt modes of thought, and provide mood- and emotion-congruent coding and retrieval of information.'[30] Fridja asserts that emotions are a functional part of the cognitive process: 'They can be considered the mechanisms whereby the organism signals to its cognitive and action systems that events are favorable or harmful to its ends. It is the relevance signaling mechanism.'[31] Daniel Goleman's best-selling book, *Emotional Intelligence*, captures the most contemporary thinking about emotions:

> A view of human nature that ignores the power of emotions is sadly shortsighted. The very name *homo sapiens*, the thinking species, is misleading in light of the new appreciation and vision of the place of emotions in our lives that science now offers. As we all know from experience, when it comes to shaping our decisions and our actions, feeling counts every bit as much – and often more – than thought. We have gone too far in emphasizing the value and import of the purely rational – of what IQ measures – in human life.[32]

---

[30]   Jaak Panksepp, 'A Proper Distinction Between Affective and Cognitive Process is Essential for Neuroscientific Progress', in: Paul Ekman and Richard J. Davidson (eds.), *The Nature of Emotion: Fundamental Questions*, New York: Oxford University Press 1994, p. 225.

[31]   Nico H. Fridja, 'Emotions are Functional, Most of the Time,' in: Ekman and Davidson (see note 30), p. 113.

[32]   Daniel Goleman, *Emotional Intelligence*, New York: Bantam Books 1995, p. 4.

Thus, we know that the emotions are neither good nor bad, but simply an inherent, critical, and even primary phase of human information processing and interaction.

In support of neuroscientific theory, a growing body of evidence reveals that the emotions guide and surround perceptions and decision-making. For instance, Chartrand and Bargh documented what they call the 'chameleon effect,' in social interaction. In three experiments, they discovered that, (1) the motor behavior of participants unintentionally matched that of strangers with whom they worked on a task; (2) that mimicking the posture and movements of a partner facilitated the smoothness of interactions and increased liking between interaction partners; and (3) that dispositionally empathic individuals exhibited the chameleon effect to a greater extent than did other people. This study confirms a fact reported in numerous other studies: there appears to be a non-conscious mimicry of the postures, gestures, and tones of interactional partners.[33] Since we know that human beings often infer their own emotional states from the behaviors they are producing, we know that they can be unwittingly 'infected' with the emotions of others, thus shaping their mood positively or negatively for the topic under discussion.[34]

McCroskey and Richmond tested a similar phenomenon known as the 'reciprocity' phenomenon; that is, the hypothesis that successful communicators adapt their communication style in order to gain approval from their partners. Applied to the workplace environment, McCroskey and Richmond discovered that supervisors who exhibit positive responsive behaviors such as mimicry and synchrony, for instance, are more likely to be perceived by subordinates as credible and attractive; in addition, highly congruent or responsive supervisors are viewed generally more favorably than low responsive supervisors by subordinates. McCroskey and Richmond conclude that, '...people who are responsive can anticipate generating more positive relationships as being the likely outcome of their behaviors.[35] That is, people like others who reciprocate their behaviors.

Hatfield, Cacioppo, and Rapson write about yet another phenomenon of emotional life, one they call 'emotional contagion.' Emotional contagion is a multiply determined, primitive, pre-conscious complimentary emotional response that some people get from others.[36] A notable instance of emotional contagion was reported by Mullen and his colleagues in 1986, in their study of the 1984 American presidential campaign between Ronald Reagan and Walter Mondale. The study determined that Peter Jennings, the anchorperson of the ABC television network, exhibited more positive and favorable facial and vocal expressions (affect) when referring to Reagan compared to counterparts Tom Brokaw from NBC and Dan Rather from CBS, whose emotional displays did not exhibit a bias toward either candidate. In a follow-up telephone survey, Mullen and his colleagues discovered that voters who watched

---

[33]   Tanya Chartrand and John A. Bargh, 'The Chameleon Effect: the Perception-Behavior Link and Social Interaction,' *Journal of Personality and Social Psychology* 76 1 (June, 1999) p. 893.

[34]   Hatfield, Cacioppo, and Rapson (see note 23), pp. 51-52.

[35]   Virginia P. Richmond and James C. McCroskey, 'The Impact of Supervisor and Subordinate Immediacy on Relational and Organizational Outcomes,' *Communication Monographs* 67, 1 (March, 2000) p. 86.

[36]   Hatfield, Cacioppo, and Rapson (see note 23), p. 5.

ABC News were more likely to vote for Reagan than those who watched either NBC or CBS. As psychologist Elaine Hatfield notes, 'Subtle differences in the affect of the three famous anchors were apparently sufficient to influence viewer's preferences and voting behavior.'[37]

With so much evidence of emotion operating in our social interactions, at work, and in the media, is it not logical to conclude that it must be at work in the courtroom? And if it is, why do judges themselves either not understand this fact, or deny it? Could Quintilian, after a career spent as an advocate and a teacher of rhetoric be so wrong? While empirical and experimental research is needed as a follow-up on our survey, the following observations seem reasonable.

Emotional display of the kind Quintilian favors is less effective in the courtroom today than it was in Quintilian's. Because of the prevailing philosophy of law that dominates western legal tradition, a philosophy that has led to rules and procedures intended to segregate and vitiate emotional appeals, judges suppress them, both their own and others' in the courtroom. When judges are asked about emotions, they often respond 'You can feel them, but you can't show them.' Quintilian's Rules regarding how to present an emotional appeal may need minor revision today given the transformations that have taken place in the courtroom since Roman times.

Emotional proof, however, remains a powerful force in the courtroom. Research strongly supports the notion that, rather than being a distinct entity, knowing is always channeled through the emotional corridor of the brain.[38] While they may not show their emotions or allow them to be displayed in their courtrooms, judges still feel strongly about those who appear before them, and they use those feelings to make decisions.

In fact, by driving emotional display underground, today's magistrates may have unwittingly made emotional appeal an even more powerful force than in Quintilian's time, operating as an enthymeme or suppressed premise. We may even say with some assurance that the 'Peter Jennings' effect is alive and well in the courtroom.

For attorneys interested in persuasion as well as argument;[39] that is, as we are discussing the courtroom in this essay, the implications are clear. While emotional proof may appear today in a more nuanced fashion, it may nevertheless play as determinative a role as it did in Quintilian's time. There is every reason to suspect that emotional proof may be the courtroom 'wild card,' a proof that, because it is not studied in law schools nor understood very well in its manifestations, is persuading, but in such a manner that the judge may claim immunity from its influence. Great lawyers such as Gerry Spence and Johnnie Cochran use it masterfully through post-modern techniques such as the moving narrative drawn from popular culture, or the wink of an eye, the subtle gesture, or turn of phrase. Great attorneys understand that

---

[37]   Hatfield, Cacioppo, and Rapson (see note 23), p. 129.
[38]   Goleman (see note 32), pp. 16-29.
[39]   Persuasion is defined as the art of using primarily extralogical appeals to secure decisions. Argumentation gives priority to logical appeals while taking cognizance of ethical and emotional appeals. Persuasion gives priority to ethical and emotional appeals while taking cognizance of logical appeals. The difference is one of emphasis; thus, if one looks at the courtroom as a 'rhetorical' site, as this essay does, one is concerned with persuasion as much as argumentation. Cf. Austin Freely, *Argumentation and Debate*, 3rd edition, Belmont, CA: Wadsworth Publishing 1971, p. 7.

they may not see a tear in the judge's eye, but that one may still have fallen quietly onto his or her heart.

Recent research into the role of emotion in the courtroom would be kind to Quintilian, showing him to be a prescient thinker on the phenomenon. Writing about his experiences and the experiences of his great role models, people like Cicero and Demosthenes, Quintilian put into his own terms much of what contemporary psychology offers today based upon neuroscience and social scientific experimentation. And while his Rules for emotional display in the courtroom would be viewed today as archaic, his belief that emotions are affecting the outcome of a trial from the opening to the closing argument remains viable. Hyperides did not have Quintilian's wisdom to guide him in his defense of Phryne. He knew, however, what all astute students of human behavior know: that try as we might to suppress them, our emotions are at work in all we do, flooding our perceptions and surrounding our judgments.

POSTSCRIPT

A postscript must be added to this essay based upon interviews I have conducted with a number of judges since the distribution of the survey. Recent legislation (circa 1985) in the United States known as 'victim impact' law, is changing the tone of America's courtrooms as we speak. Several judges with whom I spoke noted that, while emotional display has been checked during the trial, it has become the centerpiece, the proof of choice one might say, of the victim impact phase of the proceeding that occurs between the decision of the judge or jury and the sentencing.

Just prior to sentencing a convicted defendant, the court now allows the victims, their relatives, friends, and sometimes even counselors and therapists, to address the now-convicted criminal about the personal pain and anger they feel about the crime. Victim impact statements are often delivered with copious amounts of emotion often accompanied by tears and crying. They have occasionally even caused violence to erupt in the courtroom. Cathartic though they may be for the victims, for the judge the victim impact statement can be a real problem. The anguish of the victims often leads them to ask for punishments far beyond what the law allows, in some cases life imprisonment or death when the sentencing guidelines call for 10-15 years. The judge is now caught between the law and the demands of the victims. The result, oftentimes, is that the victims leave the court believing that justice has not been done and the criminal leaves the courtroom believing that the judge piled on a few more years to appease the victims.

Most judges with whom I spoke agree that victim impact legislation is necessary since a victim's anguish is often marginalized during the fact-finding phase of the trial. However, while judges are supposed to adhere to sentencing guidelines set by law, some find themselves moved to assessing longer sentences as a result of the victim impact statements, decisions that are then appealed. Other judges noted that they determine their sentence before the victim impact phase so as not to be moved by the courtroom pathos to decisions not mandated by the crime and the law. Regardless of the outcome, victim impact legislation is changing the climate of

America's courtrooms, having the direct effect of restoring victims to the center of the judicial process, but having the side-effect of bringing emotional display back into the trial with all the vicissitudes attendant thereto. While our courtrooms remain places where we argue the law and argue the facts, recent transformations in the judicial proceeding we call a 'trial,' suggest that we have begun now to 'pound the table,' with more frequency and effect.

JOSÉ-DOMINGO RODRÍGUEZ MARTÍN

MOVING THE JUDGE[1]

A Legal Commentary on Book VI of Quintilian's Institutio Oratoria

1. PROLOGUE

Quintilian's students must have waited anxiously for the lessons included in Book VI, having studied the five previous books on basic (Book I) and rhetorical (Book II) education and, in Books III to V, on the searching for arguments for a technical speech (*inventio*). Book VI would have seemed to them an oasis in the middle of their laborious studies since its central theme is laughter.

Therefore, we can easily imagine the great interest of the students in such an attractive programme: they were going to learn all the instruments that lead to laughter or tears while acting in court: how to respond with humour to the attacks of the opposing advocate and how to rouse the audience to applause after their speech, all that, spiced up with the substantial examples that Quintilian takes from his experience, and to which his students are already accustomed. But this time, the examples will consist of a selection of the best jokes, word play, and witty answers, rescued from legal history by the old master. What student could resist such an attractive study offer?

So when we begin to read, eagerly, Book VI, the last thing we expect is to find good old master Quintilian - who is normally in such a good mood - in a state of infinite sadness. At the moment when he begins to write this book, Quintilian tells us that he has lost his young wife, and his two sons, who were five and ten years old.

This preface seems to have been written at the point when his sadness was at its deepest, since the melancholic description he draws of his beloved family shows a beauty that only sincere care can express: the master tells us that, his wife being so young, losing her was as painful as the loss of a daughter (VI.pr.5); that the death of his youngest child took one of the lights of his life away (VI.pr.6). He also describes his total distress caused by the death of his other son, young Quintilian, after a long illness (VI.pr.12):[2]

> *Tuosne ego, o meae spes inanes, labentis oculos, tuum fugientem spiritum vidi?*
> Object of my vain hopes, how was I able to see your eyes fade, your soul fly away?

After reading the previous books, it was already clear that Quintilian was a master with a deep vocation. Now, we can do nothing but to admire it: because, since his

---

[1] I would like to thank Joanna Gould for her useful corrections and the time she dedicated to the revision of the English version of this article.
[2] I use the text edition by Winterbottom (see 'Introduction, note 26); all translations are my own.

love for his students is stronger than his own sadness, he decides to dedicate to his pupils the book that was meant for his son (VI.pr.16). And, although he has lost his interest in finishing his great work,[3] he is also conscious of the fact that many young students are waiting for his advice (VI.pr.16). Thus, the lesson begins.

2. THEMES OF THIS COMMENTARY

I could not resist making my little commentary on these touching, beautiful paragraphs, just like my compatriot Quintilian was not able to begin his work without expressing first his own feelings, so let me explain with no more delay the purpose of my work: whenever a jurist reads this book of the *Institutio oratoria,* he, or she, will get the feeling that something is wrong with the text, since the impression we get is that the power of oratory is so effective that the role of Roman jurisprudence is reduced to the minimum. This is surprising, since Roman jurists do not pay much attention to this question; on the contrary, they concentrate their works on the technical aspects of court actions. Their books are full of legal techniques, extremely subtle and highly developed, in order to assure the aim of justice throughout a controlled procedure which leaves little room for oratory. In this essay, I will try to give arguments and examples on both sides of the question, trying to describe the real role and opinion of both jurists and advocates at the time of Quintilian, when dealing with the power of feelings.[4]

Nevertheless, the aim of this project is not only to study the *Institutio oratoria* in detail, but also to encourage the reader to enjoy Quintilian's wonderful lessons. Therefore, while I discuss the main theme of my article, I will also try to highlight many moments of this book which display the sense of humour, sensibility, and legal abilities of the master from Calagurris.

3. QUINTILIAN'S LEGAL KNOWLEDGE

It could perhaps be said that Quintilian gives so much importance to oratory simply because he was not a jurist himself. But, as is commonly known, the first point to be set is that Quintilian himself had a more than acceptable knowledge of the norms

---

[3]   Although he says this in VI.pr.16, let us also read VI.pr.3, of moving beauty: 'Unum igitur optimum fuit, infaustum opus et quidquid hoc est in me infelicium litterarum super inmaturum funus consumpturis uiscera mea flammis inicere neque hanc impiam uiuacitatem nouis insuper curis fatigare'. ('The only good attitude would have been to throw this unfortunate work, and any remaining inspiration, into the fire in which these entrails of mine will burn in premature flames, and not to exercise in new projects this vitality which should be considered, in moments like these, even impious'.)

[4]   Throughout this essay, I will use these two general terms to distinguish the experts in law from the experts in oratory, although the terminology of these categories was no longer accurate in Quintilians's time. In fact, he uses other denominations which were also common in his time: *accusator* (see VI.1.36), sometimes also *patronus* (for example, in VI.1.24-25), a term which reminds one of the obligation of former owners of slaves (*patroni*) to assist their *liberti* in court. The same term was used in the public procedures against provincial governors who had been accused of corruption. Since the inhabitants of the province could not themselves act in court, they needed a Roman *patronus* to plead their case in Rome.

that ruled the law of his time, and this is especially obvious in Book VI. First of all, we find many technical words that are used with the accuracy of a jurist: the reader will find, among the explanations of Roman procedural law, a whole series of legal examples, in which Quintilian shows his knowledge of substantive law. Thus, he will speak about the waste of the *bona paterna* (VI.3.44), about commodate (VI.3.64), interdicts (VI.3.79), testaments (VI.3.92), heritage acceptance (VI.3.97), legacy (VI.3.100), etcetera. A whole life dedicated to law also allows Quintilian to use technical words as literary speech,[5] or to joke and play with their meanings.[6]

His knowledge of technical matters is also guaranteed by his long extensive professional experience, shown through many comments in which we can guess that only those who have spent their whole life in the courts could have such a deep vision of the essence of trials. He uses a surprisingly modern terminology. Both old and modern trials mean the substitution of self-help for legal procedures, but they still wear the indelible imprint of the disputes they substituted. Thus, Quintilian uses war terms to describe court situations, which have the same descriptive force today: especially when dealing with the *altercatio* or forensic debate (Chapter 4) and *consilium* or strategy (Chapter 5) as discussion techniques. Quintilian uses expressions such as 'to defend oneself or to attack' (*ad resistendum vel lacessendum*, VI.3.104), since debates are like battles (*pugna*, VI.4.15; 4.21; 5.5; *acies*, VI.4.17; *rixa*, V.4.13-14), even like slash fight (VI.4.4); and he adds that surprising our *adversarius* with our speech is like laying an ambush for him (VI.4.14). Therefore, the master not only displays to his expectant pupils his deep knowledge of the judicial framework, but also life-long experience in the courts.

4. THE INFLUENCE OF ORATORY ON THE JUDGE'S DECISIONS

It is therefore clear that Quintilian must have good reasons to give so much importance to oratory, and that these are not actually based on ignorance of legal techniques. So, before comparing his opinions with the texts of Roman jurists, let us dedicate some lines to some selected points of Quintilian's explanations, to give an accurate idea of the power of oratory to move the judge.[7]

He introduces the subject, the conclusion of the speech or *peroratio* (VI.1ff.), by listing the two ways for the advocate to make the judge pronounce himself in the advocate's favour, after having heard his speech.

The first of these two ways is the enumeration of facts (*res*). Quintilian explains that, at the end of the speech, it is very important for the advocate to show again to

---

[5] It is absolutely impressive to see how Quintilian is able, in the middle of his terribly sad *proemium*, to play with these literary resources: with terms from the law of succession, he explains how he was going to leave his work to his son, but that now he will have to leave it to others (VI pr.16): 'sicut facultates patrimonii nostri... aliis relinquemus'.

[6] See the example about ambiguity as an oratorical instrument in *Inst. or.* VI.3.51

[7] The reader may have noticed that the quotations do not follow the order of Quintilian's Book VI; my idea is to gather some appropriate examples that illustrate each point I make, rather than to summarize the chapter, in order to make my commentary more lively and to lead the reader's attention to interesting points of the text.

the judge, briefly, the complete list of arguments that he has used. However, it is necessary to be very careful: it is useful to refresh the judge's memory and put the whole case before his eyes,[8] but not to the extent of making him think that the orator does not trust the judge's memory! (VI.1.2; 1.8). He also points out that the delivery is as important as the contents: adding a brilliant conclusion to the enumeration of the facts will have an irresistible effect on the judge. An example of this is taken by Quintilian from his admired Cicero: while the republican orator was talking directly to Verres, in reality he was trying to influence the senators who were listening, so the conclusion was as follows: 'After hearing these arguments, the judge should condemn you, even if he were your own father!' (VI.1.3).[9]

The students would ask themselves: 'Apart from enumerating the facts, what is the second way to convince the judge?' The answer of the master is astonishing: appealing to the emotions. You must play with the feelings of the judge if you want to win the cause; facts are not enough.

This advice is even more surprising for the importance that Quintilian gives to it, since, in Book VI, much more space is given to the matter of feelings than to the question of facts. While facts are found only in the first six paragraphs of the first part, dedicated to *peroratio*, the study of emotions covers not only the rest of this part, but also the whole of Chapter 2[10] and the long, central Chapter 3, dedicated to laughter (*De risu*).

The question is so important that Quintilian undertakes, in this Book, a very detailed study of human nature. Throughout these pages, he studies the origin and meaning of laughter, he classifies the emotions, he analyses the methods (and excesses) of other advocates. The importance of the question, on the other hand, requires the high learning that his expressions reveal: opinions of Greek philosophers about the convenience, or inconvenience, of provoking emotions (VI.1.7ff.), his critiques of other schools (VI.1.42-43); the classification of passions into *êthos* and *páthos* (VI.2.8 ff.), etcetera.

However, his explanations do not belong to the field of theoretical oratory. Every concept, every idea comes with a different example, displayed with a descriptiveness that only the old teacher could articulate, mixing his own court recollections with his literary ability. He reveals, in the end, his own experience, in order to show his students that he is teaching not mere academic theory, but daily practice. As a result, we can see, passing before our eyes as in an old film, advocates who bring the relatives of the victims to the court, or even lift them in their arms while speaking, or show the murder weapon still bloodstained - or sometimes even a bone of the victim! - in order to move the judge. In his examples, there are advocates for whom the court bursts into applause, while others have to escape from the laughter, having made fools of themselves. Accusers who know how to bring the judge to tears

---

[8]   In the master's own words (VI.1.1): 'memoriam iudicis reficit et totam simul causam ponit ante oculos'.

[9]   Quintilian's quotation of Cicero is taken from Cicero, *In Verrem actio*, V.136; note that the orator's words are not literally quoted.

[10]   Called *De divisione adfectuum et quomodo movendi sint*, ('On the classification of passions and how they are to be roused') in some manuscripts in which his work has come down to us.

because of the gravity of the cause, defenders who appeal to the judge's clemency, and both parties attempting to prevent the judge from becoming affected by the emotions that the advocate of the opposing party will try to arouse in him. Quintilian advises to establish the alibi in close collaboration with the defendants, and to break that of the other advocate, and to come out with flying colours using an appropriate joke when one's own arguments are refuted. Laughter, tears, mercy, and (why not?) the social image of the judge are the aim of the advocate who has a good grasp of oratorial techniques.

Among all these resources, Book VI is first of all famous for its third chapter, *De risu*. I especially advise the reader to enjoy the wonderful selection of jokes and witty answers contained in VI.3.22-103. Just to give an example (and to make the reader curious), it is worth quoting VI.3.73, where Quintilian repeats Cicero's comment about Fabia, the wife of Dolabella, who said that she was thirty years old:

> *'Verum est', inquit, 'nam hoc illam iam viginti annis audio'.*
> 'That is true', he replied, 'I have been hearing her say that for twenty years'

Or that moment in which the accusing advocate sharply asked Cicero, who was the defender, what he knew about a certain S. Annalis, and he replied, quoting from memory, the beginning of Ennius' *Annales: Quis potis ingentis causas euoluere belli?*, ('Who can the causes vast of war unroll?', VI.3.86). As Quintilian says, it's better to stop here and refer the reader directly to the jokes in the book, because if not, it is going to be difficult for me to restrain myself from telling too many (VI.3.65)!

5. PARTICULARITIES OF ROMAN PROCEDURAL LAW

At first sight, it may not seem very 'professional' to us, as continental lawyers, that an advocate would attach more importance to provoking the emotions of the judge or rousing the laughter of the audience rather than presenting the facts as proved, since our system of professional judges does not leave much room for brilliant orators. However, jurists who are familiar with the common law system, in which juries are much more in use than in civil law courts, may find it more acceptable to attach so much importance to these emotions (the success of some trials on US television come to mind). Quintilian wrote his *Insitutio oratoria* after a long judicial career, and knew what he is talking about. It is worth highlighting a few characteristics of the trials that Quintilian describes, that may help to explain the efficacy of oratory to influence the final verdict of the jury, in comparison with the technical methods of the jurists.[11]

First of all, it must be said that the greater part of Quintilian's examples are taken from criminal procedures (in which there was a jury), rather than civil ones, since civil procedures before a *iudex unus* would not give much scope for oratory; in fact, displaying rhetorical skills may even have been considered ridiculous. Quintilian explains this with a funny comparison: making a tragedy out of a little civil dispute

---

[11]   See in this book, 'Introduction', about the legal procedures in Rome.

would be like trying to disguise a little boy with high *cothurni* and a big mask of Hercules (VI.1.36).[12] Quintilian states that oratorical techniques are more effective in criminal cases than in civil ones, because of the importance of what is discussed; indeed, he designates the criminal cases by the word *pericula*, 'dangers' (or 'risky situations'), and the accused, by *periclitans,* 'the one in danger [of being strongly punished]' (VI.1.21-22; 1.36), in contrast to the *privatae causae* (VI.1.36), in which the verdict is mostly pecuniary (VI.1.50, *pecuniaria litis*).[13] The master even distinguishes between the kind of advocate who is suitable for each of the two procedures (VI.4.7), and also between the diverse techniques of fact enumeration, depending on the length of each case (VI.1.1 and 8) or on the kind of object in dispute (general procedures, definition cases, fact cases, and processes which may or may not require the proofs to be technical proofs; see VI.4.4).

Here we find the first distinction between the themes studied by the legal experts and those of Quintilian: the great majority of texts that have come down to us refer to Roman private law, gathered by Justinian's compilers in the Emperor's Digest. In those civil procedures, the *probatio* should be almost exclusively technical, since it was a question of documents or witnesses. If we read, for example, D.22.5, *De testibus,* or Inst. 4.17, *De officio iudicis,* there is no mention of the influence of orators but only technical commentaries on the value of different proofs.

Nevertheless, there were some civil procedures in which the judge was not *unus,* but a jury of *centumuiri.* Those were cases which could allow the orators to display their skills (for example, discussing the state of liberty or slavery of a person), as maybe they also could in problematic civil procedures.[14]

On the other hand, it is known that, in Rome, as is the case nowadays, laws were subject to interpretation, to the extent that different judges could reach very different conclusions when applying a rule. This problem was avoided by the Romans through a wise measure: allowing the litigant parties to choose their own judge, so that afterwards none of them could complain about the decision of someone they trusted.[15] In these cases, there was also a place for orators, who could fill the little

---

[12]   Cicero gives another good and funny example in *Orator,* 72 (English translation by H.M. Hubbell, in Loeb Classical Library): 'Quid enim indecorum est, de stillicidiis cum apud unum iudicem dicas amplissimis uerbis et locis uti communibus (...)!' ('How inappropriate it would be to employ general topics and the grand style when discussing cases of stillicide before a single referee (...)!') See also Cicero, *De optimo genere oratorum,* 10.

[13]   I want to point out here that among the *privatae causae,* there were also some offences which were simply considered 'civil offences': *furtum, rapina, iniuria, damnum,* and those prosecuted by the *praetor* in his *Edictum.* On the contrary, offences of 'public' gravity, the *crimina,* were prosecuted by criminal law. While looking for examples for his lessons, Quintilian offers cases from both kinds of trials; but since a special place is reserved for his idol Cicero, there are also lots of examples from his speeches before the Senate, an organ in charge of many political procedures. On these questions, see O.F. Robinson, *The Criminal Law of Ancient Rome,* London: Duckworth 1995 and B. Santalucia, *Diritto e processo penale nell'antica Roma,* 2nd edition, Milan: Giufrrè 1998.

[14]   On this question, see W. Kunkel, *Herkunft und soziale Stellung der römischen Juristen,* 2nd edition, Graz-Vienna-Cologne: Böhlau 1967, rpt. Cologne-Weimar-Vienna 2001, pp. 328-329.

[15]   In Emperor Justinian's Digest (533 AD), there is a text of the jurist Ulpian, which is categorical, i.e., D. 4.8.27.2 (text and translation from A. Watson (ed.) *The Digest of Justinian,* Philadelphia: University of Pennsylavania Press 1985): 'Stari autem debet sententiae arbitri, quam de ea re dixerit, siue aequa siue

holes left by the jurists when they tried to reduce the possibilities of parties contesting decisions, writing almost perfect *formulae*. However, as we jurists know, reality is always more flexible than the *formulae* or articles we write, and language is a poor instrument that cannot contain all the possibilities of daily life. As a result, every jurisprudential text could always be liable to different interpretations, which was in the end the task of the orators.

The last particularity is that, in Rome (at least until the development of the imperial *cognitio extra ordinem*), there were no professional judges, in today's meaning of the word. On the contrary: even if it was a criminal procedure, the judge was a common citizen, chosen to act as the judge for a trial. That was the logical consequence of the concept that the Romans had about law: *ius civile* was, as its name reveals, the law of the *cives*, of the citizens. As a matter of fact, *ius civile* could be created by laws, which were approved by *cives* meeting in the assemblies, or as a result of the *mores maiorum*, which consisted of customs, created and observed by citizens since time immemorial. The civil law could even be created by citizens without any special power, the so-called *iuris prudentes*; their decisions were only valid if other citizens considered them to be right and reasonable: only then did their opinions become *ius*, invested with *auctoritas* (the equivalent of 'social prestige').[16]

Therefore, only the rules that passed the filter of civic control became effective law. Was not it therefore logical, that citizens themselves were the ones who should put them into effect by acting as *iudices*? Maybe here lies the explanation of the perfection of Roman law, a system which consists of such fair laws, so well-adapted to human nature, that people still consider them 'natural', in the sense that it is difficult to imagine different laws ruling daily life: the secret of the success of the system was that the creator and the addressee of the law were the same person: the citizen. As a matter of fact, *sententia* just means 'opinion', but an opinion of a citizen in a case becomes, automatically, Law (and Truth: *sententia pro veritate habetur*).[17]

---

iniqua sit: et sibi imputet qui compromisit. Nam et diui Pii rescripto adicitur: 'uel minus probabilem sententiam aequo animo ferre debet'' ('Moreover, the award which the *arbiter* makes in a particular case ought to stand whether it is just or unjust; the person who referred the arbitration to him has himself to blame. For a rescript of the deified Pius adds: 'Or you ought to bear with an undisturbed mind an unjustifiable opinion'.). This text refers to arbitration, but is also entirely suitable for the classical judicial procedures, since the two systems share the same basic idea (and, probably, a common origin): because the parties freely choose the person who is to resolve their dispute, they cannot argue afterwards that his decision was not right.

[16] Examples of the term *auctoritas* being used in the sense not of an special power, but of social respect for the wisdom of a personal opinion, can be found in *Inst. or.* VI.3.30; 3.33; 4.17 and 5.10, where it means simply 'to be right'. The word *auctoritas* has a more legal sense in VI.5.9, where Quintilian is talking about the mother's *auctoritas* over her son: it is not actually a legal power, but a prestige status that leads to respect and obedience. See also in this book J. Fernandez' comment on the concept of *auctoritas* in Book I of the *Institutio oratoria*.

[17] The term *sententia* has different meanings in Latin. Quintilian also uses it in different ways. Book VI provides examples of its technical-legal sense (e.g., in VI.2.7). It is used in a rhetorical sense in VI.3.36 and with the meaning of 'ideas' (in opposition to *verba*) in VI.1.52. Obviously, the term *sententia* was a common word for the Romans, and it underlines the private character of the judge's decision; in the same way, to give a *'iudicium'* is nothing else but to give an opinion (see VI.1.37). In this respect, paragraph VI.5.1 is of special interest, since the author uses *iudicium, opinio* and *sententia* with different meanings.

It is also true that usually the judges were chosen among the *equites* or the senators, and obviously the citizens belonging to those social classes received a good education including Rhetoric and Law.[18] However, there is a great difference between this education and that of our modern professional judges. Therefore Quintilian is very conscious that the advocate not only can, but even must profit from the judge's condition of *privatus*:[19] he can convince the judge more easily with feelings than with technicalities. He justifies it by an appropriate parallel: 'It is like lovers, who are not able to judge with objectivity the beauty [of the beloved person], because passion prevails over the eye' (VI.2.6). Who could deny that his example remains fresh today?

6. DIFFERENT ROLES OF JURISTS AND ORATORS

So what role did jurists play in this aim of convincing the judges? Does the fact that they did not write about rhetorical matters mean that they thought that justice should be achieved only through technical methods, like in an ancient version of modern positivism? Let us give some clues to clarify the relationship between the art of the orators and that of the jurists.

I have already said that the main *arena* of the jurists was the civil procedure, so their possibilities to influence the final decision of the judge were restricted to the composition of the *formula* (in the first part of the trial, *in iure*), which limited the decisions of the judge to those within that document. Once the trial entered its second part (*apud iudicem*), they could only influence the judge by defending their clients themselves.[20]

In fact, we know that some jurists were also advocates, and developed rhetorical skills. Some examples include Titius Aristo, Opellius Macrinus, Iulus Paulus, or Papinian himself.[21] Q. Mucius Scaevola was considered by Cicero as the most eloquent among the jurists.[22] The fact that jurists acted as advocates was quite common, since the participation in civil procedures was considered normal for someone who wanted to begin a political career. The opposite case (orators who became jurists) was rare: maybe the most famous exception is that of S. Sulpicius Rufus, who was 'the best orator after Cicero' (cf. D.1.2.43), but not being able to understand some legal explanations of the jurist Q. Mucius Scaevola, thereby wounding his professional image, he decided to leave the profession of orator and become a jurist.

However, the original situation, as far as we know, was that of a clear difference between the roles of the two professions: orators, in the beginning, did not have to learn the law: at the time, that was a bare *nescentia,* not the criticized *ignorantia* of

---

[18] See O.E. Tellegen-Couperus, *A Short History of Roman Law,* London-New York: Routledge 1998, pp. 57-59
[19] Indeed, Quintilian considers it as an *officium* for the advocate (VI.1.9).
[20] See F. Schulz, *History of Roman Legal Science,* Oxford: Clarendon Press 1953, pp. 53-54.
[21] About these and other examples, Kunkel (see note 14), p. 326.
[22] Cicero, *Brutus,* 145: *Iuris peritorum eloquentissimus.* About this question, see K.Z. Méhész, *Aduocatus Romanus,* Buenos Aires: Víctor P. de Zavalía 1971, p. 61.

later times,[23] a logical consequence of the separation of roles: let me remind the reader that, in early times, the jurists were the *pontifices*, and therefore did not act as advocates in courts.

This distinction was maintained throughout the republican time, but in the last two centuries BC, things began to change, as the new formulary procedure gradually replaced the old *legis actiones* system, and jurisprudence was already open to lay-men. While the rhetorical arts reached their highest level, orators began to enter the domains of the jurists, since they realised that a good orator should also have a sound knowledge of the legal aspects of his client's case: indeed, what Q. Mucius Scaevola reproached S. Sulpicius Rufus for, was his ignorance of the law of the city.[24] Quintilian himself advises his students to study Law (XII.3.1-2), in order to become capable of distinguishing good from evil (cfr. II.21), or to avoid the embar-rassing situation of having to ask for advice in the middle of a trial, when a new legal aspect of the case appears (II.12.3).[25]

But this golden moment of Quintilian, in which a good orator was one who had a solid education not only in Rhetoric, but also in Law and Philosophy, did not last long. In later times, legal education was considered as a heavy load for an orator, to such an extent that some authors criticized jurisprudence as a task for duller minds. Maybe it was the consequence of the new times, in which the free creativity of jurists was little by little controlled by the emperors; but it also meant the final vic-tory of a conception of court acting in which legal techniques were considered as useless in comparison with effective playing on the feelings of the judges.[26]

Maybe we can find here the final answer to this study: such a conception of law had nothing to do with the traditional *reverentia* that jurists always gave to *ius*. Maybe Roman legal scholars, rather than being conquered by orators, preferred to stay out of the arena and continue preserving the technical aspects of the law, sepa-rated from alien factors such as the feelings of the judge. Schulz describes the situa-tion this way:[27] 'They stood fast and refused to suffer the noisome weed of rhetoric, which choked so much else that was fine and precious, to invade their profession'. It is clear that his opinion is expressed in too sharp a way, but the underlying idea, that the jurists just intended to protect the purity of their own *ars* from pernicious influ-ences, may be right. This was a fortunate decision, since in this way, they preserved and developed the law, something that Hellenistic forensic rhetoric was incapable of producing.

They were too loyal to the pure idea of their art to pay attention to rhetorical methods, something more appropriate to politicians or advocates than to jurists. That is why they did not write about the influence of feelings in the final decision of the

---

[23] See Méhész (previous note), p. 59.
[24] Pomp. D.1.2.43: 'Namque eum dixisse turpe esse patricio et nobili et causas oranti ius, in quo uer-saretur, ignorare'.
[25] Cicero, along the first chapter of *De oratore,* criticizes some orators of his time who try to defend their clients without knowing the first thing of Roman law.
[26] Schulz (see note 20), p. 108. See also this German author's clever comparison of Quintilian and Liba-nius on p. 338, note Q.
[27] Schulz (see note 20), p. 55.

judge; that was left for other kinds of literature.[28] Quintilian's lessons show us the point in which jurists and orators were able to work together, the moment in which justice could be achieved through the efforts of both specialists put together: going on with the comparison between trials and fights, Quintilian's favourite model, Cicero, says that jurists 'provide the ammunition' for the battle that orators have to undertake.[29] But jurists did no more than that: as Quintilian says, 'Proofs make the judge see that our position is the best; but emotions make him support it himself' (VI.2.5). However, that battle was beyond the purposes of the jurists.

7. CONCLUSION

As a conclusion, outside the main aim of this article and in parallel to my introduction, I would like to underline a last moving point of Quintilian's theories about law. Apart from comparing trials with battles, the master reveals what, in his opinion, is the essence of the advocate's *officium:* if the judge's emotions are so overwhelming, if the task of the advocate is to play with his listener's emotions, then the advocate is not a fighter, but an actor.

Thus, Quintilian speaks about the 'scene' when referring to trials (VI.1.38; 1.49), and says that the advocate must laugh and cry even more than actors do (VI.2.35). Calling the court audience *theatrum,* he even says that the advocate should develop such a touching performance that, to conclude, he could say: 'Now you can clap!' (VI.1.52). Also using theatre terminology, he establishes the limits of this scenic vision of the *apud iudicem* process, preventing it from falling into farce (VI.3.29) or easy parody (VI.1.47). Maybe the most surprising proof of how accurate his idea is, is the fact that, both in Latin and in modern languages, we use the verb 'to act' equally for the theatre 'actor' and for the judicial *actor.*[30]

Therefore, Quintilian reveals himself in Book VI as a master of the human soul, a deep *connoisseur* of the mechanisms that work inside every person. Quintilian is not talking about alien things, since he is also a victim of passions: let us remember once more the state of sadness in which he wrote this book. However, after having read the whole display of instruments that an expert orator (such as he) is able to use, is it not natural to suspect that the moving beginning of this book is only a demonstration, to prove how the master is able to touch our hearts? In other words, was it real sadness, or only a new proof of the efficacy and power of a good rhetorical discourse that the master gives to his students? That is to say... was he acting?

There is no doubt that the inclusion of that beautiful *proemium* at the beginning of a book dedicated to feelings was intentional, but my admiration for the master of Calagurris, borne of hours and hours of reading and enjoying his masterly prose, is

---

[28]   And not only rhetorical literature, but also philosophical: see, for example, Aulus Gellius, *Noctes Atticae,* XIV.2, about the *officium iudicis.*

[29]   Cicero, *De oratore,* I. 242; 253; *Topica,* 65: *hastas ministrare.*

[30]   See VI.1.26, which includes a comparison between the oratorical techniques of the advocates, and the masks used by actors on stage.

stronger than my scientific criticism. I would rather believe that Quintilian was sharing his feelings with his readers.

For that reason, I prefer to think that the master was indeed acting, but in a different way: better than anyone else, Quintilian personifies his own vision of the advocate as an actor, since, all through this book, he has surprised us and made us laugh with his examples, just as if he had been feeling equally happy when he wrote them.

He teaches us, thus, a lesson about professionalism: as advocates, our mood does not matter, but that of our defendants does; as teachers, that of our students. His litigation, his education, his laughter matters. Therefore, both on the courtroom and classroom stages, in both of which settings Quintilian was an expert, the only criterion will always be the same and today it still rules the honourable profession of those who, day by day, climb on the stage to awaken feelings: *the show must go on.*

DAVID PUJANTE

THE ROLE OF *DISPOSITIO* IN THE CONSTRUCTION OF MEANING: QUINTILIAN'S PERSPECTIVE

1. INTRODUCTION: THE SCOPE OF *DISPOSITIO* IN QUINTILIAN

Book VII is the only book in the *Institutio oratoria* dedicated to *dispositio*. Given that Quintilian's work encompasses twelve books and that there are five parts or canons of rhetoric (*inventio, dispositio, elocutio, memoria* and *actio*), a simple mathematical calculation indicates that little space is dedicated to this second canon of classical rhetoric. This seeming lack of attention becomes even more evident when we compare the many books dedicated to the other two parts involved in textual construction (*inventio* and *elocutio*). Is *dispositio* perhaps of secondary importance or is it that, despite being fundamental, it is so simple that no further explanation is necessary? When we read the book Quintilian dedicates to *dispositio,* we find that, quite to the contrary, it is one of the most complex sections of the treatise, where the stasis theory (conjecture, definition, quality, jurisdiction) is explained.[1] In the tenth and final chapter, we find a possible explanation as to why so little space is dedicated to *dispositio* in the *Institutio oratoria*. According to Quintilian, in VII.10.7:

> *Hoc est quod scriptor demonstrare non possit nisi certa definitaque materia.*
> It is precisely this (the structure of the speech) which is impossible to demonstrate other than by reference to some definite and specific case.[2]

Thus, Quintilian clarifies that *dispositio* goes beyond the theoretical scope of his work. The writer of a handbook on rhetoric such as he cannot discuss the structuring of discourse in abstract terms. He must deal with specific and clearly defined material. If a method for structuring this material exists, it is learned from successive practical applications in specific cases. Quintilian goes on to explain that such a method (of arrangement) does not depend on the teacher, but on the learner. Physicians teach the symptoms of illnesses and the known remedies, but the capacity to

---

[1] Quintilian examines the relationship between different modes of discourse and stasis in Book III (III.8.4). See J.W. Basmore on the stasis theory in Quintilian and the influence of his work: 'Quintilian on the status of the later comic stage', *Transactions & Proceedings of the American Philological Association* 40 (1901), pp. 21-22; J. Cousin, *Études sur Quintilien*, 2 Vols., Paris: Boivin 1935-1936, rpt. Amsterdam: Schippers 1967; J. Cousin, 'Quintilien, 1935-1959', *Lustrum* (1962) pp. 289-332. J. Cousin, *Recherches sur Quintilien*, Paris: Les Belles Lettres 1975. L. Calboli Montefusco, *La dottrina degli "status" nella retorica greca e romana*, Bologna: Università degli Studi di Bologna 1984; A.C. Braet, Variationen zur Statuslehre von Hermagoras bei Cicero', *Rhetorica* 7, 3 (1989) pp. 239-259.
[2] I use the edition by Winterbottom (see 'Introduction', note 26) and the translation by Butler (see 'Introduction', note 27).

perceive and understand the type of illness one is dealing with is determined by the
aptitudes each individual possesses (VII.10.10). *Dispositio* is clearly a critical part of
rhetoric since it links the different aspects of stasis, thus determining the key issues
in a case. Although Quintilian acknowledges the importance of *dispositio*, he concedes that its mastery depends exclusively on the capacity of the individual orator, a
natural talent that should be practised and its development encouraged and cultivated. Quintilian is not concerned with theory, his focus is on practice: concrete and
specific cases. Resorting to a classical dichotomy well-known in literary theory,[3] we
can say that, in *dispositio*, *ars* (an acquired skill) gives way to *ingenium* (a natural
talent). Precisely as a result of this pragmatic approach, in Book VII, Quintilian
relies on specific examples to develop his ideas.

Thus, it is evident that *dispositio* has to do with structure as well as with the elucidation of the distinct stasis of the specific situation. How are the two related? The
answer to this question will provide a definition of this second canon of rhetoric.

2. REDEFINING THE SECOND RHETORICAL OPERATION IN THE *INSTITUTIO ORATORIA*: ORDER AND MEANING

While *inventio* provides a series of referential elements albeit lacking a significantly
clear structural design, *dispositio* places us fully within the realm of discourse,
which is the realm of interpretation. If by *inventio* we mean the discovery of material, the method by which subject matter is chosen and how it is treated and presented within a coherent framework (III.1.1),[4] to begin to construct the text is to
begin to fit together the elements at our disposal. If the referential world offered us
a clear design of reality, there would be no need for rhetorical discourse. There
would be no point in having an interpreter of facts were it not possible, for example
in judicial discourse, for one interpreter to design a coherent argument asserting an
individual's guilt, while another is able to design an equally coherent argument for
the accused's acquittal using the exact same set of facts. The order of the world is
not given; it is determined by us. Interpretation requires a specific design, order and
arrangement of ideas, creating an indissoluble link between *inventio* and *dispositio*.[5]

---

[3]   See the application of this dichotomy by Antonio García Berrio in his books: *Formación de la teoría
literaria moderna, 1. La tópica horaciana en Europa*, Madrid, Cupsa, 1977; *Formación de la teoría literaria moderna, 2. Teoría poética del Siglo de Oro*, Murcia, Universidad de Murcia, 1980.
[4]   Cousin translates the passage from Quintilian 'quo quaeque in ea modo inuenienda atque tractanda
sint' as 'de la méthode pour trouver et traiter ses matériaux', cf. M. F. Quintilien, *Institution Oratoire.
Livres II et III*, Vol. 2, edited and translated by Jean Cousin, Paris: Les Belles Lettres 1976, p. 140.
[5]   Although in Quintilian's treatise *dispositio* follows *inventio*, this does not correspond with actual practice since, in composing a speech, all of the five canons of rhetoric apply simultaneously. Quintilian simply follows his predecessors' attempts at establishing theoretical constructs in which the different parts or
canons of rhetoric are rigidly separated into distinct categories. Antonio García Berrio has proposed distinguishing between the actual specific application of rhetorical canons and the theoretical model on
which they are based, cf. A. García Berrio, 'Poética e ideología del discurso clásico', *Revista de Literatura* XLI 81 (1979) pp. 36-37; Id., 'Lingüística, literaridad/poeticidad (Gramática, Pragmática, Texto)',
1616. Anuario de la Sociedad Española de Literatura General y Comparada 2 (1979) pp. 156-157. T.
Albaladejo, *Retórica*, Madrid: Síntesis 1989, p. 61 suggests that rhetorical communication is efficient

Classical interpretation of Quintilian already recognised the direct relationship existing between order and *dispositio*. Next, in order to respond to the question posed
above, we must consider the relationship between order (*ordo*) and stasis (*status*).
In terms of the relationship between *ordo* and *dispositio* Josef Martin explains:

> Quintilian scheint den Unterschied zwischen *dispositio* und *ordo* nicht erkannt zu
> haben, wenn er als Neuerungssucht empfindet, neben der *dispositio* noch vom *ordo* zu
> sprechen. [6]

Quintilian does make a theoretical distinction between *ordo* and *dispositio*: *ordo* is
defined as the correct ordering of the parts and elements in such a way that they are
coherent, and *dispositio* as their useful or expedient distribution (VII.1.1). However,
according to Martin, Quintilian, who is the first to discuss *dispositio* and *ordo*
together, considers the two to be inextricably related. *Dispositio*, then, can be said to
be a useful ordering of material.

This ordering is useful as long as it allows us to establish the facts and issues,
the rhetorical points, that will lead us to a resolution of the case. It seems that
rhetorical ordering is required of us exactly when we are faced with the problem of
elucidating the questions of stasis: What are the facts? Are they certain or uncertain? Is it necessary to define the facts? Once defined, do they need to be qualified? To resolve these issues we will need to construct or design a suitable interpretative framework. To design such a framework, it is necessary to begin by
posing the right questions. A good question is worth as much as a good answer
since the one depends on the other. In the book on *dispositio*, Quintilian deals with
stasis, that is, the formulation of the questions that need be raised in order to identify the key point on which the case hinges. The proposed questions or *proposita*
(VII.1.4) are: Is there a conflict that must be resolved? (conjecture); What is it?
(definition); What is it like? (quality); and finally: What is the legal situation in
this case? (jurisdiction and a consideration of the problems that arise from ambiguities in legal texts and the problem of establishing intention). This is one of the
ways in which structure and stasis interact. However, the complexity of *dispositio*
is great and we must distinguish among different levels of structure, each of which
is designed to achieve different aims.

3. THE DOUBLE SIGNIFICANCE OF *DISPOSITIO*

It is possible to identify a double usefulness of *dispositio*: 1) *dispositio* must lend
coherence to the facts; and 2) *dispositio* must serve to persuade. As we have seen,
dispositio provides the interpretative framework for the case in question. However,
it also determines the persuasive strategies to be employed. Following Celsius and
Cicero, Quintilian explains that he agrees with placing strong arguments first, the

---

when the three canons that constitute discourse intersect, entering into a relation of simultaneity. For a
discussion on the extent to which Quintilian is conscious of such a distinction between the reality of
application and the theoretical model, see D. Pujante, *El hijo de la persuasión. Quintiliano y el estatuto
retórico*, 2nd edition, corrected and revised, Logroño: Instituto de Estudios Riojanos 1999, p. 134.
[6] J. Martin, *Antike Rhetorik. Technik und Methode*, Munich: Beck 1974, p. 217.

strongest arguments last, relegating weaker arguments to the central part of the discourse. Along the same lines, he also agrees that the most serious accusations should be dealt with first (VII.1.10-11). These and many other aspects of *dispositio* are combative strategies. We thereby can deduce that there are two ways of organising material. One type of organisation provides an interpretative framework, which I will term 'interpretative disposition'. The other way of structuring the discourse is designed to demonstrate to the audience that things are exactly the way the interpreter (*orator*) presents them (and no other), which I will call 'strategic-persuasive disposition'.

Therefore, given that *dispositio* initiates the structuring of the oration, it also initiates the act of ordering the discourse, an order that is related to 1) the elucidation of the cause of the conflict or dispute and 2) the manner in which the audience can be persuaded that this is so. Here we have two useful types of ordering that serve a dual purpose: designing the structure of the truth and persuading others of its veracity. All this is designed to achieve a yet higher purpose: to establish within a given social context our elucidation of truth so that justice is served. It is not ethical to use persuasive strategies to put forward a twisted interpretation of the facts. This would go against Quintilian's concept of morality and his definition of the orator as a *vir bonus dicendi peritus* (XII.1.1), a good man skilled in speaking. The orator should abstain from resorting to arguments that may be effective but not serious. Cousin explains:

> (L'orateur) s'abstiendra de recourir à des arguments inattendus, destinés à frapper l'esprit du vulgaire, mais non à convaincre les gens sérieux. [7]

Discourse may employ strategic-persuasive disposition aimed at presenting the view of events of which the orator is fully convinced. In this way, disposition is a means of shedding light on the truth, and of communicating this truth in a convincing and persuasive manner. *Dispositio,* then, is a basic element in the rhetorical scheme. It is, in fact, the rhetorical canon with the widest sphere of influence since it is in the structuring of all the different elements that make up the speech that we discover the essential point that determines the nature of the discourse. In this way, *dispositio* encompasses both the realm of matter (*res*) and that of words (*verba*).

4. *DISPOSITIO* IN *RES* AND *VERBA*

Thus, language gives shape to the world, and there are few occasions where this is so evident as in the rhetorical experience. The interpretative framework referred to manifests itself within a pragmatic textstructure. Quintilian argues that *dispositio* interacts with thoughts, words, figures, and linguistic colour (VII.1.40 and VII.10). This could be understood in simplistic terms to suggest that disposition acts as a device that simply orders the elements once these have been established, strategically dispersing them throughout the speech to serve a variety of expressive functions. However, in both the first and tenth chapters, Quintilian explains that the dis-

[7] Cousin (see note 1), I p. 351.

position of *verba* also requires talent (*ingenium*), the ability to perceive and understand the essential cause of the dispute: the points that give rise to disagreement. Since talent is a basic requirement for the disposition of both realms, there is a clear relationship between the disposition of the *verba* and the disposition of the *res*, from which it follows that it is not possible to consider the disposition of *verba* as a simple dissemination of stylistic devices. Disposition designs linguistic colours and figurative schemes as the only means of expressing the interpretative framework that will elucidate the essential questions of stasis. Once again we are confronted with a theoretical division that does not correspond to reality. The distinction between disposition of the *res* and disposition of the *verba* is possible only in theory. In practice, one cannot be separated from the other. Ultimately, the orator is only able to express his thoughts on stasis through a series of rhetorical devices.

Although Quintilian discusses disposition in the section on *verba* (for instance in his study of analogy), the main focus of Book VII is on the role of disposition in terms of *res*. The argumentative order derives from the rhetor's skill in correctly formulating the right questions which will give rise to a discussion based on: 1) human logic, verisimilitude or coherence (arguments should be posed in such a way as to lead to a coherent understanding of the main point or issue in question and to the acknowledgement of the facts on the part of the audience); and 2) equity (our final interpretation should also rest on the conviction that the logic of the argument does not go against the sense of fair play among the opponents).

The questions Quintilian formulates are based on different argumentative principles and take into account different points of view, all of which are aimed at designing a structure that allows for the discernment of truth, truth that is derived from this examination, a truth that is not evident before the act of composing the speech (which would otherwise render this act futile), but is a result of the process. The greater the orator's commitment and natural talent, the more forceful the speech. The most forceful speech is the one that best accomplishes its aims, with no evident lapses, not always through deductive reasoning though touching on all the points and, consequently, other rhetorical elements come into play. Reasoning is more timid and proceeds step by step while the rhetorical perspective accepts the fact that being practical often involves taking a giant leap forward, relying on other elements such as intuition, equity, and emotional persuasion. Arguments should be precise, but logical argument is not the only resource at hand.

5. THE STASIS OF CAUSE: ON CONJECTURE

Most of Book VII is dedicated to establishing the questions of stasis. Quintilian opens Chapter 2 with a discussion of conjecture and, from the very beginning, he indicates that the best way to structure an argument is to begin by asking pertinent questions in a pertinent order. This explains Quintilian's interest in developing a comprehensive and complex classification of questions. Their order is the key to credibility. In *Inst. or.* VII 2.56, he proposes:

> *Ordo quoque rerum aut adfert aut detrahit fidem: multo scilicet magis res prout <ponuntur> congruunt aut repugnant.*

... the order in which the facts are stated may either contribute to or detract from the credibility of our case; for consistency and the reverse depend to a very great extent on the way the circumstances are presented.

Quintilian sets out to organise these questions in terms of conjecture. There are general questions which apply to any type of conjectural speech and questions that apply in specific cases.

Questions that may apply to any type of conjectural discourse	Questions about the facts (de *re*)	General Questions (on the past) (Is the world ruled by providence?)
		Specific Questions (on the past) (Has Roscius committed parricide?)
	Questions about intention (de *animo*)	Past Intention (What was Scipio's attitude when he first set foot in Africa?)
		Present Intention (What is the intention behind Pyrrhus' request for peace?)
		Future Intention (How will Caesar react if Ptolemy has Pompey murdered?)

Questions about specific cases	Who?
	Why a thing exists (Origin: Is the plague a result of the wrath of the gods?)
	Cause (Why was something done? Had they sworn to do it?)
	Quality (Is the sun larger than the earth?)

Quintilian's model posits different types of questions. There are questions on the *conditions that give rise to conjecture* (a combined question in which both parts are denied, a separate query that questions whether or not the deed has actually taken place). There are also questions about the *deed* itself (simple questions: Did the person die?; compound questions: Was he poisoned or did he die of an illness?). When there is evidence to substantiate the deed, but not *who* is responsible for it, then the accused may simply deny having committed the act, or he may accuse another. In the second case, the accusation may be reciprocal (an anti-category) or a new, third party may be accused. The accusation against someone who is not part of the original case may be explicit or not. If explicit, it may simply be extraneous or arise from the wishes of the victim or deceased. Finally, the questions may deal with the *intentions* of the person who committed the act (Did he want to do it? Could he have done it? Did he actually do it?).

Providing further details would entail rewriting Quintilian's book, so I will simply outline Quintilian's guidelines for drawing the map that allows one to survey the territory being explored and identify our present position and circumstances. Quintilian seeks to show us that the best way to structure the arguments in a case is by asking pertinent questions. It is important to clarify the proper subjects for conjecture: Has it taken place? Is it what it is said to be? Is the person allegedly responsible for the act actually responsible? In each case we are confronted with a series of sub-questions. This chapter sets out to provide the ideal approach to composing a discourse that will lead us to the correct interpretation of a given problem or situation. It is *dispositio* that leads us to definition.

6. THE STASIS OF DEFINITION

By delimiting conjecture, we arrive at definition. The third chapter of the book is dedicated to definition. What distinguishes conjecture from definition? The genre adopted. (A) I did not steal; I did not receive money in deposit; I did not commit adultery; (B) This is not stealing; this money is not a financial deposit; this is not adultery. The distinction lies solely in the focus of our defence. Likewise, the method applied may involve moving from quality to definition, for instance, in cases concerning mental illness, cruelty and offences against the State (VII.3.2).

According to Quintilian, definition is the appropriate expression of the matter in question using clear and concise language.[8] Definition, then, is a linguistic approach to reality: a clear and brief statement that is appropriate to the subject at hand, not simply a statement of the *facts* (for we can never be certain if the linguistic expression corresponds exactly to the fact being referred to), but a statement that is appropriate to the *subject*. Definition is the result of the use of language in its intent to organize reality. At times, the terms are clear and what is questioned is the reality referred to (What is God?) or the quality (What is rhetoric? The power to persuade or the science of speaking well?). There are other cases in which the terms are disputed but the facts are clear (Is he who commits suicide a murderer?).

For Cicero, whom Quintilian greatly respects, definition affects both what is defined and what is excluded (VII.3.8). It is the linguistic need for fencing in the *continuum* of reality. Quintilian describes three types of questions of definition (VII.3.8-10): 1) Is it this? (Can an act committed in a brothel be considered adultery? If the answer is negative, there is no need to define anything); 2) Is it this or is it something else? (Is it stealing or sacrilege? Saying what it is not is insufficient; whatever it is must also be defined; 3) Is it this and something else? (Is it a love potion and a poison?). Sometimes the definitions do not contradict each other, but are simply expressed in different words (VII.3.12-13). In contrast to the philosophers who favour a single definition, Quintilian believes that the orator should offer several; one should not be enslaved by certain words. He proposes that a definition be presented first, followed by an explanation: a detailed complementary definition (VII.3.16). The following factors help to elucidate a good definition: properties and differences, occasionally etymology, equity always, and conjecture sometimes (VII.3.25). Fundamental to definition is quality, and so Cicero holds that the arguments which rely on definition are typically those that are drawn from 'antecedents, consequents, adjuncts, contraries, causes, effects and similarities'. Quintilian refers to this earlier in Book V (V.10.73 *passim*).

---

[8] *Inst. or.* VII.3.2: 'finito igitur rei propositae propia <est> et dilucida et breviter comprensa verbis enuntiatio'.

7. THE STASIS OF QUALITY

When both parties agree on a definition, the final judgment is based on quality, which is the focus of Chapter 4 of Book VII. Quintilian begins by discussing quality in suasive speech, controversial themes and epideictic speeches (VII.4.2-3). The chapter is dedicated to the question of quality in judicial speeches. Every legal case is about some form of compensation or penalization, or the amount of the penalty or compensation to be awarded. When the issue at hand is the penalty, possible approaches are: 1) a defence of the illegal act that has been committed; 2) a discourse in favour of extenuating circumstances or the accused's exoneration or acquittal (pleas on behalf of the accused). There are also different types of defence: 1) the action itself is defended (the absolute justification of the action due to the accused's honour or other inalienable circumstances); 2) the action is defended in terms of another action (an action may be indefensible in itself, but justified by other extraneous circumstances); 3) the action may be defended on the grounds of its usefulness to the community or the State. When none of these apply, either the blame is shifted onto another action or it is attributed to ignorance or necessity and thus lacks criminal intention. The following is an outline of Quintilian's model.

	COMPENSATION			
The question of quality in legal cases revolves around	PENALTY	DEFENCE	Defence of the case	KAT'ANTÍLEPSIN: The action itself is defended.
				KAT'ANTÍTHESIN: The action is defended in terms of another action.
				ANTÍSTASIS: The action is defended because it is useful to the community.
			The blame is shifted	METÁSTASIS: Blame is shifted to another action (or person).
				JUSTIFICATION: (The action is excused on the grounds of ignorance or necessity)
		EXTENUATION	PELIKÓTETA or PESÓTETA	
		EXONERATION OR ACQUITTAL	Due to background circumstances (the life history of the accused).	
			For having already been sufficiently punished.	
			Due to extraneous circumstances: titles, dignity, rank, family and friends.	
	QUANTIFICATION OF THE COMPENSATION OR PENALTY			

8. JUDICIAL PROCEDURE

It is the first part of the book that gives rise to the greatest number of reflections and interpretations. In Chapter 5 legal issues are addressed, and the question of quality focuses on legal matters. Even if the accused does not deny committing the act, nor does he admit to having carried out another action different from the one of which he is accused, nor does he try to justify himself, there still exists a legal procedure to which he is subject. Questions about the jurisdiction of the tribunal and the legal process arise. That is, irrespective of the specific circumstances surrounding the action (whether it was actually committed or not, whether justifiable or not), there are established procedures for trials, and the administration and implementation of these may be questioned. This leads us to consider the matter of legal stasis. Questions on legal points refer to: 1) conflicts that arise from a given law, and/or 2) conflicting laws. A series of questions about the legal text may arise (in terms of its clarity, obscurity, or ambiguity) and the issue of intention may also be called into question. Quintilian briefly discusses these core conflicts in the following chapters. Chapter 6 focuses on legal text and intention: questions about the letter of the law and its underlying intentions; questions about texts which are clear and intentions that are manifest but nonetheless pose conflicts; questions about other different intentions that are manifested in certain expressions within a given text. Chapter 7 describes various legal conflicts that may arise. Antinomy or the conflict of authority is discussed. This is an issue since legal conflicts may arise between similar laws, within a given law, or between different laws. A law may be accepted or challenged by both litigants. When legal points are at issue, either one or both laws may be challenged. Legal conflicts always hinge on the following question: Does this law apply?

To resolve any of the legal conflicts mentioned above, Quintilian relies on syllogism (Chapter 8), which contrasts the letter of the law with a series of rational universal conclusions that ultimately annul the text. This is similar to the procedure that contrasts a text with the intention for which it was written, except that in this case the scope is wider. The intention of the text and the legislator are not contrasted; instead, what is contrasted is the letter of the law and the irrefutable rational universal conclusion that overrides and cancels the actual text. We find that syllogism is related to definition. The basis of litigation is derived from the corresponding texts, which is why we speak of conclusions based on reasoning (*ratiocinatio*). The syllogistic argument derives from what is written in the text, but also draws on what is not stated but can be deduced by analogy.

9. ON ANALOGY: *DISPOSITIO* AND *VERBA*

It is especially interesting that Quintilian's discussion of analogy considers how expressive elements are embedded in the overall framework of constructed meaning. From a discussion on *dispositio* in relation to *res* Quintilian leads us once again to a consideration of the relationship between *dispositio* and *verba*. In this way, it becomes clear that the two domains, *res* and *verba,* are, in fact, inseparable and that one inevitably leads to the other. Analogy is ultimately concerned with establishing similarities between things, and so we can say that the relational understanding of the different elements of a conflict is clearly based on metaphoric meaning.[9] The discussion of *dispositio* in relation to *verba* is once again taken up in Chapter 9, which is dedicated to ambiguity or double meaning. We are shown how problems regarding the interpretation of the causes that give rise to the dispute centre around elocutionary aspects, making up a web of diverse interpretations and intentions from old and new words and meanings. In this chapter, Quintilian limits his discussion to providing possible alternative solutions to ambiguous expressions (words and phrases) that may lead to ambiguity, without any further analysis of the problem.

The book ends with Chapter 10, which is also quite brief. Here Quintilian reflects on the relation among the questions of stasis. He discusses how, in actual practice, we find that the elements which theoretical models tend to classify as separate entities do, in fact, intersect. Quintilian ends with a reflection that has served as the point of departure for this brief journey through the world of *dispositio*; a reflection on the retreat of the rhetor to winter quarters based on the conviction that a rhetorical treatise cannot substitute for natural talent, the capacity of each individual to question the state of things, to examine in depth the problems of our day-to-day existence in this world in an unstable social union with our fellow citizens. In *Inst. or.* VII.10.10, he states: *Quaedam vero non docentium sunt, sed discentium*, 'there are, however, some things which depend not on the teacher, but on the learner'.

---

[9]   In terms of rhetorical tradition it is important to reclaim the conception of analogy as a similarity between things, which is the general modern tendency; cf. the description of *Analogía* in J. Ferrater Mora, *Diccionario de Filosofía*, Barcelona: Círculo de Lectores 1991: a conception which acknowledges its metaphoric meaning and edits out metaphysical referentiality.

MAARTEN HENKET

STATUS AND *LOCI* FOR THE MODERN JUDGE
From Voluntas to Purpose and Beyond

1. INTRODUCTION

Quintilian's *Institutio oratoria* is accessible to modern law students, whether or not they are proficient in Latin. But should we advise our students to read Quintilian? Can reading Quintilian help them to become good jurists? No doubt, generally speaking, the answer to this question is yes. But if we go more into detail, the use of Quintilian's theory - if we may call it that - for modern law is perhaps less clear.

In this paper I want to address the question to what extent, if at all, Quintilian's system of *status* and *loci* can be useful for the theory of adjudication and for the training and practice of the modern judge.

Since an answer to this question is dependant on one's view of adjudication, I will begin, in the next two sections, by indicating my position on this point. In section 2 I will discuss the relationship between the legislator and the judge, and in section 3 I will discuss the task of the judge as it follows from that relationship. In section 4 I will briefly introduce the concepts of *status* and *loci*, and indicate some relevant aspects of Quintilian's theory, and in section 5 I will indicate in what respect *status* and *loci* can be of interest for contemporary adjudication.

When I speak of adjudication in this paper, I have in mind adjudication as we know it on the European continent, that is adjudication within a system of statutory law. However, I think that my conclusions are, *mutatis mutandis*, also valid for common law systems.

Given the fact that this paper is intended for a mixed audience of classicists, historians and jurists, I feel obliged to give explanations here and there that for some readers might be trivial and unnecessary.[1]

2. STARTING POINT: ADJUDICATION IN A STATUTORY SYSTEM

Many people believe that in a statute-based legal system, the legislator should make the rules and the judge should merely apply them. Applying the rules may not always be easy, since it involves, among other things, determining which rule should be applied in a given case, and interpreting that rule. But it does not involve the

---

[1] For quotations from the *Institutio oratoria* I have used the Oxford edition by M. Winterbottom (see 'Introduction' note 26). For the English translations I have used the translation by Butler (see 'Introduction' note 27).

kinds of choices a legislator faces as to what law is best for the community, nor does it involve the kind of creativity that a legislator needs in order to make those choices.

Not only do many people believe that the legal system *should* work in this way, they also believe that to a large extent it *does*. Not withstanding the overwhelming amount of evidence to the contrary, in the form of an almost weekly supply of judicial decisions, both by domestic and by international courts, that deeply affect existing law and are presented as such in the media. Apparently, the existence of a separation of powers is to many citizens what the existence of God is to a religious person: an article of faith.

In modern legal theory, however, it is almost commonplace that the judge can not be as docile as would fit the picture sketched above. Choosing the applicable rule, interpreting that rule, determining the facts, all this requires a fair amount of creativity. Also, there are cases where the applicable rules seem to be in conflict, and even cases where existing law does not provide a solution. In such cases, it is almost universally recognized that the judge does not apply law, he makes it.[2]

Though most legal theorists nowadays recognize the law-making aspect of adjudication, they differ as to the extent of this aspect. Many authors are of the opinion that in the average case, where, it is said, the facts and the applicable rule are clear, no judicial creativity and choice are involved. To borrow Hart's terminology, every legal term in this view has a core of meaning which is clear, and a penumbra where there is room for dispute, and, accordingly, for choice (no doubt an automobile is a vehicle, but what about a skateboard?).[3]

My position on this subject is as follows. Though it may be true that there is a whole body of standard cases where the judge does nothing but routinely apply existing law, in the final analysis every instance of adjudication implies the making of choices, of decisions.[4] To apply a rule in its standard meaning to a set of clear facts involves at least three decisions. First, that the facts are in fact clear. Second, that the rule applied is indeed the appropriate rule. And third, that the standard meaning of that rule is indeed the right meaning for the case at hand. These three decisions, or choices, may be made automatically and unwittingly, but they are made. Each case of this kind could have turned out differently, had the judge chosen a different option in one or more of these three choices. Had he done so, his judgement would be recognized as creative and would perhaps be published and commented upon in the law journals.[5]

---

[2] The most notable exception is Ronald Dworkin, with his much debated 'one right answer thesis'. See, e.g., the essays 'The Model of Rules I', and 'Can Rights be Controversial?', in R.A. Dworkin, *Taking Rights Seriously*, London: Duckworth 1977.

[3] See H.L.A. Hart, *The Concept of Law*, 2nd edition, Oxford: Clarendon Press 1994, Chapter 7.

[4] For criticisms of Hart's position from a semiotic perspective, see P.J. van den Hoven, 'Hard cases, do they exist?', *International Journal for the Semiotics of Law* 3, no. 7 (1990) pp. 55-63, and Bernard S. Jackson, 'Literal meaning: Semantics and Narrative in Biblical Law and Modern Jurisprudence', *International Journal for the Semiotics of Law* 13, no. 4 (2000) pp. 433-457.

[5] For a recent discussion of these issues in the Netherlands, see M.J. Borgers, et al., 'Een alternatieve visie op de functies van de redelijkheid en billijkheid en de taak van de rechter', *Nederlands Juristenblad* 75 (2000) pp. 2029-2031, and M.W. Hesselink, 'Wat is recht? etc.', *Nederlands Juristenblad* 75 (2000) pp. 2032-2040. My position is very much in line with Hesselink's.

To put it differently: to *treat* a case as a standard case is to *make* that case into a standard case. Also: each decision in which the judge clearly uses creativity and by which he clearly changes existing law could also have been treated as a standard case, in which case it would probably have passed unnoticed. To give an example: in the 1980s the Dutch Supreme Court created, in a number of decisions, the possibility of euthanasia by a physician under strict conditions. These decisions became notorious and much debated. Instead, the Court could very well have declared the physicians to be guilty of murder and have left it to the legislator to change the law.

The legal system does not dictate the one and only solution to a legal case. If that were the case, we could leave adjudication to clerks or computers, and would not need the wisdom of human judges. There is always more than one possibility, and which of the possibilities best fits in the legal system, is always debatable.

3. SYLLOGISM, OR *PHRÓNÊSIS*, OR WHAT?

If the above is true, and adjudication involves judicial creativity and choices, this has possible consequences for (a) the knowledge and skills required of a judge and (b) the form of judicial opinions. As to knowledge and skills: if we do not want the choices of the judge to be arbitrary, we should provide him as far as possible with tools that can help him to make good choices. As to the form of judicial opinions: if the judge makes choices, then presenting the resulting judgment in the form of a mere syllogistic subsumption of the facts under the rule is misleading, because it suggests that the decision is inevitable.[6] Should the judge not present the choices he has made, and give arguments in favour of those choices? I will return to both these points (a) and (b) when I discuss the possible use of Quintilian's system of *status* and *loci*. But first a little more about the form of judicial decisions.

To a certain extent, the possible choices lie within the legal system and can, as such, be said to be governed by that system. So, for instance, when the judge makes a choice between two applicable rules and bases his choice on some higher rule or principle of existing law. In that case, the higher rule or principle provides an objectively valid argument for the choice made. But not all choices can be based on objectively valid arguments. What if the judge's decision is determined by his weighing of the interests of the parties? What if it is based on considerations of equity? Can such decisions be made to rest on objectively valid arguments?

Most contemporary legal theorists feel they can not. Which brings some of them to the conclusion that we should put our faith not so much in sound argumentation but more in the judge's practical wisdom, or, to borrow a term from Aristotle,

---

[6] In the usual sense, a syllogism is a form of reasoning whereby the conclusion necessarily follows from the premises (Aristoteles, *Topica*, I.1). It can be noted that Quintilian's *syllogismus* (*Inst. or.* VII.8.1-7) is something different. His 'syllogism' serves to deduce from the letter of the law that which is uncertain ('ducit ex eo quod scriptum est id quod incertum est') and to infer what is doubtful from what is certain ('ex eo, quod manifestum est, colligitur quod dubium est'). A contemporary legal theorist would rather call this reasoning by analogy.

phrónêsis.[7] Wise and experienced judges, it is said, take good decisions, even if their final choices are not based on arguments but on intuition.

In this paper I want to argue that it is dangerous to put too much trust in the judges' intuition. We may, I think, ask from the judge that (a) he takes into consideration all relevant factors when he makes his choices, and that (b) in his published decisions he presents rational arguments for the choices made. In the remainder of this paper we will discuss to what extent Quintilian can help him to do so. In the next section I will introduce the notions of *status* and *loci*, and give some relevant characteristics of Quintilian's treatment of these notions. In section 5, I will then discuss what *status* and *loci* can mean for the modern judge.

4. *STATUS* AND *LOCI* IN CLASSICAL RHETORIC

Although the theory of *status* and *loci* is a standard part of classical rhetorical theory, each of the important authors on classical rhetoric provides his own variant. In this section I will first give a very short introduction to the notions *status* and *loci*, followed by some relevant characteristics of Quintilian's system of *status* and *loci* as presented in the *Institutio oratoria*.

4.1. Status *and* Loci

As to the term *status*: Butler, in his well known Loeb-translation of the *Institutio oratoria*, remarks that there is no exact English equivalent of that term. He suggests *basis* and *ground* as 'perhaps the nearest equivalents'.[8]

What it means can best be clarified by an example. Someone is prosecuted for theft. Several questions can be raised, among which:

- 'Did he do what he is accused of?' (*status coniecturalis*),
- 'Was what he did indeed theft?' (*status definitivus*),
- 'Can his deed be justified?' (*status qualitatis*),
- 'Should the case be brought before this court?' (*status translationis*).

Each of these questions can become the object of dispute between the prosecutor and the defence. Depending on the circumstances of a particular criminal case, the defendant will choose one of these questions as a basis for his defence, and that will then become the central issue or *status* of that particular case.

Different authors present different sets of *status*. Most authors distinguish two kinds: *status rationales* ('factual' status) and *status legales* ('legal' status), though the latter type is sometimes regarded as pseudo-status and sometimes treated as a sub-status of the *status rationales*. I will clarify this further, as far as necessary, below.

Sometimes a status is divided into sub-statuses. For example, in a criminal case the *status coniecturalis* ('did he do it?') can, among other things, give rise to questions about the accused's character, his motives, and his opportunity to commit the

---

[7] Aristoteles, *Rhetorica*, II.I.1378a. 8.
[8] Butler (see note 1), III. 6.1, at note 4.

crime. So 'character', 'motive' and 'opportunity' can be regarded as sub-statuses of the *status coniecturalis*.[9]

Locus (Greek *tópos*), means *place*, more specifically: a place to find arguments. There are common places, where one finds arguments suitable for all kinds of discussions (the modern term 'commonplace' has a different meaning) and special places, where one finds arguments for particular types of dispute.

Sometimes a status or sub-status has its own particular set of *loci*. For example, the sub-status *character* of the *status coniecturalis* ('did he do it?') can, among other things, give rise to arguments regarding the accused's education, his natural disposition, and his way of life. So 'natural disposition', 'education' and 'way of life' belong to the *loci* that belong to the sub-status *character*.

4.2. Status *and* Loci *in the* Institutio oratoria

In this section I will discuss a few characteristics of Quintilian's version of the theory of *status* and *loci* that are relevant for my argument.

What Quintilian offers in the *Institutia oratoria* is not a fully-fledged theory of *status* and *loci*, in the sense of a closed system comparable, for instance, to that ascribed to Hermagoras. His treatment is less systematic and less complete than would have been appropriate had he had that ambition. A few examples may suffice to make this clear.

Firstly, the treatment of *status* and *loci* is scattered over several books. The *status* are treated in Book III and VII. The treatment of this subject in Book VII seems somewhat odd, since *status* theory is usually regarded as belonging to the theory of invention (*inventio*), whereas the subject of Book VII is order (*dispositio*). Moreover, the *status*-system presented in Book VII differs from that in Book III. The main difference is the status (!) of the *status legales*: are they, or are they not part of, or related to, the *status rationales*?[10]

Confusing also is Quintilian's treatment of the *status translationis*. After telling us in III.6.66 that, like most other authors, he used to incorporate it as a sub-status of *status legalis*, in III.6.68 he excludes it from his new system of *status* (*Ex iis... remoui tralationem*). In III.6.84, however, he includes it once again (*hinc illae quaestiones siue actionis siue tralationis*) for didactical reasons in a special version of his theory, intended for those who are engaged in instructing the ignorant, *instituentibus rudes* (III.6.83).[11] Finally, in the preface to Book VIII, where he gives a summary of his theory, he again incorporates *translatio* as a separate line of defence: *depulsionem... praeterea defensione ac tralatione constare* (VIII. pr.9).

---

9 For Quintilian, see *Inst. or.* VII.2.27ff.

10 That Quintilian's theory is not clear on this point can be further illustrated by the fact that different commentators interpret Quintilian differently. According to A.D. Leeman and A.C. Braet, *Klassieke retorica*, Groningen: Wolters-Noordhoff / Forsten 1987, p. 36, Quintilian treats the *status legales* as genuine separate *status* in Book VII, but not in Book III; however, P. Gerbrandy, *Quintilianus, De opleiding tot redenaar*, Groningen: Historische Uitgeverij 2001, p. 162 n. 94, states that the *status legales* are taken together in Book VII as one of the *status rationales*.

11 See, however, J. Adamietz, 'Quintilian's 'Institutio Oratoria', in: H. Temporini and W. Haase (eds.), *Aufstieg und Niedergang der römischen Welt* II, 32, 4, Berlin-New York: Walter de Gruyter 1968, pp. 226-2271, p. 2262, n. 162.

As to his lack of completeness, Quintilian indicates, for instance, that he does not want to give detailed rules for the use of *loci communi*, 'a task requiring infinite detail', but that he only wishes to sketch the general line and method (V.1.3).

All in all, the parts of the *Institutio oratoria* that are devoted to the treatment of *status* and *loci* make difficult and rather technical reading and, taken together, are not easily made into a coherent system. However, this is not sufficient to discard Quintilian's theory as useless. I will come back to this in section 6, but first I will discuss the utility of *status* and *loci* for modern adjudication.

5. *STATUS* AND *LOCI* FOR MODERN ADJUDICATION

What can *status* and *loci* mean for contemporary adjudication? Regarding *loci*, this question has been the subject of a lively debate ever since Viehweg published his *Topik und Jurisprudenz*, some fifty years ago.[12] As the title indicates, this book is not a treatise on adjudication - it is about jurisprudence or legal science. It advocates a problem-directed approach to legal questions, as opposed to the system-directed or 'deductive-axiomatic' approach which was prevalent at the time in European continental law, especially in Germany. Indirectly, however, such an approach would have consequences for adjudication, which was one of the reasons why Viehweg's book met with so much opposition: critics were afraid that the 'topical approach' would lead to an excessive use of judicial discretion, in violation of fundamental principles of separation of powers and the rule of law.[13]

If one believes in law as a closed and complete system which contains a solution to every legal question, and if one believes accordingly in the possibility to find the solutions by subsumption (the system-directed or deductive-axiomatic approach), then indeed a topical approach to legal problems is unnecessary and a possible danger. But if one believes that a complete separation of powers is an illusion and that judicial discretion is inevitable, then the topical approach can be regarded not as a threat to legal certainty, but as a weapon against judicial arbitrariness, and thereby an instrument of legal certainty. Nowadays, many Dutch legal scholars take that position, and the usefulness of a topical approach as well as the desirability to develop modern legal topics are recurrent themes in the literature. An important *desideratum* for such modern topics is, in the words of Nieuwenhuis, to 'make sure that the combination of topoi becomes indeed a system, and does not remain a brantub'.[14]

One tool for systematizing is to order the various topoi pertaining to the same question hierarchically.[15] Another one is, I suggest, to take up the classical idea of linking topoi to *status*.

---

[12] English translation by W. Cole Durham Jr.: *Topics and Law*, Frankfurt am Main: Peter Lang 1993.
[13] See, e.g., F. Wieacker, 'Zur Topikdiskussion in der zeitgenossischen deutschen Rechtswissenschaft', in: E. von Caemmerer *et al.*(eds.), *Xenion: Festschrift für Pan. J. Zepos*, Athens etc.: Ch. Katsikalis 1973, pp. 391-415, 397-399.
[14] J.H. Nieuwenhuis, 'Hoi topoi', in: J.H. Nieuwenhuis, *Confrontatie en compromis*, Deventer: Kluwer 1992, pp. 109-122, at p. 120 (my translation, M.H.).
[15] Nieuwenhuis (see note 14), p. 118.

So far, the *status* theory has not received nearly as much attention in contemporary legal theory as has the theory of *loci*. An exception in Dutch literature is Antoine Braet, not a legal scientist but a scholar of rhetoric, who has convincingly shown the correspondence between classical *status* systems and Dutch criminal procedure.[16]

Though the classical *status* theories were developed primarily with criminal procedure in mind, there is no good reason to limit their scope to criminal law.[17] To illustrate that, I can take an example from Dutch civil law. In a Dutch tort case a number of distinct questions may keep the parties divided:

- Did the defendant do what the plaintiff accuses him of? (cf. *status coniecturalis*),
- Is what the defendant did illegitimate? (cf. *status definitionis*),
- Is the defendant liable? (cf. *status qualitatis*),
- Is the damage suffered claimable? (no separate parallel criminal *status*),
- Did the act of the defendant in fact cause the damage? (no separate parallel criminal *status*),
- Is the norm violated by the defendant intended to protect the interests of the plaintiff? (no separate parallel criminal *status*).

In arguing about each of these questions, legal and extra-legal *loci* might come into play. Ordering these according to the question (or *status*) they belong to would be an attempt to bring more system in the bran-tub. Historically, the theories of *status* and of *loci* were developed separately. Aristotle 'invented' the topics, but the theory of *status* was developed later. Systematically, however, it seems fruitful to take them together and to look at *status* as an ordering device for *loci*. The relationship between the *status* and the *loci* that play a role in a concrete case can be described as follows: the *status* determines the conclusion one chooses to defend, and the *loci* serve to locate the arguments to be used in that defence.

On a more abstract level the difference between *status* and *loci* is less straightforward and, I think, less important. *Status* and *loci* are both means to direct one to relevant questions, and to relevant answers (in the form of relevant arguments). There is a second argument in favour of relativizing the difference between *status* and *loci*. Whether we should regard something as a *status* or as a *locus* may vary with the circumstances, or, to use a term from semiotics, with the pragmatics of the case at hand. As an example take 'character', presented by Quintilian as a sub-status of *status coniecturalis* (see section 4.1 above). However, it is clear that 'character' can equally well function as a *locus*. This is an instance of the more general phenomenon that, in concrete discussions, a certain utterance may function as a reason, or as a conclusion, or both.

---

[16] Antoine Braet, *De klassieke statusleer in modern perspectief*, Groningen: Wolters-Noordhoff 1984, Chapter 7. Braet refers to only two publications by legal theorists on the subject: E. Meyer, 'Die Quaestionen der Rhetorik und die Anfänge juristischer Methodenlehre', *Zeitschrift der Savigny-Stiftung für Rechtsgeschichte* rom. Abt. 68 (1951) pp. 30-73; and F. Horak, 'Die rechtstheoretische Statuslehre und der moderne Aufbau des Verbrechensbegriffs', in: F. Horak and W. Waldstein (eds.) *Festgabe für Arnold Herdlitczka*, Munich-Salzburg: Fink 1972, pp. 121-142.

[17] In fact, the classical authors realized this also. Among other things, they sometimes use other than criminal examples. For Quintilian, see, e.g., *Inst. or.* VII.6.9 (on the *causa Curiana*, a famous dispute over an inheritance).

Status and *loci* can be of use with respect to both questions of law and to questions of fact. As to questions of law: The more statutes contain vague terms and open norms, the more freedom the judge has in choosing the 'right' solution. Some modern codes show a development in that direction. Extreme examples are the Dutch statutory civil law standards of 'redelijkheid en billijkheid' (reasonableness and equity) and 'belangenafweging' (weighing of interests). What is equitable in a concrete case? How does one weigh interests? Certainly there are no objective scales for doing that. To make the application of such standards less subjective and more controllable, a system of *status* and/or *loci* may be helpful.

As an example, I take the following provisions in the Dutch civil code (BW; my translation, M.H.)

> BW art. 6:248, section 1
> A contract not only has the legal consequences agreed upon by the parties, but also those which, given the character of the contract, follow from statutes, customs and reasonableness and equity.
> BW art. 3:12
> In determining what is reasonable and equitable, the following should be taken into consideration: generally acknowledged principles of law, convictions regarding the law that exist in the Netherlands, and the social and personal interests that are involved in the case at hand.

Here we see that art. 3:12 gives a few topoi (*loci*) to assist in the application of art. 6:248, section 1. But art. 3:12 does not assist all the way: what if relevant principles of law are in conflict with each other, or with social or personal interests? How does one weigh the conflicting personal interests? Here additional topoi can be helpful. For example, the question whether or not one of the parties is insured against certain forms of damage may influence the weight that should be attached to his interest in compensation.[18]

In this context it is interesting to note some differences in abstraction between classical and modern standards for the interpretation of legal documents, primarily statutes (but also contracts, testaments). First, classical rhetoric speaks of a possible conflict between *verba* (or *scripta*) and *voluntas*, that is: the intention of the author (legislator, contracting parties, testator). Nowadays, quite often a topos is invoked which abstracts from the intention of the author, namely the purpose of the text. Second, in classical rhetoric, equity is almost exclusively linked to the *status legales*, that is to the interpretation of - primarily - statutes.[19] It is, as it were, a standard to be taken into consideration in interpreting a statute, but it cannot set the statute aside.[20] Nowadays, equity is an independant standard which stands on an equal foot-

---

[18]   I derive this example from Nieuwenhuis (see note 14), at p. 116-117.

[19]   An exception can be found in the example in *Inst. or.* V.10.109-118, but, as Quintilian indicates, that has to do with the special procedure before the *Amphictyonas*: 'Sed uel potentissima apud Amphictyonas aequi tractatio est' ('as the case is being pleaded before the Amphictyonic council, we shall find that the most powerful plea that can be urged is that of equity').

[20]   Since the line between interpreting a statute and setting it aside is not always clear, and since it is therefore quite possible to interpret a statute in such a way as to ignore it, it is perhaps better to say that in antiquity *equity* could not *openly* be used to set the statute aside. The practical difference with our own use of equity may not be so great, but the theoretical difference remains important, because it reflects a different attitude towards statutes.

ing with statutes, or even higher (if used as a principle of law). Hence the subtitle of my paper ('From *voluntas* to purpose and beyond'): from *voluntas* to purpose (the 'modern' variant of *voluntas*) to equity is a development towards more and more abstract norms and thereby, towards more and more room for judicial choice. If we regard the theory of *status* and *loci* as a means to prevent choice from becoming arbitrariness, this tendency towards greater abstraction is a stimulus for further developing that theory. One of the aims could be a movement back to more concreteness or, to put it differently, to more differentiation.[21]

As I said before, *status* and *loci* can be of use with respect to questions of law and questions of fact. As to questions of fact: In criminal adjudication there are examples of decisions that have clearly been taken without paying enough attention to relevant factual data. A notorious example from Dutch criminal adjudication is the so-called Leiden ball-point case. A young man was convicted of murdering his mother by shooting a ball-point pen into her eye with a crossbow. The evidence was extremely scant and all experts thought that it was physically impossible that the pen had been shot into the eye, but the judges were 'convinced' by a declaration by a psychologist, and the man was convicted (he was later acquitted on appeal).[22]

An adequate system of (status and / or) loci could, if accepted as a standard, perhaps make it more likely that the relevant facts receive the attention they deserve. This is especially important where, as in the Netherlands, the law of evidence gives the judge a great deal of freedom. I will come back to this point in the next section.[23]

Just now I used the phrase 'if accepted as a standard'. For, of course, non-statutory *status* and *loci* do not automatically bind the judge. As we saw, positive law itself also contains *status* and *loci*, although they do not bear that name. The difference between statutory and extra-statutory *loci* is a difference in status(!), and accordingly the arguments found there differ in their degree of validity. A statute-based argument is, *prima facie* at least, valid. What makes a non-statute-based argument into a valid argument? Factors like public morality, legal dogmatics, precedent and legal theory come into play here.

Who are the addressees of a theory of *status* and *loci*? Classical rhetoric, and Quintilian is no exception, was intended for the speaker, and as far as legal practice is concerned, the addressee was not the judge or jury but the pleader. It is, however, easy to see how a system of *status* and *loci* can be useful for the judge as well. First of all, the judge who knows his *status* and *loci* will be better able to keep in mind all the factors that are relevant to the case, and to judge the quality of the arguments brought forward by the pleaders, as well as their relevance for the particular question

---

[21]   A recent example in Dutch jurisdiction is a differentiation in the interpretation of contracts (more or less literal'), depending on the question to what extent the interests of third parties come into play. See C.E. Drion, 'Kroniek van het vermogensrecht', *Nederlands juristenblad* 76 (2001), pp. 435-433, at p. 430.
[22]   District Court of The Hague, 13-10-1995 (unpublished). This case has provoked many critical reactions. In English: E. Feteris, 'What went wrong in the ballpoint case', in: M. Malsh & J.F. Nijboer (eds.) *Complex Cases*, Amsterdam: Thela Thesis 1999, pp. 159-178. See also Hendrik Kaptein, 'Jumping to Conclusions in Criminal Law', *Rechtstheorie*, Beiheft 18 (1998) pp. 385-394.
[23]   For a critique of the treatment of facts in criminal law cases in the Netherlands and elsewhere, see H.F.M. Crombag, P.J. van Koppen & W.A. Wagenaar, *Unsafe Justice: The Psychology of Criminal evidence*, Harvester: Wheatsheaf 1993.

under discussion.[24] And secondly, this knowledge can help him in finding and formulating a reasoned decision. In that last role, by the way, the judge is no longer an
arbiter, but a speaker who tries to convince an audience: he must make his decision
acceptable to the appellate court, the legal community and if possible to the parties.

To conclude this section, a warning against too great expectations is perhaps in
place. The development of a system of *status* and *loci* for contemporary law can aim
at channelling the way judges use their discretion, but cannot take away that discretion. It cannot lead to a closed and complete system of law. This is inherent in the
character of topical argument, it is inherent in the nature of adjudication, and to take
away discretion would, even if it were possible, mean regress instead of progress.
Our modern system of law is an open system, and as such cannot completely prede-
termine the judges' decisions.

6. WHY QUINTILIAN, AND HOW?

Having discussed the usefulness of a system of *status* and *loci* in general, the question arises what classical rhetoric can teach us in this respect. After all, contemporary law already works with *status* and *loci*, although they are not referred to by
those names. Besides, the treatment of these subjects in classical rhetoric is not
entirely satisfactory and has left many a problem unsolved. In many ways, modern
jurisprudence and modern philosophy have advanced beyond classical rhetoric.[25] A
system of *status* and *loci* for modern adjudication can and should not be a copy of a
classical system. Still, classical texts can do more than provide an historical background. They can be rich and important sources of inspiration for furthering the
quality of contemporary theory and practice. But why, out of all the available classical texts, should we chose Quintilian?

Generally speaking, the *Institutio oratoria* is a highly readable book. Though
Quintilian is a real schoolmaster who patiently explains what he has to say in such a
way that even a dull student can follow him, it is not a dull book. The examples
Quintilian chooses and the rich metaphors he employs make the *Institutio* good reading. Also, it is the most comprehensive of the classical treatises on rhetoric. Generally speaking, therefore, it is an excellent means to acquaint oneself with the subject,
both for law students and for legal theorists. It is both inspiring and accessible. However, the parts on *status* and *loci* are less accessible. As we saw, they are scattered
over various books, not entirely consistent, not always clear, and generally difficult.[26] For these reasons I tend to think that if we wish to confront our law students
with a classical treatise on this subject, it is perhaps wiser to turn to Cicero.

---

[24] Certainly, the *status*-concept should be adapted for this purpose, in the sense that, in criminal cases,
the judge must take into consideration *all* relevant *status*, not just the one(s) chosen by the defence. In the
same sense: Braet (see note 16), pp. 98-99. See also Meyer (see note 16).
[25] For examples, see Braet (see note 16), Chapter 7.
[26] Butler (see note 1), III.6.1 at note 3: 'This chapter is highly technical and of little interest for the most
part to any save professed students of the technique of the ancient schools of rhetoric. Its apparent obscurity will, however, be found to disappear on careful analysis'.

What is wise for legal education and what is wise for legal theory are two different questions. As said before, reading the classical authors can serve as a means to become accustomed to the approach, as a source of inspiration, and as a basis for building a theory. But the following question arises: does Quintilian's treatise in this respect offer certain advantages over other classical texts on rhetoric? To put it differently: are there reasons for the legal theorist who wishes to acquaint himself with classical *status* and *loci*, not to limit his reading to Aristotle and Cicero? I think that the answer is yes, and I will now give a few reasons why.

First of all, Quintilian makes a habit of discussing the opinions of earlier authors before explaining and defending his own. This procedure, which is constantly repeated, keeps the reader aware of the fact that there is no such thing as THE rhetorical system, but that various theories, each with their own strong and weak points, have been defended. This in turn can be an important point of departure for developing one's own system or systems. A related point is the relative flexibility of Quintilian's system as compared to, especially, that of Hermagoras.[27]

A second point of interest is Quintilian's treatment of *status* in Book VII. As indicated earlier (section 4.2), many commentators find this odd, since *status* theory is usually regarded as belonging to the theory of invention (*inventio*), whereas the subject of Book VII is order (*dispositio*).[28] From a modern, or perhaps post-modern point of view, one could argue, however, that linking the treatment of *status* and *loci* to *dispositio* is the proper thing to do. If we take seriously the idea that facts are not given but constructed in a narrative, we must acknowledge that order (*dispositio*) is an important aspect of such a construction.[29]

Finally, I want to draw attention to Quintilian's treatment of the so-called inartificial proofs or means of persuasion (*inartificiales*). To these belong witness evidence, rumours, declarations under oath, torture, precedent, and documents. Since finding these proofs did not belong to the art of rhetoric, some earlier authors payed relatively little attention to them. Quintilian, however, explicitly stresses their importance for the orator because 'all the powers of eloquence are as a rule required to disparage and refute them'.[30] He discusses these proofs in Book V, Chapters 1-7. With reference to what I said above (section 5) about questions of fact, this is an interesting aspect of Quintilian's approach.[31]

---

[27] Quintilian himself brings this to our attention, e.g., in *Inst. or.* III.11.21 where he criticises the exaggerated terminological subtlety of, especially, Hermagoras ('adfectata subtilitas circa nomina rerum').

[28] Braet (see note 15), p. 122 calls it 'less self-evident' (minder vanzelfsprekend). Adamietz (see note 10), p. 2257 suggests that, perhaps, the subject matter of *dispositio* was not extensive enough, in comparison to *inventio*, to fill a whole book, and that therefore other subjects were added by Quintilian.

[29] In this sense, see in this book D. Pujante, 'The Role of *dispositio* in the Construction of Meaning: Quintilian's Perspective.'

[30] 'Sed ut ipsa per se carent arte, ita summis eloquentiae uiribus et adleuanda sunt plerumque et refellenda. Quare mihi uidentur magnopere damnandi qui totum hoc genus a praeceptis remouerunt.' (*Inst. or.* V.1.1-3)

[31] Surely, a good knowledge of rhetoric is not the most important condition for dealing with questions of fact in a responsible way. Modern insights from psychology (e.g. regarding the reliability of the human memory) and proof theory are at least equally important.

7. CONCLUSION: NO *PHRÓNÊSIS* WITHOUT ARGUMENTATION

I have tried to show that *status* and *loci* can be useful elements in a theory of adjudication for contemporary law, that they can function as tools for modern pleaders and judges, and that the *Institutio oratoria* is a valuable source of inspiration for this subject.

There is no reason to think that a judge who neglects his argumentation has enough common sense or *phrónêsis* to take good decisions. On the contrary: why would he neglect his argumentative tasks if he had so much common sense? In other words, no *phrónêsis* without argumentation.

I conclude with two quotations. The first one is from Nieuwenhuis:

> 'Judges make choices, but *Einzelfallgerechtigkeit* does not exist. No matter how unique a case may seem to be, the decision can only be called just if it can be repeated in cases that are not essentially different. Topics play an important role as mediators between the special circumstances, on the one hand, and generally accepted opinions of reasonableness and equity on the other'. [32]

My final quotation comes, of course, from Quintilian:

> 'Let us now turn to consider the 'places' of arguments (...) in the sense of the secret places where arguments reside, and from which they must be drawn forth. For just as all kinds of produce are not provided by every country, and as you will not succeed in finding a particular bird or beast, if you are ignorant of the localities where it has its usual haunts or birthplace, as even the various kinds of fish flourish in different surroundings, some preferring a smooth and others a rocky bottom, and are found on different shores and in divers regions (you will for instance never catch a sturgeon or wrasse in Italian waters), so not every kind of argument can be derived from every circumstance, and consequently our search requires discrimination. Otherwise we shall fall into serious error, and after wasting our labour through lack of method we shall fail to discover the argument which we desire, unless assisted by some happy chance. But if we know the circumstances which give rise to each kind of argument, we shall easily see, when we come to a particular 'place', what arguments it contains'. [33]

---

[32]   *Op. cit. supra* n. 14, p. 120; my translation, M.H.
[33]   *Inst. or.* V.10.20-22.

JAN WILLEM TELLEGEN

THE RELIABILITY OF QUINTILIAN FOR ROMAN LAW: ON THE CAUSA CURIANA

1. INTRODUCTION

The main purpose of this book is to increase the interest of jurists in classical rhetoric with the help of the *Institutio oratoria* of Quintilian. This is a very good source to choose because it is considered to be one of the most important works on rhetoric dating from the early Empire. It ranks as one of the basic textbooks on rhetoric and is renowned for its clear argumentation and its completeness and for its well-considered and independent views. However, if we are to achieve our aim we need to do more than simply choose a suitable source-text. The problem is that jurists, and in particular legal historians, still base their views on the theories of the German Historical School of the 19th century. Consequently, they normally approach a source of the kind we have chosen on the assumption that in Roman times there were two distinct disciplines that were mutually exclusive. For legal historians, therefore, the *Institutio oratoria* is unreliable from a juridical point of view.

Modern classicists too are influenced by this interpretation and assume that there was a fundamental distinction between law and rhetoric in Roman antiquity. In the Preface to his new translation of Quintilian's *Institutio oratoria*, Gerbrandy also makes the distinction and bases his view – incorrectly in my opinion – on the formulary procedure of Roman law.[1] In this way but without any justification he marginalises the significance of the *Institutio oratoria* for law. As a result this misunderstanding about law and rhetoric drags on like a chronic illness ('eine ewige Krankheit').

In this essay, I will try to demonstrate that the *Institutio oratoria* of Quintilian is an indispensable supplement to older Roman sources, both with regard to our knowledge of rhetoric and of the law.[2] For this purpose I will look closely at the *causa Curiana*, the famous lawsuit which is nowadays considered to represent the triumph of rhetoric over law and I will show that this modern interpretation is incorrect.

---

[1] *Quintilianus. De opleiding tot redenaar*, vertaald, ingeleid en van aantekeningen voorzien door Piet Gerbrandy, Groningen: Historische Uitgeverij 2001, pp. 17-18
[2] The same holds for our knowledge of, for instance, *memoria*. Of the three sources dealing with *memoria*, the *Rhetorica ad Herennium*, III.28-40 is the most informative, Cicero, *De oratore*, II. 350-360 is the most thorough and Quintilian, *Institutio oratoria*, XI.2 the most detailed and the most critical. Concerning these sources see F.A. Yates, *The Art of Memory*, London: Routledge&Kegan Paul 1966, rpt. Pimlico 1992, pp. 1-41. According to A.D. Leeman and A.C. Braet, *Klassieke retorica*, Groningen: Wolters-Noordhoff / Forsten 1987, p. 123, we would not even be able to understand Cicero's account without the treatises of the *Rhetorica ad Herennium* and Quintilian.

2. THE *CAUSA CURIANA*

The *causa Curiana* was a lawsuit that took place about 92 BC; the details have
come down to us mainly via the rhetorical works of Cicero.[3] Quintilian also refers
to this lawsuit. The relevant passages give us the following information. A man
called Marcus Coponius made a will in which he instituted his son or sons as heir
or heirs. At the time when he drew up his will, however, he did not have a son but
took into account the possibility that he might still have a son or sons. He might
even have a *postumus*, i.e. a son who was born after the testator had drawn up his
will or after he had died. In addition to the institution of his heir, Coponius had
incorporated in his will a *substitutio pupillaris* in which he stated that if his son
should die before reaching adulthood a certain M. Curius was to be heir in his
place. When Coponius died and the will was opened no son had been born. Curius
received the inheritance because it was assumed that the condition relating to the
substitution had been fulfilled. The heir *ab intestato*, however, who was also
called Coponius, was of the opinion that the condition in question had not been
fulfilled and that he should have received the inheritance. He summoned Curius to
appear before the court of the *centumviri* and laid claim to the inheritance by
virtue of the *hereditatis petitio*. Q. Mucius Scaevola was the advocate who represented the plaintiff, Coponius, and L. Licinius Crassus represented the defendant,
Curius.

Scaevola's plea can be summarised as follows. It was essential to interpret the
will according to the letter and it was not permissible to depart from this literal interpretation purely on the basis of assumptions. He based his assertion on the special
nature of the law of succession, on old formulations, on the authority of his father
and on legal security. He maintained that in this case the condition relating to the
substitution had not been satisfied because, in his view, a person who had not been
born could not die. Scaevola indicated how the will should have been formulated if
the testator had really wanted Curius too to be instituted as heir if no son were born.

Crassus began his plea by ridiculing Scaevola's 'discovery' that a person had to
be born before he could die. He also argued that the intention of the testator should
be respected on the grounds of reasonableness and fairness. The testator had desired
and intended that Curius should be his heir if there was no son who reached adulthood, either because he had not been born or because he died while still a minor.
Even if the will had not been formulated absolutely clearly, anyone could understand
what the testator had intended. Not every testator was as well-versed as Scaevola in
the law of succession, and a formulation such as that used by Coponius had always
been regarded as valid. Crassus invoked to a large number of precedents and the
authority of famous jurists. The court of the *centumviri* decided in favour of Curius
and declared Crassus to be the winner.

---

[3]   The most important are: *De oratore*, I.180 and 242-244; II.140-141; *Brutus*, 144-145, 194-198 and
256; *Pro Caecina*, 53 and 69. For a complete overview see H. Malcovati, *Oratorum romanorum fragmenta liberae rei publicae* I, Textus, 4th edition, Turin: Paravia 1976.

3. MODERN INTERPRETATIONS OF THE *CAUSA CURIANA*

In the last 50 years there have been numerous interpretations of the *causa Curiana*. Almost without exception these are reactions to an article written in 1926 by the German philologist Johannes Stroux. In that article, Stroux stated that the rhetoric that had originated in Greece supplied the archaic formalistic Roman law with a much needed method for arriving at an interpretation that was in accordance with the ideas of the time.[4] According to Stroux, law and rhetoric were not separate disciplines but they supplemented each other and were practised by the same group of people. Stroux referred to the *causa Curiana* and Cicero's speech *pro Caecina* as excellent examples of the application of this new method of interpretation.

Stroux' view triggered a great variety of reactions because it was used in the discussions about interpolation-research. The latter was a movement that had developed at the time among Romanists who sought to reconstruct classical Roman law by removing later additions and amendments from the juridical sources. The relationship between Roman law and rhetoric was interpreted by each 'camp' in its own way and was used as a decisive argument in these discussions. Supporters of the interpolation research such as Beseler and Albertario regarded references to terms like *aequitas* and *voluntas* in the juridical sources as additions dating from the time of Justinian.[5] In their opinion these were rhetorical concepts that had nothing to do with classical law. Riccobono, on the other hand, supported the view that these concepts had been incorporated in Roman law in the 2nd century BC, under the influence of Greek rhetoric.[6]

The *causa Curiana* became part of these discussions about 50 years ago as a result of Schulz' book entitled 'History of Roman Legal Science'. Schulz regarded the *causa Curiana* as a dispute between two advocates, one being a *iurisconsultus* and the other an orator, and considered that their pleas reflected their respective professions.[7] Later authors like Wieacker questioned this interpretation to a certain extent but not fundamentally.[8] All modern authors writing about the *causa Curiana* are in agreement on the following points:

---

[4] J. Stroux, '*Summum ius summa iniuria. Ein Kapitel aus der Geschichte der interpretatio iuris*', intended for the Festschrift P. Speiser-Sarasin, Leipzig 1926, which never appeared in its entirety. The work was reprinted in J. Stroux, *Römische Rechtswissenschaft und Rhetorik*, Potsdam: Eduard Stichnote 1949, pp. 7-80.

[5] G. Beseler, *Beiträge zur Kritik der römischen Rechtsquellen* IV, Tübingen: Mohr 1920, p. 197 and *Juristische Miniaturen*, Leipzig: Mohr 1929, rpt. Aalen: Scientia 1987, p. 53; J. Himmelschein, 'Studien zur antiken *Hermeneutica iuris*', in: F. Pringsheim (ed.), *Symbolae Friburgenses in honorem Ottonis Lenel*, Leipzig: Tauchnitz 1935, pp. 391ff; E. Albertario, *Studi di diritto romano* V, Milan: Giuffrè 1937, pp. 91ff.

[6] S. Riccobono in his preface for the Italian edition of Stroux' monograph in the *Annali del Seminario Giuridico dell'Università di Palermo* I (1934), also (in German) in the re-edition mentioned in note 4, pp. 69ff. In the same vein, for instance, C.A. Maschi, *Studi giuridici sull'interpretazione dei legati*, Milan: Giuffrè 1938, pp. 38ff and L. Wenger, *Die Quellen des römischen Rechts*, Vienna: Adolf Holzhausens Nfg. 1953, pp. 235ff.

[7] F. Schulz, *History of Roman Legal Science*, Oxford: Clarendon Press 1946, pp. 79ff.

[8] F. Wieacker, 'The *causa Curiana* and Contemporary Roman Jurisprudence', *The Irish Jurist* 2 (1967) pp. 151ff. For a review of the most important interpretations see J.W. Tellegen and Olga E. Tellegen-Couperus, 'Law and Rhetoric in the *causa Curiana*', *Orbis Iuris Romani* 6 (2000) pp. 174-181.

a. The formulation of the substitution in Coponius' will was clear and conclusive and could not be interpreted in two different ways.
b. The substitution does certainly not indicate that Coponius wanted his inheritance to go to the substitute Curius if no son was born. The testator could have avoided all uncertainty in a simple way if he had incorporated a vulgar substitution in addition to the pupillary substitution.
c. In the lawsuit, two advocates faced each other; one was Q.M. Scaevola, the most important jurist of his day, and the other was M.L. Crassus, the finest orator of his day.
d. Because Scaevola was a jurist, he interpreted the will according to the letter. Because Crassus was an orator, he interpreted the will according to its intention.
e. The verdict never had any influence on later law.

This interpretation, however, is problematical because it contradicts what Cicero writes. Modern authors attribute this discrepancy to the fact that Cicero was an orator and therefore his rhetorical works are unreliable. In their view, the same applies to Quintilian and his *Institutio oratoria*. In my opinion, the *causa Curiana* can be explained satisfactorily on the basis of Cicero's account and this account is reliable. Recently my wife and I wrote an article about Cicero and the *causa Curiana*. Not surprisingly, our interpretation is totally different from the prevailing view.[9] I am now going to deal with Quintilian and the *causa Curiana*.

In this paper I want to make it clear that what Quintilian writes about the *causa Curiana* not only closely corresponds to Cicero's description but also supplements it in a surprising manner. Cicero becomes absolutely clear with the help of Quintilian, whereas what Quintilian writes on the subject only becomes meaningful in the light of Cicero's description. As a result, I conclude that the *Institutio oratoria* is reliable and a valuable source of our knowledge about Roman law.

4. QUINTILIAN AND THE *CAUSA CURIANA*

Quintilian writes about the *causa Curiana* in Book VII.6 in connection with the status theory and particularly the *scriptum/voluntas* status. In VII.6.1 he begins with the following statement about this status:

> *Scripti et voluntatis frequentissima inter consultos quaestio est, et pars magna controversi iuris hinc pendet.*
> Lawyers frequently raise the question of the letter and the intention, in fact a large proportion of legal disputes turn on these points.

To me what is significant here is not only that the *scriptum/voluntas* status was used frequently but also that it was used *inter consultos*, i.e. among jurists. Quintilian here does not mention any distinction between jurists and orators but uses the general term *consulti*, jurists. This corresponds entirely to Cicero's use of the term. In *Brutus*, Cicero praises both advocates for their juridical knowledge and for their rhetorical skill and also refers to both advocates as *oratores*.[10] It can therefore be con-

---

9   See Tellegen and Tellegen-Couperus in note 8.
10 *Brutus*, 145-148, 194 and 198.

cluded that the *causa Curiana* was certainly not a dispute between a jurist and an orator. Therefore the prevailing view on this matter definitely contradicts these sources.

Quintilian goes on to mention a number of cases in which the law was unclear and the *scriptum/voluntas* status had to be applied. It can happen that the law is not clearly worded. It can also happen that the wording is clear but cannot be applied literally. The law can then be challenged in three ways: (1) the law cannot always be upheld, (2) the case itself makes this evident, or (3) there is something in the wording of the law that suggests that its intention might have been different. Finally, in VII.6.9, Quintilian states that the person who interprets according to the intention must question the wording, but the person who interprets according to the wording must also try to find support in the intention. This situation arises mainly in connection with wills. Quintilian then gives two examples, the first one being the *causa Curiana*. In VII.6.9 and 10 he writes as follows:

> *In testamentis et illa accidunt, ut voluntas manifesta sit, scriptum nihil sit: ut in iudicio Curiano, in quo nota L. Crassi et Scaevolae fuit contentio. 10. Substitutus heres erat, si postumus ante tutelae annos decessisset. Non est natus. Propinqui bona sibi vindicabant. Quis dubitaret, quin ea voluntate fuisset testantis, ut is non nato filio heres esset, qui mortuo? Sed hoc non scripserat.*
>
> Again, in cases concerned with wills it sometimes happens that the intention of the testator is clear though it has not been expressed in writing: an example of this occurs in the trial of Curius, which gave rise to the well-known argument between Lucius Crassus and Scaevola. 10. A second heir had been appointed in the event of a posthumous son dying while a minor. No posthumous son was born. The next of kin claimed the property. Who could doubt that the intention of the testator was that the same man should inherit in the event of the son not being born who would have inherited in the case of his death? But he had not written this in his will.[11]

According to Quintilian, in the case of the *causa Curiana* the words of the will were not clear, but the testator's intention was clear. As we have seen, modern authors writing about the *causa Curiana* give precisely the opposite interpretation. Which interpretation is correct? Let us first look at the words of the will and then try to find out what the testator's intention was.

In Quintilian's view, the words of the will were not clear but he fails to explain why they were not clear. However, the reason they were not clear can be deduced from what Cicero tells us about the institution of the heir and the substitution. These parts of the will can be reconstructed as follows:[12]

> *Si mihi filius genitur unus pluresve is mihi heres esto; si filius ante moritur quam in tutelam suam venerit tum mihi M'' Curius heres esto.*
>
> If a son were to be born to me, one or more, he must be my heir; if the son were to die before adulthood then Marcus Curius must be my heir.

---

[11]   Text and translation by Butler (see 'Introduction', note 27), III p. 141. In his recent Dutch translation of the *Institutio oratoria*, Gerbrandy (see note 1), p. 381 makes two errors in translating this fragment: he translates *scriptum nihil* in VII.6.9 by: 'maar dat er niets op schrift staat' ('but there is nothing in writing'), and *testantis* in VII.6.10 by 'van de erfgenaam' ('of the heir').

[12]   Cf. *De inventione*, II.122 and *De oratore*, II.141.

The first point to notice is that the institution of the heir here is conditional: if no son is born, i.e. if the condition is not fulfilled, the institution of the heir no longer holds. Then a pupillary substitution becomes operative, i.e. someone is instituted as heir in case the child who has been instituted as heir should die before reaching adulthood. The substitution is a conditional institution of an heir, which only becomes operative if the first institution is invalid; the substitution serves as a replacement. If there is a substitution in a will it is assumed that there is someone who can be replaced, in other words that there is an heir. Thus a substitution is based on the assumption that the institution of the heir is unconditional. In this case, however, a substitution was combined with a conditional institution of an heir. In fact this was illogical; it was impossible to draw up an unambiguous formulation that combined a conditional institution of an heir with a substitution. Coponius had made such a will, and his will was therefore unclear. When Quintilian writes in his *Institutio oratoria* that in the *causa Curiana* the words of the will were unclear, this corresponds to the interpretation given by Cicero. It would seem therefore that the interpretation given by the modern authors is totally incorrect.

Now we come to the intention of the testator. Quintilian was of the opinion that the intention of Coponius was absolutely clear. Everybody knew what he had intended: the inheritance was to go to the substitute. The modern authors, however, believe that Coponius did not want his inheritance to go to the substitute, for if he had wanted this to happen he would have stated this clearly. They therefore base their view on Scaevola's plea as reported by Cicero. Certainly, according to Scaevola, the will did not indicate that the testator wanted the substitute to receive the inheritance. Consequently, the modern authors paid no further attention to the fact that the institution of the heir was conditional and that this was the particular point that had caused the problems.[13] Cicero also reproduces the plea of Crassus, and states that the *centumviri* declared Crassus to be in the right. He does not comment on whether the testator's intention was clear; Quintilian, however, does express his view on this point; he maintains that the testator's intention was absolutely clear. Thus, on this particular point he clarifies Cicero's account of the *causa Curiana*.

On the basis of the arguments given above, we can conclude that what Quintilian writes about the *causa Curiana* not only corresponds to Cicero's account of the lawsuit, but it also supplements it. One obtains a much clearer picture by combining the two accounts than by relying on one account only.

It should now also be clear that the account of the *causa Curiana* in the modern literature contradicts the sources. As stated earlier, this discrepancy is usually attributed to the oratorical and thus unreliable nature of the works concerned. Let us assume for a moment that the modern authors are correct and that the *causa Curiana* was in fact a dispute between a jurist and an orator; in that case, the plea of Scaevola would have been typically juridical and that of Crassus typically rhetorical. There is some difference of opinion about the plea of Crassus: according to Schulz, Crassus' plea was typically rhetorical, but according to others like Wieacker it was partly

[13] It is significant that P. Voci, *Diritto ereditario romano*, II, 2nd edition, Milan: Giuffrè 1963, pp. 215f deals with the *causa Curiana* only in the chapter on substitution.

juridical and partly rhetorical. With regard to Scaevola's plea, however, all agree that it was purely juridical. In order to ascertain whether the plea of Scaevola was typically juridical we must look carefully at the arguments he used: you can recognise the true jurist from the arguments, just as you can recognise a tree from its fruits. Both Cicero and Quintilian supply us with valuable information on this matter.

5. SCAEVOLA'S PLEA IN THE *CAUSA CURIANA*

According to the modern authors, Scaevola stated that the testament had to be interpreted solely according to the letter and he supported his view with juridical arguments. Let us see whether these two assumptions are correct.

Although all the modern authors assume that Scaevola considered that a will should be interpreted solely according to the letter, they provide a variety of explanations. I will restrict my comments to the interpretations given by Schulz and Wieacker. According to Schulz, Scaevola based his view on the following principle: if a clear meaning emerges when the words are interpreted according to their normal usage, then that meaning must be accepted even if it does not correspond at all to the intention of the testator. In this case, it could have been Coponius' intention to let Curius inherit if no son was born, but he did not write these actual words and therefore Curius was not entitled to inherit. According to Schulz, Mucius' standpoint undoubtedly corresponds to the tradition that prevailed in jurisprudence at the time of the Republic.[14]

In Wieacker's view, it was not the real intention that was under discussion here. The testator failed to consider the possibility that he might not have a son. What was under discussion was the hypothetical intention, namely what the testator would have wanted if he had considered the possibility of not having a son. In his capacity as a jurist, Scaevola stated that the hypothetical will should not be taken into account.[15]

In my view, these interpretations are incorrect. Cicero's account shows that it was impossible for Scaevola to interpret the will purely according to the letter. Coponius' testament was basically unclear because of the conditional nature of the institution of the heir and therefore Scaevola had to invoke the *voluntas testatoris*. What had to be considered here was the genuine intention of the testator, and not the hypothetical intention. This was confirmed by Quintilian. At the beginning of VII.6.9, which was mentioned above, he writes:

> *Sed ut qui voluntate nitetur scriptum, quotiens poterit, infirmare debebit, ita, qui scriptum tuebitur, adiuvare se etiam voluntate temptabit.*
>
> But just as the advocate who rests his case on the intention must wherever possible impugn the letter of the law, so he who defends the letter must also seek to gain support from the intention.

---

[14] Schulz (see note 7), pp. 78-79.
[15] Wieacker (see note 8), pp. 156-157.

According to Quintilian, the *causa Curiana* illustrates this point. Scaevola interpreted the testament of Coponius both according to the letter and according to
the intention. The fact that Scaevola also interpreted the testament according
to the intention is totally in keeping with Cicero's account, namely that
Scaevola had stated that the testator could not have intended the substitute to be
his heir.

The second assumption was that Scaevola used purely juridical arguments to
demonstrate that Coponius' testament had to be interpreted according to the letter.
Schulz does not comment on this point but Wieacker thinks that the arguments were
typically juridical. According to Wieacker, Scaevola tried, at least in the beginning,
to accommodate himself to the rhetorical style, but at length the jurist broke
through.[16]

Unfortunately, Quintilian does not discuss Scaevola's arguments, so we have to
rely on Cicero's account. In the plea of Scaevola we are first struck by the fact that
he concentrates on the substitution and ignores the institution of the heir. His main
reason for stating that the condition relating to the pupillary substitution had not
been satisfied was as follows: 'The heir did not die before reaching adulthood
because someone who has not been born cannot die.' This argument is based on the
following reasoning: 'An heir can die if he has been born; the heir has not been
born, therefore he cannot die.' This type of reasoning is known as a *modus tollendo
tollens* and is derived from Stoic logic. Is it therefore a specifically juridical way of
reasoning? The prevailing view is that the Roman jurists did not take over this
method from Greek rhetoric but they took it from Greek philosophy and particularly
from the Stoa. The fact that Scaevola used a type of reasoning from Stoic logic
would demonstrate that he was a jurist and not an orator. I do not think this is a correct conclusion. The *modus tollendo tollens* may have been of Stoic origin but reasoning of this kind was commonplace among orators. This is evident from the fact
that such argumentation was discussed in the rhetorical literature such as Cicero's
Topica.[17]

The other arguments used by Scaevola, namely the special nature of the law of
succession, old formulations, the authority of his father, and the preservation of the
ius civile are not specifically juridical; they are both juridical and rhetorical, since
they are *topoi*.[18]

Finally, it is interesting to note that in his plea Scaevola indicated what kind of
formulation the testator should have used. Cicero does not give details of the formulation, but he does report on the reaction of Crassus. He had said to Scaevola:
'Scaevola, if no will is correctly worded unless you have drawn it up, we, as citizens
of Rome, will all come to you, and you, all on your own, will put our wills in writing.'[19] In the *causa Curiana*, Crassus himself referred to precedents, i.e. to other
cases in which a conditional institution of an heir in combination with a substitution

---

[16]   Wieacker (see note 8), p. 158.
[17]   *Topica*, 54.
[18]   See, for instance, Cicero, *De inventione*, II.143.
[19]   Cicero, *De oratore*, II.24.

had been regarded as valid.[20] Apparently, this type of will was fairly common. Scaevola would not or could not regard as invalid a conditional institution of an heir when combined with a substitution. His plea is not typically juridical in this respect either.

It should now be clear that Scaevola interpreted the testament of Coponius not only according to the letter but also according to the intention, and that for this he used general arguments that were not typically juridical.

Why then do all the modern authors regard Scaevola's interpretation and arguments as being typically juridical? In my view this is because of Scaevola's status and reputation. In Schulz' view, Scaevola was the most important jurist of the Hellenistic period. By virtue of his *Ius civile libri XVIII* Scaevola was the designer of the system of the Institutes of Gaius, the work that formed the basis for later European civil law.[21] In Wieacker's view too, Scaevola was the most important jurist of his day; it was Scaevola who introduced Greek theory of science such as Stoic dialectics into Roman law. In this way he paved the way for the development of Roman legal science.[22] Because one of the advocates in the lawsuit was none other than Q.M. Scaevola, his plea must have been typically juridical.

The juridical problem in the *causa Curiana* consisted of the unclear wording of the will and the clear intention of the testator. Evidently, therefore, Scaevola's decision to interpret the testament of Coponius according to the letter was based not on his profession but on the interests of his client.

6. CONCLUSION

In my introduction I stated that the *Institutio oratoria* of Quintilian is a suitable source for increasing jurists' knowledge about rhetoric, but I stressed that more is needed than a suitable source. Modern jurists in general and legal historians in particular are still strongly influenced by the Historical School. This means that they assume that law and rhetoric are two distinct disciplines and that sources that are regarded as rhetorical are not reliable. In my opinion, this view is not based on the sources but stems from a *petitio principii*. The *causa Curiana* makes this very clear.

According to the prevailing view, this lawsuit became famous because it was the scene of a dispute between law and rhetoric, conducted between two advocates, one being a jurist and the other an orator. However, the sources that deal with the *causa Curiana*, namely the rhetorical works of Cicero and Quintilian, make no reference to a dispute of this kind, and therefore the modern authors regard these sources as unreliable.

---

[20]   According to Cicero, *Topica*, 44, Crassus had another example of a conditional institution of an heir, namely one to which a time-limit had been added. This was also regarded as valid.

[21]   Schulz (see note 7), p. 94. Because of the lack of sources this theory is generally no longer adhered today. See, for instance, H.L.W. Nelson, *Ueberlieferung, Aufbau und Stil von Gai Institutones*, Leyden: Brill 1988, p. 598.

[22]   F. Wieacker, *Römische Rechtsgeschichte*, I, Munich: Beck 1988, p. 597.

The sources mentioned, however, indicate that the lawsuit was about the interpretation of a testamentary disposition in which the wording was unclear but the intention clear. Both advocates were *iurisprudentes* as well as *oratores*, and the lawsuit was won by the person with the strongest case and the best plea. The *causa Curiana* owes its fame to the fact that it was the finest example of the use of the *scriptum/voluntas* status in the history of Roman law.

I have used the *causa Curiana* to demonstrate that the widely held view that jurists and orators represented different disciplines which were poles apart is incorrect. I have also shown that a source like the *Institutio oratoria* of Quintilian is an indispensable supplement to the older Roman juridical and non-juridical sources. However, if such a source is to be used to make modern jurists more familiar with rhetoric, then it will have to be underpinned by a fundamental discussion of the influence exerted by the Historical School on modern legal science.

FRANCISCO CHICO-RICO

SOME (SEMIOTIC) ASPECTS OF *ELOCUTIO* IN QUINTILIAN

More about Latinitas, Perspicuitas, Ornatus, *and* Decorum

1. INTRODUCTION

As is well known, *elocutio*, which the Greeks called *phrásis*, is the rhetorical operation responsible for the linguistic formulation or the outward expression through
means of a language of the ideas found in *inventio* and organized by *dispositio*;[1] in
other words, it is the rhetorical operation responsible for the conversion of the textual macro-structure, which results from the rhetorical operations of *inventio* and *dispositio*, into the textual micro-structure or textual linear manifestation.[2] *Elocutio* is,
therefore, together with *inventio* and *dispositio*, a discourse-building rhetorical operation, because its activity results in the construction of a level of discourse, i.e., the
level of the micro-structure of the text or textual linear manifestation.[3]

   Book VIII of Quintilian's *Institutio oratoria*, the object of the present study, is
dedicated, together with Book IX, to the treatment of the rhetorical operation of *elocutio*. The stylistic expressiveness, which results from the author's artistic success in
the realization of this rhetorical operation, is a unique characteristic not only of
rhetorical discourse (rhetorical expressiveness) but also of poetic discourse (poetic
expressiveness).[4] The rhetorical and poetic theories of these two books have fed
upon each other during centuries, so as to create one of the best compendia of
ancient knowledge about rhetorical imagery.[5]

---

[1] H. Lausberg, *Manual de Retórica literaria. Fundamentos de una Ciencia de la Literatura*, 3 Vols.,
Madrid: Gredos 1966-1968, §§453-457.
[2] F. Chico-Rico, *Pragmática y construcción literaria. Discurso retórico y discurso narrativo*, Alicante:
Universidad de Alicante 1987, pp. 49-63; Id., '*Elocutio* e componente linguistico-testuale di lessico',
Studi Italiani di Linguistica Teorica ed Applicata 17, 1 (1988) pp. 77-92; T. Albaladejo-Mayordomo,
Retórica, Madrid: Síntesis 1989, pp. 117-127.
[3] Albaladejo-Mayordomo (see note 2), pp. 57-64, 117-127.
[4] A. García-Berrio, 'Retórica como ciencia de la expresividad. (Presupuestos para una Retórica General)', *Estudios de Lingüística. Universidad de Alicante* 2 (1984), pp. 7-59; Id., *La construcción imagi-
naria en ' Cántico'* , Limoges, Université de Limoges 1985, pp. 49; Id., 'Qué es lo que la poesía es',
Lingüística Española Actual 9, 2 (1987) pp. 177-188; Id., *Teoría de la Literatura. La construcción del
significado poético*, Madrid: Cátedra 1994, pp. 69-244; A. García-Berrio & M.T. Hernández-Fernández,
La Poética: tradición y modernidad, Madrid: Síntesis 1988, pp. 89-100.
[5] B. Mortara-Garavelli, *Manual de Retórica*, Madrid: Cátedra 1991, pp. 40-43; J.A. Hernández Guerrero & M.C. García-Tejera, *Historia breve de la Retórica*, Madrid: Síntesis 1994, pp. 62-66; D. Pujante-
Sánchez, *El hijo de la persuasión. Quintiliano y el estatuto retórico*, 2nd edition, corrected and aug-
mented, Logroño: Instituto de Estudios Riojanos 1999, pp. 159-166.

In an attempt to present synthetically the content of Book VIII, I will say that the author of the *Institutio oratoria* begins his argument in the preface to this book with the recapitulation of the fundamental principles of the rhetorical theory described and explained throughout the earlier books. His purpose is to coherently and solidly associate them with the treatment of the rhetorical operation of *elocutio* (VIII.pr.1-12). One of the tasks of the orator, as Quintilian reminds us in this context, is that of delighting his hearers. This point allows him to introduce directly the rhetorical operation of *elocutio*, since delight depends primarily, though not solely, on style (VIII.pr.7).[6] Immediately thereafter, he deals with the doctrine of style, a doctrine which is, for most orators, the most difficult of all (VIII.pr.13). Following Cicero, the author of the *Institutio oratoria* affirms that while invention and arrangement are within reach of any intelligent man, eloquence belongs only to the true orator (VIII pr.14). In this sense, Quintilian defines the rhetorical operation of *elocutio* in the following manner (VIII.pr.15).

> For the verb *eloqui* means the production and communication to the audience of all that the speaker has conceived in his mind, and without this power all the preliminary accomplishments of oratory are as useless as a sword that is kept permanently concealed within its sheath.

Elocutio is, as the author of the *Institutio oratoria* tells us, that part which is most needy of learned art, of great effort, of training, and of imitation (VIII.pr.16), since both the efficiency and inefficiency of rhetorical discourse depend, to a large extent, on rhetorical expression (VIII.pr.17).[7] That fact does not mean, however, that one must place concern for the words above concern for the ideas: for Quintilian, the formal and sonorous appeal of words is extremely beautiful in discourse, but only when it is consistent with the power of ideas, which are like the soul of discourse (VIII.pr.18-22). The fact that the author of the *Institutio oratoria* appreciates the relationships between ideas and words in the discourse, between its background and its form, is very important for understanding the relevance of Quintilian's thought for our times; it also explains how it has become distorted throughout history, leading to the absolute and undeserving impoverishment of Rhetoric as the classical science of persuasive discourse, which has resulted in the separation and disconnection of the five traditional rhetorical operations and the exact hypertrophy of the rhetori-

---

[6] Quintilian explains it as follows (*Inst. or.* VIII.pr.7): 'I attempted to show that the duty of the orator is composed of instructing, moving and delighting his hearers, statement of facts and argument falling under the head of instruction, while emotional appeals are concerned with moving the audience and, although they may be employed throughout the case, are most effective at the beginning and end. As to the element of charm, I pointed out that, though it may reside both in facts and words, its special sphere is that of style'. In this essay, I use the text edition and the English translation by Butler (see 'Introduction', note 27).

[7] For Quintilian, (*Inst. or.* VIII. pr.17): 'the failure of the orators of the Asiatic and other decadent schools did not lie in their inability to grasp or arrange the facts on which they had to speak, nor, on the other hand, were those who professed what we call the dry style of oratory either fools or incapable of understanding the cases in which they were engaged. No, the fault of the former was that they lacked taste and restraint in speaking, while the latter lacked power, whence it is clear that it is here that the real faults and virtues of oratory are to be found'.

cal operation of *elocutio*.[8] Using the image of the healthy body, the author of the *Institutio oratoria* alludes to the necessary preeminence of ideas over words in the following way (VIII.pr.19-20).

> 19. Healthy bodies, enjoying a good circulation and strengthened by exercise, acquire grace from the same source that gives them strength, for they have a healthy complexion, firm flesh and shapely thews. But, on the other hand, the man who attempts to enhance these physical graces by the effeminate use of depilatories and cosmetics, succeeds merely in defacing them by the very care which he bestows on them. 20. Again, a tasteful and magnificent dress, as the Greek poet tells us, lends added dignity to its wearer: but effeminate and luxurious apparel fails to adorn the body and merely reveals the foulness of the mind.

In order to do so, Quintilian demands that the orator will be careful in his choice of words, but that he will have deep concern about the ideas: *Curam ergo verborum, rerum volo esse sollicitudinem* (VIII.pr.20 *in fine*).

The author of the *Institutio oratoria* also proposes the adaptation of the ideas and the words in discourse, because the best expressions depend on the ideas, i.e., on the best ideas, and are those which seem natural and are modeled on the reality and on the truth of all things (VIII.pr.21,23). Remembering Cicero,[9] Quintilian is of the opinion that 'the worst fault in speaking is to adopt a style inconsistent with the idiom of ordinary speech and contrary to the common feeling of mankind' (VIII.pr. 25). Words which do not correspond to ideas are devoid of strength and virtue.

The necessary conditions for the orator to attain the best expression will be, in this sense, the constitution, through study, of 'a true conception of the principles of eloquence', the accumulation of 'a copious supply of words by wide and suitable reading', the application of 'the art of arrangement to the words thus acquired', and the development, through exercise, of the necessary faculties 'to use his acquisitions so that every word is ready at hand and lies under his very eyes' (VIII.pr.28). He who follows these instructions will see that his ideas will spontaneously present themselves together with the most appropriate words for their expression (VIII.pr. 29).

For this reason, the final advice of the author of the *Institutio oratoria* is to take great care with style, and yet realize that 'nothing should be done for the sake of words only, since words were invented merely to give expression to things: and those words are the most satisfactory which give the best expression to the thoughts of our mind and produce the effect which we desire upon the minds of the judges' (VIII.pr.32). Only then will words guarantee a pleasant and admirable style which is 'praiseworthy and dignified' (VIII.pr.33).

In the first Chapter of Book VIII, Quintilian divides the treatment of style in two ample sections, since style manifests itself not only in individual words but also in groups of words (VIII.1.1): *Ea spectatur verbis singulis aut coniunctis*. Individual words should be Latin or pure, clear or transparent, elegant, and accommodated or

---

[8]   G. Genette, 'Rhétorique et enseignement', in: G. Genette, *Figures II*, Paris: Seuil 1968, pp. 23-42; Id., 'La rhétorique restreinte', in: G. Genette, *Figures III*, Paris: Seuil 1972, pp. 21-40; García-Berrio, 'Retórica' (see note 4).

[9]   *De oratore*, I. 12.

well-adapted to produce the desired effect. Groups of words, on the other hand, ought to be correct, aptly placed, and adorned with suitable figures. This is how the author of the *Institutio oratoria* introduces the four traditional qualities of the rhetorical operation of style, without which rhetorical discourse would have deficiencies that would impede the attainment of its persuasive objective: *latinitas* (VIII.1), *perspicuitas* (VIII.2), *ornatus* (VIII.3), and *decorum*.

2. *LATINITAS*, OR *PURITAS*

The first of these qualities of style, *latinitas*, or *puritas*, corresponds to the appropriate use of the Latin language, to the linguistic purity of language, and consists of the use of the correct expressions in the frame of the language in which the rhetorical discourse is constructed.[10] As Quintilian recognizes (VIII.1.2), this quality of style responds to the need to follow the rules of Grammar, understood as *recte loquendi scientia* (I.4.2), the indispensable condition for achieving good speech that is unique to Rhetoric, understood as *ars bene dicendi* (II.17.37) or *bene dicendi scientia* (II.14.5).[11]

3. *PERSPICUITAS*

The *perspicuitas* of style corresponds, in general, to the clarity or transparency of the expression used in the construction of the micro-structure of the text.[4] The clarity or transparency of the textual micro-structure is fundamental in order for the rhetorical discourse to be understandable to the receiver, and therefore, for the orator to reach his persuasive objective. It deals with a quality of style based on *latinitas*, because to achieve the clarity or transparency of the expression, it is necessary to use the correct expressions in the frame of the language in which the rhetorical discourse is constructed.[12] However, *perspicuitas* adds to *latinitas* the propriety in the use of words (VIII.2.1), a propriety which will always be the fruit of the linguistic effort of the orator,[13] in some cases to call the items dealt with by their own names and in other cases to avoid obscene, rude or sordid terms because of its inadequacy to the dignity of the themes and/or to the dignity of the persons to whom the rhetorical discourse is directed (VIII.2.1-2).

Very close to *perspicuitas* we find *urbanitas*, the quality understood as elegance of style, and *venustas*, the quality understood as beauty in speech, upon which depends the pleasure that the rhetorical discourse will produce in the receiver. While Quintilian does not consider these to be qualities belonging exclusively to *elocutio*

---

[10] If the Latin designation of *puritas* is *latinitas*, the Greek designation of this quality of *elocutio* is *hellênismós*. This corresponds to the appropriate use, respectively, of Latin and Greek. Cf. Lausberg (see note 1), §§463-527; Albaladejo-Mayordomo (see note 2), pp. 124-125.

[11] Mortara-Garavelli (see note 5), pp. 134-152; Albaladejo-Mayordomo (see note 2), pp. 124-125; J.A. Mayoral, *Figuras retóricas*, Madrid: Síntesis 1994, pp. 18-20; Pujante-Sánchez (see note 5), pp. 172-173.

[12] Lausberg (see note 1), §§528-537.

[13] Albaladejo-Mayordomo (see note 2), 125-126.

(in fact, the author of the *Institutio oratoria* treats them in Book VI, dedicated to the peroration and the excitement of the emotions or the feelings), they are considered to be general qualities of the rhetorical discourse that affect not only the syntactical-semantic range of the words but also the pragmatic-communicative dimension of the act of expression; in other words, not only the rhetorical operations of *inventio*, *dispositio*, and *elocutio*, on the one hand, but also the rhetorical operation of *actio* or *pronuntiatio*, on the other. However, they are general qualities of the rhetorical discourse centered on the syntactical-semantic range of the words and, above all, on the rhetorical operation of *elocutio*, since style constitutes the focal point of these qualities, as is shown in the following fragment from Quintilian's work (VI.3.17-18).

> 17. First, there is *urbanitas*, which I observe denotes language with a smack of the city in its words, accent and idiom, and further suggests a certain tincture of learning derived from associating with well-educated men; in a word, it represents the opposite of rusticity. 18. The meaning of *venustus* is obvious; it means that which is said with grace and charm.

With style as the focal point, these general qualities of the rhetorical discourse are those which guarantee that, according to the principle of *decorum*, the referential construction of *inventio* and the macro-structural organization of *dispositio* appear with an appropriate textual micro-structure at the discourse level of *elocutio* and with an appropriate oral and gestural realization on the performative level of *actio* or *pronuntiatio*. As general qualities of the rhetorical discourse which are very close to *perspicuitas*, *urbanitas* and *venustas* are, like the former, based on *latinitas*, which provides a necessary grammatical base for the orator to achieve the textual micro-structure which is not only correct but also elegant and beautiful in its formal aspect and in its expressive aspect.[14]

4. *ORNATUS*

The appropriate use of the Latin language and the clarity or transparency of the expression are basic to the construction of the micro-structure of the rhetorical discourse, since *latinitas* and *perspicuitas*, as qualities of *elocutio*, belong to the utility of the cause (VIII.3.2). Yet, on the basis of *latinitas* and *perspicuitas*, the true orator, the consummate orator, can and ought to seek *ornatus*, a 'plus' (significant, if not rationally, at least sentimentally), as David Pujante-Sánchez labels it.[15] *Ornatus* is that which guarantees the success of persuasion by means of adornment of words,

---

[14]   Mortara-Garavelli (see note 5), pp. 152-156; Albaladejo-Mayordomo (see note 2), pp. 126-127; Mayoral (see note 11), pp. 20-27; Pujante-Sánchez (see note 5), pp. 173-175.

[15]   Pujante-Sánchez (see note 5), pp. 167-168, 181ff. According to Quintilian, *Inst. or.* VIII.3. 61: 'The ornate is something that goes beyond what is merely lucid and acceptable. It consists firstly in forming a clear conception of what we wish to say, secondly in giving this adequate expression, and thirdly in lending it additional brilliance, a process which may correctly be termed embellishment. Consequently we must place among ornaments that *enárgeia* which I mentioned in the rules which I laid down for the statement of facts, because vivid illustration, or, as some prefer to call it, representation, is something more than mere clearness, since the latter merely lets itself be seen, whereas the former thrusts itself upon our notice'.

excellence of expression, and, finally, artistic efficacy.[16] We must stress the fact that *ornatus*, as a quality of *elocutio*, is not to be understood as an ornamental addition, since it is not possible to add new elements to a linguistic construction without the substantial modification of its nature due to the systematic character of language; *ornatus* is understood as the result of the transformation of the linguistic code into its different levels so as to achieve the sublimity, the splendour, the brilliance, and the authority in the words.[17] Along these lines, the following considerations of Quintilian prove to be of indubitable interest (VIII.3.1-4).

> 1. [...] For a speaker wins but trifling praise if he does no more than speak with correctness and lucidity; in fact his speech seems rather to be free from blemish than to have any positive merit. 2. Even the untrained often possess the gift of invention, and no great learning need be assumed for the satisfactory arrangement of our matter, while if any more recondite art is required, it is generally concealed, since unconcealed it would cease to be an art, while all these qualities are employed solely to serve the interests of the actual case. On the other hand, by the employment of skilful ornament the orator commends himself at the same time, and whereas his other accomplishments appeal to the considered judgment of the learned, this gift appeals to the enthusiastic approval of the world at large, and the speaker who possesses it fights not merely with effective, but with flashing weapons. 3. If in his defence of Cornelius Cicero had confined himself merely to instructing the judge and speaking in clear and idiomatic Latin without a thought beyond the interests of his case, would he ever have compelled the Roman people to proclaim their admiration not merely by acclamation, but by thunders of applause? No, it was the sublimity and splendour, the brilliance and the weight of his eloquence that evoked such clamorous enthusiasm. 4. [...] In my opinion the audience did not know what they were doing, their applause sprang neither from their judgment nor their will; they were seized with a kind of frenzy and, unconscious of the place in which they stood, burst forth spontaneously into a perfect ecstasy of delight.

The author of the *Institutio oratoria* concludes Book VIII with the description and explanation of various ornamental resources, among which stand out amplification (*amplificatio*) and attenuation (*abbreviatio*), the 'sentence' (*sententia*), and the tropes. The tropes may be one of two types. First, there are those which are used to help out our meaning: metaphor, synecdochè, metonymy, antonomasia, onomatopoea, catachresis or abuse, and metalepsis or transumption. Second, there are those which are used to adorn our style: epithet, allegory, riddle, irony or *illusio*, periphrasis, hyperbaton, and hyperbole (VIII.4- 6).

5. *DECORUM, ACCOMODATUM* OR *APTUM*

Finally, *decorum, accomodatum* or *aptum*, corresponds to the necessary adaptation which must take place between the ideas and the words of discourse, between its background and its form, between the macro-structure and the micro-structure. Let us remember what we said a moment ago: 'the best expressions depend on the ideas, i.e., on the best ideas, and are those which seem natural and are modeled on the real-

---

[16]   Lausberg (see note 1), §§538-1054.
[17]   Mortara-Garavelli (see note 5), pp. 157 ff.; Albaladejo-Mayordomo (see note 2), p. 132; Mayoral (see note 11), pp. 20-27; Pujante-Sánchez (see note 5), pp. 181-213.

ity and on the truth of all things [...]. Words which do not correspond to ideas are devoid of strength and virtue'.

But *decorum* also corresponds to the necessary adaptation between the rhetorical discourse and the general communicative context in which it is produced or delivered by the orator and received by the public. This adaptation should take place, on the one hand, on all the levels which pertain to the referent of the text and to the text itself or the rhetorical discourse and, on the other hand, on those levels and the distinct elements of the rhetorical fact. The latter includes not only the rhetorical discourse but also the interaction between that discourse, the orator, the public, the referent of the text, and the context in which the rhetorical communication takes place.[18] In other words, *decorum* corresponds to the necessary adaptation which takes place in two ways. First, between (a) the constructive level of *inventio* which semiotically is of a semantic-extensional nature and corresponds to the referent of the rhetorical discourse, (b) the constructive level of *dispositio* which is of a syntactical-semiotic nature and which is equivalent to the textual macro-structure, and (c) the constructive level of *elocutio* which is equally syntactic from a semiotic point of view and is identified with the textual micro-structure. Second, adaptation should take place between those levels and the pragmatic-communicative level of *actio* or *pronuntiatio*, i.e., the orator's oral and gestural realization of the micro-structure of the rhetorical discourse.

Decorum is, then, a principle of structuralization of the textuality and of the rhetorical communication; it is a principle of coherence which dominates the totality of the rhetorical fact and affects the interaction between the distinct elements of the rhetorical fact - the rhetorical discourse, the orator, the public, the referent of the text, and the context in which the rhetorical communication takes place. Moreover, upon *decorum* depend the suitability and the effectiveness of rhetorical discourse. We are dealing then with a characteristic, a quality or a principle, not only of the rhetorical operation of *elocutio* but also of the rhetorical operations of *inventio*, *dispositio*, *memoria*, and *actio* or *pronuntiatio*. Therefore, it determines the internal coherence as well as the external coherence of the rhetorical discourse. In other words, it determines the semantic-semiotic or semantic-extensional coherence derived from the adaptation of the text to the referent, the syntactical-semiotic coherence derived from the adaptation of one linguistic level to another in the interior of the rhetorical discourse, and the pragmatic-semiotic or pragmatic-communicative coherence derived from the adaptation of the text to the general communicative context, and, especially, to the orator and the public.

For this reason, Tomás Albaladejo-Mayordomo understands *decorum* as the support of an authentic semiotic coherence in the field of Rhetoric, which constitutes a proof of the importance of the coordination of all the elements, textual as well as extra-textual, within the rhetorical conscience. This has become one of the most solid and reliable theories of discourse available.[19]

---

[18] Mortara-Garavelli (see note 5), pp. 129-133; Albaladejo-Mayordomo (see note 2), pp. 43-53; Id., 'Estructuras retóricas y estructuras semióticas. (Retórica y hecho literario)', in: VV.AA., *Investigaciones Semióticas, III. Retórica y Lenguajes (Actas del III Simposio Internacional de la A.E.S.)*, I, Madrid: U.N.E.D. 1990, pp. 89-96; Mayoral (see note 11), pp. 20-27.

[19] Albaladejo-Mayordomo (see note 2), p. 53.

In this sense, all the rhetorical operations are led or driven in their development by the principle of *decorum*. In that which deals with the rhetorical operation of *elocutio*, which is the one that most interests us, on *decorum* depends the value which the rest of the stylistic qualities can achieve, *latinitas*, *perspicuitas*, and *ornatus*: the first, in its search for the linguistic purity of language; the second, in its search for the propriety in the use of words; and the third, in its search for the excellence of expression and, more specifically, for artistic efficacy.

6. *DECORUM* AND *INTELLECTIO*

In this revisionist context, in which, from a semiotic point of view, I deal with the conception of *elocutio* as described and explained in the *Institutio oratoria*, I would like to take advantage of this occasion to propose, even if just in summary, the idea that the search for and the preservation of *decorum* as a traditional quality not only of the rhetorical operation of *elocutio* but also of the rhetorical operations of *inventio*, *dispositio*, *memoria*, and *actio* or *pronuntiatio* constitutes one of the fundamental objectives of the rhetorical operation of *intellectio*.[20]

It is generally recognized that *intellectio* allows the orator to initiate and regulate the rhetorical operations of *inventio*, *dispositio*, *elocutio*, *memoria*, and *actio* or *pronuntiatio* within a systematic strategy of textual production in which all the elements that compose the rhetorical fact must be taken into account. It is the mission of *intellectio*, then, to begin the activity of the series which is integrated by the five traditionally established rhetorical operations and the preservation of the same in the communicative conditions most conducive to the communicative situation in general and to each of its components in particular. Thus, *intellectio* has been described and

---

[20] This idea has been put forward by T. Albaladejo-Mayordomo in two essays: 'El texto político de escritura periodística: la configuración retórica de su comunicación', in: Joaquín Garrido Medina (ed.), *La lengua y los medios de comunicación*, Madrid: Universidad Complutense de Madrid 1999, pp. 390-396; Id., 'Sociolingüística en Retórica: alteridad y diversidad en la acción discursiva', in: Pilar Díez de Revenga & José M. Jiménez Cano (eds.), *Estudios de Sociolingüística. Sincronía y diacronía*, II, Murcia: Diego Marín 1999, pp. 35-51. Starting with the review of historical texts on rhetorical theory like the *Institutiones oratoriae* by Sulpitius Victor and *De rhetorica liber* by Aurelius Augustinus and agreeing with the principle of recuperation of historical thought which dominate some of the most contemporary, committed, and responsible neo-rhetorical positions [García-Berrio, '*Retorica*' (see note 4); Id., *Teoria* (see note 4); Id., 'Retórica general literaria o Poética general', in: VV.AA. (see note 19), pp. 11-21], the model that is made up of the five traditionally established rhetorical operations (*inventio*, *dispositio*, *elocutio*, *memoria*, and *actio* or *pronuntiatio*) has been expanded to include the special operation of *intellectio* and its subsequent elaboration. Cf. Chico-Rico (see note 2), pp. 93ff.; Id., 'La *intellectio*. Notas sobre una sexta operación retórica', in: *Castilla. Estudios de Literatura*, 14 (1989) pp. 47-55; Id., '*Intellectio*', in: Gert Ueding (ed.), *Historisches Wörterbuch der Rhetorik*, IV, Tübingen, Niemeyer 1998, pp. 448-451; Id., 'La *intellectio* en la *Institutio oratoria* de Quintiliano: *ingenium, iudicium, consilium* y *partes artis*', in: Tomás Albaladejo-Mayordomo, Emilio del Río Sanz & José A. Caballero (eds.), *Quintiliano: historia y actualidad de la Retórica. Actas del Congreso Internacional 'Quintiliano: historia y actualidad de la Retórica'*, Logroño: Instituto de Estudios Riojanos 1998, pp. 493-502; Albaladejo-Mayordomo (see note 2), pp. 65ff.; Albaladejo-Mayordomo & Chico-Rico, 'La *intellectio* en la serie de las operaciones retóricas no constituyentes de discurso', in: Tomás Albaladejo-Mayordomo, Francisco Chico-Rico & Emilio del Río Sanz (eds.), *Retórica hoy*, Alicante-Madrid, Universidad de Alicante-Verbum = *Teoría/Crítica* 5 (1998), pp. 339-352.

explained as an instructive rhetorical operation which yields not a constructive level in the field of the rhetorical construction but an instructive level in the domain of the rhetorical fact. This level would contain the totality of the instructions described as semantic-semiotic or semantic-extensional, syntactical-semiotic - macro-structural and micro-structural - and pragmatic-semiotic or pragmatic-communicative which, guided towards *inventio, dispositio, elocutio, memoria,* and *actio* or *pronuntiatio,* would contribute, among other things, to the achievement of *decorum* which is necessary to guarantee the suitability and the effectiveness of the rhetorical discourse.

We affirmed in another place that a rhetorical operation like *intellectio* belongs more to *ingenium* (talent) or *natura* (nature) than to *ars* (art) or *doctrina* (learning).[85] This is the reason that it has commonly been excluded from the traditional rhetorical system of the *partes artis* and connected, mistakenly, with *inventio, dispositio, elocutio, memoria,* and *actio* or *pronuntiatio.* According to rhetorical tradition, *ingenium* is one of the natural qualities of the orator and, in general, of writers and poets. Together with *iudicium* (judgment) and *consilium* (sagacity), it is a quality which cannot be substituted by *ars.* To speak of *ingenium* must necessarily mean making reference to *iudicum* and *consilium,* natural qualities of the orator that are closely related to *ingenium.* Although we cannot affirm that those qualities are one and the same with the latter, we can at least say that the latter - together with *ars* - is led and guided towards *decorum* by the former.

In effect, *iudicium* (judgment) is the principle which leads to the achievement of internal *decorum* for the rhetorical construction, a *decorum* which we could call semantic-semiotic or semantic-extensional and syntactical-semiotic, macro-structural and micro-structural.[22] *Consilium* (sagacity), on the other hand, is a principle which leads to the achievement of external *decorum* for the rhetorical fact, a *decorum* which we could call pragmatic-semiotic or pragmatic-communicative.[23] From

---

[21]   Chico-Rico (see note 20).

[22]   It would seem evident that *iudicium* is one of the essential principles of *intellectio,* precisely that which explains the fact that this is a rhetorical operation which initiates and regulates the totality of the constructive-communicative rhetorical process, once it has allowed the orator to examine the cause and the communicative situation in which he finds himself as well as the possible changes in the course of the communicative-textual activity which may arise. For this reason, *iudicium,* through *intellectio,* is incorporated in *inventio, dispositio, elocutio, memoria,* and *actio* or *pronuntiatio* and is inseparable from them. On this subject, see Lausberg (see note 1), §§1055-1062.

[23]   Quintilian writes the following on the matter of *consilium* (*Inst. or.* VI.5.4-11): 'But here again you must not expect me to lay down any general rules. For sagacity depends on circumstances and will often find its scope in something preceding the pleading of the acuse [...]. And again in the actual pleading sagacity holds the first and most important place. For it is the duty of sagacity to decide what we should say and what we should pass by in silence or postpone; whether it is better to deny an act or to defend it, when we should employ an exordium and on what lines it should be designed, whether we should make a statement of facts and if so, how, whether we should base our plea on law or equity and what is the best order to adopt, while it must also decide on all the nuances of style, and settle whether it is expedient to speak harshly, gently or even with humility. But I have already given advice on all these points as far as each occasion permitted, and I shall continue to do the same in the subsequent portions of this work. In the meantime, however, I will give a few instances to make my meaning clearer, since it is not possible, in my opinion, to do so by laying down general rules [...]. It is enough, I think, to say that there is nothing not merely in oratory, but in all the tasks of life that is more important than sagacity and that without it all formal instruction is given in vain, while prudence unsupported by learning will accomplish more

this point of view, as Heinrich Lausberg very adeptly states, *iudicium* is led by *consilium* toward *utilitas*.[24] We would add that *intellectio*, by means of its essential principles (*iudicium* and *consilium*), is led toward the principle of *decorum*, which the rhetorical operations of *inventio*, *dispositio*, *elocutio*, *memoria*, and *actio* or *pronuntiatio* ought to have qualitatively materialized at their corresponding levels: poietical and practical, constructive and performative.

7. CONCLUSIONS

This approach leads us inevitably to considering *elocutio* as a rhetorical operation which is intimately linked to and absolutely dependent upon the other rhetorical operations. Although *elocutio* is responsible for the linguistic formulation (or the outward expression through means of a language) of the ideas found in *inventio* and organized by *dispositio*, it cannot be separated from these in the practice of linguistic communication in general and of rhetorical communication in particular. The linguistic formulation of the ideas found in *inventio* and organized by *dispositio* responds always, in virtue of the rhetorical operation of *intellectio*, to a general plan of micro-structural construction of rhetorical discourse in close connection with the general processes of textual construction and rhetorical communication between orators and hearers. In this sense, not even *elocutio* is separable from *intellectio*, *inventio*, *dispositio*, *memoria*, and *actio* or *pronuntiatio*; even its four traditional qualities (*latinitas*, *perspicuitas*, *ornatus*, and *decorum*) can be considered as exclusively dependent upon the rhetorical operation of *elocutio*. We appeal, therefore, to the universal principle of the inseparability of ideas and words, of background and form, of macro-structure and micro-structure.

If we focus on the traditional quality of *ornatus* - this 'plus' which guarantees the success of persuasion by means of adornment of words, excellence of expression, and, finally, artistic efficacy - this approach makes us consider *ornatus* as the result of the discovery of the reality which one desires to communicate. Therefore, we also consider it as the result of the interaction of *elocutio* with *inventio*, upon which depends the finding of the ideas for rhetorical discourse as well as for poetic discourse, and with *dispositio*, which permits and explains its macro-structural organization. In this context, metaphor, for example, cannot be seen as a form of linguistic-material embellishment which has been added to the discourse with the object of substituting the canonical or direct form or word, but as the result of the discovery of the proper or true form or word, as the only means of expressing the truth of reality through language. Metaphor is, in this sense, an expressive-communicative means which is necessary in rhetorical and in poetic discourse; it is the only way to represent by means of language that which one desires to express communica-

than learning unsupported by prudence. It is sagacity again that teaches us to adapt our speech to circumstances of time and place and to the persons with whom we are concerned. But since this topic covers a wide field and is intimately connected with eloquence itself, I shall reserve my treatment of it till I come to give instructions on the subject of appropriateness in speaking'.
[24]   Lausberg (see note 1), §1154.

tively.[25] For this reason, *ornatus* in Quintilian's *Institutio oratoria* is understood not as an ornamental addition, but as the result of the transformation of the linguistic code into its different levels (phono-phonologic, morpho-syntactic, and semantic-intensional) for the purpose of achieving the sublimity, the splendour, the brilliance, and the authority in words.

[25]   T. Albaladejo-Mayordomo, 'La conciencia lectora ante José Hierro', in: Martín Muelas Herraiz & Juan J. Gómez Brihuega (coords.) *Leer y entender la poesia: José Hierro*, Cuenca Universidad de Castilla-La Mancha 2001, pp. 15-43. This is one of the most solid and contemporary approaches to the study of metaphor in particular and of rhetorical figures in general. Along these same lines, see, among others, García-Berrio, *Cántico* (see note 4); Id., *Teoría* (see note 4); Id., *Forma interior. La creación poética de Claudio Rodríguez*, Málaga, Ayuntamiento di Málaga 1998; S. Arduini, 1998; 1999; 2000; 2001. Stefano (1993), 'La figura retórica como universal antropológico de la expresión', *Castilla. Estudios de Literatura* 18 (1993), pp. 7-18; Id., 'El concepto de 'figura' en la *Institutio oratoria* de Quintiliano', in: *Quintiliano: historia y actualidad* (see note 20), pp. 125-140; Id., 'Sociosemiótica de la metáfora', in: *Estudios de Sociolingüística* (see note 20), pp. 53-60; Id., *Prolegómenos a una teoría general de las figuras*, Murcia: Universidad de Murcia 2000; Id., 'Parménides y la metáfora de las dos vías, *LOGO. Revista de Retórica y Teoría de la Comunicación*, 1, 1 (2001) pp. 43-52.

OLGA TELLEGEN-COUPERUS

A CLARIFYING *SENTENTIA* CLARIFIED: ON *INSTITUTIO ORATORIA* VIII.5.19

1. INTRODUCTION

In Book VIII of his *Institutio oratoria*, Quintilian deals with *elocutio*, style. In antiquity, in Greece as well as in Rome, this was considered a very important part of rhetoric. A good orator should not only know what he would say and in what order he would say it, but he should also use such ornate and appropriate language that he would convince his audience. As Quintilian points out, without eloquence, all the preliminary accomplishments of oratory are as useless as a sword that is kept permanently concealed within its sheath.[1]

Eloquence was considered as the most difficult task of the orator. Few people have a natural talent for speaking well. It is possible to learn to be eloquent, but that takes a lot of study and exercise. That is why teachers of rhetoric concentrated on formulating rules on style and developed an extensive theory of style. Quintilian also pays a great deal of attention to this subject. He devotes more than three of the twelve books in his *Institutio oratoria* to style: Books VII, IX and X and a part of Book XI.

For present-day lawyers, style is not considered very important. In law schools, most attention is paid to teaching the system of law. This is particularly common practice in those countries of Europe where Roman law forms the basis of civil law. The last ten years or so, however, have seen an increasing interest in rhetoric. Books have been published about how to structure a proper legal argument. Law schools organise 'moot courts' in order to teach students how to speak in a court of law. It is striking that, in this context, very little attention is given to style. In the books, it is only pointed out that the style should be simple, clear, and vivid. And yet, in most legal texts that are produced every day, ample use is made of stylistic means like metaphors and rhetorical questions. These texts are frequently meant to convince the reader or the audience, for instance a judge, an official, a board of directors, or a political meeting. Apparently people realise that simple words in themselves are not enough to convince. Therefore it can be very useful to study the rules of style as they have been developed by the ancient teachers of rhetoric. Since Quintilian in his *Institutio oratoria* gives the most complete survey of style and style figures, it makes sense to begin the study of style by reading his work.

---

[1]   *Inst. or.* VIII.pr. 15. Unless indicated otherwise, I use the translation in the Loeb Classical Library by Butler (see 'Introduction', note 27).

Quintilian discusses the four traditional parts of *elocutio* in the usual order: *latinitas, perspicuitas, ornatus,* and *decorum.* In other words, a text should be formulated in proper Latin, be clear, be ornate (by means of tropes, figures of thought, and figures of speech), and be decorous. Of these, *ornatus* is by far the most interesting and also the most controversial topic because it is the most powerful weapon an orator can use. According to Quintilian, 'ornamentation of a speech contributes not a little to the furtherance of our case. For when our audience find it a pleasure to listen, their attention and their readiness to believe what they hear are both alike increased, while they are generally filled with delight, and sometimes even transported by admiration'.[2] He then refers to Cicero and Aristotle, who also thought that inspiring admiration should be one of our first aims.

Ornamentation, he continues, must be bold, manly and chaste, free from all effeminate smoothness and the false hues derived from artificial dyes and must glow with health and vigour.[3] It should also be varied to suit the type of speech to which it is applied, for the same form of ornamentation will not suit demonstrative, deliberative, and forensic speeches. Quintilian writes about this difference in VIII.3.14 as follows:

'For whereas in deliberative oratory the senate demand a certain loftiness and the people a certain impetuosity of eloquence, the public cases of the courts and those involving capital punishment demand a more accurate style. On the other hand, in private deliberations and lawsuits about trifling sums of money (and there are not a few of them) it is more appropriate to employ simple and apparently unstudied language. For we should be ashamed to demand the repayment of a loan in rolling periods, or to display poignant emotion in a case concerned with water-droppings, or to work ourselves into a perspiration over the return of a slave to the vendor.'

Quintilian then discusses several forms of ornament that can make a plea vivid: *evidentia* or illustration, *amplificatio, sententia* or reflection, and tropes. He gives many examples for all of them, often taken from work by Roman poets like Virgil, Ovid, and Horace, sometimes also from that by earlier orators like Cicero and sometimes by contemporary advocates like Domitius Afer. The examples from poetry often speak for themselves, and if they do not, they are usually clarified by the modern translators in the notes.

However, the examples taken from forensic speeches are not always clear either. In this essay, I want to discuss one of those unclear examples, namely, an example of a *sententia*. Quintilian deals with the *sententia* in Chapter 5 of Book VIII. Originally, he says, this was a sensual perception: it referred merely to the senses of the body. However, 'modern usage applied *sensus* to concepts of the mind while *sententia* is applied to striking reflexions such as are more especially introduced at the close of our periods, a practice rare in earlier days but carried even to excess in our own'.[4]

Quintilian then deals with the various forms such reflexions may take and the manner in which they should be used. This reflexion is most beautiful, he says in

---

2   *Inst. or.* VIII.3.5.
3   *Inst. or.* VIII.3.6.
4   *Inst. or.* VIII.5.2.

VIII.5.19, when it begins to sparkle by the introduction of a comparison. And, as usual, he gives an example of such a sparkling *sententia*. However, to the modern reader it is completely unclear why this sentence is regarded as beautiful or sparkling. Modern literature does not provide a conclusive explanation, either. Several attempts have been made to explain its legal background but, first, they contradict each other and, second, they do not explain why this text should be sparkling.

In this paper, I would like to submit my own explanation of this sentence. I shall approach the text in a different way than has been done until now, namely by taking into account its legal *and* oratorical background. I think that I will then be able to explain what the advocate in question meant and why, according to Quintilian, his sentence 'sparkled'.

2. *SENTENTIA*

The text I would like to discuss is VIII.5.19. I shall first render the text and give my own translation:

> *Ea vero fit pulcherrima, cum aliqua comparatione clarescit. Trachalus contra Spatalen: 'Placet hoc ergo, leges, diligentissimae pudoris custodes, decimas uxoribus dari, quartas meretricibus?'*
>
> But this reflexion is most beautiful when it begins to sparkle by the introduction of a comparison. For instance, when Trachalus said, in his speech against Spatale: 'Is this then acceptable, ye laws, the most scrupulous guardians of decency, that a tenth be given to wives and a quarter to mistresses?'

The text refers to a trial which took place in the second half of the first century. We know this because Quintilian here quotes an advocate called Trachalus. This was M. Galerius Trachalus, an important Roman senator who was consul in 68. He was also a famous advocate and, in that capacity, was very much admired by Quintilian.[5] In this case, he was acting as advocate for the plaintiff.

The other person mentioned in the text is the defendant, a woman called Spatale. Her name suggests that she was of Greek origin and that she was a woman of disreputable habits, Spatale meaning 'voluptuous'. The trial must have been about an inheritance. This can be deduced from the reference to 'the laws'. It is generally taken for granted that these laws are the *lex Iulia et Papia,* which contained sanctions relating to the law of succession. The inheritance must have been a large one, for a 'v.i.p.' like Trachalus would not have bothered to act as an advocate when only small money was involved.

In order to understand Trachalus' comparison, we must first know what this *lex Iulia et Papia* was about. Actually it is not one law, but a combination of two. In 18 BC, the Emperor Augustus introduced the *lex Iulia de maritandis ordinibus,* containing rules on marriage and divorce. Twenty-five years later, in 9, the rules of this law were mitigated somewhat by the *lex Papia Poppaea*. These two laws were, and still are, usually referred to in one breath with the *lex Iulia et Papia*. They were

---

5 So W. Eck in H. Cancik - H. Schneider (eds.), *Der neue Pauly: Enzyklopädie der Antike,* IV, Stuttgart-Weimar: Metzler 1998, p. 757.

designed to encourage marriage and improve the birthrate, with the purpose of restoring the population of Italy, the nucleus of the Roman empire.[6]

In this law, three sets of rules can be distinguished. First, they required all men aged between 25 and 60 and all women aged between 20 and 50 to be married. Second, they forbade marriages between freeborn citizens and women of dubious reputation like prostitutes and actresses. Third, they contained a system of privileges and sanctions meant to stimulate the birth of legitimate offspring. These privileges and sanctions mainly related to the law of succession. They were taken seriously because getting (part of) an inheritance or a legacy was the chief way of acquiring wealth. Since these sanctions are relevant in this connection, I shall summarise them here.

1. An unmarried person (*caelebs*), who, under this law, should be married, was *incapax*, i.e. he or she could claim nothing under a will unless he or she was a close relative of the testator.
2. Persons who were married but had no children (*orbi*) could take only half of the inheritance or legacy left to them, and, from each other, they could inherit only one tenth.
3. Everything which, due to *incapacitas*, could not be acquired was qualified as *caducum*.
4. This part of the inheritance was passed on to the other testamentary heirs with children; failing these, to legatees with children; and failing these, to 'the people'.

Let us now return to our text. It is clear that, in the first part of his comparison, when he says that 'a tenth be given to wives', Trachalus is alluding to the second sanction of the *lex Iulia et Papia* (people who were married but had no children could inherit from each other only one tenth).

The second part of Trachalus' comparison (*quartas meretricibus*), however, is rather obscure. In modern literature, it is taken for granted that the *lex Iulia et Papia* also contained a rule as to how much could be given to a *meretrix*, a prostitute. The fact that the prostitute is mentioned immediately after the wife may suggest that the law allowed prostitutes to receive a quarter of an inheritance. Therefore, romanists have tried to explain why, in this case, a prostitute could get a quarter.

In his recent book on prostitution, sexuality, and the law in ancient Rome, Thomas McGinn discusses and criticises these explanations and adds one of his own.[7] I will restrict myself to summarising some older views; then I will deal more explicitly with McGinn's interpretation, and finally I will submit my own explanation of this comparison.

The oldest view on this text mentioned by McGinn dates from 1866; it was Hartmann who then suggested that Spatale had been a *concubina* of the testator and that the law would have granted a one-fourth capacity to concubines.[8] McGinn rightly

---

[6] R. Astolfi, *La Lex Iulia et Papia,* 3rd edition, Milan: Cedam 1995, XIII. See also P. Csillag, *The Augustan Laws on Family Relations,* Budapest: Akadémiai Kiadó 1976, pp. 77ff.
[7] Th. McGinn, *Prostitution, Sexuality, and the Law in Ancient Rome,* New York-Oxford: Oxford University Press 1998, pp. 94-99.
[8] G. Hartmann, Ueber die Voraussetzungen und Grenzen der Incapacität nach der lex Iulia et Papia', *Zeitschrift für Rechtsgeschichte* 5 (1866) pp. 219-255, in particular p. 221f. He, in his turn, refers to Heineccius, *Ad legem Iuliam et Papiam lib. II,* Leipzig: Teubner 1778, p. 196.

objects to this hypothesis by pointing out that, in the text, Spatale is simply identified as a prostitute, not as a concubine.

In 1942 another view was presented, namely, by Solazzi. He thinks that Spatale was an unmarried mother and that the *lex Iulia de maritandis ordinibus* contained a special rule for unmarried fathers and mothers. The *pater solitarius* and the *mater solitaria* were not married but they did have children and as such were partly *capax*.[9] He bases this reconstruction on a late classical work called the Epitome of Ulpian. This jurist, who lived around 200, mentions the *pater solitarius* in the heading or *rubrica* of section 13. However, he does not refer to such a person in the section itself, nor does he specify how much this person would be capable of acquiring. Solazzi explains Quintilian's text thus that Spatale may have been a *mater solitaria* and that she was therefore capable of acquiring a quarter of her lover's inheritance. This explanation is not very convincing, either. McGinn rightly points out that there is no indication in the text that Spatale had children. I would add that there also is no source in which the term *mater solitaria* occurs. Besides, this interpretation does not explain Trachalus' remark. If the law had allowed a *mater solitaria* to inherit, he would not have reproached Spatale for receiving a quarter but he would have reproached the *lex Iulia et Papia* for creating such an unfair situation and so have said something which was not politically correct, and he might even have put his own position in jeopardy.

A third variation is based on a theory which was put forward by Savigny but which Savigny did not apply to Quintilian's text. That was done only much later. According to Savigny, the *lex Iulia et Papia* forbade *feminae probrosae* like prostitutes and actresses to marry freeborn men but, in return, it allowed them full capacity to inherit.[10] He bases this hypothesis on two texts by Suetonius. The most important one is Suetonius' remark in his biography of Emperor Domitian that, in 83, this emperor deprived infamous women of the right to receive inheritances and legacies.[11] Savigny concludes from this text that, before that time, those women were fully capable of acquiring an inheritance. Astolfi follows Savigny in that he also thinks that Spatale as a *femina probrosa* was allowed by law to inherit but, on the basis of Quintilian's text, he thinks that infamous women were entitled only to a quarter of what was left to them in a will.[12]

---

[9] S. Solazzi, 'Attorno al 'caduca'', in *Atti dell'Accademia di scienze morali e politiche della Società reale di Napoli* 61 (1942) 71-225 = *Scritti di diritto romano* IV (1938-1947), Naples: Jovene 1963, pp. 265-379, in particular pp. 334ff.

[10] F.C. von Savigny, *System des heutigen römischen Rechts*, 2nd edition, Berlin: Veit 1856, rpt. Aalen: Scientia 1981, pp. 555ff. It is not clear to me how this view relates to Savigny's theory that a marriage contracted against the rules of the *lex Iulia et Papia* was valid except for the sanctions of this law; for instance, when a freeborn man married an actress, their marriage was valid but, at the same time, they were regarded as *caelebs* and therefore were *incapax* to take under a will. E. Nardi, *La reciproca posizione successoria dei coniugi privi di conubium*, Milan: Giuffrè 1938, pp. 20ff, rightly challenged this theory of Savigny's and showed that these marriages were entirely invalid. See also E. Nardi, 'La incapacitas delle *feminae probrosae*', *Studi Sassaresi* 17 (1938) pp. 151-178. Unfortunately, I have not been able to read this article.

[11] Suetonius, *Domitianus*, 8. The other text is Suetonius, *Tiberius*, 35. However, as far as I can see, this second text does not have any bearing on the *lex Iulia et Papia* but refers to the *lex Iulia de adulteriis*.

[12] Astolfi (see note 6), p. 61. In note 31, he adds that there are romanists who link this quarter to the *lex*

McGinn partly agrees with Astolfi but wants to modify his view in two respects. First, he thinks there is no justification to extend the application of the regime for the *quarta* to all *feminae probrosae*; this *quarta* is only mentioned by Quintilian and then only in connection with a prostitute. Furthermore, he thinks it is unlikely that all prostitutes would have been punished by this limit of one-fourth on their testamentary eligibility. Such a measure would be at odds with the spirit of the law, which permitted them to marry freedmen and adopted a neutral, at times even benevolent approach toward the lower classes.

According to McGinn, Trachalus when contrasting *meretrices* with *uxores*, was thinking of unmarried prostitutes. They of course were *caelibes* and as such would be completely incapable of receiving an inheritance. However, McGinn thinks that the *lex Iulia et Papia* allowed the unmarried prostitutes one-fourth as a mild form of encouragement not to marry. I'll try to explain his way of reasoning. In his law, Augustus had permitted prostitutes to marry freedmen, but at the same time he regarded such unions as dishonorable and wanted to discourage them. He did so by making unmarried prostitutes partly, i.e., for one fourth, capable of inheriting. On the other hand, if a prostitute married a freedman and had children, then, as an *uxor*, she would not fall under the law and would be completely capable of inheriting. If she was married but had no children, then, like the other *uxores* in this position, she would be entitled to receive only one tenth of her husband's inheritance. Only the unmarried prostitute could claim a *quarta* from a generous lover. That is why, according to McGinn, in the case against Spatale, Trachalus could say that the laws allowed a quarter to prostitutes.

The interpretations of Quintilian's text by Astolfi and McGinn are not convincing either. They make the same mistake as the other authors, i.e. they do not take into account the context of Quintilian's example. They all concentrate on the question of why the *lex Iulia et Papia* allowed prostitutes to receive (a quarter of) an inheritance or a legacy. They obviously assume that this law contained such a rule. However, there is no source confirming this assumption and it seems to me that such a rule would be completely at odds with the spirit of the law. Prostitution may have been widely tolerated in Rome, but that does not mean that prostitutes were exempted from a law which was meant to stimulate marriage and procreation. If that had been the case, satirists like Martial and Juvenal would certainly have written about it. Apparently, the text must be tackled in another way.

I think it may be more useful to concentrate on the question of what Trachalus meant in this sentence. Why does he compare the wife receiving a tenth part of the inheritance with the mistress receiving a quarter? And why does Quintilian consider this comparison sparkling and the *sententia* beautiful? In order to answer these questions, we have to try and reconstruct the case which led to this trial.

Falcidia of 50 BC, but he does not mention any names, nor does he criticize their view. This law protected testamentary heirs from being obliged to pay more than three-quarters of the inheritance to legatees. However, this law cannot be relevant here, because Trachalus is accusing Spatale of receiving too much, not of wanting to pay too little.

3. ANOTHER *SENTENTIA*

Outside the *Institutio oratoria,* there is no information to be found about the trial against Spatale. However, Quintilian himself refers to this case one more time, namely, in VIII.5.17, i.e., two sections before the Trachalus one. Here he mentions another form of *sententia,* namely, the reflexion which is transferred from one context to another. As an example, he quotes the advocate who acted on behalf of Spatale, Q. Vibius Crispus. Like Trachalus, he was a leading Roman senator with an important political career who was also a famous advocate.[13] The text runs as follows.

> *Et aliunde petita, id est in alium locum ex alio translata. Pro Spatale Crispus, quam qui heredem amator instituerat decessit, cum haberet annos duodeviginti, 'Hominem divinum, qui sibi indulsit'.*
> Others still, depend on the fact that they are transferred from one context to another. Crispus, in his defence of Spatale, whose lover had made her his heir and then proceeded to die at the age of eighteen, remarked: 'What a god-like fellow to gratify his passion thus!'

From this text, it can be inferred that someone had made a will in which he instituted his mistress, Spatale, as his heir and then, at the age of eighteen, he had died. Spatale's right to the inheritance was challenged and, during the trial, her advocate, Crispus, made the following striking remark: 'What a godlike fellow to gratify his passion thus!' Crispus probably meant that, during his lifetime, Spatale's lover gratified his passion by keeping her as a mistress and, after he died, he did so by making her his heir. Crispus therefore transferred the gratification of the lover's passion during his lifetime to the time after he had died.

What extra information can we deduce from this text with regard to the trial against Spatale? Firstly, we can establish that the testator was a young Roman citizen who was 18 years old when he died. Secondly, he had made a valid will and therefore he must have been *sui iuris,* i.e. independent, and he must have been older than 14 when he made the will.[14] Thirdly, he named his mistress Spatale as his heir. The text it is not clear as to whether Spatale was the only heir and would get the whole estate, or that she had to share with others. However, here the first text may help us out. According to Trachalus, a quarter of the inheritance was given to a mistress. It is obvious that this mistress is Spatale herself and that her lover had left her

---

[13] See M. Deissmann-Merten, in: K. Ziegler-W. Sontheimer (eds.), *Der kleine Pauly* V, Munich: Deutscher Taschenbuch Verlag 1979, pp. 1248-1249.

[14] Being *sui iuris* meant that he was not under the *potestas* of a *pater familias* and that he was able to have an estate. Being *sui iuris* had nothing to do with age. At birth, sons or daughters came immediately under the paternal power of their father or grandfather and they could still be so when they were grown up. However, in Roman law, there were several ways of ending the *patria potestas.* It usually terminated either at the death of the *pater familias* or by emancipation, a formal release from *potestas* by the *pater familias.* Very often, children who left their paternal home were emancipated, for instance when they got married or when they settled elsewhere. On the other hand, it could also happen that children became *sui iuris* because their *pater familias* died. If he left them a fortune, they could not dispose of it until they were *pubes,* grown-up. For girls, that happened when they reached the age of 12 and for boys the age of 14. Then they could also make a will. It was usual for young Romans of wealthy families who were *sui iuris* to draw up their wills when they reached the age of 14 or soon after.

a quarter of his inheritance. This means that there must have been other heirs. It is most likely that they were relatives of the testator. Theoretically, it is possible that he was married but did not have children yet, and that he had left one tenth to his wife and the other 65% of his estate to his relatives. However, the testator being only 18 years old when he died, I think it a bit more likely that he was not married yet and that he had left the rest, i.e. three quarters of his estate, to his relatives.

Spatale was probably not married, and therefore, by law, she was not able to receive her share in the inheritance. According to the law, it should go to the other testamentary heirs, provided they had offspring. From the fact that they sued her, it can be deduced that she had already taken possession of her share or of part of it, and refused to hand it over to the other testamentary heirs.[15]

Now we come to the plea Trachalus made against Spatale. He claimed that she was not entitled to receive her share of the inheritance. He could and probably did refer to the fact that she was unmarried and therefore, by law, *incapax* to take under a will. That would have been a convincing argument in a legal sense, but it would not convince morally.

On the other hand, Vibius Crispus also had a very powerful argument in the fact that it was the intention of Spatale's lover that she would be his heir. The law was clear in that she could not be his heir, but the testator had indulged in such a god-like manner in his passion during his lifetime that it was only right that his wishes in this respect should also be fulfilled after his death.

Consequently, Trachalus had to use an extra argument, a moral one, and he did so by including in his plea the *sententia* quoted by Quintilian. He compared the share the testator had left to her with the maximum share that he could have left to a wife. He could not have left more than one tenth to his wife, therefore it was not only unfair but even a shame that he would leave more than twice that amount to his mistress. The laws on marriage and divorce were meant to be the faithful guardians of decency, and the testator had acted entirely against their intention by putting his mistress in a better position than he could have put a wife.

We do not know whether Trachalus was successful, but he certainly had the stronger position in the trial. He could base his claim on the *lex Iulia et Papia*, and there was no ambiguity as to the interpretation of this law. For Romanists, it may be remarkable that there was a trial at all, since, according to the law in the books, Spatale had no right whatsoever to this inheritance. Apparently, in real life, things went differently than we read in the Digest or Gaius' Institutes. There we only find the results; here, in Quintilian's *Institutio oratoria,* we find the law in action.

Now that we know the legal background to the trial and, in particular, the position Trachalus had in this case, we can understand why he made this comparison: he used a strong moral argument which was much more convincing than the legal one. We can now also understand why Quintilian called the sentence most beautiful: it gave a surprising turn to the situation.

---

[15]   The action they had to use was the *caducorum vindicatio*. Cf. Gai. *Inst.* 2.207; *Ulpiani Epitome*, 17.2 and 25.17; *Fragmentum de iure fisci*, 3.

4. CONCLUSION

I hope I have shown that an example such as Quintilian gives in *Inst. or.* VIII.5.19 can only be understood and valued properly if it is read in its context. This means that classicists have to realise which legal question was behind this sentence of Trachalus, and that romanists have to realise that they cannot isolate the reference to the *lex Iulia et Papia* from its forensic context and then try and explain it. Only when we reconstruct the legal and the oratorical background to the sentence can we understand the comparison. Only then does it become clear why Quintilian used Trachalus' words as an example of a sentence which lights up by a comparison.

BAREND VAN HEUSDEN

THE SEMIOTIC MINUET IN QUINTILIAN'S RHETORIC: ON THE TREATMENT OF FIGURES IN BOOK IX OF THE *INSTITUTIO ORATORIA*

1. INTRODUCTION

The reading of Books VIII and IX of Quintilian's *Institutio oratoria* (on eloquence or *eloquentia*)[1] may cause, in today's readers, a strong sense of both familiarity and strangeness. The sense of familiarity comes from the fact that working on the style of a text is something we all know from experience. Most of the sentences in this text, for instance, were rewritten a number of times. What words should I choose and how should I arrange them in sentences? What would be the right tone, what would be convincing examples? And how should I present my thoughts? You certainly know what it feels like, sitting in front of a piece of paper or screen, thinking about right formulations, about what sounds better, about your audience, about what could eventually be the cause of misunderstandings. And this work on the style of a text is not restricted to the preparation of a text for oral presentation or publication in written form. Even while we are speaking before an audience we may reflect upon the way in which we are saying things. Moreover, some of us teach it to students: be clear and precise, avoid commonplaces and cliché's, do not use the same expressions too often, and try to diversify the grammatical forms.

But the treatment of style in the *Institutio* also confronts us with a foreign world. We are not used to long speeches anymore. Ours is a culture of shock - of short, quick and concise communication. Brief notes have taken the place of long letters, debate and discussion that of long and elaborate oral presentations. We are witnessing today, in the Western world at least, a 'corrosion of the symbolic' (the reference is to Richard Sennett's *The Corrosion of Character*).[2] Language, in its symbolic form, has lost ground to visual and sound communication (and one may wonder whether this still is communication!). We watch life images on TV and cinema screens, photographs and drawings in newspapers and magazines, as well as on billboards. All sorts of 'graphics' and patterns of sound fill our environment. Symbolic language, supplanted by sensations and facts, is 'out', and so is the content of symbolic language: concepts, opinions, and points of view. But language and opinions always were the domain of the rhetorical. Does this mean that rhetoric is 'out' too?

---

[1]   All references are to Butler's edition of the *Institutio oratoria* (see 'Introduction', note 27).
[2]   R. Sennett, *The Corrosion of Character. The Personal Consequences of Work in the New Capitalism*, New York: Norton 1998.

Style', however, is certainly alive. Not in the traditionally rhetorical and linguistic realms of celebrations, political debate and the field of the law, but in entertainment, publicity (advertisement), marketing, fashion and design. The goals, however, are fundamentally different from the rhetorical. Fashion does not want to convince; it wants to seduce. Communication tends toward either, indeed, seduction (and the advent of the audio-visual media certainly had a major influence on this development) or, on the other hand, toward formal argument and proof. In between these two options, little space is left for that which is the main field of rhetoric, that is, the realm of opinions, points of view, pros and cons. Today, both the deliberative and the demonstrative rhetoric are in an anaemic condition. The political has started borrowing devices from publicity, marketing, and entertainment. This may be true also for forensic rhetoric. Even if a brilliant orator would stand up today, whom would he (or she) speak to?

Quintilian's way of argumentation, based on the use of comparisons and the reference to authorities, reflects a rhetorical way of thinking to which we are no longer used. 'Metaphors are no arguments, my maiden...' His metaphors are seldom creative, they are unambiguous and easy to understand. Also, his rhetoric does not apply to dialogue. The rhetorical perspective presupposes a monologue followed, sometimes, by another monologue. Nowhere is debate or discussion the central issue. Although the speech is meant to influence others, these others are not partners in a dialogue or research, nor can one identify with them. They are, really, adversaries (or public) in a verbal fight. This, too, puts Quintilian at a great cultural distance from us.

What may also strike us as strange, or at least as different, in Quintilian's approach, is his carefulness. The *Institutio* is about carefulness in its original sense of doing things with care (which is not exactly the same thing as being precise). Taking care of the words one uses, in view of both the subject matter at hand and the people involved. It is this sense of care, of taking time before one utters a statement, and taking time for exercise and practice, which has become rare in our time of quick pace and information overload.

Finally, we may wonder about the elaborate categorising and classifying of figures of style, or about the systematic use of comparisons as arguments. What we are used to are either easy-to-remember rules of thumb, or systematic (in the sense of logical, scientific) treatises. Quintilian's *Institutio* is mainly, as so many other rhetorical treatises of his time and later, a taxonomic endeavour - and taxonomy, in general, precedes analysis. Reading this text, however, one gets the impression that the taxonomic approach is in a sense already waning. Quintilian is full of contempt about the endless lists of rhetorical species and subspecies, which he finds in the books by his colleague-orators. He tries to limit the number of distinctions to the minimum and to focus instead on the analysis of effects. Names are not that important.

Thus Quintilian, in these two books, deals with what would seem to be the most common of subjects, that is, style - the way in which one presents a text. And yet, the whole endeavour has a foreign taste.

2. THE SEMIOTIC PERSPECTIVE

In order to analyse Quintilian's stylistics from a systematic perspective, which would also allow us to relate his work to contemporary rhetorical culture, we have to take a step back. It will be a *reculer pour mieux sauter*: I will briefly sketch a general semiotic framework that allows us to characterise the rhetoric as a specific form of representation or, in jargon, as *semiosis*.

As all other organisms, humans live in a world of representations. These representations are determined by our physical constitution, that is, by our perceptual and neurological apparatus. The whole of these representations constitutes the *Umwelt* - the world in which we live (the term was coined by the biologist Jakob von Uexküll).[3] Organism and *Umwelt* interact with each other in closed loop. Thanks to these representations, certain events - or signals - elicit appropriate reactions in the organism. If the reactions do not fit, the organism will perish and, if this happens all too often, the species risks extinction.

These representations that constitute the organism's *Umwelt* become signs, and culture, when they are experienced as such, that is, as something which is not the world, but something which stands for, which re-presents. I leave aside discussions about culture defined as non-genetically transmitted behaviour,[4] as well as discussions about the use of signs by primates - these issues are of no importance here. In order to become a sign, a representation must be separated from the actuality it represents. Let me give a simple example: the image you have of a room (that is: the representation of it) becomes a possible sign once you can represent a room to yourself without having to be there. The important consequence of this ability is that now, once you enter a room (any room!), you will be able not just to know that it is a room, but to recognise it as a room. To recognise means: you know this is a room and at the same time, you know it is not the representation of a room. Thus, to be able to signify is to be able to recognise. Signification (or *semiosis*) is nothing but this ongoing process of bringing together memory and actuality. Semiotic artefacts, such as gestures, language, pictures, etc., are mainly mnemonic devices that facilitate the semiotic process. Oratory is no exception to this general semiotic process. It is but one of the many ways in which humans represent their environment.

Humans only dispose of a limited number of semiotic strategies. These strategies form the building blocks of human culture. As we can remember and represent the world in basically three different ways, I speak about a semiotic minuet. First, the representation can be of a concrete event. We may represent an event as an event, that is, as we perceive or imagine it. You have this kind of representations of your family members, your home, of the places where you live and work. In our daily life, most of the semiotic work we do concerns this kind of signs. Also when reading a novel, for instance, or when seeing a film, we use them to construct imag-

---

[3] On Von Uexküll, see 'Jakob von Uexküll: A Paradigm for Biology and Semiotics'. Special issue of *Semiotica*, 134 – 1/4 (2001). Guest editor: Kaevi Kull.
[4] F. de Waal, *The Ape and the Sushi-master. Cultural Reflections by a Primatologist*, New York: Basic Books 2001.

inary situations. These representations of events in terms of concrete time, place, and persons or characters are called icons. Sometimes they are also called figures - which is important for our discussion of Quintilian. The iconic representation, or iconic sign, or icon, has a one-place structure, because representation and meaning coincide.

The second type of representation makes things a little bit more complicated. It brings together a number of concrete events under one umbrella. This umbrella can be a gesture, a visual or an acoustic sign. Language certainly is the best known system of this kind of signs. Thus with the word 'hat', for example, we refer to an infinite number of concrete events. That is, the use of the acoustic representation 'hat' allows for the creation of what is called a concept or category. These signs are called symbolic signs or symbols. It should be clear that symbols allow for easy communication, as they do not require some form of re-enactment of the situation we are communicating about (as the citizens of Gulliver's Laputa knew so well). Symbolic signs have a two-place structure: they always consist of an expression or *signifier* and a content or *signified* - the first being an acoustic or visual or tactile image, the second a concept.

A number of things about symbolic signs are of importance for the discussion of Quintilian. Symbols may facilitate communication, but they also require it. Symbol systems are conventional (no concept arises as such), and have to be learned. Each language (the term is here used as synonym for symbol system) constitutes a culture or a cultural realm. This is true for national languages but also for professional jargon (such as, for instance, juridical language). Symbolic signs are intricately related to the social world and to communication, as it is the communication that legitimises and continuously confirms them. Without communication, the symbolic world loses its ground.

Secondly, symbolic signs build upon iconic signs. They do so both on the level of the expression and the content. As an acoustic, visual or tactile image, an expression is always an iconic sign, that is, the representation of a concrete event - a sound, a rhythm, a pitch, a font, a style of writing, a colour, etc. In terms of what was said above, the expression, apart from referring to a concept, is always also a figure and can be dealt with as such. But even on the level of the content, the iconic representation is never far away. If we say, for instance, 'A tall woman with red hair, carrying a baby, came walking into the room', most of us will immediately construct a mental image - an icon! - of this situation, although all the words used in the sentence are symbolic representations. A related fact is that most of us represent concepts in a prototypical form - that is, as a more or less concrete event. Thus the concept of 'bird', in Dutch, is represented as an animal looking somewhat like a sparrow. The same is true for most concepts. Even when we deal with abstractions such as love, or hate, or equality, we tend to represent them as concrete - iconic - situations.

A third type of representation refers to the structure of an event, that is, to abstract relations. These relations (of causation, for instance, or of number) are not a part of our sensory experience, nor are they conceptual, that is, a matter of putting together events under one name. On the contrary, discoveries about the structure of the world have often had disastrous consequences for our conceptual systems. These indexical signs, or *indices*, have a three-place structure. To our images and concepts, they add a world of relations and structures, a world which we do not perceive but which determines appearances. The indexical sign is not based on individual experience (as the iconic sign is), nor is it based on conventions (as the symbolic sign). Instead, it is necessary, logical, determined. It does not come about in perception or communication, but in thinking. With the advent of the indexical sign, humanity entered the era of science and philosophy. But, as with the symbolic sign, indexical signs are built upon icons and symbols. Even in abstract science, we need symbols, and we use images. Indexical relations are often represented with iconic signs. This is done with graphs, for instance, and with models or sketches. These iconic indexical representations are also often called figures. Complex and abstract indexical representations seem to have their origin in simple drawings, and indexical culture only takes off with the invention of drawing.

Thus humans dispose of a relatively simple semiotic infrastructure which determines their very complex *Umwelt*. Although the theory cannot be worked out here in any detail, it provides us with a simple model of the semiotic process. With the help of this abstract model, we can analyse Quintilian's discussion of figures as presented in the *Institutio*. It will also enable us to relate his discussion of oratory to present day culture.

As Quintilian says in Book III, every speech consists of signs and that which the signs refer to (III.5.1). The three sign types that we have distinguished above, however, serve different functions. These functions can be described very roughly as: perception, conceptualisation and analysis (or structuring). From images, via concepts to structures, the relation between the sign and what is represented (its referent) becomes increasingly abstract. The three semiotic functions can be related to the three functions of oratory: *delectare* (the demonstrative), *movere* (the deliberative), and *docere* (the forensic). In other words: to show (and to tell), to interpret (and to give meaning - we still speak about a political or rhetorical 'move'), to explain (and to structure). It is not so strange, therefore, that Quintilian judges this triad to be 'logical' (III.4.12). The three genres of oratorical speech (VIII.1.6-12; but see also III.4) have their semiotic logic. Every situation is represented according to the three semiotic modalities. In Book III, Quintilian discusses the question. First he mentions those (Cicero, among others), who criticised the three-partition of rhetoric. Then, however, he proceeds to explain its logic. He puts forward a number of arguments: one can distinguish between three kinds of public: those who come to enjoy a speech, those who want an advice, and those who have to judge. Another point of view distinguishes past, present and future: the juridical deals with the present, the deliberative with the future and the praise or laudation with the past. A third criterion is that which distinguishes between certainty and doubt: the laudatory speech is about what we know for sure, both the deliberative (choice) and the juridical concern things about which we are in doubt. The categorisation of Anaximenes is a further specification of these three main genres (cf. III.4.9). Moreover, the semiotic triad is reflected in the well-known rhetorical triad of pathos, ethos and logos.

3. FIGURES

As we argued above, all our representations are figures insofar as they are sensory images ('sensory' taken in its broad sense, including real and imagined sensory impressions). A text, here defined as a more or less coherent whole of representations, or signs, is always also figurative. Texts can consist of behavioural, verbal, acoustic, or visual signs, or a combination of these. Figures occur on all three levels of semiotic abstraction: as concrete images, as images of symbolic concepts, and as images of indexical structures: images can be perceived events, perceived concepts and perceived structures. Figures of speech, of meaning and of thought have to do with the way in which a representation (a *text* in the broad semiotic sense) is presented and perceived. Now this is exactly what Books VIII and IX of the *Institutio* are about.

Rhetorical speech is conceived as a fight by Quintilian (IX.1.20). The metaphor has become a commonplace today - ARGUMENT IS WAR is one of the 'metaphors we live by'.[5] Speech is like a fictional character, with an attitude, gestures, with a face even. One almost has the vision of a puppet, the strings of which the orator is pulling. This puppet is fighting its fight, and apart from that, it must make an agreeable impression on the audience. Therefore, the way in which something is said may seem utterly unimportant but, says Quintilian, it is definitely not. Style makes what we say trustworthy and enters the thoughts of the judges without being noticed. In other words: form is invisible, but it works. It is a hidden weapon, a disguise.

Quintilian distinguishes between three broad types of stylistic devices, which he identifies as, respectively, tropes, figures of speech, and figures of thought (IX.1.1). Each type of device corresponds to one of the iconic representations identified above: figures of speech to the iconic on the level of symbolic expression, tropes to the iconic on the level of symbolic content, and figures of thought to the iconic on the level of indexical structure. Nowhere Quintilian deals with the iconic *pur sang*, which is the consequence of his focussing on language and argument, that is, on the symbolic and the indexical. Crucial, however, is the perceptual aspect of the representation, the way in which a text is present, as well as presented, to our eyes, ears and other senses.

Before we proceed to take a closer look at the three types of figures, we must tackle a more general issue, which is that of the opposition between figures and normal, non-figurative representations. Is it not the case that every representation is already a figure, simply because it has to be perceived in one way or another? The question pertains to a general discussion on perception. Normally, it would seem, we do not perceive our world very consciously. We are not aware of what we perceive until we are confronted with a deviation, with a difference. As perception always implies a deviation, however small, from what we expect, this amounts to saying that in fact, most of the time, we do not perceive, we do not re-present, but we live and act in a pre-established world of representations. We do not really see what is

---

[5]   G. Lakoff and M. Johnson, *Metaphors we live by*, Chicago-London: The University of Chicago Press 1980, pp. 77-86.

happening around us - the world is replaced, or substituted, by a more or less complex construction of our memory. Thus, difference is eliminated, and with difference, 'true', conscious perception.

Quintilian's analysis of tropes and figures antedates deconstruction philosophy by some 2000 years. Neither tropes nor figures (nor tropes *as* figures) can easily be distinguished from non-figurative, so-called literal speech. Figures are forms, but can one imagine a text without form? At the same time, they are deviant, new forms. But deviations become customary in the course of time. Which makes the opposition, rather than a question of systematic differences, a matter of memory versus actuality. Quintilian deconstructs the opposition between figurative and non-figurative speech, where he defines the figure as 'form' (*qualiscumque forma sententiae*). The figure is of course always there but it is perceived as such only when it deviates from the standard. So the figure is at the same time both everything[6] and only part of everything - it refers more to a temporal phase than to a specific group of linguistic forms. The 'logocentric' distinction or opposition between the literal or normal (grammatical) and the figurative (poetical and/or rhetorical) is 'deconstructed' by revealing the thoroughly figurative nature of the literal, as well as the literal fate of the figurative.

It is not so strange therefore, to hear Quintilian argue that of course, all speech is (or has) a figure but that, on the other hand, figures come to life only where deviations from a normal way of talking stand out. As he himself notices (IX.3.1): 'Figures of speech have always been liable to change and are continually in process of change in accordance with the variations of usage. Consequently when we compare the language of our ancestors with our own, we find that practically everything we say nowadays is figurative.' His comparison of speech to a human face is also telling (IX.3.101-102). A non-figurative speech is compared to a lifeless face, whereas a completely figurative speech would be similar to a face in constant movement (and as we know, a face that is alive, will always be moving...). At the same time, the figure is something that is eye-catching. The passage is important enough to be quoted in its entirety. 'Therefore in the first and common sense of the word everything is expressed by *figures*. If we are content with this view, there is good reason for the opinion expressed by Apollodorus (...) to the effect that he found the rules laid down in this connection quite incomprehensible. If, on the other hand, the name is to be applied to certain attitudes, or I might say gestures of language, we must interpret *schema* in the sense of that which is poetically or rhetorically altered from the simple and obvious method of expression. It will then be true to distinguish between the style which is devoid of figures (or *aschêmátistos*) and that which is adorned with figures (*eschêmatisméiê*). (...) We shall then take a *figure* to mean a form of expression to which a new aspect is given by art' (IX.1.13). The unnoticed figure thus becomes a zero-degree figure.

Quintilian thus compares, more than once, a speech to the human (male) body. Figures are the attitudes, the gestures, and the general shape of the body of speech.

---

6   R. Granatelli, 'Le definizioni di figura in Quintiliano Inst.IX.1.10-14 e il loro rapporto con la grammatica e le *controversiae figuratae*', *Rhetorica* 12-4 (1994) p. 402

It is as if we witness how, in his discourse, the thinking about speech and figures is not yet thoroughly conceptual. Images are still strongly present as such, as images. The concept of figure is still in the making.

Books VIII and IX are certainly the most 'literary' part of the *Institutio*. It is no coincidence, of course, that many of the examples of stylistic devices Quintilian gives, are taken from literary sources. Also, an important part of the reading sources of the young rhetorician is literary. Virgil is one of the important authors to whom Quintilian continuously refers for stylistic examples, and so are Homer, Seneca, Terentius and others.

The argument about figurative language brings to mind the debate in the study of literature that was triggered by Viktor Shklovsky's essay on 'Art as Technique'.[7] In this short, but ground breaking paper, Shklovsky, who was one of the leading figures (no pun intended) of the Russian Formalist movement, argued that the basic function of art was to restore true perception. Art does so by confronting us with deviations ('estrangement') on the level of our representations of the world. Years later, the great literary theorist Roman Jakobson defined the poetic function in communication as the reference of a message to itself as language - that is, in Quintilian's terms, as a figure.[8]

The iconic belongs, in principle, to the realms of concrete experience and the representation of that concrete experience in art. Quintilian's reference to Cicero is very adequate and telling, where Cicero says that in a figure, we are able to see the occurrences as if we had them in front of us (IX.1.27). Quintilian also compares the figures to the breath the body needs to move (IX.2.4). From a semiotic point of view this is precisely what figures always do: they bring movement in the process of representation. All the stylistic devices come down to this one thing: to force the audience (judges, juries) to become active in the process of *semiosis*, by making or creating a concrete situation in which the more abstract, the conceptual and logical meanings will function. 'For eloquence delights in variety, and just as the eye is more strongly attracted by the sight of a number of different things, so oratory supplies a continuous series of novelties to rivet the attention of the mind' (IX.2.63). 'The facts themselves must be allowed to excite the suspicions of the judge, and we must clear away all other points, leaving nothing save what will suggest the truth. In doing this we shall find emotional appeals, hesitation and words broken by silences most effective. For thus the judge will be led to seek out the secret which he would not perhaps believe if he heard it openly stated, and to believe in that which he thinks he has found out for himself' (IX.2.71).

4. THREE TYPES OF FIGURES

In its first sense, as a figure of speech, the figure is simply the way a text looks and sounds. Although Quintilian discusses sound and rhythm in a separate chapter, it

---

[7]   V. Shklovsky, 'Art as technique' in: L.T. Lemon-M.J. Reis (eds.), *Russian Formalist Criticism. Four Essays*. Lincoln-London: University of Nebraska Press 1965, pp. 3-24.
[8]   R. Jakobson, 'Linguistics and poetics' in: D. Lodge (ed.), *Modern Criticism and Theory. A Reader*. London: Longman 1988, pp. 32-57.

also belongs, systematically, to the realm of language as a figure. Figures are not just visual; they are also acoustic. The musical qualities of words are not linguistic in the strict sense. They pertain to the iconic, not to the symbolic. Language is now used as a musical instrument. And still, Quintilian assumes that power of rhythm and melody is at it strongest in eloquence. I consider the whole fourth chapter of Book IX, which deals with sound and rhythm, as an integral part of the treatment of the figures of speech. Our modern sense of prose has come a long way since prose was still considered to be rhythmical and melodic. In part this must have to do with the dominance of the written word in our culture, and with the decline of oratory in its various forms (liturgical, political, juridical). Probably we still hear the difference, but we are no longer in grade of constructing it consciously or name it.

The concept 'figure of thought' refers to the perceived structure of the thought in speech. As such it pertains to the indexical but, similar to a sketch, it is the iconic, the 'sensory' side of the indexical. The figure of thought is what the thought 'looks like' when it is presented in discourse, it pertains to its appearance. In the figures of thought there is lyric, as well as drama (prosopopeia) and epic (painting with words) - in short, one could say, there is literature.

The third meaning of the term figure, as it is used today, for instance, when we speak about 'figurative language' is that of trope. Quintilian himself states that 'There are some again who call tropes figures, Artorius Proculus among them' (IX.1.2). And he also remarks that it is not easy to distinguish between figure and trope because the resemblance is so close. Our semiotic analysis corroborates this and allows us to systematically relate the two devices. Quintilian gives the following definition of the trope: 'It is the transference of expressions from their natural and principal signification to another, with a view to the embellishment of style or, as the majority of grammarians define it, the transference of words and phrases from the place which is strictly theirs, to another to which they do not properly belong. A figure, on the other hand, as is clear from the name itself, is the term employed when we give our language a conformation other than the obvious and ordinary' (IX.1.4). Now tropes fit the definition of the figure equally well. The difference between tropes on the one hand and figures of speech and thought on the other has to do with the fact that tropes are a matter of conceptual meaning, whereas figures are not. But distinguishing meaning from form (either form of speech or form of thought) we tend to forget that meaning has a form as well - one could even define meaning as 'a choice of form'. The meaning we attribute to a form is, in fact, another form, and it is this substitution of one form for another that, in tropes, is strange and deviating from the ordinary and obvious. The trope is thus basically a figure, but a figure of meaning. The three functions of metaphor are necessity, understanding, and beauty. Quintilian thus distinguishes tropes that are used for their meaning and tropes used for the sake of beauty (VIII.6.3). 'We do this either because it is necessary or to make our meaning clearer or, as I have already said, to produce a decorative effect' (VIII.6.5). A trope adds a more or less strong iconic dimension to the conceptual content of an expression. This iconic dimension can be limited to an emotional value, as when we say that there is strength in a speech, but it can also create a very palpable and concrete image. This is the case, for instance, when a metaphor is creatively used. Such a metaphor really offers a new perspective (a new perception). Apart from adding value to a concept or a new perspective, metaphors can also be used for their explanatory value, as is often the case in science. The concept and image of the 'metaphor' itself once probably functioned as such.

What blurs the picture, however, at least where figures of meaning, or tropes, are concerned, is the fact that there is another difference - gradual this time - that interferes with the one between figurative and non-figurative. This is the distinction, briefly referred to above, between the figurative and the conceptual. A concept is not a figure. It has a different semiotic quality - symbolic instead of iconic. Thus the opposition between figurative and literal seems to hide at least two distinctions: that between old and new semantic forms, and that between iconic and symbolic, that is, between a one-place and a two-place representation. Both the prototypical meaning and the metaphor are situated in between the 'purely' figurative and the conceptual. Whereas the latter is sometimes new and creative (but does not need to be so), the other is generally extremely conservative and stable.

The movement from figure to concept is an extremely important one. An event or situation is less and less understood as this or that concrete situation, but is brought under the umbrella of a general concept. This movement necessarily entails a choice both of perspectives and values. Concepts are seldom neutral. This process of conceptualisation, that is, of naming concrete situations and thereby putting them in a certain perspective, categorising them and valuing them, is probably one of the main endeavours of rhetoric. Words are all-important, and so are images, but only insofar as these images have an unmistakable symbolic - conceptual - content. They must be easy to understand. Thus in rhetorical discourse, metaphors are actually transferred concepts. The iconic is at its best a nice extra. In a sense, therefore, Quintilian is right not to count the rhetorical trope as a figure. Insofar as the tropes he considers are basically substitutions of concepts, and not substitutions of the images of concrete situations or events, he is right in doing so. An artistic, poetic metaphor endangers the rhetorical position[9].

5. RHETORIC AND ORATORY AS A SEMIOTIC PROCESS

How can we characterise the rhetoric itself from a semiotic point of view? As communication, it is basically a social process, in which something is 'done with words'. Rhetoric is the domain of language, and in general sense, of symbolic representation. It is the domain of choices and values, of conceptualisation. The way in which a situation or event is interpreted, that is, conceptualised, will determine the way in which we act. This conceptualisation of our *Umwelt* is done with and through language. Which is why language is also the domain of rhetoric... After the terrorist

---

[9] It should be noticed that what Quintilian discusses as *emphasis* not always really fits his definition of the figure of thought. It is rather a matter of tropes, that is, of content. It is also very close to irony and does not need a specific 'figure' to be successful. Can one say that the decoding of an ambiguous message is a thought figure? In a sense it is, but then all tropes are so too. The point is that in emphasis we are dealing with meaning, more than with form. The figure is 'the way in which', whereas the trope is more 'the what'.

attacks in New York and Washington, the United States asked Afghanistan for the expulsion of Osama bin Laden. The Taliban, however, replied that they considered Osama bin Laden to be their guest. Now their culture forbids them to send a guest away. It was therefore up to the Pakistani diplomats to convince them of the fact that this rule did not apply to guests who are criminals, or that for once, they had to disregard the rules of their culture. An international expert described terrorism as a cancer. In our culture it is accepted that cancers have to be removed quickly, while otherwise they might kill the organism. And another example, also taken from the recent events in the United States, is the choice we have between calling terrorism either a crime, or an act of war. It is clear, I think, that the two conceptualisations entail completely different reactions.

In order to impose a certain conceptualisation (and interpretation, and valuation), we seduce, we fight, we argue - with words. We delight, we move, and we instruct in function of this overarching goal, which is to convince our audience of an opinion, of *doxa* and *mores*. Once we have achieved this interpretation, it is our culture, system of law, or tradition, which tells us what the correct behaviour should be.

We can now understand why from a rhetorical perspective, poetry (and, *a fortiori*, figures) are seen as a deviation (French: *écart*) from normal speech. As rhetorical thinking is thinking in terms of conventions and concepts, of choices and ensuing actions, and *not* so much in terms of perceptions of concrete situations and events, its main goal is not, as it is in art, perception and experience. Quite the contrary: rhetorical thinking is directed towards what is meaningful and already has acquired a certain positive or negative value. In rhetoric, the concrete event is always subsumed under one or more general categories. Rhetorical thinking is therefore thinking in terms of choices. And choices imply oppositions. The dichotomous thinking is in itself a solution to the problems of interpretation created by concrete reality, as poetical, figurative language tries to represent it. Figures, which constitute the backbone of art, seem to be of secondary importance in rhetoric. They embellish, they may create a favourable impression of the speaker, but as iconic signs they may even threaten the basic goal of rhetoric. Quintilian himself is quite clear about the fact that figures are not a 'doing with words' (IX.1.23). The figure seduces, and by seducing, it may support rhetoric.

'Real' figures, on whatever level one finds them (form, meaning, structure) are potentially dangerous for rhetoric. Being concrete, they generate ambiguity, uncertainty, and doubt, which are not directly qualities of a rhetorical text. Thus, most rhetorically used figures tend to be only mildly creative, and have, at most, an ornamental character. There is thus a tension inherent in Quintilian's view of rhetorical style: as a figure, in order to be pleasing, style must be deviant, but as a rhetorical weapon, it must not attract too much attention. Beauty yes, but never too much of it… Which is basically the tension between rhetoric and art. The tension is mirrored, on the other side of the semiotic spectrum, in that between rhetoric and science, between opinion and truth.

Style is not about facts (instruction) or meaning (moving), but about appearance (delight). Style, Quintilian says, is extremely difficult to acquire (VIII.pr.14). It is necessary, however, if one wants to communicate successfully. 'And without this power (of eloquence) all the preliminary accomplishments of oratory are as useless as a sword that is kept permanently within its sheath' (VIII.pr.15). Beautiful language is sparkling and glittering (twinkling even). It shines - all these images refer to a certain movement - brilliance, the sublime - it is never static (VIII.2.1-6). Not only the image of the situation and the accused person is important, but also the image the defender gives of him or herself and his or her opponent, as well as the court (the judges). Apparently, however, style does not come naturally. 'It is this, which is the chief object of our study, the goal of all our exercises and all our efforts at imitation, and it is to this that we devote the energies of a lifetime; it is this that makes one orator surpass his rivals, this that makes one style of speaking preferable to another' (VIII.pr.16).

At the beginning of Book IX, Chapter 4, Quintilian tells us: 'I am well aware that there are certain writers who would absolutely bar all study of artistic structure and contend that language as it chances to present itself in the rough is more natural and even more manly. If by this they mean that only that is natural, which originated with nature and has never received any subsequent cultivation, there is an end to the whole art of oratory. For the first men did not speak with the care demanded by that art nor in accordance with the rules that it lays down. (...) No, that which is most natural is that which nature permits to be done to the greatest perfection. How can a style which lacks orderly structure, be stronger than one that is welded together and artistically arranged? (...) Why then should it be thought that polish is inevitably prejudicial to vigour, when the truth is that nothing can attain its full strength without the assistance of art, and that art is always productive of beauty?' (IX.4.3-7).

There are a few points to be made. First there is the fact that rhetoric pertains to civilisation and civilisation is a form of ordering the natural world. One may ask, of course, whether there is a continuum from the natural to the more civilised state. Quintilian seems to suggest that this is indeed the case. He represents a view of culture in which what is done is done with care, with utmost precision and eye for detail. Civilisation brings with it a strong control over the environment, the body (in all its manifestations), language, and thought. In Book VIII, Quintilian emphasises 'that the precepts of which I have spoken may be regarded not so much as having been discovered by the professors of rhetoric as having been noted by them when they presented themselves' (VIII.pr.12). At the end of the book, he once again stresses that everything should look natural, though it is highly constructed. It may remind one of the Zen-culture of Japan: years of exercise must lead to a perfect naturalness of movement (in painting, for instance, in fighting with swords, or in the arrangement of flowers). This ideal of the total control of action corresponds to the spontaneous perfection that must be achieved in great oratory.

A second point is the question of 'measure' and beauty. Beauty is allowed, as long as it is not overdone. It functions as a kind of gateway through which the hearers are introduced to the argument. The position is well known: from a rhetorical perspective, art is mainly an extra, a means to achieve the rhetorical end, it is not (yet) considered an autonomous semiotic force. His elaborated example of the olive trees is again telling – the analogy serves as argument (VIII.3.8-11). 'In fact, true beauty and usefulness always go hand in hand'.

6. THE RHETORIC OF ANTI-RHETORIC

One gets the impression that Quintilian's is, in a sense, an anti-rhetorical rhetoric. He strongly focuses on argument and style. But argument and style belong to the realms of proof and beauty, that is, in the end, to the domains of science and art. He also stresses the fact that speech should be 'natural', clear, and as simple as possible. Quintilian always tries to avoid the cheep, the too overtly rhetorical. He stresses the openness and earnestness of the orator. No tricks, no lying, at least in principle. His rhetoric is one of caution and discreteness. Discreteness can be achieved with the different figures - of speech and thought. His example-argument of the decorated body is telling (VIII.pr.18-22): the rhetorical should enforce what is already naturally there, it should not deform it. The best choice of words is the most simple and straightforward (VIII.pr.23). Style has to be natural (VIII.pr.19), and it must have the same source as the argument. 'Therefore I would have the orator, while careful in his choice of words, be even more concerned about his subject matter. For, as a rule, the best words are essentially suggested by the subject matter and are discovered by their own intrinsic light' (VIII.pr.20-21). In Book VI, where he moans the death of his wife and his two sons, he demonstrates this himself. Quintilian is the Mies van der Rohe of oratory. His suspicion of what is generally associated with the rhetorical makes him very 'modern'. It is the suspicion toward rhetoric that is akin to the scientific mind. Quintilian's is an almost rational rhetoric, well suited, therefore, to the modern mind.[10] According to Seel, the *Institutio* was meant for the education of the humanist, not for the rhetorician.[11] But then, of course, anti-rhetoric is rhetoric too. It is the rhetoric, for instance, of King Lear's daughter Cordelia.[12] Choices cannot be avoided. However, it probably is the more clever form of rhetoric in a culture in which 'good speaking' is looked upon with distrust. There may have been historical reasons for this drift toward the aesthetic and the juridical. As Seel notices, with the advent of the Roman emperors, rhetoric lost much of its political functions. It kept permeating Roman culture, though.

7. CONCLUSION

Whereas rhetoric is prominent in post-structuralist theory, it is virtually absent in contemporary European culture. And although it would seem to be a sort of common wisdom that we live in a world that is our own construction, and that facts are human-made, the role of symbols and language has become marginal. If one would have to characterise 'post'-postmodernism, that is, European culture as it changed in the eighties and nineties of the past century, this would certainly be one important aspect of this culture: the decline of the symbolic in favour of the iconic and the indexical. We live, today, in a culture of soaps and genes, a culture dominated by

[10]   O. Seel, *Quintilian oder die Kunst des Redens und Schweigens*, Stuttgart: Klett-Cotta 1977, pp. 9ff.
[11]   Seel (see note 10), p. 16.
[12]   P. Valesio, *Novantiqua. Rhetorics as a Contemporary Theory*, Bloomington: Indiana University Press 1980.

images and theories. The realm of traditions, conventions, choices, opinions and action has shrunk, it has lost much of its importance. One of the basic tenets of post-modernism was that our world is fundamentally symbolic, that is, based on (systems of) conventional signs. In our daily lives, we experience exactly the opposite: life is subjectively experienced and it is genetically determined (cf. the novels by Michel Houellebecq, or the film *Code inconnu* by Michael Haneke), but it is only marginally social... Most of the signs, to the scandal of the elderly, have lost their meaning. For humanistic scholars, there may still be meanings to discover, but from the perspective of most inhabitants of our culture, meaning has vanished. Communication and conceptualisation have become the domain of a very few.

It is one of the main issues in the contemporary political debate: the absence of meaning. The demonstrative (for instance in publicity and marketing) and the juridical have taken over - in fact very much of what should be political is interpreted as a mix of demonstrative and forensic - of 'image' and 'fact' (mainly economic and biological fact...). There is little space for the truly political, and, therefore for the truly rhetorical. The adventures of the Norwegian ship with refugees in the Australian territorial waters is just one example of this trend - the juridical and the political tend to merge... when what is a political decision is masked as a juridical point.

Manipulation and facts have become more important than argumentation. Seduction, coercion and the logic of necessity have taken the place of debates. We are influenced by facts and by appealing and threatening images, but are we still influenced by meaning, by concepts and values, by shared goals and standards? Or by something as old fashioned as ideology?

The quest for a new form of rhetoric may have directed our attention toward Quintilian. If we want to restore rhetoric, however, our culture must allow us to do so. That is, we have to re-value the realm of meaning - of symbols, language, and choices. It is our task to point out how certain aspects of culture can never be reduced to experience or fact, but will always remain a matter of meaning and choice. And what is more, we must also make it clear that it is very dangerous to view these matters of choice as question either of taste or of logic. If we want to restore a humanist, 'quintilian' rhetoric, we must strive for a culture of balance and complexity, in which the rhetorical is again an (important) aspect of all communication. With Quintilian, we must plead for a revival of social communication, a revival of the debate on opinions, values, and tradition, as well as for a careful (in both of its senses) use of symbolic signs.

OLGA TELLEGEN-COUPERUS

STYLE AND LAW: HOW TO WIN A CASE BY MEANS OF *EMPHASIS*

1. INTRODUCTION

In the ninth book of the *Institutio oratoria*, Quintilian continues the discussion of style which he began in Book VIII. He now concentrates on a group of stylistic phenomena, viz., figures of style. Here, the orator does not manipulate the meaning of the words but the connection between words and syntax.

Traditionally, a distinction is made between figures of speech and figures of thought. In this chapter, I will pay attention to one particular figure of thought, viz., that of *emphasis*. Quintilian (IX.2.65-66) tells us that *emphasis* is a figure

> 65. ... *in quo per quandam suscipionem quod non dicimus accipi volumus, non utique contrarium, ut in ironeíai, sed aliud latens et auditori quasi inveniendum ... 66. Eius triplex usus est; unus si dicere palam parum tutum est, alter si non decet, tertius qui venustatis modo gratia adhibetur.*
>
> 65. ... whereby we excite some suspicion to indicate that our meaning is other than our words would seem to imply; but our meaning is not in this case contrary to that which we express, as is the case in irony, but rather a hidden meaning which is left to the hearer to discover. ... 66. This class of figure may be employed under three conditions: first, if it is unsafe to speak openly; secondly, if it is unseemly to speak openly; and thirdly, when it is employed solely with a view to the elegance of what we say.[1]

It may be clear that the first situation occurs frequently in law and politics. This was particularly true of Quintilian's own time, the early Empire. It is obvious that it was unsafe for Quintilian to refer to the political situation of the day, but he states that this type of *emphasis* was very popular and that it was commonly practised in the schools.

However, according to Quintilian, when an orator employs *emphasis* in a court of law, he will only be successful if he can make the judge think that he is reluctant to use *emphasis*. He illustrates this statement with an example from legal practice. The lawsuit in question, which he describes in IX.2.73-74, is rather special because he himself had acted as an advocate for the defendant. In this case, a wife was charged with forging her husband's will. Quintilian describes how he won the case by using the figure of thought of *emphasis*.

As usual, Quintilian's description is very brief. This may have been all right for his contemporaries, but for modern readers it is not. Several scholars have tried to

---

[1] I use the text edition and translation in the Loeb Classical Library by Butler (see 'Introduction', note 27), p. 415.

translate and interpret the text, but Russell, in his new translation of Quintilian, still concludes that the situation is unclear. In this essay, I want to explore what the legal problem exactly was and how Quintilian succeeded in winning the case by using the figure of *emphasis*. To this end, I will first quote the text, give the most recent English translation, and assess the facts of the case as Quintilian presents them. Then I will summarize the interpretations by modern classicists and romanists, and show how they interpret the legal problem and the *emphasis* as used by Quintilian.

My conclusion is that neither the classicists nor the romanists have been able to reconstruct the case properly because they have some preconceived ideas about the text and because they do not at all, or at least not enough, take account of the rhetorical context of Quintilian's story. Therefore, in the last part of my paper, I will try and make my own reconstruction of the legal problem and of the rhetorical device of *emphasis* as used by Quintilian.[2]

2. THE TEXT, THE TRANSLATION, AND THE FACTS

Quintilian describes the case of the forged will in *Inst. or.* IX.2.73-74. I will quote the text and give the most recent translation, i.e., the one by Donald Russell:[3]

> ... *Ream tuebar, quae subiecisse dicebatur mariti testamentum: ea dicebat chirographum marito exspiranti heredes dedisse, et verum erat.* 74. *Nam, quia per leges institui uxor non poterat heres, id fuerat actum, ut ad eam bona per hoc tacitum fideicommissum pervenirent. Et caput quidem tueri facile erat si hoc diceremus palam, sed peribat hereditas. Ita ergo fuit nobis agendum ut iudices illud intelligerent factum, delatores non possent apprehendere ut dictum; et contigit utrumque. Quod non inseruissem veritus opinionem iactantiae nisi probare voluissem in foro quoque esse his figuris locum.*[4]
> ... I was defending a woman who was alleged to have forged her husband's will. She alleged that the heirs had given a bond to the husband on his deathbed. This was true. 74. Since the wife could not legally be the heir, this procedure had been adopted in order to allow the property to come to her by this tacit *fidei commissum*. It was easy to save the woman from conviction if we said this openly, but the inheritance was then lost. I therefore had to plead in such a way that the judges understood what had happened, but the informers could not seize on any explicit statement. I succeeded on both counts. I should not have put this in for fear of being thought to boast of it, if I had not been anxious to prove that there is a place for these Figures even in the courts.

Before we start discussing the translation and interpretation of this text, we must determine what facts can be deduced from the text. First, we know that the following persons were involved: a man, his wife, and several heirs of the man. However, we know nothing about the relationship between the heirs and the man (or the wife). Second, we know that the husband had made a will. The word 'subiecisse' suggests

---

[2]   This paper is the result of a discussion 'à trois' with José Luis Alonso, who originally was to 'do' Book IX, and Jan Willem Tellegen. I am very grateful to them both for their critical comments and valuable suggestions.
[3]   Russell (see 'Introduction' note 27), IV, pp. 77-79.
[4]   I use Winterbottom's edition of the text (see 'Introduction', note 27). In the first sentence, other editions read 'et dicebatur' or 'et dicebantur' instead of 'ea dicebat'. This difference does not seem to affect the reconstruction of the case.

that his will had been forged and that a second document was involved.[5]

The third fact is that the heirs presented a *chirographum* to the husband when he was about to die. A *chirographum* is a handwritten document which was commonly used to acknowledge a debt. From the phrase 'id fuerat actum, ut ad eam bona per hoc tacitum fideicommissum pervenirent', it can be inferred that, in this document, the heirs promised to pay over the estate to the wife.

Fourth, we know that the wife was accused of having forged her husband's will, in other words, that she had acted contrary to the *lex Cornelia de falsis*.

Finally, Quintilian tells us that, in his plea, he signified to the judges what had been done, but that he took care that the accusers could not use his words against him. In doing so, he used the figure of *emphasis*.

Unfortunately, these facts do not provide us with a complete explanation of the legal problem, nor do they make clear how Quintilian exactly used the figure of *emphasis*. So, let us see how the modern classicists interpret the text.

3. MODERN CLASSICIST INTERPRETATIONS OF *INST. OR.* IX.2.73-74

The oldest of the modern translations of Quintilian's *Institutio oratoria* is the one made by Butler in 1921 for the Loeb Classical Library. His translation of IX.2.73-74 as well as his comment on the text have inspired all later translators and almost all commentators. Therefore, I will begin by quoting Butler's comment on the text. In a note, he explains the text as follows.

> The bond was to the effect that the heirs would make over the property to the wife. The existence of such a bond proved the wife innocent, since it was a virtual confirmation of the will, of which it showed the husband to have cognisance. But the bond was not valid in the eye of the law and such *tacita fideicommissa* were illegal, since the wife could not inherit; consequently the admission of the existence of the bond would have involved the loss of the inheritance which on information being laid (cp. *delatores*) would have lapsed to the state. [6]

According to Butler, the contents of the bond were the main problem of the case. In the bond, the heirs promised to pay over the inheritance to the wife. However, this promise was invalid in the eye of the law because the wife could not inherit. Butler does not explain why the wife could not inherit. The only laws restricting the right of a wife to inherit are the *lex* or *leges Iulia et Papia*. In these laws, Emperor Augustus denied or restricted the right of certain categories of people, particularly the unmarried and childless, to inherit.[7] Apparently, Butler assumes that the words 'per leges' in the sentence 'quia per leges institui uxor non poterat heres' refer to these

---

[5]   The term *subicere* indicates that a false document was presented to replace the true will; cf. F. Marino, 'Il falso testamentario', *Zeitschrift der Savignystiftung*, rom. Abt., 105 (1988) pp. 653-655. See also M.P. Piazza, *La disciplina del falso nel diritto romano*, Padua: Cedam 1991, pp. 135ff.

[6]   Butler (see note 1), p. 418, note 2.

[7]   On this law, see R. Astolfi, *La Lex Iulia et Papia*, 3rd edition, Milan: Cedam 1995. See also in this book, Tellegen-Couperus, 'Sententia'.

laws.[8]

I have several objections to this explanation. First, Butler confuses two different legal notions, i.e., to institute an heir and to inherit. In Roman law, instituting an heir was an activity of someone who made a will. A testator was not completely free as to whom he could institute as heir.[9] The main category of persons who could not be instituted was that of the people who did not have Roman citizenship (the *peregrini*). All other people, men and women, could be instituted as heirs.[10] Even a slave could be instituted as heir, provided he was manumitted first. So, generally speaking, a testator was free to institute a Roman woman as his/her heir.

The second notion, i.e., to inherit, was an activity of an heir, either on the basis of a will or, when there was no valid will, on the basis of the law. Since the time of Emperor Augustus, there had been a law denying or restricting the right of certain categories of people to inherit: the *lex Iulia et Papia* mentioned above. It seems that Butler, in his comment, confused the ability to be instituted as heir and the ability to inherit because he interpreted the words 'per leges institui uxor non poterat' in the sense that a wife could not inherit because of the *lex Iulia et Papia*.[11] This is obviously not correct because the text is about a wife who could not be instituted as heir. However, the question then is what the words 'per leges' mean. I will return to this question later.

My second objection is that Butler does not explain the use of *emphasis* in connection with the accusation of forgery. He states that Quintilian had to keep the bond secret because its contents were illegal, i.e., in violation of the *lex Iulia et Papia*. However, in this case, the wife had been accused of forgery, i.e., of acting contrary to the *lex Cornelia de falsis*. It seems that Butler has confused the *lex Cornelia* with the *lex Iulia et Papia*. Therefore, the question remains what Quintilian had to conceal in his plea.

There is another classicist who has interpreted the text, namely Cousin. He interprets the legal problem and the way in which Quintilian used the figure of *emphasis* as follows.

> Or, le fideicommis tacite, c'est-à-dire l'héritier qui promet au testateur, verbalement ou par écrit, de remettre tout ou partie de la succession à un incapable est déchu pour indignité comme fraudeur (*Dig.*, XLIX, 14, 3 et 4); les biens sont dévolus au fisc ou aux *Patres* (*Dig.*, XLIX, 14,48). Il faut donc démontrer que le terme de chirographaire a été

---

[8] Russell (see note 4), p. 76, note 124, seems to do so too; he writes: 'If the marriage was 'iniustum' (for instance with a noncitizen) it would be illegal for the wife to be the heir.' The wife would then be legally unmarried and so be barred from inheriting under the *lex Iulia et Papia*.

[9] For a full survey, see P. Voci, *Diritto ereditario romano*, I, 2nd edition, Milan: Giuffrè 1967, pp. 401ff.

[10] Only once, in the history of Roman law, the ability of women to be instituted as heirs has been restricted, viz., in the *lex Voconia* of 169 BC. This law forbade men from the first census class (i.e., with an estate worth more than 100,000 sesterces) to institute a woman as heir. However, this law soon lost its 'raison d'être' and certainly was no longer used in Quintilian's day. On the rights of women to inherit, see L. Monaco, *Hereditas e mulieres. Riflessioni in tema di capacità della donna in Roma antica*, Naples: Jovene 2000, and on the question of how long the *lex Voconia* was applied, O.E. Tellegen-Couperus and J.W. Tellegen, 'La loi Voconia et ses séquelles', *Tijdschrift voor rechtsgeschiedenis* 66 (1998) pp. 65-95.

[11] This confusion also shows in the discrepancy between Butler's translation and his interpretation of the sentence 'quia per leges institui uxor non poterat heres': he translates it as 'since the wife could not legally be appointed his heir' but interprets it as 'since the wife could not legally inherit.'

employé par erreur, que ce que les héritiers avait reçu était bien l'héritage, mais que leur dette à l'égard de la veuve, dette reconnue par écrit, devait être remboursée. La femme était donc délivrée du soupçon de faux; il n'y avait pas de fidéicommis ni de testament supposé. Mais pour résoudre la question, il a fallu que tout le monde mit de la bonne volonté.[12]

According to Cousin, the wife was causing problems because she was incapable to inherit. However, the heirs were also causing problems: by having promised to pay over the inheritance to the wife, they had made themselves guilty of *indignitas*, unworthiness, and ran the risk of losing the inheritance to the *fiscus* or the *aerarium*. Therefore, Quintilian had to show that the term *chirographum* had been used by mistake and that there was no trust or forged will.

I am afraid Cousin's interpretation is not convincing either. First, it is based on the same mistaken idea that the wife in this case could not inherit. Second, even if she had been *incapax*, it is not at all certain that a trust in her favour would have been against the law and that the heirs' promise to pay over the inheritance to her would have been an infringement of the law. Originally, the concept of *indignitas* was applied to the heirs of someone who had been murdered, if these heirs did not take steps to have the culprits prosecuted.[13] Later, it was extended to other cases of 'unworthy' conduct of the heirs towards the deceased. In the middle of the second century, Emperor Antoninus Pius ruled that someone who had taken on a secret trust to pass on the inheritance to another person who was *incapax* under the *lex Iulia et Papia* should be deprived of all interest in the property under trust. Nowadays, it is assumed that this rule introduced a new type of *indignitas*.[14] It is unlikely that it already applied in the middle of the first century, when this trial took place. Consequently, Quintilian cannot have used the figure of *emphasis* only in order to deny the existence of the bond.

We must conclude that neither Butler nor Cousin has given a convincing interpretation of the legal problem and that, so far, no one has been able to explain the use of *emphasis* satisfactorily. The main reason is that both interpret the legal problem in terms of the *lex Iulia et Papia*, although this law is not mentioned in the text. Let us now see whether the romanists have done any better.

4. MODERN ROMANIST LITERATURE ON *INST. OR.* IX.2.73-74

Two modern romanists have paid some attention to our text: in 1935, Albert Levet wrote an article on the incapacity of husbands and wives to inherit from each other because of the *lex Iulia et Papia*, in which he mentions Quintilian's text.[15] More

---

[12] J. Cousin, *Quintilien, Institution oratoire*, V, Paris: Les Belles Lettres 1978, p. 314 [Notes complémentaires (IX)].

[13] Voci (see note 9), pp. 465ff.

[14] The sources are not very clear in this respect, cf. Paul. D. 49.14.49, Mod. D. 35.2.59.1, and Paul. D. 22.1.17.2. On this question, see D. Johnston, *The Roman Law of Trusts*, Oxford: Clarendon 1988, pp. 58ff. with literature.

[15] A. Levet, 'La quotité disponible et les incapacités de recevoir entre époux d'après les lois caducaires', *Revue d'histoire du droit* 14 (1935) pp. 195-238, particularly p. 230.

recently, David Johnston has mentioned it in his book on the Roman law of trusts.[16] They both seem to assume that, in Quintilian's case, the husband had made a trust in which he asked the heirs to pay over the inheritance to his wife. He had done so in order to circumvent the *lex Iulia et Papia*. She did not have full *capacitas* because she did not have any children in common with her husband, nor did she have the *ius liberorum*. Because the trust was against the law, it had to be kept secret: it was a *tacitum fideicommissum*. Levet and Johnston both interpret the words 'per leges' as referring to the *lex Iulia et Papia*.

Levet and Johnston explain the situation as follows. At first, the husband could still leave his estate to his wife by making a *fideicommissum universalis*, i.e., by asking his heirs to pass on the inheritance to her. However, when, in the time of Vespasian. an *SC Pegasianum* extended the limitations of the *lex Iulia et Papia* to trusts, this escape route was blocked. From then on, the husband could only leave his property to his wife by means of a secret trust. If the trust became known, anyone could act as a *delator* using the *vindicatio caducorum nomine populi* against the widow, and so obtain the substantial premium of a quarter of the inheritance.[17] In the Digest, several texts can be found which contain references to tacit trusts made to avoid the restrictions of the *lex Iulia et Papia*. Such trusts were generally formulated as an acknowledgment of a debt.[18] According to Levet and Johnston, Quintilian's words 'per hoc tacitum fideicommissum' refer to a similar secret trust.[19]

There are several reasons why I cannot accept the interpretation given by Levet and Johnston. The first is that the *lex Iulia et Papia* did not bar spouses from inheriting from each other or to institute each other as heir. It stated that they could receive one tenth of the other's estate and the usufruct of one third. If they had children from a former marriage, there were some additions and if they had one child between them, they were fully capable of inheriting from each other.[20] Quintilian would have been grossly inaccurate if he really had meant that the laws, i.e., the *lex Iulia et Papia*, barred a husband from instituting his wife as heir. Quintilian knew quite well what this law was about, as appears from his story in Book VIII about the young Roman who had left a quarter of his estate to his mistress.[21] Therefore, the words 'per leges' must have a different meaning.

Second, there is no evidence that the *SC Pegasianum* actually did extend the limitations of the *lex Iulia et Papia* to trusts in favour of a husband or wife; the sources only mention the unmarried and the childless.[22] Moreover, the earliest reference to

---

[16]   Johnston (see note 14), pp. 43 and 62.
[17]   Nero reduced the unknown initial premium to this amount, cf. Suetonius, *Nero*, 10; Tacitus, *Annales* III.25.1 and III.28.3.
[18]   A *chirographum* is mentioned in Iul. D. 30.103, Gai. D. 34.9.10 pr., and Call. D. 49.14.3.3; a *cautio* - here the written documentation of a *stipulatio* - is mentioned in Julian's text ('domestica cautione') and also in Paul. D. 49.14.48 pr.
[19]   In the same vein, U. Manthe, *Das Senatus Consultum Pegasianum*, Berlin: Duncker&Humblot 1989, p. 89, note 18, who mentions Quint. *Inst. or*. IX.2.73-74 as an example of such a secret trust.
[20]   Cf. *Ulpiani Epitome* 15 and 16. On the rights of husband and wife to inherit from each other, see S. Treggiari, *Roman Marriage*, Oxford: Clarendon Press 1991, pp. 69ff and 379ff.
[21]   See in this book, Tellegen-Couperus, 'Sententia'.
[22]   See, for instance, Gai. *Inst*. 2.286 and 286a.

the *tacitum fideicommissum* as a new legal institution dates from the time of Trajan, whereas the bulk of the texts on this subject is from the Severan period.[23] In my view, there is no reason to assume that Quintilian used the words 'per hoc tacitum fideicommissum' in the sense of a secret trust, made to circumvent the law. Therefore, these words must have a different meaning, too.

My third and most serious objection to the interpretation given by Levet and Johnston is that they completely ignore the context in which Quintilian tells his story. They look at the words 'leges' and 'tacitum fideicommissum' and interpret them as if they were part of a Digest text. Apart from the fact that their interpretation does not fit the law of Quintilian's day, they do not try to explain how Quintilian could win this case by using the figure of *emphasis*. I therefore think that the text has to be interpreted in a different way.

5. HOW TO WIN A CASE BY MEANS OF *EMPHASIS*

In order to find a better way to explain Quintilian's text, I will concentrate on the two weak spots in the traditional interpretation.

My first point of criticism was the translation and interpretation of the words 'per leges' in IX.2.74. I pointed out that, in this case, they cannot be taken to mean 'according to the law' or 'legally' because there was no law prohibiting a wife from being instituted as heir by her husband. However, the word 'lex' can also have other meanings, for instance, that of an agreement or of a condition to an agreement, an autonomous declaration, or even a last will.[24] In my view, the words *per leges* in this text refer generally to autonomous declarations. Such a declaration could be made in various ways: in a handwritten document, a *chirographum*, or a codicil. If we interpret the words 'per leges' in this sense, Quintilian states that the wife could not be instituted as heir in a handwritten document, i.e., other than in a formal will. What did he mean by that?

In Roman times, it was always a rule that a testator could institute an heir only in a valid will, i.e., in a *testamentum per aes et libram*.[25] This was an oral, formal act. In its original form, it appears to have implied the *mancipatio* (sale and transfer) of the testator's property to a *familiae emptor* who then allowed the testator to make his will before five witnesses. During the Republic and the early Empire, it was customary for a last will to be written on wax tablets. The *mancipatio* still took place as an oral act but now the *familiae emptor* joined the five witnesses. The testator declared that these tablets contained his last will and he asked the witnesses to seal it. In this way, secrecy could be preserved and proof could be produced more easily later.

---

[23] See Val. D. 49.14.42 pr.-1. In Trajan's time, even the regular *fideicommissum* was not yet very popular. Pliny the Younger, for instance, does not mention it in his letters. Cf. J.W. Tellegen, *The Roman Law of Succession in the Letters of Pliny the Younger*, I, Zutphen: Terra 1982, p. 103.

[24] Cf. C.T. Lewis and C. Short, *A Latin Dictionary*, Oxford (i.e. London): Clarendon 1879 (rpt. Oxford 1969), p. 1055; see also H. Heumann and E. Seckel, *Handlexikon zu den Quellen des römischen Rechts*, 10th edition, Graz: Akademische Druck- und Verlagsanstalt 1958, p. 312.

[25] Cf. P. Voci, *Diritto ereditario romano*, II, 2nd edition, Milan: Giuffrè 1963, pp. 64ff, and M. Kaser, *Das römische Privatrecht*, I, 2nd edition, Munich: Beck 1971, pp. 678ff.

In Quintilian's case, the husband must have made a will. As I mentioned before, this can be inferred from the fact that his wife was accused of 'subiecisse ... mariti testamentum', 'having forged her husband's will'.[26] It is very likely that he had not instituted her as heir in his will. If he had, Quintilian would have mentioned it. It is not likely, either, that he had made a *fideicommissum* in favour of his wife, for Quintilian does not say so.

That brings us to the second point, the 'tacitum fideicommissum'. It is clear now that these words cannot refer to a secret trust made to circumvent the *lex Iulia et Papia*. What do they mean then? A *fideicommissum* was a request in a will or a codicil (originally a letter). The testator asked a beneficiary of his estate to do something for or give something to a third party. It might comprise the whole estate, part of it, or individual items. There were no formalities attached, not at the time of Augustus when it became enforceable in law, nor in Quintilian's day. From the words 'per hoc tacitum fideicommissum' in IX.2.74, two conclusions can be drawn. First, the word 'hoc' apparently refers back to a word, or rather, a document, mentioned earlier in the text. The only word that is relevant in this connection, is *chirographum*. Therefore, the words *chirographum, leges,* and *fideicommissum* all refer to the same thing, i.e., the document in which the heirs promised to pay over the inheritance to the wife. Second, the word 'tacitum' cannot be taken to mean 'secret', as some authors do. However, 'tacitum' can also mean 'tacit'. In that sense, it can very well refer to the way in which the *fideicommissum* had been made, i.e., that it was supposed to have been tacitly acknowledged by the husband when it was offered to him on his deathbed.

It now becomes clear what sort of legal problem Quintilian was faced with and how he solved it. When the husband in this case made his will, he instituted certain persons as heirs but he did not leave anything to his wife. She somehow persuaded the heirs to make a deal and to promise to pay over the inheritance to her.[27] A bond to this effect was drawn up and was offered to the husband, on his deathbed, for the purpose of obtaining his approval. Moreover, in this way, they could also make it clear that nothing was done behind the husband's back. However, the bond changed the husband's last will fundamentally and could therefore be seen as a new will. This 'second will', however, had not been made by or at the request of the husband and it had not been presented to witnesses during a formal *mancipatio*. That is why the *delatores* had accused the wife of having forged her husband's will.

Quintilian states that he could successfully have denied the charge of forgery by telling openly what had been done. However, then it would also become clear that the initiative to make the bond had not come from the husband but from the wife and/or the heirs. Therefore, the document could not really be considered to represent the husband's last will; it could not even be seen as a valid *fideicommissum*. As a result, the bond would no longer entitle the wife to claim the inheritance.

---

[26]   See note 5.
[27]   She may have promised them a quarter of the estate, the part to which they would have been entitled if it had been a regular *fideicommissum*, and/or she may have promised them to make a will and leave the estate to them.

Quintilian solved this problem by emphasising the fact that the heirs offered the bond to the husband, thereby suggesting to the judges that it was acknowledged by him and that, therefore, there had been no forgery. Everything had been done in accordance with the wishes of the husband and everybody was happy that the wife would get his estate. This interpretation would fit well into the common practice that husbands wanted to leave their wives suitably provided for.[28] However, he took care not to refer to any reaction of the husband, for then the *delatores* would immediately conclude that the bond was presented as the husband's last will. They would stress the fact that this bond had not been drawn up by or at the request of the husband and that there had been no witnesses to verify it as his last will. In fact, the bond did not represent his last will at all: it was a forgery.

Therefore, Quintilian stuck to the one fact that was at the same time useful and harmless, namely, the fact that the heirs had presented the bond to the husband. The hidden meaning of his plea was that the bond could be considered as a *fideicommissum*, but he took care to avoid any discussion of the legal nature of the bond. This is how he successfully employed the figure of *emphasis*.

---

[28]   Cf. J.F. Gardner, *Women in Roman Law and Society,* London-Sydney: Croom Helm 1986, pp. 163ff. and E. Champlin, *Final Judgments. Duty and Emotion in Roman Wills 200 B.C.– A.D. 250*, Berkeley-Los Angeles-Oxford: University of California Press 1991, pp. 120ff

JAMES J. MURPHY

QUINTILIAN'S ADVICE ON THE CONTINUING SELF-EDUCATION OF THE ADULT ORATOR: BOOK X OF HIS *INSTITUTIO ORATORIA*

1. INTRODUCTION

For the adult speaker, Book X of Quintilian's *Institutio oratoria* is undoubtedly the most important one.[1]

Book X offers a plan for the lifelong self-education of a practicing speaker. Just as a physician may recommend physical exercise as a means of enabling someone to do a better job, Quintilian recommends rhetorical exercise to enable the courtroom pleader to do a better job. And just as physical exercise requires energy and time to make it worthwhile, rhetorical exercise demands a commitment by the speaker. It is always easy to postpone any kind of exercise, to think that it's too hard or too time-consuming, but its real value comes only when there is a strong personal resolution to do what is necessary.

Clearly, then, a mental decision about exercise has to precede any discussion of the specific details of what to do. Quintilian is of course aware of this. In order to understand what he has in mind, it will be useful to examine not only the purpose of Book X but its position in relation to the other eleven books of the *Institutio*.

Recall what has preceded Book X. Books I and II treat the elementary education of boys, while the following seven books handle the first three of the five 'parts' of rhetoric – that is, Invention, Arrangement, and Style.

Some modern scholars, including George A. Kennedy, have been perplexed by the fact that after completing the lengthy discussion of Style in Books VIII and IX, Quintilian does not go on in the customary fashion to take up the next two 'parts' of rhetoric, namely Memory and Delivery.[2] Yet there is good reason for the position of Book Ten, as Quintilian points out in his opening sentence (X.1.1):

> But these precepts of being eloquent, though necessary to be known, are not sufficient to produce the full power of eloquence, unless there be united to them a certain Facility, which among the Greeks is called *Hexis*, or 'habit.'

---

[1] Citations are from James J. Murphy (ed.), *Quintilian On the Teaching of Writing and Speaking: Translations from Books One, Two and Ten of the Institutio Oratoria,* Carbondale, Illinois: Southern Illinois University Press 1987. This is a revision of the 1856 translation by John Selby Watson. There is a separate Latin edition of Book X by W. Peterson (Oxford, 1891), with an excellent discussion of literary criticism in the book.

[2] 'It seems rather strange, therefore, to find the whole discussion inserted into the middle of the account of style.' George A. Kennedy, *The Art of Rhetoric in the Roman World: 300 B.C.-A.D. 300,* Princeton, New Jersey: Princeton University Press 1972, p. 500.

In other words, mere knowledge of what to do is never enough. Quintilian's Latin term for what is needed is *facilitas*. While it is often translated by the English term facility, its real meaning is closer to what Aristotle terms a dúnamis, faculty[3] – that is, an almost inherent ability. Quintilian, like Aristotle, wants the speaker not just to act rhetorically, but to be rhetorical.

All the precepts of Invention, Arrangement and Style have been rehearsed in the preceding six books; these are things that children too can learn. But how does the adult speaker acquire the deeply-ingrained capacity for improvisation? How become rhetorical? Quintilian's response is that the adult must consciously undertake a career-long continuation of the interrelated learning activities once forced on him by the schoolmaster when he was too young to understand the process he had to undergo in school. If the adult learner does not do this, he will not benefit from the precepts of Memory and Delivery which are shortly to follow Book X.

2. BOOK X AS ADULT COMMENTARY

In this sense Book X is an adult commentary on the training exercises laid out in Books I and II, because here Quintilian explains in greater detail the rationale of the school regimen. The difference is that now the adult must know the 'why' of what he does; as a child he needed only to follow the master's directions. Quintilian clearly assumes that the adult speaker will have undergone the elementary training exercises laid out in the first two books (X.1.4):

> I am not here saying how the orator is to be trained – for this has been told already, if not satisfactorily, at least at well as I could – but by what kind of discipline an athlete, who has already learned all his exercises from his master is to be prepared for real contests.

Moreover, there is much more in Book X than just a review of the earlier books. Indeed the second sentence introduces explicitly what had been merely implied before – that is, the close relationship of writing, reading, speaking, and listening in the education of the orator (X.1.1-2):

> I know that it is often asked whether more is contributed by writing, by reading, or by speaking. This question we should have to examine with careful attention if in fact we could confine ourselves to any one of these activities; but in truth they are all so connected, so inseparably linked with one another, that if any one of them is neglected, we labor in vain in the other two – for our speech will never become forcible and energetic unless it acquires strength from great practice in writing; and the labor of writing, if left destitute of models from reading, passes away without effect.

What may not be immediately apparent to a modern reader is that Quintilian includes listening as one of the major elements here. For the Romans, listening is closely related to reading, because in ancient times the act of reading itself had an auditory aspect. Today we are accustomed to silent reading, but silent reading is mainly a post-printing phenomenon. During ancient and medieval times, when there were few texts for reading, people read more slowly and carefully. And it was common to vocalize while reading – that is, to pronounce the words out loud as they

---

[3]   Aristoteles, *Rhetorica,* I.1.1355a 26.

were read. (Note that Quintilian himself points out the auditory aspect of reading in Chapter 8 of Book I; the Latin term for reading, *lectio*, makes no distinction between reading for a single reader or for an audience.) Punctuation as we know it was unnecessary in a text read aloud, because the normal pausations and parallel constructions of oral style made meanings clear without the commas and semi-colons we now regard as essential in our silent reading. Much Roman writing does not even have the most primitive punctuation - spaces between words.

What many modern readers do not know is that the nature of reading changed radically with the advent of printing. The mass production of texts by mechanical means made faster reading methods necessary, and the habit of vocalization virtually disappeared by the early sixteenth century. It has been estimated that as many as a million books were printed in the forty-odd years from the Gutenberg bible in the 1450's to the year 1500. The slowness of vocalization could not keep up with this new demand, and silent reading has been common ever since. Modern readers unaware of this change therefore would not know that Quintilian means both 'listening' and 'reading' when he uses the term 'reading'.

Listening for Quintilian is not a passive act. It requires as much positive application as reading, speaking, or writing. In the eight-part formal exercise known as Imitation (*imitatio*) the student is first asked to listen to a model text read aloud, then dissected in grammatical detail by the master; then he is asked to listen to his fellow students' paraphrases and transliterations of the text (for example, from prose to verse, or Latin to Greek).[4] Quintilian argues in Book X that a good stock of words comes not from a memorized vocabulary but from 'reading and listening to the best language' (X.1.8). Though he concedes later that what the eye sees is easier to remember than what the ear hears – 'the perception of the eye is quicker than that of the ear' (XI.2.34) – it must be remembered that the whole educational program begins with concern for what the child hears at home before ever going to a school (I.1.1). The task of the adult is to continue, on his own, to utilize active listening just as he continues purposefully to read, speak, and write so he may gain that *facilitas* which is the purpose of all his self-training.

Even though he continually stresses the interrelationship between the four modes of learning, Quintilian is particularly interested in the writing-speaking connection. For example he says at one point that writing makes speaking precise; speaking makes writing easy (X.7.29). At another point he says 'In writing are the roots, in writing are the foundations of eloquence' (X.3.3). Yet here, as always, he is quick to interpose a caution about writing well rather than writing quickly; he notes that a hasty draft will always look hasty even after careful editing.

3. PLAN FOR SELF-EDUCATION OF THE ORATOR

What we have seen so far is that Quintilian urges the adult to practice constantly in the four modes of reading, writing, listening, and speaking. But how?

---

[4]   For a detailed discussion of ancient *imitatio*, see Donald L. Clark, *Rhetoric in Greco-Roman Education*, New York: Columbia University Press 1957, pp. 177-212.

Quintilian is extremely difficult to summarize, because he often discusses several viewpoints before providing his own conclusions.

Nevertheless it might be useful at this point to furnish a brief overview of the seven chapters in Book X so that we may have a better understanding of the full scope of his plan for the self-education of the adult orator.

Chapter 1 opens, as we have seen, with the call for the acquisition of habit, using the four modes of learning just discussed. Then he says that the orator can acquire a copious store of words and matter through deep reading of good writers and speakers. Thus the choice of models for reading and imitation is critical. An important principle is that the use of many different models will equip the orator to use many different styles himself.[5] Thus the orator should read not only orators, but both ancient and modern poets, historians, dramatists, and philosophers for their various modes of expression. Quintilian regards the choice of models as so important that he devotes more than four fifths of his first chapter (sections 23 to 130) to a detailed discussion of scores of particular models.[6]

Chapter 2 stresses the value of imitation of models. What Quintilian means by imitation here is a very specific, eight-part set of exercises which the Roman adult would remember from his school days. The first step is reading the text aloud, followed by analysis of the texts – its form, grammatical features, style – and then memorization of at least part of the text; the next two phases, paraphrase and transliteration, involve re-casting the text into other forms (for example, prose into verse); the final stages are recitation of the paraphrases and transliterations. In the school situation the master would then correct the recitations publicly. The adult is encouraged to do all this either by himself, or, if possible, in the presence of others. Again, Quintilian's constant principle is one of purposeful activity: everything is done for a specific purpose, to gain a specific skill useful in the courtroom. He points out again that the use of numerous models helps to acquire numerous ways to say things.

Chapters 3 and 4 address some practical aspects of writing. It should be careful rather than quick. Self-correction – addition, erasure, or alteration – is quite as important as the actual writing. We must therefore write as much as possible and with the utmost care (X.3.2).

Chapter 5 again emphasizes the value of formal imitation, but Quintilian goes on to recommend that the adult practice several more learning methods once learned in the schools.[7] The first exercise he recommends is called a Thesis, in which the writer is asked to write an answer to a general question, that is, a question not involving individuals. An example would be: Should a man marry? Since both positive and

---

[5] This key issue of single versus multiple models erupted during the European Renaissance, with some humanists arguing that Cicero alone was the only model to follow. See Izora Scott, *Controversies Over the Imitation of Cicero in the Renaissance as a Model for Style, and Some Phases of Their Influence on the Schools of the Renaissance*, Davis, California: Hermagoras Press 1991.

[6] The essay by Sanne Taekema, in this volume, analyzes the modern implications of Quintilian's choice of models for imitation.

[7] They are from a standard set of graded learning exercises called *progymnasmata*, originally devised by the Greeks but popularized by the Romans; they were so efficient that European and American schools employed them right down to the twentieth century. See the essay of Serena Querzoli in this volume.

negative answers are possible, the exercise calls on the writer to marshal arguments to support the chosen answer; the exercise is intended to encourage both analytic thinking and the adroit use of evidence. The other exercise is called a Commonplace, which asks the writer to 'color,' that is, to cast a favourable or unfavourable light upon an established fact, a thing admitted. An example would be a prosecutor's description of an admitted theft in a manner to exasperate and incite a jury; using methods such as comparisons with other crimes, conjectures as to the past life of the accused, repudiation of pity, and concluding remarks on justice, decency, respect for law, and the consequences of the theft. Another exercise is the Declamation, a formal oration supporting one side or another in a fictitious court case; Quintilian recommends writing out such speeches, for this will accustom the orator to the actual skills used in the courtroom. He also recommends visiting courts to observe real cases, and then writing out their own speeches as if they had been participants.

Chapter 6 discusses the value of meditation as training for extemporaneous speaking. In a particular case, having a well thought-out plan in advance will free the orator to improvise additional ideas during the course of his speech.

Chapter 7, the last, continues his thought about extempore speaking. Quintilian declares that the power of improvisation is the highest achievement of the orator – an echo of his opening statement at the beginning of Book X that *facilitas* is the aim of his whole program. He says that the man who fails to achieve this had better abandon the task of advocacy and devote his powers of writing to some other form of expression. This *facilitas* must be maintained by constant practice, so daily speaking and writing are valuable. If we cannot find an audience, we should prepare whole cases in our mind silently. He concludes with the admonition that we must study always and everywhere, and think about cases even while doing other things.

All this may seem to be a forbidding and almost impossible set of tasks, tasks to be undertaken in addition to the everyday work of an active courtroom pleader. But just like the physical exercise that a physician might recommend to make a worker healthy, so these rhetorical exercises can improve the efficiency of one who works with ideas and words before juries and other audiences. Quintilian recognizes that it may be hard to find time to do these exercises, and makes several suggestions on this score. For example he says that night time is best for thoughtful exercises, but if that is not possible one can draw up mental exercises while walking, or meditate toward planning a case silently in the midst of other people.

4. SOME SPECIFIC ADVICE FROM BOOK X

The modern reader of Book X at first may not recognize the purposeful plan Quintilian presents, because he writes in any easy and apparently casual style. The same style which makes it difficult to summarize him also makes the reader want to continue reading. Moreover, his pages are studded with practical advice, memorable aphorisms which speak out to everyday problems of the adult orator.

For these reasons I urge you not to accept my short summary of Book X as the totality of its valuable advice for you. You must read the book yourself. Only in this way can you get its full flavor. Quintilian, after all, was the most famous teacher in first-century Rome, a successful lawyer who turned to teaching and then, after twenty years of service, spent two years preparing the *Institutio oratoria*. This remarkable combination of legal practice and successful teaching made him the ideal writer for a book like this. One would expect much from him, and one does get much from him.

If everything I have said so far still leaves you, as an adult orator, unimpressed by Book X, let me conclude with some sample statements from it that may give some hint of the perceptive mind of this writer:

- Every case has its own peculiar nature, or matter common to it with but few others; (but) words are to be prepared for all kinds of cases (X.1.6).
- Some speeches contribute more to our improvement when we hear them delivered, others when we peruse them (X.1.16).
- Reading is free, and does not escape us with the rapidity of oral delivery, but allows us to go over the same passages more than once (X.1.19).
- The whole conduct of life is based on the desire of doing ourselves what we approve in others (X.2.2).
- It is dishonorable even to rest satisfied with simply equaling what we imitate (X.2.7).
- Every species of writing has its own prescribed law, its own appropriate dress (X.2.22).
- Nature has herself appointed that nothing great is to be accomplished quickly, and has ordained that difficulty should precede every work of excellence (X.3.4).
- By writing quickly we are not brought to write well, but by writing well we are brought to write quickly (X.3.10).
- We must strive against inconveniences, and acquire such habits that our application may set all interruptions at defiance – for if we direct our attention, with our whole mental energy, to the work actually before us, nothing at all of what strikes our eyes or our ears will penetrate into the mind (X.3.28).
- To the time allotted for corrections, there must be a limit (X.4.3).
- I would not have our paraphrase be a mere interpretation, but an effort to vie with and rival our original in the expression of the same thoughts (X.5.4).
- The great proof of power is to expand what is naturally contracted, to amplify what is little, to give variety to things which are similar, attraction to such as are obvious, and to say with effect much on little (X.5.11)
- Meditation may in a very few hours embrace all points of the most important cases (X.6.1).
- We must study at all times and in all places (X.7.26).
- By writing we speak with greater accuracy, and by speaking we write with greater ease (X.7.29).

These brief examples of Quintilian's realistic approach to public advocacy may provide some motivation for readers to look more closely at Book X as an important guide for the continuing self-education of the adult speaker.

SANNE TAEKEMA

REASONS FOR READING

Quintilian's Advice on 'What to Read' in Book X

1. INTRODUCTION

The *Institutio oratoria* is a comprehensive treatise on rhetoric, covering everything from rhetorical theories to educational aspects and practical advice on public speaking. The education of an orator does not only include teaching the basics of designing and delivering a speech, it also concerns developing and polishing one's ability to speak well. In Book X, Quintilian addresses the question of whether oratorical power is best achieved by reading, writing, or speaking. His answer is given directly: all three are indispensable and closely connected. He discusses each in turn: what and how to read, how to practice writing and how to practice speaking. My interest is in the first issue — what to read — and this is fueled by present-day concerns about a lawyer's training.

Education in rhetoric as treated by Quintilian is no longer an integral part of a lawyer's studies. Nowadays, the emphasis is on the content of the law books, on landmark cases, and some attention is paid to the theoretical and historical background of law. The isolation of this training of law as a specialized profession has given rise to a plea for a broader education for lawyers, and especially to a plea for the reading of literature. The scholars who make this plea are united in the movement of *Law & Literature*. They concern themselves both with the general argument that lawyers should read literature and with more specific recommendations about the literary works that should be read.

Both issues are also dealt with by Quintilian in Book X: he discusses the necessity of reading, and a number of authors, both Greek and Roman, in different genres. He also pays attention to what it is exactly that an orator can learn from these works. These reasons are interesting from a modern perspective: how do Quintilian's reasons for reading compare to those given by *Law & Literature* scholars nowadays? My hypothesis is that modern scholars focus on moral reasons for reading, while Quintilian focuses on stylistic reasons.

In order to test this thesis, I will examine Quintilian's advice on what to read in detail and compare this advice to that of two key figures of the *Law & Literature* movement: Martha Nussbaum and James Boyd White (§2 and 3). I will then attempt to explain the differences or similarities between Quintilian and these modern authors (§4) and, finally, consider what we can learn from Quintilian for present-day education in the law (§5).

2. READING ACCORDING TO QUINTILIAN: DEVELOPING CRITICAL JUDGMENT

Quintilian begins his discussion of reading with the general subject of its benefit: why read at all? His starting point is the idea that an orator who prepares himself for actual practice needs resources, needs a supply of words, expressions, even subject matter, ready for use whenever he needs it (X.1.5). In addition, reading will sharpen his judgment: it can help him to decide in what context a word or expression is appropriate. Precisely for this reason, reading is to be preferred to listening to an oral presentation: it is easier to be critical of a text when you are at leisure to read at your own pace than when influenced by the delivery of a speaker (X.1.17). For the development of one's oratorical skills, Quintilian believes in learning by example (X.1.15). The best way to broaden one's vocabulary and to learn how to use it well is by reading different texts; in this way, a student can see directly how others apply oratorical devices, which provides more insight than learning the rules.

In the context of Quintilian's project, a program to train an orator, it makes sense that a young orator should read the works of other orators in order to perfect his own power of speaking. However, Quintilian also prescribes other reading material than oratory: he includes the genres of poetry, history, and philosophy as well. Of these, the immediate relevance for an orator is less clear: why read such works as well? Quintilian is aware of the doubts one might have about other genres of literature, and gives a qualified recommendation: however excellent a poet, historian, or philosopher may be, an orator should not follow them in everything.[1] Poetry aims at aesthetic pleasure, it is fictional and uses figures of speech, features that make it unsuitable for direct imitation in oratory. Similarly, the historian writes primarily to tell an interesting story, not to prove a point, which makes his style freer than the appropriate style for an orator.[2] Philosophy is closer to oratory, but still there are important differences that require caution when using philosophy as an example, most importantly, philosophy's theoretical character.

In Quintilian's positive recommendation of these three genres, the range of reasons for turning to them is striking. Poetry, history, and philosophy together cover most of the aspects of a legal speech. A sublime style, the approach to the subject, a triggering of emotions, the treatment of character can all be found in poetry, while history provides a healthy and pleasant style and knowledge of historical facts. Philosophy is useful both for arguments on virtue and for forensic debates and the examination of witnesses. Thus, we can recognize *pathos*, the appeal to the emotions, and *ethos*, the presentation of a positive or negative character as reasons for reading poetry, and *logos*, rational argument as taught by philosophy: the three classical means of persuasion. In addition, in the reference to poetry and history, we can

---

[1] See *Inst. or.* X.1.28 regarding poetry, X.1.31 regarding history, and X.1.35 regarding philosophy.

[2] Quintilian saw history as the genre closest to poetry. It was not seen as aiming at scientific truth, but more as pleasant storytelling. See also A.D. Leeman, *Orationis Ratio. The Stylistic Theories and Practice of the Roman Orators Historians and Philosophers*, Amsterdam: Adolf M. Hakkert 1963, p. 329.

see different stylistic features, reminiscent of the grand and middle types of style,[3] and reference to subject matter which may be relevant for a speech in court.

Following his discussion of genres, Quintilian includes an overview of authors who should be studied, in which he returns to the different aspects that justify reading them. The result is a unique list of Greek and Roman authors critically discussed by a professor of rhetoric. Because of this list, Book X of the *Institutio oratoria* is much read, primarily by classicists, as an early example of literary criticism.[4] The overview is systematic, discussing Greek poetry, history, oratory, and philosophy in turn, and following the same structure for Roman authors. The Greek as well as the Roman part begins with their greatest epic poet, Homer and Virgil, respectively. Starting with these authors would still be a traditional way to begin such an overview. What is surprising, however, is Quintilian's generous view of other authors: even those he criticizes severely on some points, he recommends for reading because of other aspects. It is interesting to dwell a little on his argument here.

Quintilian rejects the idea that only classic works, only the best authors, should be read. His view is that every author who has stood the test of time has at least something to say that can be worthwhile for a future orator, so a student should not limit himself to great works only. However, an essential part of Quintilian's argument is that a reader should have the ability to understand the value of a text himself, so a very important element of a student's curriculum is the training of *iudicium*, critical judgment.[5] In the context of learning to speak well, the notion of judgment refers to the ability to judge the appropriateness of words and expressions in specific contexts: to know when and how to use a word. Underlying this is a different meaning of judgment: recognizing what is good and bad in an author. In the context of reading, the latter meaning is the primary one: first one needs to see what is good about a literary work in order to use literature for the development of judgment of when and how to use stylistic means. In connection to *iudicium*, Quintilian does invoke the idea of great works. A student needs to read the best authors as carefully as he can to recognize all their merits, because such profound reading of good literature is the only way to develop *iudicium*. Once his sense of judgment is formed, he can and should apply it to all kinds of literature. Thus, we see that Quintilian has a place for a concept of great works, of a canon, without limiting his advice on reading to those works only.

Quintilian does not only address the issue of reading literature in Book X of the *Institutio oratoria*: it also comes up in earlier books as part of a discussion of the curriculum of the young student. For a full understanding of the place of reading in the orator's education, these other passages need to be considered as well. First, reading is part of the studies with the *grammaticus*, the grammar teacher, and later it

---

[3] The reference to *sublimitas* in connection with poetry indicates a link to the grand style, while the expression 'iucundoque suco' may refer to the middle style, cf. Leeman (see note 2), p. 329.

[4] *Inst. or.* X.1.47-X.1.131. See George Kennedy, *Quintilian*, New York: Twayne Publishers 1969, pp. 101-115, G.M.A. Grube, *The Greek and Roman Critics*, London: Methuen & Co 1965, pp. 284-307, and Leeman (see note 2).

[5] The importance of *iudicium* in Book X is convincingly argued for by Marc Laureys, 'Quintilian's Judgement of Seneca and the Scope and Purpose of Inst., X, 1', *Antike und Abendland* 37 (1991) pp. 100-125, at p. 120.

is part of the curriculum with the rhetorician. Here he invokes a traditional division of tasks between these two teachers. It is part of the task of the grammar teacher to teach poetry, the classics most importantly. The rhetorician, on the other hand, needs to teach his students to read history, oratory, and philosophy. Quintilian hints at similar reasons why these genres should be taught as in Book X: comedy, for instance, is useful because it is so good at portraying character and emotion. What is particularly interesting is the emphasis on reading classics at an early age: for Quintilian, it is of the foremost importance that young students read honourable texts, so what better to read than Homer and Virgil? Other considerations, such as the difficulty of a text, do not seem to be much of an issue in determining what is appropriate. Both the grammar teacher and the rhetorician are instructed to point out excellences and deficiencies in the texts, so that a student trains his critical judgment from the earliest confrontations with literature.

He returns to the issue of reading in Book XII, where the knowledge needed by an orator in his lifelong efforts to be a good orator is discussed. Here, more elaborately than in Book X, reading philosophy is commended because of the need for moral instruction. This is to be combined with a practical knowledge of the law and of society: an orator should not only be morally upright but also very knowledgeable (XII.3.8). This includes historical knowledge: both regarding morality and law, an orator should be able to call on a host of historical examples (XII.2.29 and XII.4.1).

These differences in emphasis between the different books make sense in light of the structure of the whole *Institutio*.[6] Books I and II concern the earliest training in which basic skills and basic moral teaching is central. Book X is part of the discussion of *elocutio*, concerning the wording of a speech, so it is understandable that there is an emphasis on stylistic reasons for reading. It should be noted, however, that the reasons advanced in the early books and in Book XII are also mentioned, although not elaborately, in Book X.

From a present-day perspective, it is striking how much use Quintilian makes of literary examples and to what extent he commends the use of literature as a source of style and knowledge. The connection between literature and oratory in the *Institutio oratoria* can in part be seen as reflecting a general attitude at the time.[7] In antiquity, literature (*litterae*) was a cultural concept, encompassing all of what was written —be it history, philosophy, poetry, oratory or science— that could be seen as expressing the Greek and Roman cultures.[8] Although there was, of course, a distinction between poetry and prose, there was no such thing as 'literary' prose as a subcategory of prose writing in a more general sense.[9] This way of regarding all known writing as a whole is reflected both in Quintilian's use of all kinds of literature as examples in the *Institutio oratoria*, and in his generous recommendations on

---

[6] Cf. Kennedy (see note 4), p. 101-102.
[7] Cf. Leeman (see note 2), p. 13.
[8] See Wolfgang Schadewaldt, 'Der Umfang des Begriffs der Literatur in der Antike', in: Horst Rüdiger (ed.), *Literatur und Dichtung: Versuch einer Begriffsbestimmung*, Stuttgart: W. Kohlhammer 1973, pp. 12-25, at p. 14.
[9] Schadewaldt (see note 8), p. 18.

what to read: it is a way of referring to a common cultural heritage as the obvious source.

3. READING ACCORDING TO NUSSBAUM AND WHITE: STIMULATING THE IMAGINATION

In modern *Law & Literature* scholarship, there is a pronounced shift in attention compared to that of Roman times. Where Quintilian prescribed all forms of literature of his time, from poetry to philosophy, there is now a concentration on fiction, or more precisely, narrative fiction. Lawyers need to read stories, stories that say something about the law and lawyers. Here too, education is at issue: reading is necessary to prepare a lawyer for practising his or her profession well. The place and value of reading in education is very different, however.

Leading *Law & Literature* scholars advocate the reading of literature primarily because it appeals to the imagination. Using one's imagination in the way literature invites readers to do, makes it easier to understand the lives and motives of other people: it stimulates one's moral capacities. According to James Boyd White, a text invites a reader to step into another world, the world of the text, and to participate in that world imaginatively.[10] This has ethical implications: a reader has to relate to the values the text implies and make judgments about them. This active engagement with a text is something that a lawyer or law student has to learn, because a lawyer's work consists primarily of dealing with texts. Reading literature is important, because literary texts invite you to read in a way that should also be adopted for legal texts.[11]

More so than White, Martha Nussbaum narrows down the type of texts to read to narrative fiction. She emphasizes that the form of a story challenges us to recognize others, to give them our full attention, an insight which can also help a lawyer to acknowledge his responsibility for other, real, persons.[12] It is the concrete setting, the fabric of particulars that makes a story the form that is especially suited for teaching ethical understanding.[13] By knowing the circumstances of a character's life and problems, our moral judgment will be more nuanced and sensitive because we understand the complexity of the situation. By reading we learn to take the place of a central character and to acknowledge his or her humanity: we develop deep sympathy.[14] Thus, learning to use one's imagination by reading novels is good for moral development in a number of ways: it improves moral judgment, it trains one's

---

[10]   James Boyd White, *When Words Lose Their Meaning: Constitutions and Reconstitutions of Language, Character, and Community*, Chicago and London: Chicago University Press 1984, p. 9.
[11]   James Boyd White, *From Expectation to Experience: Essays on Law & Legal Education*, Ann Arbor: University of Michigan Press 1999, p. 71.
[12]   Martha Nussbaum, *Poetic Justice: The Literary Imagination and Public Life*, Boston: Beacon Press 1995, p. 99.
[13]   Nussbaum (see note 12), p. 8. Not surprisingly, Nussbaum is a defender of Aristotelian virtue ethics. Nussbaum is the most restrictive in the kind of works that should be read: she sees a special role for the novel and even more particularly for the realist novel (p. 10).
[14]   Nussbaum (see note 12), pp. 34 and 94.

capacity for empathy, and it is a step towards acknowledging real responsibility. All of these are aspects of a moral attitude needed to be a good lawyer.

Both White and Nussbaum emphasize the need to overcome the limited perspective that a profession such as the law generates. They prescribe reading as a way of learning to bring a general human capacity, that of sympathy or sensitivity, to the exercise of the legal professions. As White says, lawyers are not just lawyers, they are people, and it is important, not the least for their own well-being, that these aspects of their personalities are integrated.[15] Literature asks for a discovery of meaning, a way of engaging oneself with a text that stimulates such capacities.

Thus, the first reason White and Nussbaum advance for reading literature is that it is a good way to stimulate the moral capacities that are essential for a lawyer, but are lacking from a traditional law training. There is, however, another reason for reading. A second important reason, stressed mostly by White, is to show that law itself is an art. Comparing law to literature uncovers the similarity of the two: a legal text can be literary and a lawyer can be an artist with language.[16] By reading literature and law as literature, it will become clear to the reader that the meaning of a text in both categories is cultural and social. Texts constitute a way of being, they presuppose a cultural context, they address an audience: aspects of meaning which are not apparent in a legal text as it is usually read but which surface when a literary way of reading is applied. Somewhat differently, but with the same aim of integration, Nussbaum stresses that literary imagination is part of public and legal rationality. Imagination is not something only belonging to art, and opposed to reasoning, but necessary in order to be fully rational. They both draw attention to the continuities between law and the other humanities.[17]

This plea for integration of law and the humanities in a way brings us back to Quintilian, because it is, in a sense, a plea for returning to the kind of integrated education as a lawyer-citizen that Quintilian describes. But before I examine the relevance of that plea and Quintilian's significance for it, I want to discuss the differences and possible connections between these modern authors and Quintilian.

4. ETHICS AND ELOQUENCE

At first sight the purposes of reading literature advanced by Quintilian seem to be very different from those advanced by White and Nussbaum. The very different contexts of Quintilian's discussion of reading in Book X and the modern books on literature and law suggest various explanations. The most straightforward explanation is that Quintilian's book X has a specific function in the context of the *Institutio*: what to read in order to improve one's eloquence. This means that an emphasis on rhetorical aspects of texts and on the style in which these are put were to be expected. These are aspects of reading that are directly connected to the improve-

---

[15]   White (see note 11), p. 76, also p. 56.

[16]   White (see note 11), p. 65.

[17]   White (see note 11), pp. 89-110. Martha Nussbaum, *Cultivating Humanity: A Classical Defense of Reform in Liberal Education*, Cambridge: Harvard University Press 1997, is a general plea for a humanities education as necessary for becoming a good citizen.

ment of one's ability to speak. The aim of White and Nussbaum in their discussion of literature is much broader: they make a case for reading literature and its relevance to law and lawyers not just for practical purposes but to improve the person of the lawyer as a whole and to enlarge one's understanding of law in general. They are less specific about what we can gain by reading, although there is a definite focus on the moral dimension of reading. However, it would be too simple to leave it at that: we have seen both that Quintilian's aims are not restricted to style and that White and Nussbaum have more to say in favour of literature than its ethical relevance.

Even if Quintilian has a wider range of reasons for recommending reading than using it for acquiring facility, as passages from other books than Book X clearly show, it is striking how many specific reasons he advances for reading specific types of literature and authors. What can explain this difference with the modern authors I have discussed? At least two explanations come to mind. I have already pointed to the concept of literature in antiquity: the broad notion of literature as expressing the cultural heritage and of oratory as an integral part of it. In contrast, modern society since the Romantic period has questioned such a concept of literature and inclines towards a purely aesthetic understanding of what literature is and the way it should be read.[18] What is striking about *Law & Literature* scholars such as White and Nussbaum is that they do not embrace such an aesthetic concept.[19] They argue against it by making a case for an ethical reading of literature and the relevance of this kind of reading for law. Claiming that literature has important functions, in opposition to *l'art pour l'art*, is not acceptable to every scholar of literature: many claim that a literary work should be assessed on its own terms. Thus, an important feature of modern discussions about the relevance of reading for lawyers is that the concept of literature is problematic and the very idea that it can be useful in some sense has to be defended vigorously. This was unnecessary in Quintilian's time: he only had to stress what can be learned from literature, not that something could be learned. He could therefore turn directly to specific reasons for reading, for instance, the importance of comedy and tragedy for character portrayal.

Closely connected to the unproblematic concept of literature in Roman times is the idea of imitation: it was thought perfectly acceptable to imitate great authors in one's speeches and writing. Quintilian did not recommend a mechanical copying of stylistic features, but a creative use of a certain style, for instance Cicero's, in an appropriate place was looked upon as good use of one's knowledge of literary examples. With the rise of the value of authenticity (also a Romantic notion), being original, and finding one's own voice has become of prime importance, especially in art and literature. Here we see that White and Nussbaum have a modern perspective: their reasons for reading literature express a loose idea of inspiration for readers. They refrain from prescribing what a reader should get out of a text and refer to the possibility of personal experience in reading.[20] This can also explain the lack of specific recommendations: if the main point is that reading can inspire someone to develop his own capacities, it is less acceptable to articulate very specific reasons for

---

[18] Compare the discussion in Peter Widdowson, *Literature*, London: Routledge 1999, pp. 37-49.
[19] Explicitly, White (see note 11), pp. 60-61.
[20] See e.g. White (see note 11), p. 87.

specific reading. So we see that Nussbaum recommends a genre, the realistic novel, and discusses examples without suggesting that a specific author should be read for a specific message.[21] White is even more broad-minded: he thinks in terms of interesting texts, be they poems, novels, or political treatises. Each of those can serve to show how a community of author and reader is established. Thus, literary works in a modern perspective are to provide inspiration for a reader's own responses to texts and to life, and it is hoped that a lawyer who reads will bring these experiences to bear upon his professional life as well.

Looking at the general capacities that literature is said to develop by White and Nussbaum, we see that some of these capacities are also in some way addressed by Quintilian. The most interesting in this respect is the capacity for critical judgment, one of the main things that reading can help develop in Quintilian's view. The idea of developing judgment by reading is also present in the work of White and Nussbaum: both emphasize that it is necessary to be critical of what one reads and of what one might learn from a literary work.[22] It is also interesting to note that both authors, but White especially, emphasize that good texts themselves call for a critical appraisal of their meaning. Especially when a text addresses the boundaries of the world it has described, it invites a judgment about the meaning of that imagined world. White discusses the language of Homer's *Iliad* in these terms: this is a heroic world of specific actions and responses with its own ritual language. Homer shows the importance of glory in battle and being honored by fellow warriors, but he also questions the terms of that world and the values it holds high by hinting at the common humanity and similar grief of Greeks and Trojans. This is not something that is in itself part of that world but it is a critical note in the epic that the author hints at.[23] A good literary work, which has different layers of meaning, thus trains one's critical judgment, allowing one to explore the less obvious readings of the text. This prepares a reader for the criticism of other, less profound texts: because one is alerted to the ambiguities of language and the complexity of a good text, a critical appraisal of the meaning of other texts becomes possible. Again, the idea of critical judgment has a strong ethical flavour for White and Nussbaum: it is not criticism of the stylistic and rhetorical achievements of the text that is central, it is criticism of superficial evaluation and the ethical response to a text.

The place of critical judgment in the work of White and Nussbaum also adds a new dimension to the notion of a classic literary work. Quintilian thought classics important as the source of the standards of good writing that are necessary to train *iudicium*. Only by reading excellent works can one learn to appreciate what is truly good. Such appreciation can then be the starting point for criticism of less well-written texts and is therefore the basis of *iudicium*. For Quintilian, there were a number of authors who belonged to a well-established canon.[24] What to read in order to train

---

[21] Nussbaum (see note 12), pp. 7-11.
[22] See Nussbaum (see note 12), pp. 9-10, and White (see note 11), pp. 68 and 78.
[23] In *When Words Lose Their Meaning* (see note 10), Chapter 2, especially pp. 55-58. A similar argument about complexity of meaning is made by Nussbaum (see note 12), p. 95 in her discussion of Richard Wright's 'Native Son'.
[24] See Peter Steinmetz, 'Gattungen und Epochen der Griechischen Literatur in der Sicht Quintilians',

critical judgment was not a real issue: one had to read what was generally accepted as good. Quintilian did, however, observe the problem of determining what is really excellent in a classic work: it is always necessary to distinguish the good aspects from the not-so-good, since a completely flawless text has yet to be written. To this notion of classics, as the (acknowledged) best we have, we can add the notion of a classic as a self-referential work with complexity of meaning which White and Nussbaum hint at. Classics can then be seen as the works that defy an easy and superficial reading and stimulate critical judgment in this way.

The most difficult issue posited by this comparison of Quintilian and modern authors is the connection between ethics and rhetoric. I must confess that the merging of an ethical and a rhetorical reading of texts that can be found in White and Nussbaum makes me uneasy at times. Although I see the value of both ways of reading, the way ethics is connected to the literary language of a text is problematic: there is a risk that the dangers of rhetorically persuasive texts are overlooked. In comparison, Quintilian keeps it simple: he explicitly distinguishes the ethical value of reading from the rhetorical value and recommends both, but separately. He does stress the need for an orator to be a good man, but does not suggest that becoming a good man is achieved through rhetorical training; and this is something that sometimes seems implicit in the way of reading recommended by White and Nussbaum. I do not think there is an easy solution: one can do no more than stay alert and critical, on the basis of both one's reading and one's common sense. There is another side to the issue, however, that I want to address.

Not only can there be doubts about the integration of rhetorical and ethical aspects of texts in respect to ethics, but it also seems to underestimate the independent importance of the rhetorical function of reading. It is this message of Quintilian's tenth book that needs more attention in the present-day debate. It is a very straightforward message: a good lawyer needs to speak and write well, and to achieve this, the careful reading of literary works is a first step. Quintilian's advice to practice writing and speaking as well, should not be forgotten, but this is much more accepted as part of a lawyer's training (although it does not hurt to mention it!). The value of reading literature for the formation of one's own style is much less appreciated. Especially in continental Europe, the opinion reigns that it is enough if a lawyer can be clear, precise, and matter-of-fact, both in his style of writing and of speaking. The idea that developing one's own style and voice is important is frowned upon. Quintilian and his contemporaries were convinced that a boring speech in the court of law was less convincing than a lively and well-worded speech, a truth somehow forgotten in present-day law practice and scholarship. Reading literature can make one aware of the power of words in an easy and pleasant way. We only need to remember that one should be cautious in using literary phrases in legal writing and pleading. As Quintilian says, it has to be appropriate. However, the studying of different styles of writing and discovering what is appropriate in what context remains as useful now as it was in Quintilian's time.

in: Rudolf Stark (ed.), *Rhetorika: Schriften zur aristotelischen und hellenistischen Rhetorik*, Hildesheim: Georg Olms 1968, pp. 451-463.

5. A HUMANITIES EDUCATION FOR LAWYERS

Quintilian's relevance today can thus be translated into a plea for reading literature to improve lawyers' style and ability to write well. The most important lesson we can learn from Quintilian, however, touches a broader theme. Less explicit, but the implicit understanding not only in Book X, but in the whole of the *Institutio oratoria*, is the idea that a student needs a broad education to become a good orator. He needs to know his epic poets, to have a sound knowledge of history, understand philosophical argument, and know the law (XII.2-4). Thus, Quintilian is in favour of a broad, general education.[25] At this point, modern *Law & Literature* scholars join hands with Quintilian: the most important educational idea they promote is a broad humanities education.[26] Such a broad education, including literature, philosophy, history, and also anthropology and foreign languages, is not a generally accepted curriculum for law students today. Either it is thought that this is done at an earlier stage, in secondary education, or (in the United States) in a bachelor program. A law program at university is supposed to be a specialization, geared to the specific knowledge that a lawyer should have. The first objection to such a view of a law education is that a far-reaching specialization is not what a law education should be about. Especially in continental Europe, where all university education is specialized, a law degree should first of all be an academic degree, and prepare students to be good citizens. This was what Quintilian had in mind with his rhetorical education: a good orator should be a good man, a *vir bonus*. He did not prepare students specifically for law, although that was the most important domain for oratory in his time, he prepared them for life.[27] Nussbaum has a similar aim in her proposals for educational reform: to cultivate good citizens. It requires something more to argue that law students specifically need such a broad education. But there are good reasons to say so. The central one is White's point that law is an art: lawyers need to interpret, compare, and criticize, to write and speak, in ways very similar to the practicing of other arts. Therefore, the skills a lawyer needs are not restricted to knowledge of the law and a method for reading cases: he must know how to read, write, and speak.

A very important component of such an integrated education, a component that is most clearly advanced by Quintilian, is the development of critical judgment. Reading is a good way to learn to separate good from bad, especially when it is part of education and reading experiences are discussed and evaluated. Quintilian's reasons for reading both classics and a broad variety of modern texts from all genres still hold: classics are texts that can provide us with some of the standards of good writing, while other reading is necessary to learn to employ these standards. Even if

---

[25] This was the accepted view in Quintilian's time, see M.L. Clarke (revised by D.H. Berry), *Rhetoric at Rome: A Historical Survey*, London: Routledge 1996, p. 121.

[26] Except the works mentioned, see James Boyd White, 'What can a Lawyer Learn from Literature? Book Review of Law and Literature: A Misunderstood Relation. By Richard Posner', *Harvard Law Review* 102 (1989) pp. 2014-2047, at p. 2023.

[27] Following Cicero's ideas, see A.D. Leeman and A.C. Braet, *Klassieke retorica*, Groningen: Wolters Noordhoff 1987, p. 135.

our notion of what a classic book is has been broadened beyond Homer, Virgil, Plato, and Cicero to include Shakespeare, Dante, Tolstoy, and George Eliot, it is still worthwhile to read at least some of them. What makes a classic, is less straightforward than it was in Quintilian's time. In this, I follow White's lead and would prefer texts with different layers of meaning, raising difficult questions. There are many such multi-layered, well-written texts, and a thorough reading of some can help a future lawyer to develop his or her judgment, in both stylistic and ethical matters.

PETER WÜLFING

CLASSICAL AND MODERN GESTICULATION ACCOMPANYING SPEECH
An Early Theory of Body Language by Quintilian

1. INTRODUCTION

In the classical system of rhetoric, *actio*, delivery with instruction on voice, posture, facial expression, gesture, and so on, was the last of the duties (*officia*) of the orator; it was also known as *pronuntiatio*. Thus, *pronuntiatio* is the realization of that which was up to this point an edifice in thought and perhaps notes. The word *actio*, from *agere*, 'to perform', corresponds to the Greek *hypókrisis*, the activity of an actor.[1]

In the mature system of Quintilian's time, *actio* was divided into the topics of voice *(vox)*, hand and arm movement *(gestus)*, body movement *(motus)*, dress and outfit *(cultus)*, and finally posture *(habitus)*. In his *Institutio oratoria,* Quintilian deals with *actio* in Chapter 3 of Book XI. The topic I would like to discuss is that of *gestus*. Under this heading, Quintilian first deals with the gestures that are performed with the head, then those that show in the face (*vultus*), and the gestures of neck, arms, hands, and fingers. However, the rest of Chapter 3 also contains interesting reflections on these sophisticated trivialities as well as numerous important details of a cultural and historical kind.

Actio and its elaboration arise from the completeness of the rhetorical system itself. Historically, however, this did not happen suddenly and all at once. *Hypókrisis* was first noticed by Aristotle in his *Rhetorica*, which probably originates from about 340 BC. Aristotle, however, only described *hypókrisis* as 'very important' and immediately added that it evaded text-book treatment, since it had not yet been systematically dealt with.[2] His pupil Theophrastus wrote a book on delivery (*perì hypokríseos*), but it has not survived.

We know virtually nothing about the development of *actio* up to the Latin *Rhetorica ad Herennium*, which may have been written by a certain Cornificius, and which dates from the 80s of the last century BC and is roughly 180 years older than Quintilian's *Institutio oratoria*. Cornificius' rhetoric is a thin volume compared to Quintilian's *Institutio*. It does contain the complete rhetorical system, but only in outline.

The entire section on *pronuntiatio* consists of nine sections instead of Quintilian's 184, just one twentieth part. Consequently, the subject is treated only in a cur-

---

[1] Even today, Latin languages use *acteur*, *attore*, and English uses *actor*.
[2] Aristoteles, *Rhetorica*, III. 1. 1403b-1404a.

sory way. Its tenor is: 'Caution! Avoid exaggeration!' According to Cornificius, the main function of *gestus* and *vultus* is to gain credibility *(probabiliora reddere quae pronuntiantur)*. Two statements at the beginning stand out.[3] First, the author says that the topic of *pronuntiatio* is not more important than the other *officia*, and, secondly, he states that no one has yet written about it in detail *(diligenter)* because it defies verbalisation, an opinion that one tends to agree with.

Cornificius wrote down only short comments and, after only a few lines, is very proud of what he has undertaken,... *quantum susceperim negotii*. To him, *pronuntiatio* is a matter of practice, not at all suited for systematically written instruction. Cornificius does not, therefore, agree with the great orator Demosthenes, who, when questioned on the most important aspect of the art of rhetoric, is said to have replied: *'Hypókrisis'*. When questioned on the second most important one, he again replied *'hypókrisis'*, and the answer was the same as regards the third most important aspect.[4] Quintilian really went further. Fully aware of the difficulties, he at least attempted to describe part of the subject.

Now I would like to show that there can be fruitful historical communication between a classical and a modern topic, in roughly the following way: the classical approach, here Quintilian's chapter on *gestus*, strikes us as peculiar. We would not treat it in quite the same way today and his description has no modern equivalent: today, we would approach it differently. The topic of body language is obviously in fashion and, against this yardstick, Quintilian's treatment appears completely inadequate. But it cuts both ways. Having found the reasons for the difference, one can understand that Quintilian's exposition actually has a decisive advantage: first, it is embedded in a generally accepted system of his time, remaining somewhere between systematic representation and practice; second, it does not even appear to aim at completeness, and, finally, it is normative, not descriptive.

This part of the rhetorical system fascinates me because it belongs to the field of *oral* rhetoric, i.e., to the actual practice of speaking. Through its long tradition, rhetoric has been reduced to style and theory of argumentation. Now it no longer needs a chapter on *actio*; in his handbook on rhetoric, Lausberg does not discuss this topic. In reading about *actio*, one experiences something particularly original and at the same time eternally valid. After all, people gesticulated then as they do now. Maybe we can learn something directly from Quintilian XI.3, more precisely, from the sections 84-124, the forty sections on the *gestus* of the arms, hands, and fingers.

2. QUINTILIAN ON GESTICULATION

In *Inst. or.* XI.3, Quintilian describes approximately twenty gestures. I would like to discuss ten of them. My descriptions are obviously modern interpretations of Quintilian's text, and only a reconstruction of what was intended, errors (always possible) excepted.[5]

---

[3] *Rhetorica ad Herennium*, III.19.

[4] In Cicero, *De oratore*, III.213, and in Quintilian, *Inst. or.* XI. 3.6.

[5] My interpretations are based on the text and translation Butler, see 'Introduction', note 27, with

In XI.3.92, Quintilian describes the first gesture as follows (ill. 1).

> *Est autem gestus ille maxime communis, quo medius digitus in pollicem contrahitur explicitis tribus, et principiis utilis cum leni in utramque partem motu modice prolatus, simul capite atque humeris sensim ad id, quo manus feratur, obsecundantibus, et in narrando certus, sed tum paulo productior, et in exprobando et coarguendo acer atque instans, longius enim partibus his et liberius exeritur.*

One of the commonest of all the gestures consists in placing the middle finger against the thumb and extending the remaining three: it is suitable to the *exordium*, the hand being moved forward with an easy motion a little distance both to right and left, while the head and shoulders gradually follow the direction of the hand. It is also useful in the statement of facts [*narratio*], but in that case the hand must be moved with firmness and a little further forward, while, if we are reproaching or refuting [i.e., in the *argumentatio*], the same movement may be employed with vehemence and energy, since such passages permit of greater freedom of extension.

In XI.3.93 Quintilian warns for applying this gesture in a wrong way, for instance, by lifting the arm to the left shoulder or across the chest: this looks like gesticulating with the elbow.

The same gesture can also be performed with both middle fingers under the thumb (ill. 2). Quintilian says that this produces an even more forceful impression, *instantior*, which is why this gesture is not suitable for the *exordium* or the *narratio*.

Illustration 1 and 2

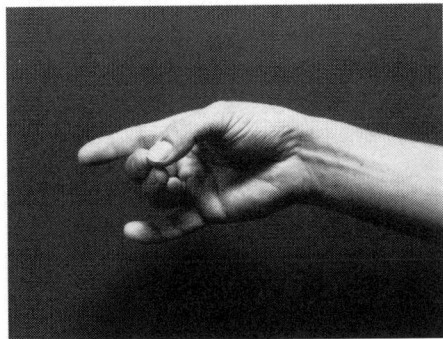

corrections where necessary, and on the treatment by U. Maier-Eichhorn, *Die Gestikulation in Quintilians Rhetorik*, Frankfurt: Lang 1989. The pictures are my own work. Note the following difficulty: for every position of the hands, there is also an associated arm movement which completes the full *gestus*. However, the text only implicitly contains arm movements; therefore, I will not describe them.

Illustration 3-8

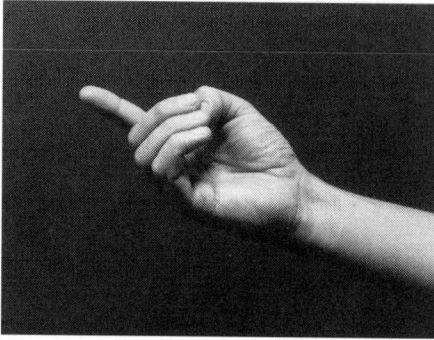

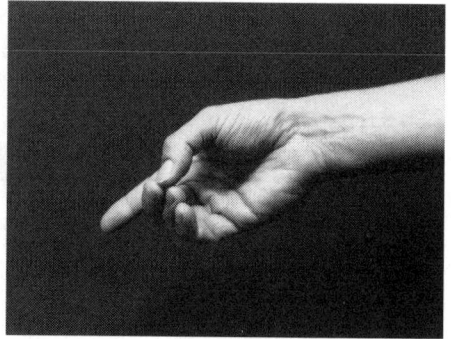

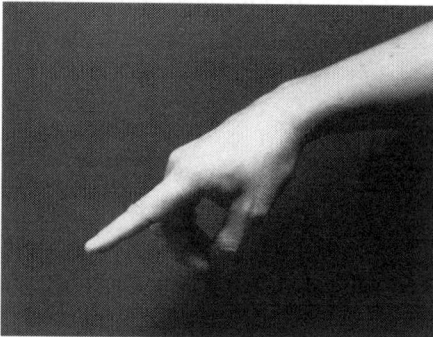

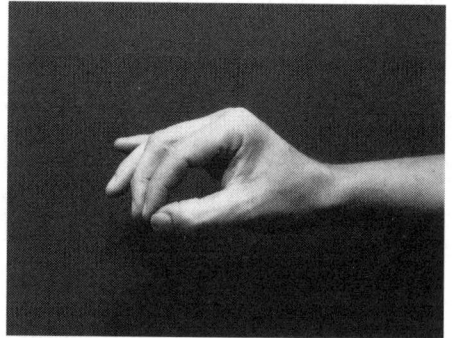

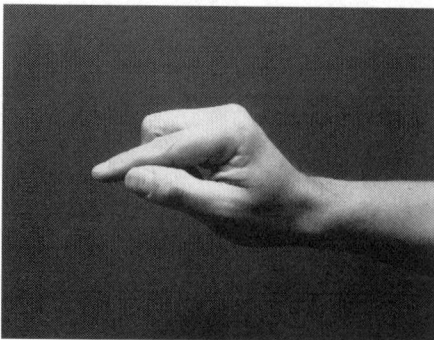

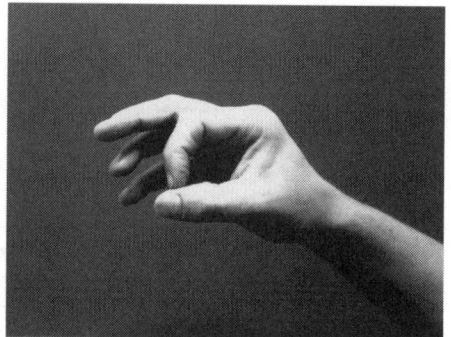

Illustration 9

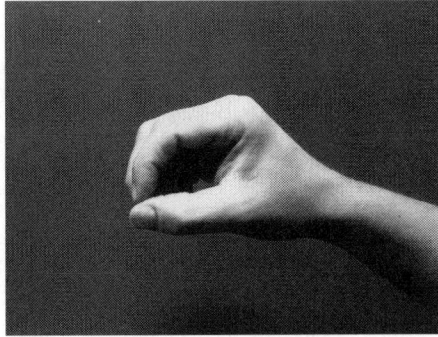

He evidently means that it is rather suited for intensive speech, for instance, when the orator is arguing or when he is summing up at the end of the speech.

In illustration 3, we see the famous raised forefinger. According to Quintilian (XI.3.94), it serves to reproach and to indicate, *exprobrari et indicare* (hence its name of *index* finger). Crassus used to use this gesture very effectively, so Quintilian reports.[6]

In illustrations 4 and 5, we can see the lowered *index*, which Quintilian says has an urgent effect, *urget* (XI.3.94, *in fine*). For us, on the contrary, the gesture of the raised forefinger is notorious: it is considered dogmatic, authoritarian, at least unpleasantly didactic and importunate. The lowered *index* is almost the strongest gesture described by Quintilian. With him as well as with Cornificius, recommendations on reserved gestures predominate.

The two gestures shown in illustrations 6 and 7 are well suited for argumentation (XI.3.95). The pointing gesture is softened on both sides. On the left, the forefinger is covered by the thumb and middle finger. On the right, the forefinger is supported by the thumb and middle finger. This gesture is suitable for energetic reasoning (*acrius argumentari*).

In illustration 8, we find ourselves on more familiar ground: this gesture is thoroughly well known (XI.3.101). The tip of the forefinger joins up with the middle of the thumbnail (that is, forms a ring), while the other fingers remain relaxed. It looks good when confirming, relating, and differentiating (*adprobantibus et narrantibus et distinguentibus*).

The gesture shown in illustration 9 is similar, but with three bent fingers. It is much used by the Greeks, says Quintilian, often with both hands, in rounding off their *enthymemes* (rhetorical conclusions), as it were one by one (XI.3.102). Here one can observe that Quintilian prefers 'broken' gestures, i.e., those in which the full execution, the full *impetus* is held back or taken back. Doubtless, this posture corresponds to the ideal of *elegantia*, the ideal of the social strata that were called upon to discourse and to which the speech was primarily directed.

---

[6]   Referring to Cicero, *De oratore*, II.188.

I would like to describe one more gesture without illustration, but on the basis of Quintilian's text, because it shows that one cannot simply label Quintilian as 'preferring restraint.' In XI.3.103, he writes:

> *Est et illa cava et rara et supra humeri altitudinem elata cum quodam motu velut hortatrix manus; a peregrinis scholis tamen prope recepta tremula scenica est. Digitos, cum summi coierunt, ad os referre, cur quibusdam displicuerit, nescio. Nam id et leviter admirantes et interim subita indignatione velut pavescentes et deprecantes facimus.*
> Again, there is the somewhat unusual gesture in which the hand is hollowed and raised well above the shoulder with a motion suggestive of exhortation. The tremulous motion now generally adopted by foreign schools [i.e., the Greek and Asianic] is, however, fit only for the stage. I do not know why some persons disapprove of the movement of the fingers, with their tops converging, towards the mouth. For we do this smoothly when we are surprised, and at times also employ it to express fear or entreaty when we are seized with sudden indignation.[7]

I interpret the whole remark as saying that other teachers have found this gesture common and vulgar, but that Quintilian, the superior judge assured in his taste, would rather prefer to sanction such a gesture, which conveys true feeling in a universal way, for he adds in XI.3.104:

> *Quin compressam etiam manum in paenitentia vel ira pectori admovemus.*
> We even clench the hand and press it to our breast when we are expressing regret or anger.

Let us be clear: this is no beating of the breast, but a gesture of self-emphasis. Emotion may and must be freely displayed. On the other hand, and herewith he finishes his discussion of *gestus*, to point to something with the thumb bent back is in general use, but according to Quintilian, it is inappropriate for the orator.

To conclude my description of the gestures, I want to make some general remarks on this section and on some sections elsewhere in Chapter 3. First, it can be established that Quintilian did not have any serious problems with the verbal description of gestures. However, he only describes a relatively small number of arm and hand postures, mainly the fine, distinguished movements. Also, there is hardly a single *gestus* recommended for the *peroratio* which, as is well known, requires high pathos and *amplificatio*. The reason is that even Quintilian tends to admonish. Theatrical displays are to be avoided at all cost. Quintilian proceeds in a pedagogical way, mainly using positive recommendations rather than prohibitions; nevertheless, he also refers several times to certain 'bad habits' (*vitia*).

Second, the gestures he describes have two functions. Some refer to the pace of speech: they give rhythm, organise the speech; these gestures are still employed in modern speech. Others underpin the spoken words with the specificity or emotion of the speaker, in contrast to the various gestures of modesty. However, classical rhetoric basically lacks an appreciation of the social differences expressed in speech and especially in gestures. Classical rhetoric is and always was an instrument of the ruling class. In this connection, Quintilian only briefly comments that the *actio* is to be

---

[7]   This gesture seems to me to correspond to that by which people in Greece and Turkey nowadays express praise and joy, accompanied by an '*oraía!*' (nice!), or rather a '*çok iyi!*' (great!). The hand is often thereby moved down from the mouth to the chest.

adapted to the speaker, the addressee, and the audience, and he explains this with a few very conventional remarks on the three basic tasks of the speaker: *conciliare, persuadere, movere* (XI.3.150-153).

Another striking feature is that basic ethnic differences are denied. The above-mentioned Greeks represent a particular school of oratory in the overall Greek-Roman culture. Quintilian only remarks in this connection (XI.3.87):

> *Ut in tanta per omnes gentes nationesque linguae diversitate hic mihi omnium hominum communis sermo videatur.*
> In fact, though the peoples and nations of the earth speak a multitude of tongues, they share in common the universal language of the hands.

After all, gesticulation has a special role whereas facial expression and voice can stress or add nuance to what is said (XI.3.85):

> ..., *hae, prope est ut dicam, ipsae loquuntur.*
> ..., the hands may almost be said to speak by themselves.

I maintain that the statement on the common speech of mankind is a *cliché* that is also often heard nowadays: 'When travelling abroad, you can get along without speaking the language' or 'You can always get by with hefty gesticulation.' On closer inspection, only the pointing gestures are international. Many other gestures may at times cause fundamental misunderstandings. One only has to think of lifting the head, which means negation for Greeks and Turks but to us means nodding assent. Or their gesture 'Come', a downward movement of the hand with the back of the hand facing upwards. We can easily mistake it for a kind of scaring away, and so on. Yet, from the same passage, we learn in an important and enduring way that a speech without gesticulation is not worth the name: it would be crippled (*trunca*) and weak. This is instantly confirmed by everyday experience: it is almost unbearable to listen to a speaker who does not move, particularly when his facial expression does not change (assuming that there is such a speaker): speech and gesture naturally belong together.

Further on in Chapter 3, the following observation catches our attention (XI.3.114):

> *Manus sinistra numquam sola gestum recte facit; dextrae se frequenter accommodat.*
> The left hand never does correctly accomplish a gesture by itself; but it will often conform its motion to that of the right.

The majority of gestures, therefore, were performed single-handedly with the right hand. The left hand was able to reinforce with a parallel equivalent. This brings us to some peculiarities of classical oratory, which we should bear in mind.
- The speaker stood alone, he did not have a desk in front of him.
- His outer gown, *himátion* or *toga*, was so arranged that one end was thrown over the left shoulder, leaving the right shoulder and the right arm free. So gesticulation with the left arm was unpractical, since it could disturb the gown. In fact, the gown was arranged as it was in order to leave the right arm free because of the general preference given to that side. Today, too, the right hand is the bearer of gestures and left-handers gesticulate on the 'wrong' side.
- Finally, the total orality of the delivery and the reception of a speech was a basic prerequisite. There certainly was the written text of the speech, *libellus*, but Quintil-

ian advised against holding it in the hand, because it would look like lack of trust in one's own memory and would impair the gestures.

3. MODERN GESTICULATION

What is the state of gesticulation nowadays? There appear to be some basic rules: we also find it hard to take when a speaker does not move. We also find lack of facial expression unnatural and very disturbing. We also wish, almost without being aware of it, appropriate gestures, neither too many nor too few. But with that, our knowledge and experience of gesticulation is almost at an end.

I have already spoken of the different circumstances: for us, speech is no longer the only medium of mass communication. Much takes place in writing or on the radio or telephone, where we do not see the speaker. In this respect, television has changed quite a lot: gesture has a function there once again and this is what seems to link our 'new oral culture' with television, not with the previous media of electronic communication, like radio or telephone. On television, however, the announcer often sits at a table or, in talk shows, on a sofa or a revolving stool. Apart from the desk, announcers have other objects to 'hang on to' that hinder gesticulation. They hold, for example, a manuscript or a ball-point pen or a microphone.

Our gesticulation is undoubtedly less conventionalised: everyone moves as they want. And yet, despite the restrictions just noted, there are basic rules. I have tried to identify them by observing people at conferences and on television, and by reading some of the specialised literature.

At conferences, there is nowadays no culture of gestures; how one speaks depends very much on the personal culture of the individual speaker. There is, however, a north-south gap here: a higher value on bodily self-portrayal, as, for example, is common among Italians, allows one to move elegantly and aesthetically, whereas in the north this would quickly be condemned as 'exaggerated'. In classical rhetoric, it is stated that the movements of the speaker must be 'masculine'. But beware! The wealth of Mediterranean gestures is in the simple people, and that is not the public speaker whom Quintilian is addressing.

Particularly on television, one is struck by the preponderance of talking while seated; this is very unclassical, it is not covered at all by classical teaching on oratory. Moreover, people who are sitting, but also people standing, obviously attempt *not* to gesticulate, that is, not to move the hands around too much. Head movements replace much of this. But the hands, obviously due to previous instruction, are kept as still as possible.

I have also collected a few ideas from modern literature. I will begin with the phenomenon of the anti-gesture. In our culture, we have a number of gestures which are there to prevent gesticulation. Franz Kiener calls them gestures of self-restraint: the speaker puts both hands together or into one another, the most common form being folded hands.[8] It has the effect of unobtrusiveness, modesty, sometimes even

---

[8] F. Kiener, *Hand, Gebärde und Charakter*, Munich-Basle: Reinhardt Verlag 1962, pp. 212ff. On modern gesticulation, see also K.R. Scherer and H.G. Walbott (eds.), *Nonverbale Kommunikation. Forschungsberichte zum Interaktionsverhalten*, Weinheim-Basle: Beltz 1979, rpt. 1984.

of submissiveness. Placing the fingertips together also belongs here. This phenomenon can clearly be seen on television, for example, in presenters of the weather forecast: apart from other gestures of self-restraint, the announcers use the button for changing the weather map. Only a few pointing gestures to the satellite picture are allowed: Azores, British Isles, Scandinavia, and the build-up of air over the Alps. In addition, there is sometimes a kind of truncated performance gesture pointing downwards, which may be connected to the fact that announcers do not *de facto* have an audience, but only a restricted space between them and the recording equipment. I have found no equivalent of this anti-gesture in classical Antiquity.

In modern literature, several types of gestures are distinguished. First, there are the 'performance gestures' which prevail in modern speaking. They are one-handed and two-handed gestures of illustration, i.e., they illustrate the process of speaking itself. This has several aspects. By their movement, these gestures should draw attention to themselves and hold it there. Then the movement, being situated in the space between speaker and listeners, fills this space, bridges it, creates a bond, draws the listeners in, lets the speaker and the speech open up to the listeners, shows them highlights and transitions. This seems to cover a basic function of gesture. Paul Ekman and Wallace Friesen call them *illustrators*.[9]

Further descriptions of 'performance gestures' are given by Kiener.[10] He describes, for example, the two-handed spherical position, as if the speaker were enclosing an imaginary balloon. It indicates that something coherent is being stated. Then there is the two-handed refined position (the speaker holds both hands in front, each with the fingers joined together). He is thereby signalling a complicated connection, which demands full attention. The single-handed refined position is the weaker, more commonly used form. These gestures also invite concentration: 'Pay attention! What I'm explaining is complicated.' Not far from this is the proverbial raised forefinger, which can mean a warning 'Be careful there' or can illustrate the speaker's claim 'I'm not just anyone standing here.' Then the open palm slanting downwards: a gesture of 'There you are...!' This gesture can also act as an invitation: 'Here you can observe everything, just take a closer look at what I'm explaining to you.' And if the hand is dropped a little, this means 'It's obvious!'

Second, there are gestures which give rhythm, divide up and count, which symbolise a sequence. Other gestures refer to globality (the hand moves to and fro or up and down). This is saying 'Everything is included' or the grand gesture is made (holding the arms out wide), which can mean 'all this is offered to you' and (with simultaneous lifting of the shoulders) add resignation. The gestures of repetition are simpler (for example, circling of the hands) and all the deictic gestures which mean 'here, there, far away.' Many of these can turn into gestures of self-emphasis and relationship: from me to you, and so on. A large group of gestures within this category are pointing gestures. They 'translate' the contents of the speech into space. They mediate between the figurative meaning and the actual meaning: the statement 'later' is accompanied by the gesture 'far away'; the state-

---

[9]   Paul Ekman – Wallace V. Friesen, 'Handbewegungen', in: Scherer-Walbott (see note 8), pp. 108-123, = 'Hand Movements', *Journal of Communication* 22 (1972), translated by H.G. Walbott.
[10]   Kiener (see note 5), p. 221.

ment 'act of God' is accompanied by the gesture of pointing upwards; the statement 'from the depth of his feelings' is accompanied by a scooping gesture from below moving upwards.

The third type of gestures are the gestures of meaning. They undoubtedly form a group of their own. Ekman and Friesen call them *emblems*. They are the kind of gestures that can, on their own and without speech, state something unambiguously: 'yes, no, maybe, don't know, watch out! take care! come! go away!' They can also accompany and illustrate speech. Precisely this group largely lacks equivalents in 'formal' speech. On the contrary, they comprise the gestures of the ordinary people. They consist mainly in repeating in gestures of what is being said, for instance, gestures of counting money, when money is being talked about; the similar gesture of rubbing the fingers together when feelings are the subject; waving the fist when we menace a person, and so on. The vulgar gestures also belong to this category. They are characterised by their proximity to the obscene: the upward-thrusting thumb and the gesture of 'finished', 'enough', 'I don't care', when both hands, alternately brushing one another, are moved away from the body; the forearm jerk or *bras d'honneur*, as it is called by the French, when a hand slaps to the opposite elbow and bends that arm; the rubbing together of the forefingers when the talk is of any kind of coupling.

When taking a look at modern literature, one is struck by the fact that scientific interest in this subject originates in several disciplines, but hardly in philology (a few exceptions prove the rule). Although the modern term is 'body *language*', it is only rarely a *linguistic* discipline that describes it. On the other hand, psychology, physiology, behavioural studies, ethnology, and art history, among other things, vie for a position in this area.

Even this observation is interesting. It is in line with current scientific conduct, for the intention is diagnostic: 'What does somebody who makes this gesture - often unconsciously - disclose about himself?' The stance of the investigator and informer quickly becomes apparent, and may be thoroughly justified, for example, when Marianne Wex writes about the gestures of men and women, and documents her observations with photographs.[11] After all, the topic often appears in books of photographs, for instance, in those by Samy Molcho[12] and Dennis Morris[13], who have 'culinary' motives, Morris more so than Molcho.

Modern science is by its nature mainly descriptive, experimental and quantifying. It deploys an extensive recording apparatus, which can capture direction, intensity, and frequency of gestures. It also concerns itself with differentiating the captured values, arranging them hierarchically, and identifying the resulting structures and groups. In the essay by Ekman and Friesen, the attitude of the investigator as well as the quantifying approach are clearly visible.[14] A large part of this article is concerned with gestures of deception, and another article by the authors is entitled

[11]   M. Wex, *'Weibliche' und 'männliche' Körpersprache als Folge patriarchalischer Machtverhältnisse*, 2nd edition, Frankfurt: Frauenliteraturvertrieb 1980.
[12]   S. Molcho, *Körpersprache*, Munich: Mosaiek 1983.
[13]   D. Morris, *Bodywatching: A Field Guide to the Human Species*, Oxford: Grafton 1987.
[14]   See note 10.

'Body Movement and Voice Pitch in Deceptive Interaction'.[15] Regarding the quantifying approach, I quote for fun: 'Among the student nurses the number of illustrative movements correlated positively under the conditions of accuracy with the fem-
ininity scale of the California Personality Inventory ($r = 0.61$) and with
cooperativeness according to the Interpersonal Check List ($r = 0.53$), but negatively
with dominance ($r = -0.45$ in CPI; $r = -0.48$ in ICL)...'.[194] These researchers are
certainly likeable people, but I do not like the purpose of their research.

4. CONCLUSION

Compared to the modern scientific literature on gestures, the partial system of classical times describing *gestus* was distinctly limited. It had undeniable deficits, several of which I have mentioned above, yet it also had several advantages that are
nowadays unmatched.

(1) It belonged to the education of all cultivated people, not only a few specialists. Nowadays, it is a forgotten part of education. As far as I know, not even lawyers
are explicitly trained in pleading: scarcely in argumentation, not at all in public
speaking.

(2) The classical teaching of this partial area was, by comparison, clear and
described a coherent whole. It required no burgeoning terminology; the parts of the
human body and a few descriptions of direction and pace were enough.

(3) It always retained its connection to the text. By comparison, modern studies
on this topic predominantly treat gestures as independent signs that replace speech or
oppose it.

(4) Moreover, classical teaching looked at what the speaking subject wanted to
express, starting from the subject's interest in representation; it did not look at the
hidden messages which an overbearing researcher now wants to deduce from the
gestures of ordinary people against their will and interests.

(5) It is also not dependent on completeness: examples suffice.
We often criticise the normative, rule-based character of classical systems. We thereby
overlook that rules of recommendation help the individual according to intention,
whereas the descriptive approach always perceives the individual as a mere object.

However, we must not deceive ourselves. The 'charm' of classical theories has
heavy drawbacks. They are always addressed to the upper social strata only, as
mediators and yardsticks. This is also very true of rhetoric.

Nowadays, we have to deal with ever more complex conditions of speech (specially in the context of a television studio where an audience may or may not be
present), and with an ever growing number of communicative situations. Therefore,
we need adequate instruments. However, these instruments might cut us off from the
valuable, enriching, human, holistic system of gesture as part of ancient rhetoric.
Maybe its very simplicity can make us think further.

---

[15]   P. Ekman, W. Friesen, and K.R. Scherer, 'Body Movement and Voice Pitch in Deceptive Interaction,
Semiotica 16 (1976), also in: Scherer-Walbott (see note 8), 271-275 translated by H.G. Walbott.
[16]   Ekman and Friesen (see note 9), p. 120.

ESPERANZA OSABA

THE RIGHT OF APPEAL IN QUINTILIAN'S *INSTITUTIO ORATORIA* XI.1.76

1. INTRODUCTION

As we know, Book XI of the *Institutio oratoria* consists of three chapters. In the first, Quintilian, in accordance with Cicero's approach, discusses the fourth virtue of *elocutio*, the *apte dicere* or form to be given to a discourse. In the two remaining chapters, he discusses the fourth and fifth parts of rhetoric, memory and *pronuntiatio* or *actio*.[1]

From a juridical standpoint, which is the one I took in examining Book XI, Chapter 1, seems the most relevant and will therefore form the core of my analysis. In his discussion of *apte dicere*, Quintilian reviews all the factors that the orator must consider when exercising his skill – i.e., his own person, the person on behalf of whom he speaks, the judge to whom the *oratio* is addressed, the adversary in the cause, and of course the circumstances of time and place in which the proceedings occur and the type of action in question. Each of these factors elicits from Quintilian comments and discussion that are highly interesting and worth studying.

I was especially intrigued by the information Quintilian provides on various actions where parents and children confront each other in the courts. He displays before us a rich tapestry in which, for example, a son might seek the incapacitation of his father (XI.1.58) and the appointment of an administrator of the father's assets

---

[1] On Quintilian: D. Pujante, *El hijo de la persuasión. Quintiliano y el estatuto retórico,* 2nd edition, Logroño: Instituto de Estudios Riojanos 1999, especially pp. 275-295; J. Cousin, *Études sur Quintilien,* I, *Contribution à la recherche des sources de l'institution oratoire,* Paris: Boivin 1935, rpt. Amsterdam: Schippers 1967, pp. 607-633; J. Adamietz, 'Quintilian's "Institutio oratoria"', in: H. Temporini and W. Haase (eds.) *Aufstieg und Niedergang der römischen Welt,* II, 32, Berlin-New York: Walter de Gruyter 1986, pp. 2227-2271; O.E. Tellegen-Couperus, 'Quintilian and Roman Law', *Revue Internationale des Droits de l'Antiquité* 47 (2000) pp. 167-177T. On *memoria* and *actio*: J.A. Hernández Guerrero, 'De la actio de Quintiliano a la "imagen" pública', in: T. Albaladejo, E. del Río, and J.A. Caballero (eds.), *Quintiliano: Historia y actualidad de la retórica. XIX Centenario de la Institutio Oratoria,* Madrid y Calahorra 1995, 3 Vols,. Logroño: Instituto de Estudios Riojanos 1998, pp. 87-100; J. Martin, *Antike Rhetorik. Technik und Methode,* Munich: Beck 1974, pp. 349-355; G.A. Kennedy, *A New History of Classical Rhetoric,* Princeton, New Jersey: Princeton University Press 1994, pp. 173-192; I. Mastrorosa, 'Appunti per un lessico giudiziario in Quintiliano', in: *Atti del II Seminario Internazionale di Studi sui Lessici Tecnici Greci e Latini,* Naples-Messina: Edizioni Scientifiche Italiane 1997, pp. 233-243; B. Steinbrink, v. 'Actio', in: Gert Ueding (ed.), *Historisches Wörterbuch der Rhetorik* I, Tübingen: Niermeyer 1992, pp. 43-52; W. Neuber, v. 'Memoria', in: *Historisches Wörterbuch* (see above), pp.1037-1047; J.C. Gómez Alonso, 'La memoria en Quintiliano', in: Albaladejo (see above), II pp. 595-604; C. Marimón Llorca, 'La especificidad pragmática de la pronuntiatio y su incidencia en la construcción del discurso retórico', in: Albaladejo (see above), pp. 649-658.

(*curator bonorum*), offset by another vignette in which a father wishes to renounce his rights of paternity and disown or formally separate himself (*abdicare*) from a son who, born of the father's marriage to a prostitute, now wishes to marry a woman of the streets in his own turn (XI.1.82-83). The emancipation of children also appears in this Book as a general cause of conflict, with even mothers and their offspring battling in court in all types of greater and lesser disputes. But there are other points of interest as well. For example, there is crucial information on the *iudicia publica*. In this respect, Book XI provides useful information on the daily practice at the courts and tribunals (XI.3.127, 130, 134, 156-157), and on the language used therein (XI.2.50).

From this interesting range of subject matter, I have chosen to focus on an issue affecting Roman procedure itself, i.e., the institution of appeal. In particular, I wish to discuss a text that has not been the object of special attention and which is found in Chapter 1, paragraph 76 of Book XI.[2]

2. QUINTILIAN, *INST.OR.* XI.1.76

Hoc et apud eos (a) quibus appellatum erit, si forte ad eosdem remittemur: adicienda ratio vel necessitatis alicuius, si id causa concedit, vel erroris vel suspicionis. Tutissimum ergo paenitentiae confessio et satisfactio culpae, perducendusque omni modo iudex ad irae pudorem.

The same method may be adopted if our case should chance to be sent back to the same judges from whom we have appealed: but we may further, if the case should permit, plead that we were forced to take the action which we did or were led to it by error or suspicion. The safest course will therefore be to express our regret, apologise for our fault and employ every means to induce the judge to feel compunction for his anger.[3]

This paragraph comes within the context of a discussion by Quintilian of the best strategy or form of discourse to adopt when an orator addresses judges who either feel hostile towards for the cause or persons involved the situation alluded to in the passage immediately preceding this one (XI.1.75),[4] or else who have had some prior association with the case, as posited in the two subsequent passages (XI.1.77 and 78).[5]

Prior association might have existed if the judge had, at some earlier time, delivered an opinion on the same matter now defended by the orator, in perhaps a

---

[2] I use the edition by Winterbottom (see 'Introduction', note 26).

[3] I use the translation by Butler (see 'Introduction', note 27).

[4] *Inst. or.* XI.1.75: 'Apud iudicem vero qui aut erit inimicus alioqui aut propter aliquod commodum a causa quam nos susceperimus aversus, ut persuadendi ardua est ratio, ita dicendi expeditissima. Fiducia enim iustitiae eius et nostra causae nihil nos timere simulabimus. Ipse erit gloria inflandus, ut tanto clarior eius futura sit fides ac religio in pronuntiando quanto minus vel offensae vel utilitati suae indulserit'.

[5] *Inst. or.* XI.1.77: 'Accidit etiam nonnumquam <ut> ea de causa de qua pronuntiavit cognoscat iterum. Tum illud quidem commune: apud alium nos iudicem disputaturos de illius sententia non fuisse, neque enim emendari ab alio quam ipso fas esse: ceterum ex causa, ut quaeque permittet, aut ignorata quaedam aut defuisse testes aut, quod timidissime et si nihil aliud plane fuerit dicendum est, patronos non suffecisse sucurret. 78: Etiam si apud alios iudices agetur, ut in secunda adsertione aut in centumviralibus iudiciis duplicibus, parte victa decentius erit, quotiens contigerit, servare iudicum pudorem: de qua re latius probationum loco dictum est'.

related or similar cause.[6] In such cases, Quintilian advises future orators to make the judge feel that, when his ruling was given, certain essential information was lacking, or some necessary witness had not been present. As a last resort and in the absence of other arguments, Quintilian even proposes that the orator should subtly lay the blame for the judge's earlier decision on the deficient advocacy of the original orators in the case. The following fragment (XI.1.78) is devoted to suits for freedom and to cases heard by a tribunal of *centumviri*. In liberty proceedings, we know that if the suit was lost on a first hearing, it could be presented on successive occasions, pursuant precisely to *favor libertatis*.[7] Concerning the tribunal of *centumviri*, composed as it was of more than a hundred judges and beloved by orators due to the solemnity conferred on the proceedings by the size of the audience, we know that a single case could apparently be heard by different sections of the tribunal and that divergent sentences could therefore be passed.[8] In this regard, Suetonius, in his *De vita caesarum*, provides us with testimony of appeals to the Emperor Domitian against rulings of this tribunal.[9] In these cases, where an orator is dealing with proceedings of this kind, Quintilian suggests that the advocate should show the greatest respect for judges who have handed down an earlier ruling on the matter.

On the whole then, in these fragments, Quintilian is dealing with cases that place the orator in the delicate position of having to address judges whose opinion, or that of colleagues on the tribunal, has been called into question. In all such cases, our expert warmly advises that the advocate avoid embarrassing the judge or making him feel that his skill or that of his colleagues is being placed in doubt. To this end, the orator must strive to lay responsibility for the judge's decision on factors beyond

---

[6] We know that, under certain conditions, e.g., when a *litis contestatio* was not considered preclusive, the action could be reintroduced or related claims could be raised. On this subject, see M. Kaser and K. Hackl, *Das römische Zivilprozessrecht*, 2nd edition, Munich: Beck 1996: pp. 301ff.; 375ff. M. Talamanca, *Istituzioni di diritto romano*, Milan: Giuffrè 1990, pp. 330ff.

[7] Kaser-Hackl (see note.6), pp. 102-103; G. Franciosi, *Il processo di libertà in diritto roman*, Naples: Jovene 1961, pp. 260 ff.; M. Brutti, *La problemática del dolo processuale nell'esperienza romana* 2I, Milan: Giuffrè 1973, p. 505 n. 215

[8] On the *centumviri*: Kaser-Hackl (see note 6), pp. 52-56; F. Gayet, v. '*Centumviri*', in: M.Ch. Daremberg- E. Saglio, *Dictionnaire des Antiquités Grecques et Romaines* 1,2, Paris: Hachette 1877, pp. 1013-1015; F. la Rosa, '*Decemviri*' e '*Centumviri*', in: *Labeo* 4 (1958) pp. 14-54; B. Albanese, *Il processo privato romano delle legis actiones*, Palermo 1993, p. 124 n 430; H. Lévy-Bruhl, *Recherches sur les actions de la loi*, Paris: Sirey 1960, pp. 147ff.; M. Wlassak, v. *Centumviri*, in: *Pauly-Wissowa's Realencyclopaedie* 3, Stuttgart (1899) pp. 1935-1952; J. M. Kelly, *Studies in the Civil Judicature of the Roman Republic*, Oxford: Oxford University Press 1976, pp. 1-39.

[9] Suetonius, *Domitianus*, 8: 'Plerumque et in foro pro (...) tribunali extra ordinem ambitiosas centumvirorum sententias rescidit'. See J. M. Kelly, *Princeps iudex. Eine Untersuchung zur Entwicklung und zu den Grundlagen der kaiserlichen Gerichtsbarkeit*, Weimar: Böhlau 1957, pp. 96-97, and review by P. Frezza, *Studia et Documenta Historiae et Iuris* 24 (1958) pp. 348-353; J. Bleicken, *Senatsgericht und Kaisergericht. Eine Studie zur Entwicklung des Prozessrechtes im frühen Prinzipat*, Göttingen: Vandenhoeck & Ruprecht 1962, pp. 142-143 n. 4, and review by W. Kunkel, *Zeitschrift der Savigny Stiftung*, rom. Abt. 81 (1964) pp. 360-377; C. Sanfilippo, 'Contributi esegetici alla storia dell'appellatio. 1 Sull'appello contro la sentenza del giudice formulare nell'impero', in: *Annali Camerino* 8 (1934) pp. 317-350, especially pp. 332-334; R. Orestano, *L'appello civile in diritto romano*, Turin: Giappichelli 1953, pp. 210ff.

his control, such as the evidence originally presented or even lack of ability on the part of the original orator.[10]

In the text I wish to analyse, the first part of the fragment concerns cases where the advocate must speak before the very judges whose sentences he have appealed, in the event that he have been sent back to the same tribunal.[11]

As we know, resort to appeal arose within the new political context created by the Principate and made it possible to apply to the Emperor for review of a case.[12] Although there has been much debate about the origin of the Emperor's right to hear appeal cases, what can be affirmed is that it was based on imperial authority itself. We know that the origin of the power to judge appeals was derived from the Emperor's assumption of different Republican powers (*tribunicia potestas, imperium proconsulare*), but it was based above all on his own prestige or personal charisma, i.e., on his *auctoritas*.[13] For the new political power, it was another form of control that could be exerted, this time over the judiciary, and constituted an entirely new situation, since as we know, no appeals could be brought against the sentences handed down by the judiciary system previously in place (*ordo iudiciorum privatorum*).[14] The process of implementing the new system of appeal was naturally

---

[10] Quintilian also discusses these matters in *Inst. or.* V.2.1-5.

[11] We know that, during that period, the term *appellatio* could be used in a sense other than that of review in second instance of a valid sentence, and mean imperial intervention in first instance or, for example, a petition of *intercessio*, as can be seen, for example, in C. Masi Doria, *Spretum Imperium,* Naples 2000, pp. 294ff. On this subject see Orestano (see note 9), pp. 197ff. However, in Quintilian's text, both the meaning and the context would seem to indicate judicial review in second instance.

[12] Kaser-Hackl (see note 6), pp. 501ff.; N. Palazzolo, *Processo civile e politica giudiziaria nel Principato,* Turín: Giappechelli 1980, pp. 29-37; L. Fanizza, *L'amministrazione della giustizia nel principato: aspetti, problemi,* Rome: L'Erma di Bretschneider 1999, pp. 11-60; R. Orestano (see note 9); Idem, v. 'Appello', in: *Novissimo Digesto Italiano* 1, Turin 1957, pp. 723-725; v. 'Appello', in: *Enciclopedia del Diritto* 2, Varese (1958) pp. 708-713; Kipp - Hartmann, v. 'Appellatio', in: *Pauly-Wissowa* (see note 8), 2, Stuttgart (1896) pp. 194-210; G. Humbert, v. 'Appellare', in: *Dictionnaire des Antiquités* (see note 8), pp. 328-330; Th. Mommsen, *Römisches Strafrecht,* Graz: Akademische Druck- und Verlagsanstalt 1955 (= Leipzig 1899), pp. 468 ff.; L. Raggi, *Studi sulle impugnazioni civili nel processo romano,* Milan: Giuffrè 1961; B. Santalucia, *Studi di diritto penale romano,* Rome, "L'Erma" di Bretschneider 1994, p. 223 and n. 222; A. H. M. Jones, *The Criminal Courts of the Roman Republic and Principate,* Oxford: Blackwell 1972, p. 91ff.; J. L. Murga, *Derecho Romano Clásico* II. *El proceso,* Zaragoza 1983, pp. 324ff.; A.W. Lintott, 'Provocatio, from the Struggle of the Orders to the Principate', in: *Aufstieg und Niedergang* (see note 1), 1.2 (1972) pp. 263-267; G. Pugliese, 'Linee generali dell'evoluzione del diritto penale pubblico durante il principato', in: *Aufstieg und Niedergang* (see note 1) 2.14 (1982) pp. 737ff.; U. Vincenti, *Ante sententiam appellari potest,* Padua: Cedam 1986. See also on the jurisdiction of the senate in matters of *appellatio,* F. de Marini Avonzo, *La funzione giurisdizionale del senato romano,* Milan: Giuffrè 1957; O.E. Tellegen-Couperus, 'Did the Senate function as a Court of Appeal in the Later Roman Empire?', *Tijdschrift voor Rechtsgeschiedenis* 53 (1985) pp. 309-320; F. Arcaria, *Senatus censuit. Attività giudiziaria ed attività normativa del senato in età imperiale,* Milan: Giuffrè1992.

[13] Palazzolo (see note 12), pp. 29-37, also Fanizza (see note 12), pp. 22ff.; Kelly (see note 9), pp. 70ff., pp. 91ff.; Bleicken (see note 9), pp. 124ff., 131ff.; Orestano (see note 9), pp. 183 ff.; Arcaria (see note 12), pp. 37ff.

[14] Against these, other remedies were possible: *Intercessio, infitiatio* against *actio iudicati, restitutio in integrum,* Palazollo (see note 12), pp. 29-37; Kelly (see note 9), p. 91ff.; Orestano (see note 9), p. 79ff.; G. Buigues Oliver, *La rescisión de los hechos y actos jurídicos en derecho romano (Premisas para un estudio de la restitutio in integrum),* Valencia: Ediciones Nomos 1992; L. Raggi, *La restitutio in integrum nella cognitio extra ordinem. Contributo allo studio dei rapporti tra diritto pretorio e diritto*

neither easy nor straightforward. The first steps were taken under Augustus and progressed steadily throughout the first century AD, until, according to Villers, appeal ceased to be a political means of pressure and became instead a right to which claimants were fully entitled under the law.[15]

Quintilian, whose writings and activity date from the second half of the first century, would, of course, have been well acquainted with the possibility of raising an *apellatio* or *provocatio* to Caesar, because, while the remedy of appeal did not take on its definitive traits until the end of the second century, appeals to the emperor against the rulings of judges must surely have been numerous since the beginnings of the Principate.[16] Indeed, even Augustus was known to have delegated the resolution of appeals due to the excess work that they entailed.[17] According to a passage in *Suetonius*, he entrusted to the urban praetors appeals by residents of Rome, and to ex - consuls appeals from the provinces.[18] [This, naturally, holds for sentences which came from trials *extra ordinem*, that is, under the new procedure of imperial cognition[19] heard by judges whose power was in fact based on imperial authority.] To this should be added the well-grounded conjecture that with time, it also became possible to appeal sentences of the previous *ordo*, but *extra ordinem*.[20]

Now then, the essence of appeal to the Emperor resided precisely in the fact that the possibility of having a sentence overturned was being sought from the pinnacle of power – from the Emperor himself. The Emperor could delegate the power to

---

imperiale in età classica, Milan: Giuffrè 1965; G. Cervenca, *Studi vari sulla "restitutio in integrum"*, Milan: Giuffrè 1965; B. Biondi, 'Appunti intorno alla sentenza nel proceso civile romano', *Scritti Giuridici* 2, Milan: Giuffrè 1965, pp. 435-517, especially pp. 505ff.; C. Buzzacchi, *Studi sull'actio iudicati nel processo romano classico*, Milan 1996.

[15]   R. Villers, 'Appel devant le prince et l'appel devant le Sénat au premier siècle de L'Empire', in: *Studi in onore di Pietro de Francisci* 1, Milan: Giuffrè 1956, pp. 375-391, especially pp. 383ff.; M. Molè, v. 'Sentenza', *Novissimo Digesto* (see note12), 16, pp. 1081-1103.

[16]   Quintilian uses the expression *appellare*, for example, in *Inst. or.* IV.1.22. A glossary of terms used in Quintilian's work can be found in J. J. Iso Echegoyen, *Index verborum y concordancia de las "Instituciones oratoriae" de Quintiliano*, Barcelona: Bellaterra 1989; E. Bonnell, *Lexicon Quintilianeum*, Leipzig: Teubner 1834, rpt. Hildesheim: Olms 1962. Also vs. 'Appellatio; Appello', in: *Thesaurus linguae latinae*, Leipzig: Teubner 1900, pp. 271-276. The use of the terms *appellare-provocare* is confusing even later; see for example F. Goria, 'Ricusazione del giudice e giudices electi da Costantino a Giustiniano', in: *Legislazione, cultura giuridica, prassi dell'impero d'Oriente in età giustinianea tra passato e futuro*, Milan: Giuffrè 2000, pp. 153-209, especially p. 174-175 n. 56; Orestano (see note 9), p. 197; Arcaria (see note 12), p. 78.

[17]   Fanizza (see note 12), pp. 38ff.; Palazzolo (see note 12), p. 35; Kipp (see note 12), p. 200; Orestano (see note 9), pp. 196ff.

[18]   Suetonius, *Augustus*, 33. Kelly (see note 9), pp. 93-96. Assuming even that the appellations discussed in the text concern the invocation of imperial intervention both in first and second instance, Orestano (see note 9), pp. 196ff.; Sanfilippo (see note 9), p. 335. See also another view in Arcaria (see note 12), pp. 38ff.

[19]   I. Buti, 'La "cognitio estra ordinem" da Augusto a Diocleziano', in: *Aufstieg und Niedergang* (see note 1) 2, 14 (1982) pp. 29-59.

[20]   A passage in Suetonius tells of the annulment of a sentence of the *centumviri*, by Domitian himself, with, however, the effect of cassation rather than reform. M. Amelotti, *La prescrizione delle azioni in diritto romano*, Milan: Giuffrè 1958, pp. 143ff.; Kelly, see note 9), pp. 96-97. C. Lécrivain, 'L'appel des juges-jurés sous le Haut-Empire', in: *Mélanges d'archéologie et d'histoire de l'École française de Rome* 8 (1888) pp. 187-212, especially pp. 209ff.; Orestano (see note 9), pp. 186ff., 209ff.; Sanfilippo (see note 9), pp. 317-350; Arcaria (see note 12), p. 37 n. 10.

abrogate or review the sentence to a given magistrate or judge, who in all cases would be the hierarchical superior of the one who had first passed sentence.[21] Quintilian, however, seems to be saying that the orator might find himself before the very judge whose sentence was being appealed. In principle, the situation strikes us as strange, since we wonder why an orator might find himself in these circumstances.

Clearly, we cannot rule out the possibility of an appeal being sent back to the same judge that had tried the case in first instance. We must bear in mind that, during these years of the first century appeals were resolved case by case in the absence of specific regulations to this effect, as certain extraordinary cases show.[22] For example, Dio Cassius relates in his *Historia Romana,* that the emperor Tiberius refused to judge appeals against the decisions of senator Marcus Silanus because of the latter's enormous prestige.[23] According to the same author, Fonteius Capito, a legatus of Germania, decided to resolve an appeal against a sentence he had passed previously by confirming the sentence and having the appellants put to death.[24]

In short, while we may surmise, given the uncertainty surrounding these early appeals, that situations such as those described here might not be absolutely unusual, they must have been quite extraordinary even for the period. However, the two incidents mentioned do show how displeased a judge could be by an appeal against his earlier sentence. It could even be considered an affront to review a sentence issued by a person of prestige.[25]

However, while we cannot entirely rule out the possibility that a judge might be asked to resolve an appeal against his own decision, another interpretation of Quintilian's text might also be possible. This would be the case of an advocate who, after having defended a cause before a judge and having appealed the sentence handed down, is again sent before the same judge on the occasion of a different suit. We know that in the *cognitio extra ordinem,* the new procedure instituted with the advent of the Principate, the parties were not allowed a choice of judges and the competent magistrate could try the case himself or else delegate his competence to a *iudex datus.*[26] This could also be the coincidence that Quintilian is referring to, wherein the orator and the judge confront each other again after the former has appealed a decision of the latter.

Nearly two centuries later, we find a text by Ulpian, included in the Digest under the title '[An appellant] may be required to plead another action before [a judge] from whom he is appealing',[27] in which the jurist argues that appeal against a sen-

---

[21] Fanizza (see note 12), p. 41; Sanfillipo (see note 9), p. 336.

[22] Orestano (see note 9), p. 194 and pp. 202ff.

[23] Dio Cassius, 59.8.4-5; 51.19.6; also Suetonius, *Caligula,* 12.1 and 23; *Nero,* 17. Tacitus, *Annales,* III.24.3; III.56.1-2; III.57.1; XIII.1; XIV.28; See Fanizza (see note 12), pp. 38ff., Villers (see note 15), pp. 375-391; Kelly (see note 9), p. 96; Arcaria (see note 12), pp. 55ff.

[24] Dio Cassius, 63.2.3, see Fanizza (see note 12,) pp. 38ff.

[25] Perhaps reasons of friendship or enmity with the judge who passed the sentence prevailed over those of justice, as hypothesised by Villers,(see note 15), p. 383.

[26] Buti (see note 19), p. 33. G. Humbert [Ch. Lécrivain], v. 'Judex, judicium', in: *Pauly-Wissowa* (see note 8), Paris 1900, 3/1, rpt. Graz 1969, pp. 632-642; Kaser-Hackl (see note 6), pp. 460ff.

[27] Ulp. D. 49.12: 'Apud eum, a quo appellatur, aliam causam agere compellendum'. I use the translation by A. Watson (ed.), *The Digest of Justinian,* Philadelphia: University of Pennsylvania Press 1985.

tence should not be an obstacle for appearing again before the same judge to plead a different case. In the words of the jurist (D.49.12.1):

> *Ulpianus libro quarto de appellationibus:*
> *Si quis ex alia causa appellaverit a iudice, an in alia causa eundem iudicem habere necesse habeat, videamus. Et hodie hoc iure utimur, et tametsi appellatio interposita sit, tamen apud eundem iudicem a quo quis provocavit, compelletur alias causas si quas habet agere: nec utetur hoc praetextu, quasi ad offensum iudicem non debaet experiri, cum possit denuo provocare.*
> Ulpian in Book IV on Appeals:
> Let us see whether, if a person appeals from a judge in one action, he is required to accept the same judge in another. We nowadays follow the legal principle that even if an appeal has been lodged, a person is still compelled to plead any other actions that he has before the same judge from whom he appealed. Nor is he to use this as a pretext on the grounds that he ought not to go to law before a resentful judge, since it is possible for him to make a fresh appeal.

Quintilian and later Ulpian could be speaking about the same situation: having to defend a cause before a judge whose sentence the advocate has appealed. It would appear that this posed a problem which in the time of Ulpian (2nd and 3rd centuries AD) still existed. Why? The jurist himself provides a clue when he notes that the judge might have been offended by the appeal against his sentence. The reason for this feeling of offence is explained by Ulpian, when, in the opening passage of Book 49 of the Digest, devoted to the subject of appeals (D. 49.1.1 pr.), he says:

> *Ulpianus libro primo de appellationibus:*
> *Appellandi usus quam sit frequens quamque necessarius, nemo est qui nesciat, quippe cum iniquitatem iudicantium vel imperitiam recorrigat.*
> Ulpian in Book I on Appeals:
> As everybody knows, the practice of appeals is both frequent and necessary, inasmuch as it corrects the partiality or inexperience of judges.[28]

That is, sentences are appealed mainly because of judges' bias, or injustice, or because of their lack of skill.[29] Thus, judges would be offended by an appeal, particularly as they were high ranking senators and *equites*.[30] Although we know that

---

[28] Despite the tempering of this opinion in the same fragment when he says: 'Licet nonnumquam bene latas sententias in peius reformet, neque enim utique melius pronuntiat qui novissimus sententiam laturus est', Not but what it may sometimes alter well-delivered judgments for the worse, for it is not [necessarily] the case that the last person to pronounce judgment judges better.

[29] Gai. D. 2.8.9; Paul. D. 29.5.21.2; Ulp. D. 47.10.1pr. On *iniuria iudicis*, see: G. Pugliese, 'Note sull'ingiustizia della sentenza nel diritto romano', in: *Studi in onore di Emilio Betti*, 3, Milan: Giuffrè 1962, pp. 727-781, especially 735ff. A different situation arises in cases where the *iudex litem suam fecit*; on this subject, see I. Cremades and J. Paricio, 'La responsabilidad del juez en el derecho romano clásico', *Anuario de historia del derecho español* 54 (1984) pp. 179-208; A. D'Ors, 'Litem suam facere', in: *Studia* (see note 9), 48 (1982) pp. 368-394; O. F. Robinson, 'The "Iudex qui litem suam fecerit" explained', in: *Zeitschrift* (see note 9), 116 (1999) pp. 195-199; Orestano (see note 9), pp. 114-115; Arcaria (see note 12), p. 35 n. 5.

[30] In this regard, see J. M. Kelly, *Roman Litigation*, Oxford: Clarendon Press 1966, p. 102ff. Regarding the competence of the prefects of the praetorium, according to a fragment by the jurist Hermogenianus (D. 4.4.17) an appeal signified a claim against the unfairness of a sentence, whereas a *restitutio in integrum*, a remedy already existing under the *ordo* leading to annulment of the proceedings, was a request for pardon of the error itself or allegation of deceit by the adversary; see Raggi (see note 14), pp. 199ff.

appeals were also raised over defects of procedure and even deceit on the part of the
adversary, and not merely against sentences considered 'iniquitous', according to
Lauria, it must have been generally considered that appeals were brought mainly due
to judges' lack of skill or unfairness.[31] This was so much the case that it finally
posed a judicial problem, which is the one addressed by Ulpian and which, in my
opinion, was detected a century earlier by Quintilian. Indeed, around the year 341,
the Emperor Constantius felt obliged to declare that judges should not consider
appeals against their sentences as injurious.[32]

Returning now to our fragment, the rhetorician from Calahorra, under this more
plausible interpretation of the second part of the passage, is recommending that,
should his pupils find themselves again in the presence of a judge they have
appealed from, they should justify themselves by blaming the appeal on imperious
need, error, or some kind of suspicion. In any event, he seems to advise them (in the
final phrase of the passage) that the safest (or most prudent) course is to show repentance[33] and to apologise for the fault committed,[34] trying by all means to make the
judge feel ashamed of showing his anger.[35] In view of this advice of Quintilian, one
immediately wonders: could the threat posed by an appeal, or the anger of an
appealed judge, have proved so serious?

The answer to this question, which should no doubt be in the affirmative, is not
to be found in literary sources, but in legal texts instead. Both in the Digest and in
the Theodosian Code, as well as in the Code of Justinian, we find texts that allude to
the situation. In fact, in both the Codes, there is a Title 'On those who failed to
appeal for fear of the judge'.[36]

This *metus iudicis* or fear of the judge appears further justified in the light of the
numerous imperial constitutions that exist on the subject.[37] For example, in one of
the earliest known today, the emperor Alexander Severus sent a rescript to the
Greeks of Bithynia stating that appeals of litigants must not be impeded for any reason, and prohibiting provincial governors and *procuratores* from using violence or

---

[31] M. Lauria, 'Sull "appellatio"', in: *Studii e Ricordi,* Naples: Jovene 1983, pp. 65-70, especially 66-67.
[32] CJ 7. 62.20 (*Imp. Constantius A. Albino*, a. 341)
[33] See also *Inst. or.* VII.4.18; IX.2.60.
[34] An acceptance of blame in this regard is found, for example, in *Inst. or.* VIII.2.24; VIII.3.45; VII.4.15. The term *satisfactio* is used with a similar meaning in *Inst. or.* VI.3.34
[35] An intervention of this sort, concerning matters outside the cause in hand, would be necessary to win over the judge. The right moment for it might have been the *exordium*. In Quintilian's view, everything pertaining to the person speaking in the cause pertains to the cause, *Inst. or.* IV.1.12: '... sed ego cum auctoritate summorum oratorum magis ducor, tum pertinere ad causam puto quidquid ad dicentem pertinet, cum sit naturale ut iudices iis quos libentius audiunt etiam facilius credant'. Indeed, we should also remember that there was a specific type of *exordium* devoted specially to matters outside the cause (*Inst. or.* IV.1.71). The idea is to make the judge well-disposed to us and, to this end, in matters that cannot be contradicted by other means, Quintilian in another passage, just as in the one we are studying, advises the orator to give the impression that amends have been made through repentance or expiation (*Inst. or.* IV.1.45).
[36] CJ. 7.67 and CT. 11.34: *De his qui per metum iudicis non appellaverunt.*
[37] See, for example, W. Litewski, 'Die römische Appellation in Zivilsachen (Ein Abriss) I. Principat', in: *Aufstieg und Niedergang* (see note 1) 2,14 (1982) pp. 81-82; Kaser-Hackl (see note 6), p. 508 n. 60-62; p. 615 n. 7; p. 619 n. 18; F. Goria, 'Ricusazione del giudice e giudices electi da Costantino a Gius-

commiting outrages against them or from holding them in a military prison to impede their access to the Emperor.[38] But such aggression was so ingrained that as late as 314 Constantine felt moved to lay down a prohibition against the imprisonment, injury, or torture of appellants in civil suits[39] or cruel acts against them. Moreover, years later, he would again order judges to refrain from frightening litigants in an attempt to avoid an appeal once sentence had been passed.[40] Along these same lines, in another constitution, the Emperor Julian addresses persons who were unable to present an appeal due to violence exerted against them by the judge when they presented their claim.[41]

3. CONCLUSION

To conclude, whether the orator is sent to defend an appeal before the very judge who handed down the sentence in the first instance, or whether the judge is one the orator previously appealed against in a different suit, or whether there is some other possible interpretation that has not occurred to me, Quintilian's advice to his pupils and readers, perhaps even those of today, does not appear to be misguided. When an advocate has to appear again before a judge against whom he has appealed, all sorts of apologies are in order, for even a few centuries after Quintilian, when resort to appeal was a fully established judicial right, doing so in certain circumstances could be risky, and even constituted a heroic act on occasions. This then was perhaps the first mention of a situation which would later be included in the Digest and in the Code.

---

tiniano', in: *Legislazione* (see note 16), pp. 153-209, especially 172.

---

[38]   Paul. D. 49.1.25. In fact, since the time of Septimius Severus, appeals were considered validly brought when, out of fear of violence on the part of the judge in question, they were held in a public place, Marci. D. 49.1.7.

[39]   CJ. 7.62.12 (*Imp. Constantinus A. ad Catullinum*, a. 314). The CT. includes constitutions of Constantine: CT. 11.34.1 (*Imp. Constantinus A. ad universos provinciales*, a. 331); CT. 11.34.2 (*Imp. Constantinus A. ad Volusianum p(raefecto) p(raetorio)*, a. 355); CT. 11.30.15 (*Imp. Constantinus A. ad concilium provinciae Africa, a. 329)* and others, see J. Gaudemet, 'Constitutions constantiniens relatives à l'appel', *Zeitschrift* (see note 9), 98 (1981) pp. 69-71; F. Pergami, *L'appello nella legislazione del tardo impero*, Milan: Giuffrè 2000, pp. 142ff. See also PS 5,4,18; PS 5,35,3. A passage in Ulpian states that magistrates who, failing to honour the right of appeal, had had a Roman citizen put to death, struck, or held by the neck for torturing, or had done so himself, would be subject to the Julian law on public violence (*Lex Iulia de vi*), Ulp. D. 48.6.7. On this text, see Fanizza (see note 12,) pp. 44ff. It is interesting to find instances showing that fear of the judge must have been used as a resort when the legal period for appeal had expired, in times, of course, when the remedy of appeal was fully configured with clearly stipulated deadlines: CJ. 7.67.2 (*Imp. Iulianus A. Germaniano pp.*, a. 362).

[40]   CJ. 7.61.1 pr. (*Imp. Constantinus A. Profuturo praefecto annonae*, a.319). Occasionally, the appellant also became violent. For example, both Paul and Ulpian have passages in the Digest stating that appellants may not shout insults at the judge, as they will be censured as infamous if they do: Paul. D. 47.10.42 (= *Pauli Sententiae* 5.4.18); Ulp. D. 49.1.8.

[41]   CJ. 7.67.2 (*Imp. Iulianus A. Germaniano pp.*, a.362).

VINCENZO SCARANO USSANI

ROMANUS SAPIENS AND *CIVILIS VIR*

Quintilian's Theory of the Orator acting for the Benefit of the Imperial Power

1. IN PLACE OF PHILOSOPHY

Even if Quintilian himself had not advised the reader of the importance of the last book in the conceptual structure of the *Institutio oratoria*, defining it as 'the most important portion of his work',[1] the reader would not have missed such characteristic.[2] It was in fact this peculiarity which distinguished, more than any other, Quintilian's work from an 'ordinary' *Ars rhetorica*[3] and which justified the title of the *Institutio*. The title in fact refers to the offer of an isagogic model combining in one expositive form the contents of a *téchnè*, or art, and the guidelines for a complete intellectual and moral training of the orator.[4] Therefore, in the twelfth book, the educational plan, already sketched in the preface of the *Institutio*,[5] was fulfilled: the education of the perfect orator.[6]

---

[1]   *Inst. or.* XII.pr.1: 'pars operis longe gravissima'. I use the edition by L. Radermacher, revised by V. Buchheit, Leipzig: Teubner 1959, rpt. 1965, and give my own translations.

[2]   According to I. Lana, *Sapere, lavoro e potere in Roma antica*, Naples, Jovene 1990, p. 281 n.1 with literature, Book XII did not stir up 'particolare interesse fra gli studiosi' of Quintilian's *Institutio*.

[3]   The *Duo libri artis rhetoricae*, circulating under the name of Quintilian, were in reality only unauthorized divulgations of notes from Quintilian's lessons collected by his pupils (*Inst. or.* I pr.7; III.6.68).

[4]   Cf. Lana (see note 2), p. 282. P. Desideri, *Dione di Prusa. Un intellettuale greco nell'impero romano*, Messina-Florence: D'Anne 1978, p. 88 stresses the circumstance that Quintilian, having mastered the subject 'della crisi dell'eloquenza per svuotarlo dall'interno' - in his *De causis corruptae eloquentiae* the problem seems to have been solved merely in a technical perspective, that is, with the analysis of the possible faults of different forms of expression - built, with the *Institutio*, 'un modello di formazione e di comportamento politico che è, come appare scopertamente nell'ultimo libro, la quintessenza dell'efficentismo tecnico e dell'arrivismo con pretese intellettuali al servizio di qualunque regime'. See also A. Manzo, 'Manente honesta voluntate (Inst. XII.1.46) tra ideologia e retorica', in: *Atti del Congresso internazionale di studi vespasianei 1979*, Rieti: Centro di Studi Varroniani Editore 1981, pp. 2.443ff. According to M. Winterbottom, *Quintilian the moralist*, in: T. Albaladejo, E. Del Rio, J.A. Caballero (edd.), *Quintiliano: historia y actualidad de la rétorica*, I, Logroño: Instituto de Estudios Riojanos1998, p. 333, 'It looks as though the book *De Causis* was the moral kernel of the *Institutio*'.

[5]   *Inst. or.* I.pr.9-20.

[6]   On the meaning of *instituere* and the isagogic model of *institutio*, see S. Querzoli, *Il sapere di Fiorentino. Etica, natura e logica nelle* Institutiones, Naples: Loffredo 1996, pp. 42ff. The difference between *ars* and *institutio* is underlined by A. D. Leeman, *Orationis ratio. The Stylistic Theories and Practice of the Roman Orators Historians Philosophers*, Amsterdam: Hakkert 1963, it.tr. Bologna: Il Mulino 1974, pp. 406f. Not without some polemic, Columella significantly had noted that the perfect orator had still not been found (*De re rustica*, 11.1 'Nam nec oratoria disciplina deseritur, quia perfectus orator nusquam repertus est...').

In order to be defined as such, he not only had to master his art, but also to be *vir vere civilis*, a man who can really play his part as a citizen, and *vere sapiens*, a truely wise man. He had to be able to manage public and private affairs, to guide towns with his advice, to found them with laws, to amend them with trials, as well as to possess all virtues of the soul, also the science of living honestly, that is the wisdom of which the philosophers had claimed to be the only *studiosi*.[7]

The orator so educated would really be, according to the Catonian definition, *vir bonus dicendi peritus*, 'a good man, skilled in speaking'.[8]

Quintilian was conscious of the novelty of his isagogical proposal and, consequently, of the difference between his educational programme and that shaped by Cicero, in particular in *De oratore*, which was the only point of reference, but towards which he claimed his more ambitious perspective.[9] In his temerity, the Spanish *rhetor* was also going to try to impart good morals to the orator and to assign him his duties.[10] It was a project which prevented him from following his predecessor, because he was determined to go further. Cicero had in mind an orator who was master of all knowledge useful for his education, and claimed the supremacy of rhetoric, but he had not considered it a 'total knowledge', which, in the first place, could replace philosophy in education.[11]

Exactly the passages of Book XII, where Quintilian repeats and encreases his criticism of philosophy, show how this new approach was functional to a fundamental aspect of the theoretical itinerary of the *Institutio oratoria*; they cannot be

---

[7] *Inst. or.* I.pr.14.

[8] *Inst. or.* XII.1.1. The question of the Stoic origin (especially from Diogenes of Babylon) of Cato's definition, with an accurate study of the various theories, is analysed by G. Calboli, *Marci Porci Catonis. Oratio Pro Rhodiensibus. Catone, l'Oriente greco e gli imprenditori romani*, Bologna: Pàtron 1978, pp. 14ff. with literature, who defends Cato's paternity of this definition: it could have been at the beginning of a work about rhetoric. Lana (see note 2), p. 289 and n.21 thinks, on the contrary, that the definition is 'certamente stoica', but Quintilian preferred to ascribe it only to Cato in order to prove to his readers that he was connected with the real Roman cultural tradition. According to G. Moretti, *Acutum dicendi genus. Brevità, oscurità, sottigliezze e paradossi nelle tradizioni retoriche degli Stoici*, Bologna: Pàtron 1995, pp. 82ff., the definition was Cato's re-elaboration 'in direzione del *mos maiorum*' of a 'suggestione stoica'. P. García Castillo, 'Influencias filosóficas en la definición del *vir bonus* de Quintiliano', in: Albaladejo (see note 4), II, pp. 891ff., finds, in the definition, Platonic, Aristotelian, and Stoic influences.

[9] *Inst. or.* XII.pr.4; XII.1.19; XII.1.21; XII.2.5.

[10] *Inst. or.* XII.pr.4: 'At nostra temeritas etiam mores ei conabitur dare et adsignabit officia'.

[11] *Inst. or.* XII.pr.4. On the 'educational' programme of *De oratore*, see A. Michel, 'La pédagogie de Cicéron dans le De oratore: comment unir l'idéal et le réel?', *Revue des Études Latines* 64 (1986) pp. 72ff. On the relations between philosophy and rhetoric in Cicero's works, see A. Michel, *Rhétorique et philosophie chez Cicéron. Essai sur les fondements philosophiques de l'art de persuader*, Paris: Presses Universitaires de France 1960, pp. 327ff. Cicero considered philosophy '*matrem omnium bene factorum beneque dictorum*' (Cicero, *Brutus*, 322). P. Desideri (see note 4), p. 89 notes that Cicero, in *De oratore*, had expressed the persuasion that rhetoric and philosophy were integrated. According to G. E. Manzoni, 'Il retore Quintiliano di fronte ai filosofi', in: P.V. Cova, R. Gazich, G.E. Manzoni, G. Melzani, *Aspetti della 'paideia' di Quintiliano*, Milan: Vita e Pensiero 1990, p. 148 with literature, Cicero tried to bridge the opposition between rhetoric and philosophy: his *De oratore* could therefore be considered 'come un manifesto dell'universalità del sapere fondato sulla sintesi di retorica e filosofia'. M. Winterbottom, 'Quintilian and the Vir Bonus', *Journal of Roman Studies* 54 (1964) p. 90 thinks that 'there is no doubt that Cicero was not primarily concerned with the moral aspects', and that being 'the leading orator of his day, he may have thought indelicate or superfluous to stress that the perfect orator must be a good man'.

interpreted merely as a renewal of the secular conflict between rhetoric and philoso-phy.[12] Quintilian's project aimed at offering, first of all, the restitution to rhetoric of those studies of wisdom of which the philosophers had become the supreme holders and which were absolutely necessary to the orator.[13]

Of course, Quintilian did not omit to declare and to argue the reasons which authorized the perfect orator to claim everything necessary for his education from the science of things divine and humane, and to restore this to the sphere of elo-quence.[14] All three parts into which philosophy was divided - *naturalis, moralis, rationalis* - in fact had important features connected to the rhetor's activity.[15] Only Academics, Peripatetics, and Stoics, among the various philosophical schools, could actually provide useful principles to eloquence.[16] Of course, the orator had to be a follower of the *leges* of none.[17]

Nevertheless Quintilian resolutely did not fall into the misunderstanding of those who, as Isocrates,[18] named philosophy the rhetoric which was the 'science of speak-ing well'.[19] Therefore, the orator did not have to become a philosopher,[20] whose way of life was in fact very far from the duties of a citizen and from the tasks of an ora-tor. Quintilian intended to educate a Roman *sapiens* who, not in the secluded dis-cussions of the study but in practice acted as a true *civilis vir*,[21] and who was nour-ished with the memorable sayings and actions of the Roman tradition, so rich in noble examples.[22]

The project of restoring to rhetoric some typical conceptual spheres of philoso-phy ànd the attempt at undervaluing this science were based on underlining the civil disengagement of the philosophers - who kept aloof from assemblies, trials, and pub-lic affairs - and on the not at all new argument of the existence of many false philosophers,[23] culminating in the famous assertion: *Philosophia enim simulari potest, eloquentia non potest*, 'Philosophy may be counterfeited, but eloquence never'.

---

[12] A synthesis of the origin and the development of the ancient conflict between rhetoric and philosophy in Manzoni (see note 11), pp. 144ff. with literature. He holds that (pp. 143f., 156f., 169ff.), although Quintilian's ideas are also expressions of it but 'non delle più rappresentative', the real object of the rhetor's polemic are the philosophers as 'concorrenti nella educazione dei giovani romani': the attacks were mainly directed against the contemporary 'teachers' of philosophy.
[13] *Inst. or.* XII.2.8 and 9.
[14] According to Manzoni (above note 11), p. 168, in Quintilian's use of the well known Stoic definition it is possible to recognize 'un atteggiamento non preclusivo' of the Spanish rhetor towards the 'scienza rivale'.
[15] *Inst. or.* XII.2.9-22.
[16] *Inst. or.* XII.2.25. Cf. Manzoni (see note 11), p. 169.
[17] *Inst. or.* XII.2.26 and 27. Cf. Manzoni (see note 11), p. 169.
[18] *Inst. or.* II.15.33. See Manzoni (see note 11), pp. 146f. On Isocrates' definition, see R. Granatelli, 'Per un ripensamento sulle radici culturali di Apollodoro di Pergamo', *AION. (filol.)*, 2-3 (1980-81) p. 89; H. Wilms, *Techne und Paideia bei Xenophon und Isocrates*, Stuttgart-Leipzig: Teubner 1995, pp. 208ff.
[19] *Inst. or.* II.15.34
[20] *Inst. or.* XII.2.6 and 7.
[21] *Inst. or.* XII.2.7.
[22] *Inst. or.* XII.2.29 and 30.
[23] *Inst. or.* XII.3.12. Cf. Manzoni (see note 11), p. 170.

It is difficult to deny the existence of a consonance between Quintilian's attitude to philosophers and the Flavian cultural policy,[24] especially with Domitian's decree which banished philosophers from Rome and Italy, probably in AD 93.[25] Domitian continued his father's policy. Vespasian, who, as is well-known, had established a salaried chair of rhetoric[26] and granted immunities and privileges to professors and physicians,[27] nevertheless banished philosophers from Rome.[28] Quintilian, a professor called to the salaried chair of rhetoric,[29] probably in AD 94 appointed educator of the sons of Flavius Clemens,[30] and honoured with the *ornamenta consularia*,[31] had always been very close to the Flavians: it was a behaviour clearly confirmed by the significant praises for Domitian in the *Institutio oratoria*.[32] His programme was undoubtedly consistent with Domitian's cultural policy and offered an isagogic proj-

---

[24] For a global description of the attitude of the Flavian emperors towards the 'intellectuals', see S. D'Elia, 'Osservazioni su cultura e potere nell'età flavia', *Quaderni di Storia* 11 (1980) pp. 351ff; S. Franchet D'Espèrey, 'Vespasien, Titus et la littérature', in: H. Temporini -W. Haase (eds.) *Aufstieg und Niedergang der römischen Welt* II.32.5, Berlin-New York: Walter de Gruyter 1986, pp. 3049ff.; K.M. Coleman, 'The Emperor Domitian and Literature', in: *Aufstieg* (see above), pp. 3087ff.; Lana (see note 2), pp. 257ff.

[25] The sources do not agree on the date: see I. Lana, *La teorizzazione della collaborazione degli intellettuali con il potere politico in Quintiliano. Institutio oratoria, Libro XII*, Turin: Giappichelli 1973, p. 12 n.2 with sources and literature, who dates the banishment to the last months of AD 93. See also G. Coppola, *Cultura e potere. Il lavoro intellettuale nel mondo romano*, Milan: Giuffrè 1994, pp. 423ff. and n.317 with other literature; P. Southern, *Domitian. Tragic Tyrant*, London: Routledge 1997, pp. 115 and 153 n.12; B. Zucchelli, 'Quintiliano e i Flavi', in: *Atti 1979* (see note 4), p. 2.583 n.58, points out that another banishment, in AD 88/89, is also mentioned.

[26] Suetonius, *Vespasianus* 18; Dio Cassius, 65.12.1a. On the meaning and the importance of this imperial decision, see V. Marotta, *Multa de iure sanxit. Aspetti della politica del diritto di Antonino Pio*, Milan: Giuffrè 1988: p. 93, and Coppola (see note 25), pp. 307ff. with literature.

[27] See the well-known edict discovered in Pergamum, which granted important privileges to *magistri, medici, iatraliptae*, in *Fontes Iuris Romani Antejustiniani*, I, 2nd edition, Florence: Barbèra 1968, p. 73; see also D.50.4.18.30. An accurate analysis of Vespasian's cultural policy is in Desideri (see note 4), pp. 28ff., pp. 51ff., pp. 61ff., pp. 144ff. A survey of Vespasian's decisions regarding privileges, is in V. Scarano Ussani, *Le forme del privilegio. Beneficia e privilegia tra Cesare e gli Antonini*, Naples: Loffredo 1992, pp. 53f.

[28] On Vespasian's edict of banishment from Rome of all the philosophers excepting Musonius Rufus (Dio Cass. 65.13.2), who was banished afterwards, but called back by Titus (Hieronymus, *Chronicon*, in Migne, PL XXVII, col. 460), cf. Desideri (see note 4), pp. 63ff.; Marotta (see note 26), pp. 95ff.; Coppola (see note 25), pp. 420f. and n. 307 with other literature.

[29] In spite of the chronological error in Hieronymus, *Int. Chron. ad ann. Dom.* 89 ('Quinctilianus ex Hispania Calaguritanus, qui primus Romae publicam scholam et salarium a fisco accepit, claruit'), Quintilian was presumably the first teacher of Latin rhetoric who received a salary from Vespasian: see G. A. Kennedy, *A New History of Classical Rhetoric*, Princeton: Princeton University Press 1994, p. 177 and n.4. See also Zucchelli (see note 25), pp. 575f. Juvenal, *Saturae*, VII.188ff. mentioned Quintilian's economic prosperity.

[30] See Lana, *La teorizzazione* (see note 25), p. 17; Kennedy (see note 29), pp. 179f.

[31] Quintilian could have obtained them by the good offices of Flavius Clemens (Aus. *Grat. act.* 7 [White] 'Quintilianus consularia per Clementem ornamenta sortitus honestamenta nominis potius videtur quam insignia potestatis habuisse'): see Lana, *La teorizzazione* (see note 25), p. 15, and Kennedy (see note 29), p. 180. It is possible that also Juvenal, *Saturae*, VII.197 referred at him.

[32] *Inst. or.* III.7.9; X.1.91; see below, nn.114, 115, 116: Manzoni (see note 11), p. 172, does not think 'di riscontrare nell'*Institutio* atteggiamenti di adulazione nei confronti di Domiziano'. An evidence of Quintilian's prestige is certainly in Martialis, *Epigrammata*, II.90.

ect, in which important educational tasks were taken away from philosophers and attributed to rhetoric, to which were also ascribed the tasks of imparting good morals and assigning duties,[33] so proposing rhetoric as a complete 'science of life'. Quintilian's attempt to marginalize, if not to expel,[34] philosophy from the education of the orator and, generally on account of the function ascribed to rhetoric, from the education of the members of the future leading classes, matched with the political censure decided by the imperial power.

2. THE JURIST'S MODEL

To the perfect orator, in order to be considered so, were also absolutely necessary deep juridical and religious notions: 'this orator will also require a knowledge of civil law, and of the custom and religion of the State which he will guide'.[35] He would not have been able to propose himself as adviser in public and private counsels if he had not known the constitutive elements of the State, that is of its institutions. This study followed the school years, when the orator was already 'dismissed by his teachers of eloquence'.[36]

The orator's necessary deep knowledge of civil law had already been emphasized, as is well-known, by Cicero who, in his *De oratore*, had discussed this matter with plenty of cultural ideas and theoretical basis.[37] They were superior to the modest and schematic considerations used by Quintilian in the attempt to demonstrate the not excessive difficulty of learning *ius*, law, which perhaps would have seemed hard to a person who observed it from far.[38] Law was in fact certain or dubious.[39] All law which was certain was either written or derived from the *mores*, customs.[40] The law which was dubious had to be treated by the standard of equity.[41] The law, written or founded on the custom of the State, was not difficult to learn: it was sufficient to study it![42] The dubious law was explained by the jurists in their opinions and consisted either in the interpretation of words or in the distinction between what was and

---

[33]   *Inst. or.* XII pr.4. Cf. Lana (see note 2), p. 287.
[34]   Lana (see note 2), p. 288 thinks that 'Quintiliano, come retore, esercitando una sorta di potere culturale, espelle la filosofia, in quanto tale dal territorio degli intellettuali'.
[35]   *Inst. or.* XII.3.1: 'Iuris quoque civilis necessaria huic viro scientia est et morum ac religionum eius rei publicae, quam capesset'. With *iuris civilis scientia* Quintilian probably referred to the jurists's knowledge, which concerned all Roman law. According to R.G. Austin, *Quintiliani Institutionis oratoriae liber XII*, 2nd edition, Oxford: Clarendon Press1954, rpt. 1972, p. 92, the rhetor meant, on the contrary, 'the 'Laws of the State', competent to *cives*, in contrast to *ius gentium*'.
[36]   *Inst. or.* XII.pr.3: '... a dicendi magistris dimissus'. Cf. Lana (see note 2), p. 325.
[37]   After the hint in Cicero, *De oratore*, I.18, it is what Cicero makes Crassus say in *De oratore*, I.159-202. Cf. V. Scarano Ussani, *L'ars dei giuristi. Considerazioni sullo statuto epistemologico della giurisprudenza romana*, Turin: Giappichelli 1997, pp. 6ff., with literature. Antonius objects to Crassus that a wide knowledge of law is not necessary for the orator (Cicero, *De oratore*, I.234-250).
[38]   *Inst. or.* XII.3.6.
[39]   *Inst. or.* XII.3.6.
[40]   *Inst. or.* XII.3.6.
[41]   *Inst. or.* XII.3.6.
[42]   *Inst. or.* XII.3.7.

what was not right.[43] The knowledge of the significance of every word was either common to wise men or peculiar to the orator.[44] *Aequitas* was well known to all the best people.[45] And the orator, who, in the first place, was supposed to be *bonus vir* and *prudens*, would not be worried if he discovered that his thought diverged from that of some jurist, because also to the jurists it was permitted to disagree.[46] If he wanted to know the jurisprudential opinions about some cases of dubious law, he could learn them by means of reading, which was, in studying, the less difficult activity.[47] For the orator it was very easy to know the law. In fact, if most jurists were people who having despaired of ever becoming able advocates decided to study law, it was very simple for him to learn a subject of which those who declared their incapacity to become orators had become experts.[48] So Quintilian repeated an opinion which already had been expressed by Cicero in his *Pro Murena*[49] and which he had quoted earlier, in Book VIII: 'so we see that those, who could not become orators, betook themselves to the study of the law'.[50]

Probably following Cicero's suggestions, Quintilian stated in Book XII of the *Institutio* that some of them, namely M. Cato, Q. Mucius Scaevola and S. Sulpicius Rufus, had been able to add the gift of eloquence to being great jurists.[51] Moreover, Cicero who, in pleading causes, never lacked legal knowledge also had begun to write on this subject in order to demonstrate that an orator was able not only to study law but also to teach it.[52]

Obviously, it was impossible for the author of the *Institutio oratoria* to expel the science of law - the real, absolutely necessary, civic knowledge in Rome - and the jurists from Roman culture, or to marginalize them. In the Flavian age, on the contrary, the great jurists, leaders of the two *sectae*, or schools,[53] began more and

---

[43]   *Inst. or.* XII.3.7.

[44]   *Inst. or.* XII.3.7. Austin (see note 35), p. 95, thinks that Quintilian, using '*prudentes*', hinted explicity at the jurists: 'if they are trained as a body in *interpretatio*, so too is the *orator* in his own way'.

[45]   *Inst. or.* XII.3.7.

[46]   *Inst. or.* XII.3.8.

[47]   *Inst. or.* XII.3.8.

[48]   *Inst. or.* XII.3.9.

[49]   Cicero, *Pro Murena*, 29. Cf. Austin (see note 35), p. 95.

[50]   *Inst. or.* VIII.3.79: '... sic nos videmus, qui oratores evadere non potuerint, eos ad iuris studium devenire'.

[51]   *Inst. or.* XII.3.9. On Cato the Censor, see Cicero, *De oratore*, I.171, and Livy, *Ab urbe condita*, 39.40.6. Q. Mucius Scaevola *Pontifex* was, according to Cicero, 'iuris peritorum eloquentissimus', cf. *Brutus*, 145 and 163, where his 'dicendi elegantia' is praised. The compliment seems very doubtful to F. Schulz, *Geschichte der römischen Rechtswissenschaft*, Weimar: Böhlau 1961, p. 65 n.1. (= *Storia della giurisprudenza romana*, Florence: Sansoni 1968, p. 106 n.1), who thinks that Cicero's opinion about the oratory of jurists was altogether unfavourable (pp. 64f. nn.6, 2, 3, = *Storia*, pp. 105ff. nn. 6, 2, 3). Lana (see note 2), p. 324 stresses the fact that Quintilian regards the jurists 'oratori falliti'.

[52]   *Inst. or.* XII.3.10. Presumably, in this passage, Quintilian refers to Cicero's *De iure civili in artem redigendo* (see Gellius, *Noctes Atticae*, 1.22.7, and also Charisius, *Ars gramm.* 175.18-19 = G. L. 1.138.13K): cf. Austin (see note 35), p. 96. Although some consider this work as one of the books of *De legibus*, which was not finished or else lost, most historians believe in its autonomy, cf. Scarano Ussani (see note 37), p. 17 and n. 16 with literature.

[53]   In the first place, I think of Caelius Sabinus, Pegasus and Iavolenus Priscus. On their biographies and respective magisterial careers, see W. Kunkel, *Herkunft und soziale Stellung der römischen Juristen*, 2nd edition, Graz-Vienna-Cologne: Böhlau 1967, pp. 131ff., 138ff.; R.A. Bauman, *Lawyers and Politics in*

more to co-operate with the imperial power, and they had very successful magisterial careers. Quintilian knew very well that the jurists differed fundamentally, in culture and activity, from Greek pragmatics[54] and from *legulei*, whom he associated with false philosophers, in looking for a refuge for their sluggishness.[55] So, in the *Institutio oratoria*, expressions of esteem towards jurisprudence are not absent. Quoting Aquilius' definition of *litus*, mentioned by Cicero in his *Topica*,[56] Quintilian described the work of the jurists on the appropriateness of words as most important.[57] Besides, he significantly described the jurist S. Sulpicius Rufus as *iuris antistes*.[58] Quintilian also did not forget to underline that 'the jurists frequently raise the question of the letter and the intention of the laws'.[59] With the exception of Aulus Cascellius,[60] Trebatius Testa[61] and Q.

---

the Early Roman Empire. A study of relations between the Roman jurists and the emperors from Augustus to Hadrian, Munich: Beck 1989, pp. 142ff, 146ff., 165ff., 176ff. with literature. L. Neratius Priscus began under Domitian his *cursus honorum* reaching the *praetura*: see V. Scarano Ussani, *Empiria e dogmi. La scuola proculiana fra Nerva e Adriano*, Turin: Giappichelli 1989, rpt. 1995, p. 22 and nn. 9 and 10, with literature. For a survey of jurisprudence in the Flavian age, see C. A. Maschi, 'La scienza del diritto all'età dei Flavi', in *Atti 1979* (above note 4), p. 1.59ff. On Pegasus, see particularly F. Sturm, *Pegaso: un giureconsulto dell'età di Vespasiano*, in *Atti 1979* (see note 4), pp. 1.8ff.

[54] A well known description of *pragmatici* is in Cicero, *De oratore*, I.198; see M. Bretone, *Storia del diritto romano*, Rome-Bari:Laterza 1992, p. 155; J. Crook, *Legal Advocacy in the Roman World*, London: Duckworth 1995, pp. 41, 150ff., who (n.215 with literature) observes that the meaning of 'supplier of material to advocates' in Cicero's passage 'does not appear in the epigraphy'.

[55] *Inst. or.* XII.3.11 and 12. The persons who 'taedio laboris quem ferre tendentibus ad eloquentiam necesse est, confugerint ad haec deverticula desidiae and se ad album ac rubricas transtulerunt' are the *legulei* or *formularii* and not the jurists - so, on the contrary, Lana (see note 2), p. 324f., thinks.

[56] Cicero, *Topica, 32* '... Solebat igitur Aquilius conlega et familiaris meus, cum de litoribus ageretur, quae omnia publica esse vultis, quaerentibus eis, quos ad id pertinebat, quid esset litus, ita definire, qua fluctus eluderet'. On Aquilius'definition of *litus*, see V. Scarano Ussani, *Valori e storia nella cultura giuridica fra Nerva e Adriano. Studi su Nerazio e Celso*, Naples: Jovene 1979, p. 32 and n. 51 with literature. The definition proposed in Book XI of Iavolenus' *Libri ex Cassio* seems to have drawn inspiration from that of Aquilius (D.50.16.112 'Litus publicum est eatenus qua maxime fluctus exaestuat'. *rell.*). A not analogous definition of *litus* was ascribed by Celsus *filius* to Cicero, as *arbiter*, cf. D. 50.16.96pr.: 'Litus est, quousque maximus fluctus a mari pervenit; idque Marcum Tullium aiunt, cum arbiter esset, primum constituisse'; cf. Scarano Ussani, *Empiria* (see note 53), pp. 67 and 123.

[57] *Inst. or.* V.14.34 '... cum etiam iuris consulti, quorum summus circa verborum proprietatem labor est, 'litus' audeat dicere, 'qua fluctus eludit'.' cf. Schulz (see note 51), p. 116 (= *Storia*, p. 178). According to M. Bretone, *Tecniche e ideologie dei giuristi romani*, 2nd edition, Naples: Edizioni scientifiche italiane 1982, p. 346 n.34, this passage has to be read together with *Inst. or.* XI.2.41 '... et poetica prius, tum oratorum, novissime etiam solutiora numeris et magis ab usu dicendi remota, qualia sunt iuris consultorum'.

[58] *Inst. or.* XI.1.69. Rather than the meaning of keeper (see Paul. Fest. *De verb. sign.* 250 L.; Columella, *De re rustica*, 3.21.6), *antistes* seems to have here that of master, a 'superintendent' (see Cicero, *De oratore*, I.102; Ovid, *Tristia*, III.14.1; Columella, *De re rustica*, 11.1.10; Mela, *Chorographia*, 1.18.90; Seneca, *De brevitate vitae*, XIV.5).

[59] *Inst. or.* VII.6.1: '... scripti et voluntatis frequentissima inter consultos quaestio est'.

[60] *Inst. or.* VI.3.87. On the biographical data of Aulus Cascellius, see R. A. Bauman, *Lawyers in Roman Transitional Politics. A study of the Roman jurists in their political setting in the Late Republic and Triumvirate*, Munich: Beck 1985, pp. 117ff. with literature. On this jurist, see also Scarano Ussani, *Le forme* (above note 27), pp. 36ff. with other literature.

[61] *Inst. or.* III.11.18; V.10.64. On this jurist, see V. Scarano Ussani, 'L'epicureismo di C. Trebazio Testa', *Ostraka* 1 (1992) pp. 151ff., with literature. E. Champlin, 'Miscellanea testamentaria', in *Zeitschrift für Papyrologie und Epigraphik* 62 (1986) p. 250, thinks it is impossible that Trebatius Testa was still alive in AD 4 and that L. Lentulus, to whom Inst. 2.25pr. refers, died '20 or 30 years before AD 4'.

Aelius Tubero,[62] however, Quintilian did not mention any other jurist who survived the fall of the Republic or flourished subsequently.[63] He never mentioned the jurisprudential schools. So it seems that he considered legal science as a whole of notions and data, and he never aknowledged that it had the theoretical stature of a science.[64] His attitude to legal science does not seem to be different from, or more polemical than, that of Cicero. In this way, he could demonstrate that, although rhetoric was unquestionably superior, legal science could exist fruitfully together with eloquence, as the famous examples of the past showed: the orator could master it to the point of trying to teach it, imitating Cicero's attempt. Whoever, in Roman culture, developed an isagogic project, aiming at the education of the *vere civilis vir*, had to hold in due consideration the peculiar importance traditionally attributed to jurists. Therefore, Quintilian's programme developing a project of cultural hegemony could not escape the comparison with the jurists and their knowledge. Perhaps the Spanish rhetor saw them as more dangerous opponents than the philosophers because of their being rooted in Roman tradition and because of the very good relations which, in the Flavian age, the group of the great jurists was able to renew, at a very high level, with the imperial power.

Quintilian's model of the *perfectus orator* was therefore conditioned by the figure of the jurist, recognizable in his repeating, not without anachronism, Cicero's suggestions. The republican jurist's model, to which these suggestions referred, clearly influenced Quintilian's directions about the activity of the old orator who decided to retire from forensic life. He could devote himself either to writing for posterity the history of his own time, or to interpreting the laws for those who asked his counsels, as Lucius Crassus proposes to do in Cicero's books, or to giving orally the best ideals of conduct.[65] Therefore, the old orator could legitimately become a jurist and interpret the law for those who asked his counsels. Anyhow, whatever his choice was, according to ancient custom, his house would be visited by promising youg men who would ask him, as an oracle, what is the path to true eloquence.[66]

The metaphor of the oracle demonstrates the undoubted influence on Quintilian's image of Cicero's very famous definition of the jurist's house in *De oratore*: 'the

---

[62] *Inst. or.* V.13.20; V.13.31; X.1.23; XI.1.78; XI.1.80. On the biographical data of Q. Aelius Tubero, historian and jurist, see R. Syme, *The Augustan Aristocracy*, Oxford, Clarendon 1986, rpt. 1989, pp. 305ff. (=*L'aristocrazia augustea. Le grandi famiglie gentilizie dalla repubblica al principato*, Milan: Rizzoli 1993, pp. 451ff.). Cf. also Bauman, *Lawyers* (see note 60), pp. 113ff., and J. M. David, *Le patronat judiciaire au dernier siècle de la république romaine*, Rome: École Française de Rome 1992, pp. 884f.

[63] Cf. Bretone (see note 57), pp. 346f., who stresses the fact that the jurists, mentioned by Quintilian in the *Institutio oratoria*, belong to the Republic or to the first years of the Principate 'e il loro ricordo è dovuto appunto all'attività svolta come oratori': Trebatius is remembered because Cicero dedicated to him his *Topica* and Cascellius as author of 'boutades'.

[64] In connection with Quintilian's silence about the jurisprudential schools, it is interesting to read *Inst or.* IV.2.5. Lana (see note 2), p. 325, thinks that Quintilian devalued the study of law, denying to it the status of a true and proper autonomous science, as he reduced it 'per un verso a puro apprendimento di dati e nozioni e, per l'altro' he related it 'interamente o alla scienza del linguaggio o a quella dell'etica', both legitimately belonging to the orator.

[65] *Inst. or.* XII.11.4. See Cicero, *De oratore*, I.199: 'senectuti vero celebrandae et ornandae quod honestius potest esse perfugium quam iuris interpretatio?...' Cf. Austin (see note 35), p. 218.

[66] *Inst. or.* XII.11.5.

house of a jurist is assuredly the oracle of the whole community.[67] The jurist's model was reflected in the figure of the *perfectus orator* whose expectations, for his old age, it deeply influenced. If he had not decided to become a jurist directly, he could imitate his behaviour, summarized in the metaphor of the oracle.[68]

3. COMMUNIS UTILITAS

Moving from the fundamental presupposition that only the *vir bonus* had the possibility to become an orator, Quintilian's ambitious project necessarily involved the attempt to offer to the *perfectus orator*, who, as such, was not conceivable apart from virtue, a 'table' of ethical values to which he had to direct all his activities.[69] Many of these values belonged to Roman tradition, which taught them better than any abstract theory, with the examples of illustrious men:[70] fortitude, justice, loyalty, continence, frugality, contempt of pain and death.[71] To them were added abstinence, temperance, piety, modesty, authority, constancy, confidence and equity.[72]

Although they were important, to none of them was recognized, in Quintilian's project, the central position, which was assigned to *communis utilitas*, or common interest. In fact, the rhetor amply analysed its meaning and relevance in a lucid reasoning, the importance of which seems to be underlined by its position in Book XII of the *Institutio oratoria*, as if it was preliminary to and paradigmatic of the whole educational programme.[73] The analysis developed with some difficulty and embarrassment from the statement that the orator had to be *vir bonus*[74] and to plead only good cases.[75] But there could be reasons for the *vir bonus* - although at first sight it seems hard to believe - to hide the truth from the judge in pleading a case.[76] Anyway, it was a statement which was not really astonishing because it went back to the greatest teachers of wisdom of antiquity and because of the consideration that, in most cases, actions become honest or base more by the causes from which the facts spring than by the facts in themselves.[77] Calling on the ancient teachers of wisdom

---

[67] Cicero, *De oratore*, I.200: 'est enim sine dubio domus iuris consulti totius oraculum civitatis'.

[68] Austin (see note 35), p. 219, connects Quintilian's image to that proposed by Seneca Rhetor in *Controversiae*, 1 *praef*. 9: 'Erratis optimi iuvenes, nisi illam vocem non M. Catonis, sed oraculi creditis. Quid enim est oraculum? nempe voluntas divina hominis ore enuntiata; et quem tandem antistem sanctiorem sibi invenire divinitatis potuit quam M. Catonem, per quem humano generi non praeciperet, sed convicium faceret?' But it seems more similar - not by chance - to the description of the jurist's house ascribed by Cicero, *De oratore*, I.199-200 to Crassus: this supposition can be linked to the influence of Cicero, *De oratore*, I.199 on Quintilian, *Inst or.* XII.11.4 (see note 65).

[69] *Inst. or.* XII.2.1.

[70] *Inst. or.* XII.2.29-30.

[71] *Inst. or.* XII.2.30: *fortitudo, iustitia, fides, continentia, frugalitas, contemptus doloris ac mortis*

[72] *Inst. or.* XII.2.17: *iustitia, fortitudo, abstinentia, temperantia, pietas*; XII.3.7: *aequitas*; XII.5.2: *constantia, fiducia fortitudo*; XII.9.12: *modestia, auctoritas, fides*.

[73] *Inst. or.* XII.1.12-44.

[74] *Inst. or.* XII.1.1-32.

[75] *Inst. or.* XII.1.33.

[76] *Inst. or.* XII.1.36.

[77] *Inst. or.* XII.1.36: 'non tam factis quam causis eorum'.

to support his thought, Quintilian presumably referred to the opinions of Panaetius mentioned in Cicero's *De officiis*.[78] So he introduced the first essential reference to *communis utilitas* as the element founding the orator's ethics in an 'oblique' way, which apparently continued to explain what he wrote before about the fundamental importance of the intention in order to qualify an action morally. In fact, Quintilian did not doubt that public interest could turn homicide into virtue, make sometimes the killing of one's sons *pulcherrimum*, the noblest of deeds, and justify deeds yet more horrible to relate.[79] The Spanish rhetor repeated, with essential hardness, a thought expressed by Cicero in *De officiis*. It was possible, Cicero wrote, that an action, usually considered base, did not reveal itself as such.[80] What was more griev-ous than the murder of a man, in particular of a friend? But was it possible to con-sider the person, who killed a tyrant, as a criminal, although he was his friend? This action did not seem a crime to the Roman people but, on the contrary, it was regarded as the finest of the illustrious actions: 'Has *utilitas*, then, prevailed over *honestas*? On the contrary *honestas* has followed *utilitas*'. Then, with philosophical strictness, Cicero dealt with the relationship between *utile* and *honestum*.

Also trusting to what the sternest of the Stoics had granted,[81] Quintilian, on the contrary, proceeded to consider the possibility, for the orator, of lying, obviously in order to pursue a noble purpose, so pleading a cause which, without any honest rea-son, he would never have accepted to defend.[82] Moreover, he had previously remarked that the *vir bonus*, when he lied, had more opportunities of being believed than the wicked man, because he was considered, obviously, as more trustworthy.[83] Quintilian did not forget to underline that it could frequently occur that the orator had to plead a case, in which only the reason was honourable. He did not only men-tion the defence of a father, brother or friend, but also that of a person who had plot-ted against a tyrant. The orator 'as defined by us', the author of the *Institutio orato-ria* specified, certainly did not want his client to be condemned and, defending him, would use arguments as false as those used by the orator who pleaded a bad case.[84] By demonstrating that acts which were rightly done and which the judge wanted to condemn had not happened, the orator could save a citizen who was not only inno-cent, but also praiseworthy.[85] On the contrary, the orator who had defended certain acts which were just by nature but useless to the State ('*quaedam iusta natura, sed*

---

[78]   Cicero, *De officiis*, II.51. See also *Inst. or.* II.17.27: '... nam et mendacium dicere etiam sapienti ali-quando concessum est'. Cf. Austin (see note 35), who remarks that Quintilian 'discriminates between action and motive', and calls Cicero, *De officiis*, III.18-19, 'a passage which goes back to Posidonius and Cicero, *Paradoxa*, 3.24'.

[79]   *Inst. or.* XII.1.37.

[80]   Cicero, *De officiis*, III.19 and 20.

[81]   *Inst. or.* XII.1.38: 'Stoicorum quoque asperrimi'; on this epithet, cf. Austin (see note 35), p. 69. The Stoics distinguished *to pseudos légein* from *pseúdesthai*. See H. von Arnim (ed.), *Stoicorum Veterum Fragmenta*, Leipzig: Teubner 1903-1924, rpt. Stuttgart: Teubner 1968-1978, III p. 148 n.554.

[82]   *Inst. or.* XII.1.38 and 39.

[83]   *Inst. or.* XII.1.12.

[84]   *Inst. or.* XII.1.40. Austin (see note 35), p. 71 observes that the hypothesis of the tyrannicide is 'typi-cal of the rhetoric schools'. Cf. Tacitus, *Dialogus*, 35; Seneca, *Controversiae exc.* 4.7; [Quint.] *Decla-mationes minores*, 288, 345, 374.

[85]   *Inst. or.* XII.1.41.

condicione temporum inutilia civitati') under existing circumstances would have
used a skill of speaking which was honourable, but which nevertheless looked like
dishonourable practice.[86]

In Quintilian's view, the interest of the State and the common interest seem to be
essentially equivalent conceptions, as the example which he used a few lines later
demonstrates. In the case of a good general whose action was absolutely necessary
to defeat the enemy but who was also accused of a notorious crime, he asks: 'Will
not the common interest summon an orator to defend him?[87]

In Cicero's view, however, in accordance with the declaredly Stoic ethics which
he proposed,[88] the existence of actions right by nature but at the same time contrary
to the common interest was impossible: 'disregard of the common interest is contrary to nature; for it is unjust'.[89]

This difference is significant because it concerns a particularly important ethical
aspect, with prominent reflexes on the choises in acting and their evaluation.
Because of this difference, Quintilian's use of *communis utilitas* does not seem to be
a simple adaptation to his isagogic project of a value which Cicero already considered very important in his juvenile *De inventione*[90] and which he later explicitly
mentioned in Book III of his *De officiis*.[91] Quintilian did not think that common
interest was closely connected with the doctrine of natural law, but he preferred to
exalt the autonomy of the *communis utilitas*, which coincided – at least in his view
– with the interest of the State; he proposed it as a value in which ethics and politics
were closely connected but in which, in reality, the latter determined the former. In
Quintilian's scheme, politics prevailed over ethics, influencing it to the point of
almost identifying itself with ethics.

When one declares that the State so became 'the source of morality',[92] one may
run the risk of modernizing too much Quintilian's thought. But there is no doubt that
Quintilian in his ethics for the *perfectus orator* used the interest of the State, being
identical to the common interest, to distinguish between honest behaviour and
behaviour which could not be considered as such. The interest of the political community - which was independent of the 'right by nature' and so, consequently, honest - allowed the orator to maintain the honesty of his purpose[93] and still speak in
defence of the guilty[94] and in defence of falsehood or even injustice,[95] it allowed him
to defend while employing falsehood,[96] and to sometimes conceal the truth from the

---

[86]   *Inst. or.* XII.1.41.
[87]   *Inst. or.* XII.1.43: 'nonne ei communis utilitas oratorem advocabit?'
[88]   Cicero, *De officiis*, III.2-4, 7-20.
[89]   Cicero, *De officiis*, III.30: 'communis utilitatis derelictio contra naturam est; est enim iniusta'.
[90]   Cicero, *De inventione*, II.160.
[91]   On this concept in Cicero's works, see V. Scarano Ussani, *L'utilità e la certezza. Compiti e modelli
del sapere giuridico in Salvio Giuliano*, Milan: Giuffrè 1987, p. 22 and nn. 46 and 47 with literature.
[92]   So Lana (see note 2), p. 296. Cf. also Manzo (see note 4), p. 456.
[93]   *Inst. or.* XII.1.45.
[94]   *Inst. or.* XII.1.34.
[95]   *Inst. or.* XII.1.34.
[96]   *Inst. or.* XII.1.40.

judge,[97] more generally, to lie. In fact, the conformity with the common interest marked the limit between a honourable *voluntas* and another *voluntas* which could not be defined as such.

The *vir bonus dicendi peritus,* so educated, was therefore called upon to correct vice and reform morals. The *vir bonus* preferred to defend but he would not object to prosecute if a public or private duty – an *officium* –obliged him to call someone to answer for his behaviour.[98] If they were not defended by the voice of a skilled accuser, the laws would be worthless.[99] And if it was a sin to demand the punishment of crimes, crimes would nearly become lawful actions, and wicked people would get free leave against honest people.[100] Therefore, it was impossible for the orator to tolerate that the complaints of the allies did not receive satisfaction, that the murder of a friend or a relative was not punished, and that the conspiracies, being on the point of exploding against the *res publica,* remained unavenged.[101] Quintilian wrote that only by fear it was possible to restrain the persons who were not directed by reason to behave well.[102] This was not, as is well-known, an original thought. The idea of the deterrent function of punishment, also connected with public interest, was already a Platonic theme.[103] According to Cicero, it was not possible to control the State without severity: punishment had to be inflicted for the welfare of the *res publica*.[104] The opinion that 'at least the *res publica* may benefit from the death' of the persons who 'were unwilling to be useful' justified, according to Seneca, capital punishment, although only in cases of extreme, incurable wickedness.[105]

But the events in the latest decades had to induce Quintilian to emphasize, presumably not without a certain embarrassment, the enormous difference between the perfect orator who, in the capacity of prosecutor, was comparable to a defender of

---

[97] *Inst. or.* XII.1.36.
[98] *Inst. or.* XII.7.1.
[99] *Inst. or.* XII.7.1.
[100] *Inst. or.* XII.7.1. According to A. Cavarzere, *Oratoria a Roma. Storia di un genere pragmatico,* Rome: Carocci 2000, p. 221, in *Inst. or.* XII.7.1 and 2, Quintilian proved to be fully conscious of the essential role of the prosecutor, during the Republic and in the Principate, 'nell'espletamento della giustizia'.
[101] *Inst. or.* XII.7.2. Quintilian specified that the orator had to be 'non poenae nocentium cupidus, sed emendandi vitia corrigendique mores'. According to Austin (see note 35), p. 112 this text shows the Stoic influence on his theories. Lana (see note 2), pp. 296f., locates, in this passage, Quintilian' s justification of *delatores,* who, being the prosecutors in trials of *maiestas* against persons disliked by the emperor, formally defended the *res publica* and it was possible that they were considered *propugnatores patriae*.
[102] *Inst. or.* XII.7.2. In this connection, Austin (see note 35), p. 112 quotes Cicero, *Pro S. Roscio Amerino,* 56: 'accusatores multos esse in civitate utile est, ut metu contineatur audacia'.
[103] Plato, *Leges,* 854e; 862e; 934e. On the Platonic theory of punishment and Plato's penology, see M. M. Mackenzie, *Plato. On Punishment,* Berkeley-Los Angeles-London: University of California Press 1981, pp. 178ff., 207ff.; T. J. Saunders, *Plato's Penal Code. Tradition, Controversy, and Reform in Greek Penology,* Oxford: Clarendon Press 1991, rpt. 1994, pp. 349ff.
[104] Cicero, *De officiis,* I.88 and 89. See M. Bellincioni, *Potere ed etica in Seneca,* Brescia: Paideia 1984, pp. 86ff.
[105] Seneca, *De ira,* 1.6.4. The manuscripts have various readings: '... qui aliis vivi noluerunt prodesse..'; '... quia vivi noluerunt prodesse..'.; 'qui alicui noluerunt prodesse..', but they do not change the global meaning of this passage. See also Seneca, *De ira,* 1.19.7; cf. Bellincioni (see note 104), pp. 74ff.

his country and a vulgar professional *delator*, comparable to a brigand.[106] In fact, Quintilian explained that to live a life of accusation and to be driven to accusing defendants by the prospect of a reward was next to highway robbery, whereas to rid one's country of interior pests was an action comparable to that of those men who defend their country.[107]

Therefore the most important men in the State had not rejected this aspect of the orator's *officium* and it was a common belief that the young men of high rank, as token of loyalty to the state, also had to bring charges against dishonest citizens, although it seemed as if they neither hated the wicked persons nor excited hatred, only by the consciousness of a good intention.[108]

Although he was the defender of the state, an implacable prosecutor of conspirators, so rescuing it from interior pests, the perfect orator nevertheless had to beware, in speaking, of that freedom of speech which usually degenerated into temerity, and could be dangerous not only to the interests of the case but also to those of the orator himself.[109] Quintilian availed himself of an illustrious but very remote example, remembering Pericles' wish not to offend the people by using an awkward word.[110] Quintilian's intention of pointing out, although with circumspection, the risks to which the orator was exposed by speaking too freely, in his age, is nevertheless clearly discernable. Pericles in fact feared the people, but Quintilian declared: 'what he felt with regard to the people, I feel with regard to everybody who can cause just as much harm', and he concluded, with crude realism, that therefore 'utterances which seemed courageous at the moment of speaking, are called foolish when it is found that they have given offence'.[111]

---

[106]   *Inst or.* XII.7.3. Quintilian underlined the contrast between the activity of delators, attracted by the reward, and that of those who out of patriotism accused the conspirators against the *res publica*. This contrast which is stressed, not without perplexity, by Zucchelli (see note 25), p. 588 and n.78, seems, at the end of the first century AD, very ambiguous and not completely credible. Moreover Quintilian included, among the best contemporary orators, two *delatores*. The first is Domitius Afer (*Inst or.* X.1.117; XII.10.11), his teacher (*Inst. or.* V.7.7), who, certainly, at least in his youth, was a *delator*. Cf. M. Winterbottom (see note 11), pp. 92ff.; Zucchelli (see note 25), p. 589; Kennedy (see note 29), p. 174; Cavarzere (see note 100), pp. 222ff, who rightly observes that Quintilian's portrait of Afer can not be 'quello tipico di un delatore.' The second is Vibius Crispus (*Inst. or.* X.1.119; XII.10.11). On this orator, see Winterbottom (see note 11), pp. 92ff.; Lana (see note 2), p. 298 n.36; Zucchelli (see note 25), p. 589 and n.82 with literature, who thinks that Quintilian's doubts about his eloquence in public trials - 'privatis tamen causis quam publicis melior' - correspond to his moral reservations; Cavarzere (see note 100), p. 222. According to Winterbottom (see note 11), p. 94, when one considers 'that the *delatores* were the most important oratorical phenomenon of the century, it becomes clear that Quintilian is glossing over the extent to which he himself is swimming against the tide in proclaming a new Ciceronianism'.

[107]   *Inst. or.* XII.7.3: 'Itaque ut accusatoriam vitam vivere et ad deferendos reos praemio duci proximum latrocinio est, ita pestem intestinam propulsare propugnatoribus patriae comparandum'. See Columella, *De re rustica*, 1.pr.9; cf. Austin (see note 35), p. 112.

[108]   *Inst. or.* XII.7.3: '.., quia nec odisse improbos nec simultates provocare nisi ex fiducia bonae mentis videbantur'.

[109]   *Inst. or.* XII.9.13.

[110]   According to Austin (see note 35), p. 130, the reference to Pericles is 'apparently a free interpretation of the story told by Plutarch, *Per.* 8'.

[111]   According to Austin (see note 35), p. 130, this expression is 'typical of Q.s common sense'.

In Book XII of the *Institutio oratoria,* this is the only specific and worried, although veiled, allusion to the political situation of the Principate and to the imperial power.[112] Throughout his work, Quintilian mentioned them, though not frequently, sometimes with emphatic praises of Domitian, undoubtedly expressions of faithfulness to him.[113] Quintilian exalted the piety of the emperor,[114] his quality of *sanctissimus censor,* he called him a prince who was pre-eminent in everything, as well as in eloquence[115] and, finally, also the greatest of poets.[116] Moreover, Quintilian's handbook was composed in the years in which Domitian's despotic policy became more evident and, for some people, intolerable.[117] The republican references and tones, with which the Spanish rhetor often tried to propose his educational theories in Book XII, are certainly not able to hide the real meaning of his project: to educate an orator who was fully acting in behalf of the imperial power, proposing himself to the prince as important collaborator and supporter. In the Principate, the common interest, the interest of the *res publica,* was identified with the imperial interest and will.[118] Whether the author of the *Institutio oratoria* was a 'conscious instrument of Domitian's despotic policy' or only 'an aligned writer' who followed the emperor's instructions,[119] the work proposed undoubtedly an isagogic project, having a clearly political meaning, which seems explicit in Book XII. This had its explanation in the political situation of Domitian's principate. Also because of its 'table' of values - Trajan emphasized the *utilitas omnium* as a characteristic of the foundation and the purpose of the imperial power![120] - the *Institutio oratoria* was

---

[112]　Lana (see note 2), p. 305 argues that, in *Inst. or.* XII.9.13, 'l'allusione al principe è chiarissima, per quanto discreta'.

[113]　*Inst. or.* V.13.6; VI.1.35. See also *Inst. or.* V.2.5; XI.1.49; XI.3.150 and 156.

[114]　*Inst. or.* III.7.9.

[115]　*Inst. or.* IVpr. 3.

[116]　*Inst. or.* X.1.91. The emphatically laudative expressions clearly prove, at least, Quintilian's 'loyalty' if not the special flattery towards Domitian: see Zucchelli (see note 25), pp. 581ff.

[117]　Not without reason Lana, *La teorizzazione* (see note 25), p. 17, dates this work between the end of 93 and the first months of AD 96. According to Kennedy (see note 29), pp. 179f., Quintilian began to write the *Institutio oratoria* perhaps in 93 and finished it 'probably before the end of 95, certainly before the murder of Domitian in 96'. For a survey of various hypotesis on the date of composition of the *Institutio oratoria,* see Zucchelli (see note 25), p. 583 nn.58 and 59.

[118]　Lana (see note 2), p. 302 rightly stresses that Quintilian knew well the political situation of the Principate and declared it explicitly in *Inst. or.* VI.1.35.

[119]　Zucchelli (see note 25), p. 590, argues that Quintilian was only 'certamente uno scrittore allineato'. According to E. Narducci, *Oratoria e retorica,* in F. Montanari (ed.), *La prosa latina. Forme, autori, problemi,* Roma: Nuova Italia Scientifica 1991, rpt. 1995, pp. 129ff., it is necessary to retrench 'gli aspetti 'collaborazionistici' of the *Institutio oratoria*: the educational task which Quintilian carried out and assigned to the orator was 'al servizio della collettività e non del principe in particolare'. But it is difficult to refute - apart from the question of his political ideas, a problem to which it is arduous to give an answer - that the rhetor was, objectively, in the culture of the Flavian age, a very important accomplice of Domitian's despotic policy anyway. He was well aware of its characteristics and he strove to help it with his work.

[120]　Trajan in fact wanted to introduce the reference to the *utilitas omnium* in the annual *vota* for the emperor's safety: Pliny the Younger, *Panegyricus,* 67.4, 8; 68.1; 80.5; 94.5. Pliny the Younger (*Ep.* III.20.12) significantly described Trajan's Principate as a situation in which 'sunt quidam cuncta sub unius arbitrio, qui pro utilitate communi solus omnium curas laboresque suscepit'. On these sources and the importance of the reference to the general *utilitas* in official phraseology, see Scarano Ussani, *L'utilità* (see note 91), pp. 24ff., with other sources and literature.

nevertheless destined to keep intact its validity later on after the fall of the regime in which and for which it was conceived. Moreover, it was said: *Domitianum pessimum fuisse, amicos autem bonos habuisse*, that 'Domitian was, indeed, a very evil man but had righteous friends'.[121]

---

[121] It is the well-known opinion expressed in *Vit. Alex. Sev.* 65.5. On this text, see H. Bengtson, *Die Flavier. Vespasian. Titus. Domitian. Geschichte eines römischen Kaiserhauses*, Munich: Beck 1979, pp. 257ff.; Zucchelli (see note 25), p. 581. Presumably, Domitian's *amici boni* were the persons allowed to be present in the *consilium* of the emperor (therefore the *amici principis*), although it can not be excluded completely that the expression, in this passage of the *Historia Augusta*, indicates more generally all Domitian's friends.

WILLEM J. WITTEVEEN

THE JURISPRUDENCE OF QUINTILIAN

1. GENERAL JURISPRUDENCE: A DISTANT IDEAL

How does the art of rhetoric relate to the professional activities of legal practitioners, such as advocates, judges, civil-law notaries, and legislators? The answer seems
straightforward: all of these professionals clearly have to use language as a means of
persuasion at one point or another in their work and so it is useful for them to know
what contributes to effective communication. The art of rhetoric seems to be integral
to law practice and it is thus likely that it occupies a central place in the curriculum
of law schools. At this point, the story becomes more complicated, however, because
only rarely does rhetoric constitute a body of knowledge functioning in precisely this
way. Rhetorical studies have in fact been relegated to the margins of legal education,
where training in communication, if taught at all, takes place in moot courts. The art
of rhetoric is almost never part of the core curriculum, and it is also only seldomly
selected as a specialized field of legal research. The causes of this intriguing state of
affairs cannot here be investigated. However, a rediscovery of the treasures of the
rhetorical tradition may be at hand. A reason for this is, on the one hand, a marked
tendency within academic circles to investigate law as part of the humanities, as witness studies in areas such as law and culture, law and literature, law and ethics, and
law and society; studies relating legal culture to other cultural domains will
inevitably lead to the rhetorical tradition. On the other hand, developments within
legal practice stimulate awareness of the dilemmas confronting practicing jurists,
some of which have been prominent in rhetorical treatises since the days of Plato
and Aristotle and certainly since those of Cicero and Quintilian. In fact, for many
practitioners, the old positivist ideal of law as a science and of legal knowledge as a
manifestation of technical rationality has been discarded and an understanding of
law as a rhetorical and hermeneutical endeavour has been established in its place.[1]
Donald Schön has elaborated a new role model: the 'reflective practitioner'.[2] This is
a professional who mobilizes his knowledge in action and is able to find moments of
reflection in the practices engaged in. In classical authors, such as Quintilian, a similar sense can be found of connectedness between practical commitment and the kind
of theoretical knowledge available to specialists in the art of persuasion.

---

[1] Peter Goodrich, *Languages of Law*, London: Weidenfeld and Nicholson 1990. Gregory Leyh (ed.),
Legal Hermeneutics, Berkeley: University of California Press 1992.
[2] Donald A. Schön, *The Reflective Practitioner, How Professionals Think in Action*, New York: Basic
Books 1983.

The circle of reflective practitioners includes legal professionals such as advocates and judges, legislators, civil-law notaries, lawyer-statesmen even (in the words of Anthony Kronman),[3] and it also embraces those who make it their business to reflect on law and its functions in society: the teachers and researchers of the discipline called 'jurisprudence'. The Latin term refers both to the realm of law and to practical wisdom, or prudence. Jurisprudence entails a comprhensive approach to law, it stimulates interdisciplinary work, upholds an interest in general themes relevant in all domains of the law (such as the topics of rhetoric and interpretation in law).

William Twining usefully defines jurisprudence as 'the theoretical part of law as a discipline' and he points out that it performs a variety of functions.[4] Jurisprudence helps survey the field, it constructs conceptual frameworks, it assists in simplifying the law. In doing so, it overcomes the artificial boundaries between disciplines and discourses as it raises general and abstract issues, such as basic problems of evidence and inference that are the concern of lawyers as well as of historians, social scientists, physical scientists, statisticians, and logicians – and indeed of rhetoricians. The most important function, however, according to Twining, is 'the sustained teasing out, articulation, and critical examination of the general assumptions and presuppositions underlying the discourse on any discipline or praxis at a given moment in history'.[5] This really is not so very different in spirit from Aristotle's famous *dictum* defining rhetoric as the knowledge of available possibilities of discourse, not only its strategic possibilities but the whole panoply of functions one can associate with language, from truth to power. As Aristotelian rhetoric (and the Roman rhetorical tradition after it) meant to promote critical investigation by aspiring practitioners of their 'art', so Twining advocates an interest by aspiring jurists in, among other things, legal history and legal theory in order to keep the discipline of law 'in a healthy state'. Presumably, the general jurisprudence favoured by Twining includes a thorough study of the classical rhetoricians, as their works illuminate many aspects of legal practice that are as troubling today as they have ever been (such as problems of evidence and inference). Quintilian should be somewhere on the list of jurisprudential authors, not too distant from authors habitually studied such as Plato, Aristotle, Hobbes, and Bentham (note that all of these authors devoted treatises to rhetorical topics).

General jurisprudence conceived in this comprehensive way is a rather distant ideal. Jurisprudential writings are usually much more limited in their range of subject matter, replaying endlessly the age-old debate between positivism and natural law. The question of what kind of jurisprudence is useful for reflective practitioners in practices of law may serve to broaden the discussion. The adherents of positivism and natural law, for instance, share an interest in the nature of rules and in the status of legal principles in the interpretation of the law, but their debate might become more stimulating if it also addressed wider issues relating to the normative and practical dimensions of the activities of jurists as 'good' professionals, as an advocate,

---

[3]   Anthony T. Kronman, *The Lost Lawyer*, Cambridge, Mass.: Belknap Press 1993.
[4]   William Twining, *Globalisation & Legal Theory*, London: Butterworths 2000, pp. 10-13.
[5]   Twining (see note 4), p. 12.

judge, civil-law notary or legislator. Of all the rhetorical authors, Quintilian is probably the best choice to approach these neglected themes. The Latin root of 'jurisprudence' is continually on his mind: *prudentia iuris*. In the *Institutio oratoria*, Quintilian shows how a prudent man can be both effectively and ethically involved in the
practice of law.

2. QUINTILIAN ON STRATEGY AND COMMUNICATION

My first demonstration of the strengths of Quintilian's approach concerns the ethics
of advocacy. The deeply problematical relation between persuasive and ethical
speech is one of the oldest dilemmas that rhetoricians have studied. Plato chose this
topic as the vehicle for the rejection of sophistic political philosophy and rhetoric (in
his dialogue *Gorgias*). Thus, the dilemma of the ethical lawyer was already at the
heart of the controversy about rhetoric before the great classical rhetorical systems
had even been developed (by Isocrates, Aristotle, Cicero, and Quintilian). The problem is that the advocate is supposed to do all he can to serve the interests of his
client, also when these are contrary to the interests of others or counter to the general interest. The advocate's effectiveness in employing the resources of rhetoric
may easily make him unethical. It may be attractive to bend the truth to further his
client's interests. If this is already problematical in itself, the problem is com-
pounded by the social norm concerning lawyers, who are expected to always abide
by the rules of due process and justice. How can an advocate be as partial as possible and also serve the interests of justice, which surely require awareness of opposite
interests and arguments and concern for impartial judgements? How can the advocate provide a selective narration of the facts and give one-sided interpretations of
legal rules, to win his case, and somehow also further due process and fairness?
Note that the social norm is ambiguous in the extreme, or rather that it is a double
standard: society expects advocates to be defenders of partial interests and it expects
them to be truthful, just, and fair. But these standards clash, and when this comes
out, the advocate is portrayed as a liar and a hypocrite or even as a danger to society.
    Is this a problem for contemporary jurisprudence? When reading the literature,
one is inclined to say that it has been overlooked entirely; unethical rhetoric is
regarded as a problem of legal practice, as if it is a problem without a theoretical
dimension. In general philosophical discussions, however, the problem does arise.
An influential case is Habermas' theory of communicative action, in which he
makes a sharp distinction between strategic and communicative action.[6] Whereas
strategic action aims at achieving a result with all the means available (i.e., it stands
for the aspect of the rhetorical effectiveness of advocacy), communicative action
aspires to be open, it must accommodate all different viewpoints, and it must aim at
conclusions that are acceptable to all concerned (i.e., it fits in with the justice and
due process aspects of advocacy). Habermas loads the dice: communicative action is
morally superior and it expresses the fundamental ideals of democracy and legality

---

[6]   J. Habermas, *Theorie des kommunikativen Handelns*, 2 Vols., Frankfurt am Main: Suhrkamp 1981.

in a better way. The reader is left with a haunting suspicion that there must be something philosophically more interesting to say about the other aspect (i.e. strategic action). Does not this ambition to achieve results also express some latent ideals? Is it in no way related to fairness, due process, and justice? It is a missed opportunity that there has been no response from jurisprudential authors defending strategic action as a morally better way to deal with values; it refers us back to classical authors, and especially to Quintilian.

What can we learn from him? Throughout the twelve books of the *Institutio oratoria*, we find both the strategic and the communicative motives and we typically find them intertwined, not in sharp opposition. For Quintilian, the art of persuasion apparently is neither fully strategic (goal-oriented) nor completely communicative (consensus-directed). There are, instead, many mixed forms in actual persuasive practices: strategic communication or communicative strategies. Socially meaningful courses of action seem to be located on a continuum between total honesty and radical manipulation.

This mixing of strategic and communicative motives can be discerned most clearly in Quintilian's (mostly implicit) model of rhetorical action, which I will term *the rhetorical situation*. This model has a triadic structure: pleader A opposes pleader B, and both try to convince a decisive audience C. The rhetorical situation offers an institutional setting for strategic action and interaction involving these three kinds of participants: pleaders, counterpleaders, and judges.

Strategy and communication are interrelated, both in the design and the maintenance of the institutional setting, which is mostly outside the scope of Quintilian's reflections, and in the actual rhetorical process itself. The institutional setting requires, for instance, some communicative ground rules, such as freedom of speech and the absence of direct threats of violence to the other participants; it also requires some procedural rules organizing the debate in a rational way in terms of time, energy, and the capability to solve problems. However, the way in which these communicative principles are actually given shape in an institutional setting may well provide one party or the other with strategic advantages, for instance, in the way rules of evidence favour the claimant or the defender. On the whole, the institutional setting of a rhetorical situation is dominated by a communicative approach, but important strategic elements are relevant as well.

At first sight, the rhetorical process of persuasion offers a predominance of strategic possibilities but, on closer inspection, contains many elements of communicative action. This seems inevitable in terms of the model of the rhetorical situation with its triadic structure. Pleaders who try to maximize their strategic options and use rhetoric as a purely manipulative technique to overwhelm the opponent and impress the audience need, at the very minimum, to be understood by all the other participants; otherwise all their subsequent strategies will fail. Pleaders aiming at influencing others will have to obey the ground-rules of the communicative framework, but they will also have to bring forward many theses about which they are in agreement with the other pleader and the audience, using these as premises for their reasoning. At some point in the strategic interaction, some form of open communication is bound to occur. Pleaders, counterpleaders, and judges, for instance, may come to refer to rules that supposedly apply to all and that can be potentially to their disadvantage as well as to their advantage. When these communicative elements emerge in strategic interaction, it is possible that the rhetorical situation - which starts out as a zero sum game (one player wins what the other loses) turns into a positive sum game (in which all players stand to gain through the strategies employed by all).[7]

The rhetorical situation is ideally structured in such a way as to balance strategies with counterstrategies, so achieving some kind of socially acceptable optimum. In this structure, a dynamics can occur which turns the partial accounts of pleaders into balanced audience judgements. Judges who are aware of the rhetorical moves of counsel and counsel for the other party can use the information that is deliberately presented to them in a biased way as materials out of which they build well-reasoned and impartial judgments.

In support of these theoretical considerations, let us now turn to the text of the *Institutio oratoria* itself. As an adviser of aspiring speakers, Quintilian often takes a clearly strategic stance, promising (again, like all rhetorical authors) to teach the aspiring advocate how to beat his opponents. Open communication is often enough, in Quintilian's view, needed precisely in order to be strategically effective.

Take the important issue of the treatment of facts in a law suit. This presents itself first in the difficulty of an *exordium* (opening statement) indicating clearly what the speaker is going to say, preparing the way for a more extended narration of the facts afterwards, but also working on the emotions of the audience, and making it inclined to reason with the speaker, rather than be critical about what is to follow. In Roman rhetoric, the moment of *exordium* is something like a miniature of the whole speech and much is seen to depend on its successful presentation. Quintilian's attitude towards the problem of the *exordium* is at first unabashedly strategic. 'The sole purpose of the *exordium* is to prepare our audience in such a way that they will be disposed to lend a ready ear to the rest of our speech'.[8] The audience must be made to listen. The speaker must therefore seem to be a good man who is most of all trustworthy. 'He must give the impression not so much that he is a zealous advocate as that he is an absolutely reliable witness'.[9] Precisely to be strategically efficacious, the pleader must impersonate the ideal of communicative rationality. It is all a matter of the 'art of impression management'.[10]

After discussing some of the technical points to keep in mind in composing an *exordium*, Quintilian again emphasizes the strategical superiority of not seeming to have made all these elaborate preparations. It is indeed very attractive for the second speaker, to let his *exordium* reflect and reverse the *exordium* of his opponent. Because it is seen to be improvised on the spot, the judge will be tricked into believing that the rest of the speech (which of course was prepared carefully beforehand) is also spontaneous; for this effect to occur, it is important to speak in a natural style,

---

[7] The model of the rhetorical situation is elaborated in W.J. Witteveen, *De retoriek in het recht*, Zwolle: Tjeenk Willink 1988, Chapter III.

[8] *Inst. or.* IV.1.5. I use the translation by Butler (see 'Introduction', note 27).

[9] *Inst. or.* IV.1.7.

[10] Erving Goffman, *The Presentation of Self in Everyday Life*, Harmondsworth: Penguin 1969.

not too eloquent or stylistically subtle, with some hesitation as if a new thought suddenly enters the speaker's mind. This is an important rhetorical effect to achieve, especially since the judge, according to Quintilian, will readily suspect that the *exordium* is used to work on his emotions. 'We should give no hint of elaboration in the *exordium*, since any art that the orator might employ at this point seems to be directed solely at the judge. But to avoid all display of art in itself requires consummate art'.[11] This last remark certainly evidences Quintilian's attitude towards strategy: the speaker should have everything under control, without showing it.

Note now the occurrence of more genuinely communicative motives in Quintilian's treatment of the *exordium*. He rejects the strategic advice of some authors who hold that the authority the speaker has construed during his exordium and the emotional appeal made to the judge should be fluently carried over into the actual narration of the facts. The transition should not be hidden, Quintilian argues, because the judge must not be deceived at this point but, on the contrary, must be warned that a new phase of the speech has begun, requiring his full attention.

> The first part of our statement of the facts will be wasted if the judge does not realize that we have reached that stage. Therefore, although we should not be too abrupt in passing to our statement of the facts, it is best to do nothing to conceal our transition.[12]

Quintilian then refers to a speech by Cicero (*Pro Cluentio*) in which the great politician warns the audience that his story will be long and complex.

In Quintilian's treatment of the statement of facts, we occasionally find the same emphasis on norms of open communication. The narration must be clear and concise, it must be well organized, and summaries must be provided to assist the hearer. Especially, all new points must be explicitly marked. 'The judge will be refreshed by the fact that we have brought our previous remarks to a close and will prepare himself for what may be regarded as a fresh start.[13] Yet, the emphasis in these considerations is on the strategical aspect. Quintilian emphasizes the practicality of open communication, not its ethics. The communicative moment in the interaction between speakers and the audience must be used to further the purposes of the speaker; communicative action is a moment of pause in a strategical performance. In the statement of facts, what is crucial is again the art of impression management, as witness these rules of thumb for the aspiring speaker.

> The statement of facts will be credible, if in the first place we take care to say nothing contrary to nature, secondly if we assign reasons and motives for the facts on which the inquiry turns (...), and if we make the characters of the actors in keeping with the facts we desire to be believed: we shall for instance represent a person accused of theft as covetous, accused of adultery as lustful, accused of homicide as rash, or attribute the opposite qualities to these persons if we are defending them: further we must do the same with place, time and the like.[14]

In these strategical considerations, we are far removed from Habermas' concern with truthfulness, without, however, having entered a realm of pure lies. What matters is

[11]   *Inst. or.* IV.1.56-57.
[12]   *Inst. or.* IV.1.78.
[13]   *Inst. or.* IV.2.50, see also IV.2.35.
[14]   *Inst. or.* IV.2.52.

that the advocate skilfully employs the right stereotypes, giving the actors in his story an appropriate and thus credible motivation. It is up to his opponent to correct this picture, using the opposite stereotypes. In the rhetorical situation, the judge then has to compare these two equally biased versions of the truth of the matter. Will he succeed in finding out what really happened and why? The truth is hard to establish on this basis, but the idea of truth must be seen in the context of the rhetorical situation. Then truth is no more and no less than a high degree of plausibility, as Quintilian underlines:

> Now I should regret that anyone should censure my conduct in suggesting that a *statement* which is wholly in our favour is *plausible*, when as a matter of fact it is *true*. There are many things which are true, but scarcely credible, just as there are many things which are plausible though false. It will require therefore just as much exertion on our part to make the judge believe what we say when it is true as it will when it is fictitious.[15]

What Quintilian is in effect saying here is that there is an economy of rhetorical energy that, within the setting of the rhetorical situation, makes the 'real' truth of the facts, narrated twice and from opposite points of view, irrelevant to the purposes at hand; judges will have to decide anyhow and they are never in a good position to really know what happened. For Quintilian, strategic and communicative action coincide in the task of the orator to convince the audience.[16]

We can now see what solution Quintilian envisages to the problem of ethical advocacy posed so incisively by Plato's *Gorgias*. It is not a personal solution, focusing on the qualities of the individual lawyer, but a structural one, relying on the dynamics of the rhetorical situation. The task of the advocate is to be partial but not too much so, opening enough possibilities for cooperation between the different protagonists in the rhetorical process. The task of the judge is, on the other hand, not merely that of the impartial spectator. Judges have to know the strategies of pleading and have to mobilize all their resources to make use of the rhetorical strategies of others. They have to delve deeply into partisan accounts before some kind of real impartiality can be achieved. So there arises a division of labour, with clearly marked-out roles for the three participants in the rhetorical situation, but there are unifying elements to the task: conceptions of justice, shared rules and principles, the ideal of decorum, communicative openness as a frame for strategic interplay. It will depend on the quality of the actual process, of its correspondence to the ideal of the rhetorical situation proper, and on the qualities of the participants whether the business of both advocacy and judging are ethical undertakings.

3. QUINTILIAN ON THE EDUCATION OF THE PRUDENT JURIST

The second area in which Quintilian rhetoric can be of value to jurisprudence is that of the education of the jurist as a special kind of orator. Again, this is a subject that falls outside the scope of the age-old debates between positivism and natural law; it

---

[15] *Inst. or.* IV.2.34.
[16] *Inst. or.* IV.2.21.

has come within the province of jurisprudence in recent years mostly through the emergence of a new generalist discipline of law: law & literature. For leading figures in law & literature, such as Martha Nussbaum and James Boyd White, the proper education of legal professionals is a central concern. Rather than summarize here the diverse approaches in this field, I will concentrate on a concern that is common to all of them: the conviction that it is important in legal education to provide training experiences stimulating the sympathetic understanding of others. I will then relate this topic to the rhetorical system advocated by Quintilian.

4. AN EXCURSUS ON PERSPECTIVISM

The logic of the rhetorical situation requires all participants (pleader, counterpleader, and judge) to be able to acknowledge and sympathetically take the point of view of all the other participants. In this way, it is possible to acquire sympathy (on both a cognitive and an emotional level) for standpoints that are not initially one's own and to make them part of one's own calculus of motives and emotional involvement with the issues at stake. This logic can be extended further towards an ethical attitude requiring all participants in a debate to be prepared to imagine themselves in the position of all the other participants. Applied to the tasks that legal professionals perform in social institutions, this expanded ethics of rhetorical interaction requires the good lawyer to be both able and willing to look at a problem from different, sometimes deeply conflicting, motivations and perspectives. I will label this attitude of cognitive and emotional standpoint-switching *perspectivism* and will call perspectivism the prime virtue of the jurist.

The idea of perspectivism as a legal virtue is not a novelty – and how could it be, since it has been contained in the rhetorical tradition since Aristotle and Isocrates? – but it has surprising and perhaps even radical consequences. Perspectivists must admit the fact that so-called facts are not really facts: it is always possible to take still other perspectives into account, to tell different stories about 'facts' and so endow them with different meanings. There is never a completely objective account of the facts framed by competing perspectives, no obvious road towards a truth that is independent of any point of view. Indeed, the language of the law is not a neutral medium in which events can be transparently depicted. Language organizes reality by its narrativity, it colours the facts and confers meanings, even though language is also influenced by forces beyond its control. The language of the law is not an autonomous phenomenon, even though it is laid down in the books and commentaries that jurists read and comment upon; it is dependent on practices. Facts are socially constructed; pure objectivity is impossible.

If these assumptions of perspectivism are true, if facts are not facts and the reality the law speaks about is socially constructed and managed, then it has to be accepted that in non-trivial cases, there will also be perspectives that provide a different, possibly relevant organization of the facts. Perspectivism adheres to an ideal of legal knowledge as forever adversarial, in which the process of reaching a judgement is not a given but the crucial and problematical factor for achieving a 'good' result. The perspectivist understands that it is not always possible to find the one perspective that is superior to all other perspectives. The idea that there is one stand-point that will automatically generate the right questions and the right answers is an illusion. Perspectivism does not only relate to the issue of the establishment of the facts, but also to the matter of the validity of the rules and principles and of the dog-matic concepts of law having to be 'applied' to the facts. The perspectivist rejects the 'right answer claim' that is central to positivism and some branches of natural law alike.[17] Excluded perspectives, that have not found recognition in the rules and principles and concepts forming part of 'valid' law, are in principle not to be excluded as irrelevant; they may contain the seeds of new law.

For the perspectivist, there are thus no 'easy cases'. The rhetorical process of judgment must always provide a space for perspectives that are out of the ordinary, but still possibly relevant. The decision must be motivated in such a way as to con-vince also those taking a perspective rejected by the judge. Even then, it is still pos-sible that not all concerns and interests have been taken care of and that there is still an unvoiced perspective that would judge the result as unfair or unjust. For the per-spectivist, there is no abstract boundary between right and wrong; the real views of people involved in the process of judgement are more important than theoretical considerations. Justice is not a grand design, but the locally managed avoidance of injustice. In her impressive study of *The Sense of Injustice,* Judith Shklar writes: Whatever decisions we do make will be unjust unless we take the victim's view into full account and give her voice its full weight.[18] It is never an easy matter for per-spectivists to decide at what point the perspectives of all 'victims' have actually received due recognition and consideration; it is a matter of practical wisdom (in an Aristotelian sense).

So, for perspectivism, there are no easy cases and no final or foundational answers. This makes the job of the jurist none the easier. Left without transcenden-tal answers, the predicament of perspectivism is well captured by Martha Minow. 'We cannot know without standing somewhere, and because we are situated some-where, we cannot see everything. Once we have considered this challenge, it is hard, if not impossible, to resume a faith in a reason that would transcend the situation of the reasoner.'[19] The inevitable 'partiality' of justice leads Minow to recommend the attitude sketched here of not excluding any perspective presented in a controversy and of opening the field for new excluded lines of argument demanding to be heard.

Perspectivism as a legal virtue thus comes to appear quite radical when we draw the implied consequences of the idea that every point of view must be taken seri-ously. But where does this consequentialism lead the jurist? If all the true accounts of law are relative to some perspective, is there no Truth at all? Is the person who is declared in the right in the rhetorical process then merely the person who simply won the debate of the day, not possessing a more stable title to her claims? Can there never be a right answer unless there is A Right Answer? Here, the abyss of a

[17] On the right answer claim, see Ronald Dworkin, *Law's Empire*, Cambridge, Mass.: The Belknap Press 1986.
[18] Judith N. Shklar, *The Sense of Injustice*, New Haven: Yale University Press 1990, p. 126.
[19] Martha Minow, 'Partial Justice', in: Austin Sarat and Thomas R. Kearns (eds.), *The Fate of Law*, Ann Arbor: Michigan University Press 1991, p. 50.

radical relativism opens itself. Fortunately, the virtue of legal perspectivism need not be taken this far. Perspectivism is not relativism, let alone radical relativism. It does not argue the relativity of all values, as if there is an insensitivity here for moral issues, quite the contrary. It does not argue that any story about the facts is as good as any other, as if there were no possibility to judge differences in plausibility and in other narrative qualities, quite the contrary. Perspectivism is a method aiming to sensitize the practicing jurist to other points of view than those that have at any moment been declared valid by the reigning social system of law. The rhetorical procedure of argument and counterargument generates a crucial question: do the officially valid norms do justice to what has emerged during the deliberations about the facts of the situation and the moral character of the actors involved in it?

Perspectivism opens the spectre of integrity in the way the community of law can deal with rules and principles and concepts of law which are acceptable and useful to all people concerned. Perspectivism, having this result of leading to a debate on what the legal community should encompass or encourage, confronts practicing jurists with the legal tradition they want to belong to and the history of that tradition leading to the issues at stake. Far from being relativist in a radical vein, perspectivism turns out to foster an attitude of *constructive interpretation*, in which the materials offered by the development of the normative legal system are used to provide solutions for pressing problems that have first been seen under all their different aspects, also those that have not yet been acknowledged in the legal rules, principles and concepts of the normative legal system. At this point, it is even possible to rejoin Dworkin in his natural law quest for integrity in law, where he argues that '[o]ur law consists in the best justification of our legal practices as a whole, (...) it consists in the narrative story that makes of these practices the best they can be.'[20] The perspectivist interpretation of this laudable aim is to put forward the ideal of first articulating perspectives in all their potential conflicts, in order to be able to collectively and through continued debate (of both a strategic and a communicative nature) elaborate a new direction for the grand narrative of a principled and just law, without, however, believing that this will be the final story and forever prepared to start all over again with the clash of perspectives. Adversarial rhetoric and constructive interpretation keep moving in circles.

5. THE PERSPECTIVIST JURIST: LAW & LITERATURE

After this excursus into the legal theory of perspectivism, we can hopefully better frame the question of how the good jurist can learn the virtue of perspectivism. As already mentioned, law & literature scholars believe that reading literary works can help prepare the law student and the practicing lawyer develop their sympathetic imagination. We have just argued that sympathy is the force driving the logic of the rhetorical situation and that it can be expanded into a much broader framework for a legal normative system developing through the mechanism of constructive interpre-

---

[20] Dworkin (see note 17), VII.

tation. But can this be taught, and how? What, if anything, can Quintilian's jurisprudence still contribute to this endeavour?

Martha Nussbaum has forcefully argued that not only lawyers but also concerned citizens should read realist novels, preferably the great 19th century ones (Eliot, James, Dickens, Proust) and those later novels that are continuations and transformations of the realist tradition (Forster). Reading and interpreting these literary works, more than any other genre, contributes to the development of sympathetic capabilities. Summarizing her experience in teaching these literary works to aspiring lawyers, she makes a general point about the usefulness of the realist novel, which deserves to be quoted in full.

> The novel is concrete to an extent generally unparallelled in other narrative genres. It takes as its theme, we might say, the interaction between general human aspirations and particular forms of social life that either enable or impede those aspirations, shaping them powerfully in the process. Realist novels present persistent forms of human need and desire realized in specific social situations. These situations (...) differ a great deal from the reader's own. Novels (...) speak to an implicit reader who shares with the characters certain hopes, fears, and general concerns, and who for that reason is able to form bonds of identification and sympathy with them, but who is also situated elsewhere and needs to be informed about the concrete situation of the characters.[21]

Especially the latter part of this passage deserves our attention. Realist novels do not only forge a bond of identification by addressing the implicit reader, they also generate in this reader the need to overcome his/her inevitable distance from the characters being sympathized with and this creates the need to be concretely informed about the situations (and the society) in which the characters are enmeshed. This is precisely the predicament of rhetorically active lawyers: they are not directly involved in the lives of the people they represent; they have this same characteristic distance, and they need to overcome it by sympathy and by getting acquainted with the concrete circumstances. They need to do this in order to be able to talk meaningfully about quite general human aspirations, needs, and desires that have motivated their clients in the conflict at issue. As Nussbaum stresses again and again, what matters in studying realist novels is 'the play back and forth between the general and the concrete', thus providing a style of ethical reasoning that is 'context-specific without being relativistic.'[22]

What is being recommended here is mostly an art of interpretation which is doubly reflective: of the situations of others but also of the situations that the interpreter herself is in. It is thus formative of a perspectivist attitude. It is also reminiscent of Book X of the *Institutio oratoria*, where Quintilian discusses the value of a good literary education for the aspiring rhetorician. Both Quintilian and Nussbaum think that reading the right kinds of materials enhances the grasp of the imagination on situations and human characteristics both familiar and alien to the reader.[23] Compared to Quintilian's approach, however, the mental exercises proposed by Nussbaum, all interpretive in character, make a more passive impression. Nuss-

---

[21]   Martha C. Nussbaum, *Poetic Justice*, Boston: Beacon Press 1995, p. 7.
[22]   Nussbaum (see note 21), p. 8.
[23]   See also the chapter by Sanne Taekema in this book.

baum basically advocates an art of reading sustaining an ethics of sympathy. Quintilian advocates practices of reading that are much more active in nature, being preliminaries for exercises in writing and speaking. Moreover, due to the different status of the technology of written communication, reading, for Quintilian, is still closely connected with listening to a text being read aloud and this ability to interpret a text through listening to it being read aloud again strengthens the abilities going with being a good writer and pleader. It is strange that Nussbaum nowhere mentions these other abilities a rhetorical jurist must have besides reading: the active abilities of listening, speaking, and writing, all three of which are very important in the art of judging in the rhetorical situation.[24] James Boyd White, in an approach to *Law & Literature* that is not so very different from Nussbaum's and underscoring, like her, the importance of ethical development, takes the wider view that reading and writing go hand in hand and are constitutive of the craft of the lawyer.[25] However, he does not go deeply into the relationship between these activities and the arts of listening and speaking either. Consequently, Quintilian still has something of importance to add to the educational programmes of these proponents of *Law & Literature*.

6. THE PERSPECTIVIST JURIST: QUINTILIAN RHETORIC

When we turn back to Book II of the *Institutio oratoria*, we can find further guidance on how to proceed in training aspiring lawyers in the interrelated arts of speaking, listening, reading and writing. Quintilian treats a number of educational techniques he considers elementary exercises. As an example, let us look into the way pupils are taught to prepare written narratives. Quintilian first makes a neat classification (II.2): these written narratives can be fictitious (as in tragedies and poems), they can be realistic (in the sense of stories possessing some measure of verisimilitude, as in comedies) or they can be historical (as expositions of actual events). These genres use slightly different conventions of narration the pupil must learn. Learning to write well, however, does not happen as an exercise in following grammatical rules or stylistical conventions; the most elementary exercise is the one in which speaking and listening skills are combined with analytical skills. Quintilian describes it thus.

> Written narratives should be composed with the utmost care. It is useful at first, when a child has just begun to speak, to make him repeat what he has heard with a view to improving his powers of speech; and for the same purpose, and with good reason, I would make him tell his story from the end back to the beginning or start in the middle and go backward or forwards (...) thereby strengthening the memory.[26]

Writing 'with utmost care', therefore, does not begin by setting pen to paper at all, but comes after an oral exercise in which a story must be listened to and retold, analytically restructuring it in such a way as to present different successions of the

---

[24] See also the chapter by James J. Murphy in this book.
[25] James Boyd White, *From Expectation to Experience*, Ann Arbor: Michigan University Press 1999.
[26] *Inst. or.* II.4.15.

events. It sounds elementary, and is intended to be, but in actual fact, it is not so easy to tell a tale in different temporal organisations, starting now at the end and then in the middle, and proceeding both ways from there. This is a training of analytical skills (plot construction) and also, as Quintilian notes, of the memory. Interestingly, this is not only an elementary exercise only but an exercise which can be done at higher levels of knowledge and experience, for instance, by complicating the story line or introducing points of view or adding a moral problem (What was the Iliad about? Can you summarize the story by starting at Hector's death? Or by taking the vantage point of the wrath of Achilles? Or by telling the tale in such a way as to provide a justification for Helen?). The arts of hearing, speaking, reading, and writing can be practiced at many levels, building up from simple exercises that have the added advantage of training logic and memory.

To better appraise the potential of Quintilian's jurisprudence, it is important to see that, in Book II, Quintilian is actually commenting upon the educational practice of *progymnasmata* which was prevalent in the Roman schools in his time.[27] This is a set of twelve interconnected kinds of exercises, all elementary in nature but capable of being developed into more complex forms, just as in the case of the writing exercise discussed above. According to Murphy, it is important to realize there is an order of increasing difficulty in the twelve parts of the *progymnasmata* and that all these exercises were practiced thoroughly before pupils were stimulated to compose their own speeches for the courtroom and the political assembly.[28] It actually was a carefully balanced educational programme, as we can see in this summary:

1. Retelling a fable
2. Retelling an episode written by a poet or historian
3. *Chreia*, or amplification of a moral theme
4. Amplification of an aphorism (*sententia*) or proverb
5. Refutation or confirmation of an allegation
6. Commonplace, or stereotyping a characteristic of a person
7. *Encomium*, or eulogy (or dispraise) of a person or thing
8. Comparison of things or persons
9. Impersonation (*ethologia, ethopoeia, prosopopeia*), or speaking or writing in the character of a given person
10. Description, or vivid presentation of details
11. *Thesis*, or argument for/against an answer to a general question (*quaestio*) not involving individuals
12. Praise or denunciation of laws.

What logic is there in the buildup of this 12-part set of exercises? It is not only a matter of increasing complexity of the verbal tasks performed. Of course, it is easier to summarize a fable than it is to speak in the character of a protagonist in a

---

[27]   *Inst. or.* IV.2 15-40. See on this subject also the Chapter by Serena Querzoli in this book.
[28]   James J. Murphy, 'Quintilian', in: Theresa Enos (ed.), *Encyclopedia of Rhetoric and Composition*, New York: Garland Publishing 1996, p. 583.

fable and it is also true that the easier exercise prepares the way for the more complex one, but there is also a movement from a pure classroom situation towards an imitation of real-life debate. The increasing complexity of the exercises reflects the increasing difficulty of the rhetorical tasks performed in the actual rhetorical situations of Roman society. It also indicates growing social importance in the kind of reasoning involved. The *progymnasmata* are designed to improve and expand step by step the rhetorical repertoire of the pupil; they are a form of socialization.

As an illustration, let us look at the way these exercises provide what Nussbaum termed the 'play back and forth between the general and the concrete'. The retelling of a story, following its plot, is more concrete than the amplification of a proverb, requiring more explicit generalizations about human characteristics, motives, needs, desires. The exercises of refutation and confirmation of commonplaces and the exercise of the *encomium* (praising persons) must also make use of generalities, usually stereotyped knowledge in a rather abstract fashion. In comparing things or persons, the movement is again towards the concrete, culminating in the precision work required for the vivid description of details. There is some kind of dialectical process at work here. It extends into the work of *thesis*, where the idea is again to abstract away from personal characteristics (these *theses* purposely do not involve individuals) and its abstraction culminates in the consideration of the imaginary advantages and disadvantages of proposed legislation.

The rising social importance of the rhetorical tasks involved is made clear by Quintilian himself when, at the end of his treatment of the *progymnasmata*, he comments on the exercise of debating the merits of laws:

> The praise or denunciation of laws requires greater powers; indeed they should almost be equal to the most serious tasks of rhetoric.[29]

Why is this so? Quintilian does not explicate this remark about the complexity of the art of legislation, but surely it is not too farfetched to make the connection with the then prevalent Roman idea of legislation as the art through which a free republic provides itself with stable laws needed for a well-governed empire. Indeed, Cicero in *De Legibus* goes even further: he claims that statutes have to give expression to the dictates of human reason. In this early statement of natural law theory, it is noteworthy that Cicero demands a high quality of legislation, especially in relation to its justice. According to him, in the very definition of the term 'law', there inheres the idea and principle of choosing what is just and true.[30] Quintilian may be taken to endorse the Ciceronian conception of legislation as a socially useful and important art, on which the survival of the republic may depend. When we look at the *progymnasmata* as rhetorical practices only, we fail to grasp their importance as elements in a jurisprudential theory of public life.

---

[29]   *Inst. or.* II.4.33.
[30]   Cicero, *De Legibus*, I.19. The complete sentence is, in the translation by C.W. Keyes, London: Heinemann 1977, p. 317: '... in our language I believe it has been named from the idea of choosing. For as they attributed the idea of fairness to the word law, so we have given it that of selection, though both ideas properly belong to Law'.

7. APPROXIMATING THE IDEAL OF GENERAL JURISPRUDENCE

At the outset of this essay, I declared an interest in general jurisprudence, following Twining. Jurisprudence should be a more broadly conceived, truly interdisciplinary undertaking, critically reflective of legal discourse. It must investigate the ways in which practices of law are being rhetorically constructed and interpreted. In the *Institutio oratoria,* I then discerned two themes (the relation between communicative and strategic interaction, the education of the good jurist) contributing to just such an enlarged, critically reflective view of jurisprudence. These themes are by no means exhaustive and I do not suggest that legal theorists should limit their attention to them. Indeed, it will be more productive for a general jurisprudence to undertake an integral reading of Quintilian's masterpiece than to focus on separate books and isolated passages.

To some specialists in legal theory, this will sound like a curious proposal. Do we really need to immerse ourselves in a technical manual of public speech, itself not obviously a philosophical text and dating back to antiquity, in order to find a stimulus for more reflective work on modern legal discourse in an entirely different society? Can we not simply read the summaries of the experts, of which there are plenty? The answer to this objection is that we do not seek information (which can be summarised) but inspiration (which can only be acquired through the hermeneutical experience of attentive reading); and that it is not isolated insights we need but an awareness of the way reflection on the workings of language in rhetorical practices brings together practical knowledge we have now relegated to separate 'fields' such as psychology, economics, politics, philosophy, science and, indeed, law. It is making the connection that matters.

Reading Quintilian and other classical authors about the art of persuasion, can, in the end, be even more valuable as a counterweight to the pressure of actuality which plagues modern intellectual life generally and which is definitely leading to an overemphasis on recent sources in the disciplines relating to law. Reading a classical book is a special achievement in a time in which there is an overabundance of materials that have the attraction of the new. The here and now is important; it is where our problems are located. Perhaps it is good to bear in mind an observation by Italo Calvino in his celebrated essay on the classics:

> The contemporary world (...) is always the context in which we have to place ourselves to look either backwards or forwards. In order to read the classics, you have to establish where exactly you are reading them 'from', otherwise both the reader and the text tend to drift in a timeless haze. So what we can say is that the person who derives maximum benefit from a reading of the classics is the one who skilfully alternates classic readings with calibrated doses of contemporary material.[31]

---

[31]   Italo Calvino, *Why Read the Classics?*, London: Jonathan Cape 1999, p. 8.

INDEX OF SOURCES

THE AUTHORS

Tomás Albaladejo is professor of theory of literature and comparative literature of the Universidad Autónoma of Madrid, Spain.

Jeroen A.E. Bons is a senior lecturer of classics and comparative literature at Utrecht University, The Netherlands.

Maria Silvana Celentano is professor of classical philology at the University of Chieti, Italy.

Francisco Chico-Rico is professor of theory of literature and comparative literature at Alicante University, Spain.

Jorge Fernández López is a lecturer of Latin language and literature, and of rhetoric at the University of La Rioja, Spain.

Maarten Henket is a lecturer of legal theory at Utrecht University, The Netherlands.

Barend van Heusden is a lecturer of semiotics and comparative literature at the University of Groningen, The Netherlands.

Richard A. Katula is professor of communication and education at Northeastern University in Boston, MA, United States of America.

Robert T. Lane is a bachelor in the Humanities; he obtained this degree at University College Utrecht, The Netherlands.

Andrew Lewis is professor of comparitive legal history at University College in London, Great Britain.

Ida Mastrorosa is a research fellow for the history of classical rhetoric at the University of Perugia, Italy.

James J. Murphy is professor emeritus of rhetoric and communication, and of English, at the University of California, Davis, United States of America.

Esperanza Osaba is a lecturer of Roman law at the University of the Basque Country, Leioa, Spain.

David Pujante is professor of the theory of literature and comparative literature at the universities of La Coruña and Valladolid, Spain.

Serena Querzoli is a research fellow for Roman law at Ferrara University, Italy.

Olivia Robinson is Douglas Professor of Roman law in the University of Glasgow, Great Britain.

José-Domingo Rodríguez Martín is a lecturer of Roman law at the Universidad Complutense of Madrid, Spain.

Giovanni Rossi is professor of the history of medieval and modern law at the University of Verona, Italy.

Belén Saiz Noeda is a lecturer of literary theory at the University of Alicante, Spain.

Vincenzo Scarano Ussani is professor of history of Roman law at the University of Ferrara, Italy.

Jan Willem Tellegen is a lecturer of Roman law and legal theory at Utrecht University, The Netherlands.

Olga Tellegen-Couperus is a lecturer of Roman law and legal history at Tilburg University, The Netherlands.

Sanne Taekema is a lecturer of jurisprudence at Tilburg University, The Netherlands.

Willem Witteveen is professor of jurisprudence at Tilburg University, The Netherlands.

Peter Wülfing is professor emeritus of classics at the University of Cologne, Germany.